Fourth Edition

Hotel and Motel Management and Operations

William S. Gray

Director-Hospitality Managment Program
Southern Vermont College
Bennington, Vermont

Salvatore C. Liguori

Upper Saddle River, New Jersey 07458

Library of Congress Cataloging-in-Publication Data

Gray, William S.
    Hotel & motel management and operations / William S. Gray, Salvatore
S. Liguori.— 4th ed.
      p. cm.
    ISBN 0-13-099089-2
    1. Hotel housekeeping—Management. I. Title: Hotel and motel
management and operations. II. Title.
    TX928 .G73 2001
    647.94′068—dc21

                      2002002152

Editor-in-Chief: *Stephen Helba*
Executive Assistant : *Nancy Kesterson*
Executive Acquisitions Editor:
  Vernon R. Anthony
Director of Manufacturing and Production:
  Bruce Johnson
Assistant Editor: *Marion Gottlieb*
Editorial Assistant: *Ann Brunner*
Managing Editor: *Mary Carnis*
Production Editor/Liaison: *Adele M. Kupchik*
Marketing Manager: *Ryan DeGrote*
Marketing Assistant: *Elisabeth Farrell*
Marketing Coordinator: *Adam Kloza*

Production Management: *Pine Tree*
  Composition
Production Editor: *Patty Donovan*
Manufacturing Manager: *Ilene Sanford*
Manufacturing Buyer: *Cathleen Petersen*
Creative Director: *Cheryl Asherman*
Design Coordinator: *Christopher Weigand*
Interior Design: *Word Crafters, Inc.*
Formatting: *Pine Tree Composition*
Copy Editor: *Laura Patchkofsky*
Cover Design: *Kevin Kall*
Cover Printer: *Phoenix Book Tech*

Pearson Education Ltd.
Pearson Education Australia PTY, Limited
Pearson Education Singapore, Pte. Ltd.
Pearson Education North Asia Ltd.
Pearson Education Canada, Ltd.
Pearson Educación de Mexico, S.A. de C.V.
Pearson Education—Japan
Pearson Education Malaysia, Pte. Ltd.

10 9 8 7 6 5 4 3 2 1
ISBN 0-13-099089-2

Contents

SECTION III   HOTEL OPERATIONS

Preface

As I complete this, the fourth edition of the book, I miss the counseling and input of my associate, Sal Liquori. Unfortunately, Sal passed away just after the completion of the third edition. However, I feel that the changes made in the fourth edition reflect Sal's high values and absolute integrity.

Since I left the hotel business (after 37 years) and became a teacher, I have always maintained an active consulting business, which has permitted me to be in contact with the continuing changes taking place in the industry. These have been incorporated in the fourth edition, and I would like to highlight the major changes.

1. Chapter 8 has been changed to "Sales and Marketing," with much more focus on advertising.
2. The chapters on reservations, front office, and income control have been updated to cover the new technology in the areas of property management systems and point-of-sale programs.
3. The Telephone Department has been renamed "Communications" and covers the broad scope of technological changes in this field.
4. The chapter on engineering has been rewritten to address the technological changes in this field.
5. Changes endorsed in the seventh edition of the *Uniform System of Accounts for the Lodging Industry* have been incorporated throughout the book with particular emphasis on financial statement impacts.

I have continued the practice in earlier editions of devoting a full section to hotel accounting. This is done in deference to the many community colleges who do not include an accounting course in their hospitality program.

Our textbook continues to:

- Cover every facet of the industry, including development, preopening, marketing, and operation of all departments, new and traditional.
- Be a step-by-step textbook that students in universities and hotel schools will find easy to follow and help them understand the organization structure within which a hotel operates.
- Recognize that hotel and motel operations must be viable from a business and financial viewpoint and that the continued growth of the industry must ultimately depend on profitability.

I would like to express my thanks to David Ingison, chef-owner of the East Arlington Cafe in East Arlington, Vermont, for updating me on the culinary scene, and to Susan Wheeler, manager of the Equinox Spa, Manchester Village, Vermont, for information on new spa treatments and exercises.

In addition, I would like to thank the following reviewers for their suggestions and comments: M.J. Linney, University of Texas at El Paso; Edward B. Pomianoski, County College of Morris; and Terrence McDonough, Erie Community College.

1

The History of the Hospitality Industry

The hotel industry should not be regarded as standing separate and unrelated to other industries, but rather as forming a part of the much larger hospitality industry. It is within this framework that the history of hotel development should be examined. After reading this chapter, the student should have a better understanding of the origins of the hotel industry.

EARLY HISTORY

Innkeeping is an outgrowth of man's urge to travel. Evidence exists of extensive travel over land and sea thousands of years ago. Roads used for intra-European traffic until the Middle Ages—and some that remain today—were the trails used by the courier and merchant in ancient times. Although there is no known reference to hotels or inns on those trails, there must have been places that were favorable for rest stops, probably near or accessible to water, and these may well have been used for this purpose for generations. Structures built later to accommodate travelers very probably occupied such sites.

Historians have uncovered evidence to suggest that a hospitality industry flourished more than 2,000 years before the birth of Christ. References are found in writings about life in Babylon, the center of the world in 2050 B.C. that refer to *alehouses*, apparently places that provided accommodations and sold intoxicating liquors. The concept of hospitality can also be found in writings of ancient Greece and Rome, and Biblical times. However, while during the Babylonian era, there was clearly evidence that the operation of alehouses was an income-producing business, the degree to which hospitality was a profit-making enterprise is less clear in the Greek era. Nevertheless, there are indications that in Athens in 400 B.C., when it was the center of seafaring enterprise, inns were operated as businesses to provide accommodations for visiting sailors.

Homer's Odyssey and Iliad suggest that hospitality, in those ancient times, became an obligation of the populace, for two possible reasons. In some instances, people felt that hospitality to strangers was necessary to their religious well-being; in others, they were hospitable only because of their own superstitious fears. Both attitudes derived possibly from the belief that a stranger was either a god or a representative of evil spirits, perhaps even the devil himself. In both cases we find, therefore, either religion or the supernatural as the principal motivating force in the concept of hospitality.

An explanation perhaps more logical—or, at least, easier to accept in our modern-day thinking—is that the providing of hospitality was merely a result of a "give-and-take" philosophy; that is, if you give a stranger food and lodging today, perhaps a stranger will do the same for you at another time. However, given the circumstances in which hospitality in ancient Greece was provided, it is understandable that certain elements of religion were intermingled with the idea. Missionaries, priests, and pilgrims formed a very large part of the traveling public. Often they were journeying to holy places, perhaps oracles or temples that had a dominant position in their religion. As a result, many of the accommodations for travelers were located in the vicinity of such places.

The accommodations were meager, providing only shelter and the barest of sustenance. In the earliest times, they were operated by slaves who belonged to the temples or holy places. Gradually, the slaves were replaced by free men, but even they were considered to be of low social prestige. In ancient Indian writings, we find that it was the duty of the priests and the holy men of the temples to arrange for accommodations and food for visitors.

Early travelers who were not on the road for religious reasons were usually on military, diplomatic, or political missions. This was particularly true during the Roman era, when the great Roman Empire extended far beyond the limits of Italy. Consuls, proconsuls, governors, and generals were constantly traveling between Rome and the many countries in the eastern Mediterranean that were part of the Roman Empire. The Bible notes that it was on such a journey that Paul was shipwrecked when, as Saul of Tarsus, he was engaged in a diplomatic or political mission.

Many military travelers disdained using the accommodations that were available along the route. Inns in the cities were of bad reputation and detrimental to travelers; outside the cities, they neither existed nor were needed. The military travelers preferred, therefore, to sleep in the tents they carried with them.

In ancient Persia, traveling was done in large caravans, which carried elaborate tents for use along the caravan routes. However, at certain points on these routes, accommodations known as *khans* were constructed. These were simple structures consisting of four walls that provided protection not only against natural enemies such as the whirling sandstorms but also against marauding enemies who attacked under cover of darkness. Within the walls, platforms were constructed upon which the travelers slept.

In the later years of the Roman Empire, taverns and inns provided shelter for traveling merchants, actors, and scholars. Accommodations were still primitive. Sometimes there were rooms for the people but no stables for the horses; more often there were stables but no rooms. The high point of that era in terms of hospitality was the development by the Persians of *post houses* along the caravan routes. These developed later than the khans and provided accommodations and nourishment for both soldiers and couriers. In his writings, Marco Polo described the post houses, known as *yams,* as apartments suitable for a king. They were located about 25 miles apart, perhaps the equivalent of a day's ride, and supplied fresh horses for the couriers carrying messages throughout the land. By Marco Polo's estimate, there were 10,000 such post houses in existence at the time of his journey to the Far East. In some writings the post houses were referred to as *tabernae,* obviously the Latin word from which tavern was derived. While wine and some nourishment were provided, it is unclear whether or not the establishments were operated with a profit-making motivation. In the Orient, many *caravansaries* were constructed. These were similar in nature to the post houses, structures constructed for overnight caravan stops. The sleeping quarters were constructed around a central courtyard. The term is still used in Turkey for inns built around the shores of Asia Minor. In any case, with the end of the Roman Empire in 476 A.D., the travel ceased, and the period known as the Middle Ages occupied the next 1,000 years.

THE MIDDLE AGES

During the Middle Ages, we again find the intermingling of religion and hospitality. It was considered the duty of Christians to offer hospitality to travelers and pilgrims. In many instances, monasteries functioned as inns, providing accommodations and food for the weary traveler. Some monasteries and churches, concerned perhaps with the invasion of private meditations by the traveling public, constructed separate buildings to accommodate travelers. These buildings were known as *xenodocheions,* a Greek word meaning inns or resting places.

Charlemagne, during his reign, enacted laws setting out the duty of a Christian to provide a free resting place for a traveler. However, in consideration perhaps of the possibility that a traveler might overstay his welcome, and also perhaps of the burden of providing free food for an indefinite period of time, the law limited the stay of any traveler in any one place to three nights.

Up to this point in our narrative, there has been no mention of the traveler's being charged for his accommodations or his nourishment. Indeed, the rendering of hospitality was considered a charitable donation, springing from religious beliefs rather than a business venture. But all this was to change in the year 1282 in Florence, Italy. The great innkeepers of the city incorporated a guild or association for the purpose of turning hospitality into a business. Inns became licensed and were permitted to import and resell wine. The inns themselves belonged not to the innkeepers but to the city, and they were operated under three-year leases sold by auction. Nevertheless, they were presumably profitable; in the year 1290, 86 inns in Florence were members of the guild.

The concept was not limited to Florence for long. Shortly thereafter, the business of hospitality spread to Rome and other Italian cities. It is interesting to note that, during that period, many of the innkeepers were German rather than Italian—possibly because many of the merchants who were traveling were themselves German and were eager to find accommodations where they would find their own language spoken and food to which they were accustomed.

THE 16TH TO 18TH CENTURIES

During this period, considerable improvement took place, particularly in England, in the quality of accommodations. The common mode of transportation used then was the stagecoach. Long journeys, such as from London, England, to Edinburgh, Scotland, covered a period of several days, so the stagecoaches were forced to make overnight stops. These called for not only food and rest for the horses but also food and accommodations for the passengers. A direct result was the construction of inns or taverns at suitable locations along the stagecoach routes. Since their passengers were mainly wealthy people, accustomed to certain luxuries, the stagecoaches contributed not only to growth in the number of inns but also to improvements in their quality.

The inns or taverns also became popular meeting places for local nobility, politicians, priests, and others. Licenses for the inns were issued by the local lord or knight within whose territory the inn lay. It is reasonable to assume that the issuance of such licenses was not without some form of patronage, as is known to occur in modern times.

The inns were built in a relatively standard design. The design was in the form of a quadrangle, with stagecoaches and people entering through a vaulted gateway. The yard within the quadrangle was used for many purposes, such as weddings or fairs, and often as a theater. The quadrangular form provided outside walls as a protection against enemies, and the single entrance was easy to control and protect. The various buildings or sections within provided sleeping accommodations for the travelers, a facility in which food and drink was served, and shelter for both the drivers and the horses. In the eighteenth century, coffeehouses became extremely popular in Europe and were incorporated into many of the inns.

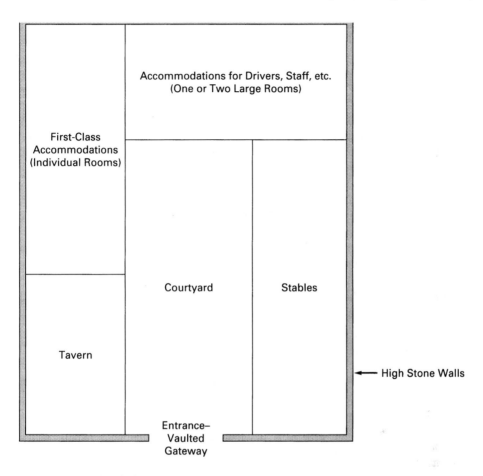

Figure 1-1 Layout of 17th Century Inn

One of the first European hotels, the Hotel de Henri IV, was built in Nantes in 1788, at a total cost of $17,500, then a tremendous sum of money. It had 60 beds and was considered the finest in Europe at that time.

GROWTH OF HOTELS IN THE UNITED STATES OF AMERICA

During the sixteenth to eighteenth centuries, early inns were built in North America in much the same fashion as in England. However, while the English inns were built along stagecoach routes, the American inns were mainly in seaport towns.

An inn in New York City played a major role in the American Revolution. Previously the DeLancey mansion, it was bought in 1762 and converted to an inn by Samuel Fraunces, a West Indian, who named it the Queens Head Tavern. The

Queens Head was a major meeting place for such organizations as the Sons of Liberty before the Revolution, and for British officers when they occupied the city. It became the scene of many dinners and parties, and in 1783, Washington bade farewell to his officers there. The building itself has been preserved as a historical landmark and now functions as a popular restaurant, known as Fraunces Tavern. In 1975, it drew particular attention when it was the scene of a bombing incident in which several people were killed.

The Queens Head was not, however, constructed specifically as a hotel. The honor of being first in this respect fell to the City Hotel, opened in 1794 in New York City, with 70 rooms. Several other, similar hotels were built in other cities in the next few years, but it was not until 1829 that a first-class hotel, Boston's Tremont House, with 170 rooms, was built. The Tremont innovated such features as private rooms with locks, soap and water for each room, bellboys, and French cuisine.

The remainder of the nineteenth and early twentieth centuries saw tremendous growth in the hotel industry, not only in the number of hotels but in the innovations designed to provide new and better comforts for the guests. Notable milestones in such growth were the following:

1834   Indoor plumbing was introduced into the hotel industry by Astor, a hotel developer in New York City.

1853   Steam elevators were first used in a hotel.

1875   The Palace was built in San Francisco, at a cost of $5 million. It was the biggest and the best of its time, with 800 rooms, and was a favorite meeting place of celebrities such as Oscar Wilde and Sarah Bernhardt. It was destroyed in the earthquake in 1906, but was immediately rebuilt in all its grandeur.

1836   The Astor House became the first hotel to be lit up by gaslight.

1894   The Netherlands Hotel in New York City became the first to have telephones in the rooms.

1896   The Waldorf Astoria was built in New York City. The next 20 years were glorious for the Waldorf, but it was razed to the ground in 1929 to make room for the Empire State Building. The new Waldorf Astoria was built in 1931 at its present location on Park Avenue.

During the same era, some of North American's most famous resorts were constructed.

1832   The Homestead in Hot Springs, Virginia.

1857   The Greenbrier, with 700 rooms, was opened in White Sulphur Springs, West Virginia, by the Chesapeake and Ohio Railroad.

1887   The Grand Hotel on Mackinaw Island, Michigan, with 275 rooms.

In the late nineteenth century, while many elegant and luxurious hotels were being built, there was also extensive construction across America of small railroad-station-type hotels catering to the commercial traveler. One of the builders of such hotels was Harvey Hotels. As the number of commercial travelers grew, so did their demands for service and comfort. A man justifiably regarded as the father of the modern commercial-hotel industry, Elsworth M. Statler, a former bellboy, had the vision to see that the growth in numbers of commercial travelers provided the opportunity for a successful hotel industry. In 1907, he built the Buffalo Statler, introducing many innovations, not the least of which was a private bath in every room. Statler must be considered the originator of the hotel-chain concept, to be followed later by Hilton, Sheraton, and many others.

The years from 1910 to 1930 saw the construction of many new hotels—nearly 100 from 1927 through 1930 alone—but very few of them were to survive the Great Depression. Nearly 85 percent of all hotels went bankrupt in the period from 1930 to 1935. These bankruptcies, however, proved to be a bonanza for the chains, giving them the opportunity to acquire quality properties at low prices—a substantial break in terms of low-cost real estate. Of particular note are the Sheraton and Hilton chains, who acquired properties during this period. In referring to the chains, note should also be made of Marriott Hotels, who became a significant part of the hotel industry.

THE MODERN HOTEL

The hotel industry will probably never again see the rate of construction that took place in the late 1920s. But new concepts in hotel design have been developed more recently in an effort to meet the changing preferences and new characteristics of the traveling public. Standard, rectangular, medium-sized, downtown hotels have been replaced (in fewer numbers) by the fine examples of new and innovative architecture. Roof-high atriums, outside scenic elevators, and other innovations have become features of such hotels as the Century Plaza in Los Angeles and the Regency Hyatt in Atlanta. Large convention hotels with extensive public areas, function space, and convention facilities have been built to meet the ever-growing group market. The New York Hilton is considered a fine example of a successful convention hotel.

There have also been great changes in the location of hotels. In the early 1900s, most of the traveling was done by train, so hotels had to be located close to railway stations. The tremendous increase in automobiles and airline travel, and the corresponding decrease in the use of railroads, opened up many new areas that could not previously be considered proper sites for hotel development. As a result, newer hotels are frequently located outside the city, at airports, and on the highways. In particular, the increase in automobile travel produced a new phenomenon in the hospitality field, the motel industry.

Motels originated as an outgrowth of increased demand by the automobile business traveler. In the early days of traveling salesmen, lodgings could frequently be found in private residences—often farmhouses near the highway—but the number of travelers soon exceeded the accommodations available. The motel became a method of providing low-cost accommodations for such travelers. Records indicate that the first motor court, the Askins Cottage Camp, was built in Douglas, Arizona, in 1901. (The development of the motel industry is discussed in detail in the following chapter.)

THE HOSPITALITY INDUSTRY

The preceding sections have traced the development of the hospitality industry and as an integral part of it, the hotel industry. Following is an examination of the hospitality industry today, both its makeup and its relationships with other industries. Most elements of the hospitality industry must be recognized as a part of the leisure industry.

The Leisure Industry

The recent years have seen many changes in day-to-day life. The reduced work week, for example, has produced the growth of an industry designed to take advantage of people's additional free time. The practice of taking short leisure vacations has also expanded the industry.

The leisure industry has been developed in many directions, such as these more significant elements:

1. The motion picture industry and the theater in its various art forms, i.e., legitimate theater, popular and classical music, comedy and magic, all benefits from the additional leisure time available.
2. Professional sports has become a major industry, both by itself and within this overall grouping.
3. The restaurant industry has benefited from an increase in the number of people eating out. This applies to both fast-food restaurants and more elegant dining facilities.
4. Additional free time has given people greater opportunities to travel. As a result, major beneficiaries within the leisure industry are:
   a. Airlines
   b. Cruise ships
   c. Motor coaches and railroads
   d. Travel agents and tour operators
   e. Last, but by no means least, the hotel industry

The Hotel Industry

Without question, the hotel industry as a whole benefits from increased travel. However, resort operations are the prime beneficiaries of increased leisure time. Facilities offering golf, tennis, skiing, health clubs, or perhaps only sun and sand, are great attractions for those who find they have more free time than they used to have.

The hospitality industry comprises those businesses that provide services, primarily accommodations, food, and beverages, not only to those traveling for pleasure, but also the business traveler. Consequently, of the elements making up the leisure industry, cruise ships, restaurants, and, to a lesser degree, airlines form a part of the hospitality industry—as do all hotels, and not only those serving the pleasure traveler.

CHAPTER SUMMARY

The early history of hospitality can be traced back to Babylon, ancient Greece and Roman times, and Persia. Religion was intermingled with hospitality not only in that era but during the Middle Ages.

Hospitality became a business in the late 1200s. In the sixteenth to eighteenth centuries, many inns and taverns were build in Britain.

Inns and ultimately hotels started their appearance in the United States around the time of the American Revolution and the 1800s saw the construction of many famous hotels and many innovations.

Construction of hotels was heavy from 1910 to 1930 but the Great Depression disseminated the industry.

Modern hotels incorporate new concepts and find new locations.

The hotel industry is a part of the leisure industry and the hospitality industry.

REVIEW QUESTIONS

1. Describe innkeeping in the Greek and Roman era.
2. Describe the various structures built as accommodations for the caravans.
3. What laws did Charlemagne enact to control the use of monasteries by travelers?
4. Describe the innovations in hotels from 1834 until 1887.
5. In the late nineteenth century, what factors were instrumental in the location of hotels?
6. What are the elements of the leisure industry?

2

Types of Hotels

As shown in Chapter 1, innkeeping has through the ages been closely associated with travel, always adapting itself to the changing needs of the traveler. In modern times, the emphasis has been on speed. Steamships, railroads, automobiles, and airplanes have all had their effect on the growth, type, and location of hotels. The tremendous increase in the world's population and the concentration of people in large metropolitan areas has also greatly influenced the hotel industry.

In today's terminology, hotels, motels, and motor hotels are practically interchangeable. In our definitions and description of the industry, we will, for brevity, use only the word *hotel*, but keep in mind that whenever it is used, it should be interpreted to mean motel or motor hotel as well.

After finishing this chapter, students should have an understanding of the various types of hotels, their facilities, and their market.

BASIC TYPES

Basically, there are only two types of hotels: transient hotels and residential apartment-hotels. *Webster's New Collegiate Dictionary* defines *transient* adjective as: "Passing . . . quickly . . . out of existence; transitory; short-lived; lasting or staying only a short time." Thus, a transient hotel is one that caters to people while they are temporarily away from home, whether for a day, week, or month, on business or for pleasure. The best definition of *residential,* and the one most easily understood, is an apartment house with full hotel services. These differ from transient hotels in that they are the official residences of the guests rather than their "home away from home." In addition, they usually require that the guest signs a lease.

Even though all hotels can be designated as transient or residential, few (excluding highway motels) cater exclusively to one class of guest. To improve occupancy and thus increase income, many transient hotels offer rooms on a permanent basis, with or without a lease. A study of the annual income per room will help the innkeeper to determine how many rooms to offer thus and at what price. Residential hotels, also to supplement their income or to accommodate guests of the permanent residents who may be in need of overnight lodging, will offer some of their rooms on a daily or transient basis.

Classification of Hotels

To classify every hotel merely as transient or residential gives the reader no idea of the many variations in size, features, or facilities offered. Nor does it provide an understanding of the reason for a hotel being what or where it is. To properly explain and so more easily define these differences, it is necessary to classify hotels in a manner that can be understood by the traveler. Several methods of classification have evolved and to some degree they interrelate.

Price

There are essentially three price categories within which hotels fall: luxury/upscale, midmarket/commercial, and budget/economy.

While this type of classification is easy to understand, it conveys a very limited amount of information specific to the hotel. Perhaps a more informative type of classification is by location.

Small Cities

By the turn of the twentieth century, most cities had one or more small hotels. They served two main purposes: they accommodated the guest who had business to transact, was traveling for pleasure, or was just passing through; and they were also social centers for the residents of the city and surrounding areas. All had at least a coffee shop; most had other catering facilities—restaurants, ballrooms, and so on. If a railroad passed through the city, the hotels were often built near the railroad station.

However, with the advent of automobile and airplane travel, the traveler who was not concerned with business in the city bypassed it. Even those who were shortened their stays; the easier the travel and the shorter the time needed for it, the less reason there was for staying that extra night in a hotel. Therefore, many of the hotels in the medium-size cities, especially those near large metropolitan areas, started to deteriorate as a result of the drop in business. Today, if they are still in existence, they are little more than second-rate rooming houses, many of them in or very close to slum areas.

Contributing to their downfall was the loss of social functions, such as weddings, anniversary parties, and dances. Since travel was easier, people holding such affairs naturally gravitated to the downtown hotels, which offered a much greater variety, better facilities, and easier access for invited guests than the suburban hotel could. Some hotels in small cities, towns, and villages, particularly those far from metropolitan areas, managed to hold onto social-event-related business, particularly when the area around the hotel had not deteriorated to any great extent.

Although old, these establishments are still well kept and relatively prosperous. Room revenue is small and rather unimportant; much of their income now comes from the sale of food and beverages. It is due to the social functions in their banquet rooms and the sales in the restaurants and bars that they have maintained their position as meeting places for the area's residents.

Large Cities

Innkeeping is truly a "people business," particularly people on the move. In our large cities, there is a great concentration of people, frequently growing in number. These cities are the commercial, industrial, financial, and cultural centers of the country and, as such, attract many people for business or pleasure. It follows, therefore, that they have a great number of hotels and there is a great variety in their size, type, and facilities offered.

Since the late 1940s, the bulk of the new construction in the industry has been of motels and motor hotels. This means that the vast majority of hotels are 40 or more years old. The upkeep and condition of these hotels generally follow the pattern set by their locations. In the poorer or slum areas of the city, they have degenerated into second-rate rooming houses. Those in the finest sections are maintained as luxury hotels. The condition of those somewhere in between depends almost entirely on the area in which they are located.

It is in the metropolitan areas that can be found a tremendous variation in size—from small hotels with less than 100 rooms, to the giants of the industry with 1,000 or even 2,000 rooms or more. Naturally, the facilities offered follow the same pattern. If we eliminate the run-down hotels in the marginal and slum areas of the city, we can say that all offer the same basic hotel services—a clean room to sleep in; telephone, maid, and bellman service; and a front office where the guest registers, with cashiers and mail and information clerks (functions performed by one to 20 or more people, depending on the size). The furnishings and appointments in the rooms vary from moderate to luxurious and are directly reflected in the rate charged. Most have at least a coffee shop; the larger hotels have one or more restaurants and some offer banquet facilities.

It is in the large cities that the apartment-hotels established themselves, and here they are found in great numbers, with a wide variety of services and appointments. Hotels are built to answer a need; the influx of people into the city created such a demand. Transient workers need furnished rooms or apartments while they look for or start new jobs. The very wealthy, staying in the city a few months each year, want their own apartments, without the trouble of having to hire staff to maintain them. Once their children have left, older citizens, particularly the rich or upper middle class, no longer need their large homes in the suburbs. Of course, they have their own furniture, so the hotel rents them an unfurnished apartment, for less money but with full hotel service, including maintenance of the furniture. When necessary, the hotel uses its own linen and replaces part or all of the furniture, with each step accompanied by an increase in rental. Some firms maintain company suites for their executives when it is necessary for them to stay in town overnight on business and for their executives from plants or other offices around the country. And finally, there are the people who want the convenience of living in the city without the bother of housekeeping. The answer to all these needs is the apartment-hotel. Thus the great variation in service and appointments, from moderate to luxurious, reflects people's needs and, perhaps more importantly, their ability to pay.

Early in the 1960s, a new concept of *apartment-hotel* was born. It followed or paralleled the trend in the apartment-housing industry away from rentals to individual ownership of the apartment. The public's reaction to these conversions was generally very favorable. The landlord received his investment back, usually with a substantial profit, and the tenants, once they purchased the apartments, received a tax benefit for the home ownership. Unlike apartment houses, a vast majority of which were converted into cooperatives, the apartment-hotels offered their apartments for sale as condominiums. The difference is that in a cooperative-type of ownership, the purchaser owns a share in the building, whereas a condominium owner has title only to his or her own apartment. The apartment-hotel operators had to retain ownership of their buildings in order to continue offering the full hotel services that their guests were accustomed to receiving. A staff was needed to maintain these services. To partially offset this expense, some of the apartments were retained by the hotel operators and offered for rental to guests of the condominium owners and the general public. Some of the hotel operators, to encourage their guests to purchase these apartments, offered to rent them on a daily basis when they were not occupied by the owner, and remit the proceeds, less a stipulated fee, to the owner. In the 1970s into the 1980s, many of the new apartment-hotels were built as condominiums and many other old hotels were converted to condominiums.

However, it is in the large so-called *convention hotels* that the whole spectrum of services is found. It has been said that they are truly small cities in themselves and that, theoretically, a person could spend a whole lifetime in one without ever having to leave the premises. They offer everything from medical services—doctors, dentists, and druggists—to entertainment in their restaurants, cocktail lounges, and nightclubs. Cable television is available for the latest plays, movies, or sports events. A snack or a sumptuous meal is easily obtained in one of the many restaurants or through room service. The shops and concessions enable the guests to buy anything from a newspaper to a diamond. How many small cities or towns can offer the same? For that matter, how many have a total population greater than the number of guests these hotels can accommodate at one time? Some can serve 4,000 to 10,000 meals at one sitting in their restaurants and banquet rooms and accommodate thousands more in meeting rooms and convention halls. With accommodations for between 2,000 to 4,000 overnight guests comes the employment of around 1,500 staff to serve these guests. Thus, there can be 20,000 people or more in the hotel at one time—truly as many as the population of a small city.

Parking has always been a major problem in our cities. Until the late 1940s, very few transient hotels provided in-house parking for their guests. But some of the better apartment-hotels did so in response to the needs of their permanent residents, and motels and motor hotels have always had parking facilities for their guests. With the growing use of the automobile, by both travelers and daily commuters into the city, the hotels again enlarged their facilities to meet a need. Hotels built since then, with very few exceptions, have garages or parking lots primarily for the use of the guests but open to the general public whenever space is available.

Resorts

A *resort hotel* may best be described as one where people go to relax and be entertained. Relaxation takes different forms for different people. It may mean just resting or sitting in the sun or sightseeing. Or it can involve swimming, boating, water skiing, fishing, golfing, mountain climbing, or skiing, one of the fastest-growing winter sports in the United States.

There is nothing new in the idea of resort areas. In ancient times, to escape the extreme weather conditions, the very rich often left the cities in both the summer and the winter. Even if they maintained their own homes in the country or at the seaside, they needed places for recreation and entertainment. The upper middle class also traveled and, particularly during vacations, needed a place to stay in which to relax. Hotels were built to cater to the needs of these people, since the average city workers spent their leisure time on nearby beaches or in the mountains, usually only for the day, and therefore had no need for a hotel.

The tremendous growth in this field during the twentieth century is probably the best example of innkeeping meeting the needs of the people. Longer vacations and shorter work weeks created more leisure time for the average worker, and higher pay and cheaper and more rapid means of transportation made all parts of the country, in fact the world, easily accessible.

People no longer had to limit their traveling to any particular season of the year. For instance, some of us can remember when Florida, especially Miami, was the playground of the 9-to-5 worker in the summer and the exclusive vacation spot of the wealthy in the winter. Today, it is a year-round resort for everyone, and this in spite of the fact that rates are generally higher in winter. The emergence of Hawaii as a vacation and recreation area is also an example of how changing travel patterns—in this case, the airplane—have helped to create new resort areas, and provided the innkeeper with new opportunities and challenges.

Resort hotels can be separated into two categories. The first is a *self-contained* unit in which the hotel provides all the recreational facilities for its guests—indoor and outdoor pools, tennis courts, golf courses, horseback riding, and some type of entertainment. The better-known hotels usually have nightclubs and hire the finest entertainers. They also show current movies and provide other forms of entertainment. Guests really have no reason to leave the hotel at any time during their stay, so food is included in the cost of the rooms, a system known as the *American Plan.* (Actually, weight-conscious Americans have been known to complain that a hotel can serve too much food—three very full meals a day plus afternoon tea, and sometimes a late evening snack. This overfeeding does not, needless to say, prevent anyone from going to such resorts.)

The other type of resort hotel is located near or at natural recreational areas such as the seashore, large lakes, national shrines, parks, or ski slopes, or in legalized gambling areas—which accounts for the popularity of Nevada as a resort area. These hotels may have their own pools and certainly restaurants, nightclubs, and other forms of entertainment for their guests, but it is the area, rather than the hotel itself, that attracts the people.

It follows that the guest need not have their meals at the hotel. In fact, many do not, preferring to try some of the other well-known restaurants in the area. In addition, since sightseeing is part of the reason for the guests' being there, many would find it very inconvenient to return to the hotel for lunch if three full meals were offered. As a result, these hotels give their guests a choice between "European Plan" (room only, with no meals) or the very popular "Modified American Plan," which provides a room and two meals (breakfast and dinner). Some hotels using the latter will even give the guest a credit against the total bill for meals that are missed.

No discussion of resort hotels would be complete without at least a mention of America's fast-growing ski areas. Skiing is an expensive sport, what with the equipment and special clothes that are needed, and the ski slope itself adds to the cost. (The operators of the ski slope have no choice. They must maintain a ski lift, and many make artificial snow when nature fails.) Nevertheless, skiing is very popular and one of the few sports that seems to attract the whole family.

Ski areas are usually far from the cities. Because of the time needed for travel and its expense, guests usually stay for two or more days, and some even spend their full vacation skiing. Again a need, and again the innkeeper has responded. New hotels, motels, and ski lodges surround the major skiing areas, and as the demand increases, more are being built.

In one respect, large resort areas are in direct competition with the cities. Both offer excellent convention facilities and actively solicit group and convention business. Although the resort hotels do not have the 1,000 or more rooms found in hotels in the large cities, they do match them in their banquet, meeting, and convention facilities. Also, they can collectively offer as many sleeping rooms as their city counterparts, since resort hotels are build in groups near each other, permitting convention guests to stay in any of them with no problems traveling to and from the convention headquarters.

Resorts have become very popular as meeting places for corporate groups. The scope of the activities keeps the attendees on premises and the convention facilities meet the needs for a proper meeting venue.

Airports

With the growth of the airline industry and the mass transportation of people by air, another need developed. An airport is usually some distance from the city. Flights may be postponed or canceled, and the airlines will have to take care of hundreds of passengers—feed them, and, if an overnight delay is involved, house them also. Previously, the passengers had to be transported to and from the city for this purpose, an expensive and time-consuming process. Again there was an opportunity and a need, and the innkeeper took advantage of it. Hotels were built around or in the major airports.

Today, their business comes not only from inconvenienced passengers. The traveler also finds a place to rest while waiting for connecting flights. Many people catching a very early flight prefer to arrive at the airport the night before and get a good night's rest at the airport hotel, thus avoiding the rush of the morning automobile traffic that is so heavy around major cities.

To cater to this airport traffic, the hotel needs a fair amount of rooms, at least 100, and some restaurant facilities, possibly a coffee shop and a main dining room. But this type of occupancy alone is not enough to run a business profitably. So most airport hotels have added banquet and meeting rooms to attract the social functions of people living in the area and business functions from firms located nearby. In certain large cities, such as Chicago, the airport hotels are favorite locations for area meetings. Personnel can fly in from several locations and meet conveniently at the airport. There are savings in taxi fares, of course, but the biggest savings is in time.

Thus, the airport hotels are also in direct competition with the city hotels and with growing success. Two problems, one in the operation and the other in the construction of the building, bear mentioning. The first relates to the transportation of the guest from the airport to and from the hotel and is easily solved. The hotel maintains a small private bus that makes frequent trips to the airport. The other is the problem of noise abatement. Modern jets are very noisy, and at an airport they take off and land 24 hours a day. But most airport hotels are relatively new, and modern technology has succeeded in insulating them to a point where few guests have had any reason to complain on this score. Many such hotels, being centrally heated and air-conditioned, therefore also have sealed windows.

OTHER METHODS OF CLASSIFICATION

Certain types of hotels are designed to meet specific needs of a certain segment of the market. We have previously discussed convention hotels. A smaller version, catering also to the group business, is conference centers. These properties are smaller than the convention hotels but have facilities specifically designed to cater to business meetings. In addition to various sizes of meeting space, they provide the ultimate in audio-visual equipment.

All-suites is a category of hotels that has become increasingly popular. The first operator in all-suites hotels was Embassy Suites, which was eventually acquired by Holiday Inns. Although they vary in format, some providing two or more rooms while others are a single room with a kitchen attached, they provide the guest with the opportunity to cook and eat in their accommodations. This is particularly attractive to long-stay guests with families—people who are temporarily located in the area. These include families in the relocation process, diplomats, or people who must stay close to loved ones who are hospitalized. The major innovator in the motel/motor inn field was Kemmons Wilson, the founder of Holiday Inns. In addition to the motorist, he also addressed the need for low-price facilities for families traveling for various reasons. Particularly he started the concepts of children staying free and children's menus.

A very basic classification is simply whether a hotel has a chain affiliation, possibly owned or leased or simply managed or franchised. Hotels not falling into this category are simply called "independents."

Motels and Motor Inns

In the earlier discussion of classification by location we did not discuss a major segment of the industry, motels and motor hotels.

The forerunners of the modern motels were small tourist cabins, usually a cluster of less than 10, mostly without baths, built by some farmer as a sideline along the road. They provided little more than a bed and overnight shelter for the passing traveler. As automobile traffic increased, these cabins grew in number, size, and appointments and became full-time businesses in themselves. Known as tourist courts, they consisted of detached frame cottages, clustered or spread over a sizable tract of land, with heated rooms and private baths. Many are still in existence along the highways, particularly on the outskirts of small cities and towns or near resort areas. Most of them now offer restaurant facilities, swimming pools, telephone service, television, and air-conditioning—improvements that make it difficult to continue classifying them as tourist courts. They seem no different from modern motels, except perhaps in the design of the buildings.

The next development, the first to be called a motel, was the roadside or highway motel. Initially, these were one-story buildings spread over a large area, containing a central office and connecting rooms on one or both sides of it. As the need for more rooms grew and land became more expensive, they became two or even three-story buildings. Much of the expansion in the number of motels occurred in the late 1940s and early 1950s; according to the U.S. Census Bureau, the number increased from 13,521 in 1939 to 41,332 in 1958.

All three types had one thing in common: very little, if any, service. The guests registered, were given the key to their room, and then were on their own. They parked their own car in front of their room, carried in their own bags, and were free to leave the following day at or before checkout time. These establishments were geared to speed automobile travelers on their way conveniently and economically. As more facilities were added, restaurants and swimming pools in particular, guests may have lingered more but, with easy access to their rooms, were still free to come and go as they pleased. And motels usually provided soft-drink and ice-dispensing machines from which the guests helped themselves.

Thus, the primary difference between a motel and hotel, until recently, was in service. In a hotel, the guest has his or her car parked by an employee, and pays extra for the garage; another hotel employee takes the guest to the room; the freedom of movement, especially by car, that the hotel guest has is restricted; and ice and soft drinks are available only from room service.

But in the early 1960s, a new trend in motels began to emerge. They grew larger and more elaborate and finally moved into the downtown sections of larger cities. Land there was very expensive, so in order to increase the number of rooms, the new motels were built 10, even 15 stories high. No longer could a guest be given a parking space near the room, and the registration process became the same as in a hotel. All the facilities offered by a hotel—telephone, television, air-conditioning, room service, coffee shops, restaurants, valet, laundry, and shops of all kinds—are duplicated in such a motel. Perhaps the only difference is that every motel has a garage, and parking is usually free in that it is included in the room rate; and most still make a few concessions to the old style by having swimming pools and ice and soft-drink machines on various floors. Because they are more truly hotels, the larger ones have become known as "motor hotels." In fact, they are hotels built primarily to cater to the motorist . However, with their numerous bedrooms, restaurants, and banquet and meeting rooms, they are in direct competition with the hotels.

In the 1970s a new trend began. No longer were people migrating to the larger cities. Instead, they were moving away from them to the suburbs and the country. Crime, high taxes, the flight of industry, and the resulting loss of jobs were the principal reasons for this reversal. The traveling public, alarmed by the crime statistics published in newspapers and repeated daily on radio and television, began shying away from overnight stays in the city.

Still, the city has too many cultural attractions to keep people from visiting it entirely. The solution: a place to sleep near, but not in, the city. A need, and again, the hotel industry met the challenge. Hotels and motor hotels were built in the suburbs surrounding the big cities. The traveler parks the car, stays overnight, and in the morning travels into the city with the family by bus or train, or even by car. They enjoy the city by day and return to the hotel or motor hotel for the night.

Here again, economics comes into play. These motorists cannot fill the hotel or make it a profitable business. However, motorists, plus the social business in the suburbs, can. The hotel is built with restaurants, banquet facilities, and meeting rooms, many with luxurious appointments to compete with the facilities offered by hotels in the city. The better city hotels will survive with large group and convention business and with the many visitors who stay in the cities (in spite of all the bad publicity). But the suburban and airport motor hotels are growing in number and popularity. Only a prosperous America can support both. The badly managed and marginal city hotels and motels are doomed and will disappear much faster than in the past with every downward cycle in the nation's economy.

By the mid-1970s, the motel had come full cycle, from the small tourist cabins to the luxurious motor hotels in the resort areas, cities, and suburbs. But a small crack had appeared in this headlong upward spiral of facilities and services. In California, a small chain was born with what is considered an entirely new concept of operation. The idea had been originally tried and discarded by the largest and one of the most luxurious chains of motels in the world, Holiday Inns, whose original properties were conceived as a group of low- to medium-priced motels. As they grew in size and popularity, however, they added restaurants, meeting and convention rooms, lobbies, and recreational facilities, and upgraded the furnishings and equipment in the bedrooms, thus completely abandoning the original concept. The general public, during a prolonged period of prosperity, was not interested in economy.

However, in the late 1960s, inflation, recession, and the resulting increase in unemployment started to take their toll. The traveling public began to question, and many could not afford, the high room rates that were necessary to charge to profitably operate these beautiful motels and motor hotels. The need grew, the time was right, and the concept started by Motel 6 in California slowly spread across the country. Whatever names they go by—Econo Travel, Days Inns, Imperial 700, Scottish Inns, and others—the operations of these budget motels were similar. Many were located in fringe areas accessible to, but not on, the main highways. They were built at the lowest possible cost to provide lodgings without frills, primarily to the commercial traveler and the family on vacation. For this purpose, the expenses of operation and the per-room cost of the building itself must be drastically reduced. Construction costs were kept low by using modular-type construction in which the entire rooms were built elsewhere, transported to the site, and placed side by side. The buildings usually had no lobbies, restaurants, or banquet, meeting, or convention rooms, and the bedrooms were very small. Many had a small office and kitchen combination where guests could get themselves a light breakfast at a minimum charge. Furnishings in the rooms were down to the bare essentials. Television, where it was provided, was usually coin-operated and usually only in black and white. Although each room had a private bath, it was outfitted with only a small standing shower, rather than a combination tub and shower. Some had small outdoor pools, but few provided any services other than an attendant to clean and make up the room. All they offered was a clean, comfortable room at a low rate.

In the late 1970s through the mid-1980s, the unemployment rate was very low, America was very prosperous, and so the budget hotels had to improve their facilities in order to attract the traveling public. A restaurant, or at least a coffee shop, was opened, a color television and a telephone was added to each room, and whatever else could be done to improve services and facilities of the budget motel was provided.

Beginning in the middle of the 1980s, *budget motor hotels* started regaining their popularity. America was still prosperous, unemployment was still low. But the middle class, which constitutes a large percentage of the traveling public, and business travelers rebelled against paying $100 or more for a room just to sleep in.

Hotel operators were quick to notice this change in attitude. As a result, they started building a new type of budget hotel. They could perhaps best be described as luxury economy hotels. Built primarily for the traveler, they omitted unneeded extras, such as expensive lobbies, large meeting and banquet rooms, and large restaurants. All featured large bedrooms, attractively furnished, with telephone service and color television. Many provided small meeting rooms and a restaurant or coffee shop, and some included a swimming pool and exercise room. All were medium priced, with an average rate around $50 to $60.

Perhaps the most startling development of the 1990s was the proliferation of new brand names on the hotel scene. The increases were not confined to any specific category of hotel but rather, with the exception, perhaps, of the luxury class, covered the spectrum from middle-range hotels and conference centers to the long-term stay and budget categories.

While the increase in brands is very visible to the average traveler, what is, perhaps, less visible is that many corporations own and operate several brands and that, in fact, there has been so many mergers and acquisitions that, in truth, there may be fewer individual corporations in the hotel field than at the advent of the 1900s.

There have been three main consolidations in the luxury category. Starwood Hotels and Resorts operates both the Sheraton and Westin properties and Four Point Hotels, mid-range properties; Canadian Pacific Hotels and Resorts have entered into a partnership with Fairmont Management—a total of 35 properties; and Hilton has merged with Promus Hotel Corporation, which has Doubletree, Red Lion, Embassy Suites, Hampton Inns, and Homewood Suites.

In the middle range, Cendent Corporation operates Wingate Inns, Howard Johnson, Ramada, Travelodge, Villager Inns and Lodges, and in the budget category, Days Inns and Super 8 Motels. Patriot American Hospitality, operator of Summerfield Suites and Sierra Suites, has merged with Wyndham International. Other consolidations include Prime Hospitality Corporation combining Wellesley Inns and Suites and Home Gate Studios and Suites; Candlewood Hotel Company combining Candlewood Suites with Cambridge Suites by Candlewood; and

Suburban Lodges acquiring Guesthouse International. It is probable that the twenty-first century will bring a whole new set of mergers and acquisitions.

Many hotel chains and independent hotels have Web sites. They provide pictures of the various types. Of particular note are Hyatt, Doubletree, Wyndham, Starwood, Renaissance, and Loews.

CHAPTER SUMMARY

There are two basic types of hotels, transient and permanent. However, hotels can be classified in many ways:

1. by price
2. by location
3. by type of clientele
4. by specific needs
5. by chain affiliation

Motels and motor inns had a major impact in the 1940s and 1950s. In the 1960s, motor hotels made the scene. The 1970s saw the advent of the budget motor hotels.

Consolidation of brands has taken place in the 1990s.

REVIEW QUESTIONS

1. What are the two basic types of hotels?
2. How are hotels classified by price?
3. What types of hotels are defined by location?
4. Describe apartment-hotels.
5. Describe resorts and identify their markets.
6. Describe all-suite hotels and identify their markets.
7. What is the history of motels and motor inns?
8. What is a budget hotel?

3

Corporate Structures and Concepts of Operation

After studying this chapter, the student should be knowledgeable of the various corporate structures used in the hotel industry.

The original concept for the operation of a hotel, particularly a small hotel, was that the owner would operate it as a *sole proprietor*. In many instances, the owner was also the manager and quite often performed other functions as well. As a sole proprietor, the owner is personally liable for the debts and losses incurred by the operation. At the same time, however, he or she is relieved from filing the documents and paying the fees that are required of an incorporated business.

But now, many owners have found it advantageous to incorporate their hotel operations. Usually, the owner forms a corporation to own and operate the hotel, although there is no reason that an existing corporation cannot be used. The creation of the corporation limits the risk and liability of the individual owner and thus protects that owner's personal assets from loss should the operation be unprofitable.

There are, however, certain options available to any individual—or for that matter, any corporation—owning a hotel. These options involve the association of the hotel with one of the many hotel chains in the country. The degree to which control of the operation of the hotel is transferred from the hands of the owner to the chain operator depends on the exact nature of that association. The relationship could be in the form of either a lease, a management contract, or a franchise agreement. The extent of the shift in the operating responsibility under such arrangements can be more clearly understood by looking at the various operating formats that the chains use.

CORPORATE STRUCTURES

Although there are many similarities in how various hotel chains function, the corporate structures under which these hotels are owned and operated are many and varied. The reasons for this are often complex and relate only to the particular circumstances of each company. There are, however, certain more common reasons.

Corporate structures that isolate the hotel operations within the corporation reduce the losses in the event of bankruptcy of an individual property. The losses can be restricted to the assets of that particular hotel, with no loss in regard to the other assets of the chain.

Similarly, the limitation of the liability of the assets of a particular hotel prevents the loss of the chain's other assets in the event of a lawsuit. Apart from legal actions by creditors, actions may be initiated by guests or clients as a result of injuries or damages incurred in or about the hotel. Labor negotiations or union agreements sometimes result in legal actions, by either the workers or the union. In certain instances, there may be lawsuits against the hotel by shop tenants, concessionaires, musicians or artists under contract, or other third parties who have a contractual relationship with the hotel. In these circumstances, the liability of the chain would also be limited to those assets held by the specific company being sued, thus preventing any risk of exposure to the other hotels in the chain.

Income tax implications are often a consideration in forming a desirable corporate structure, particularly with respect to overseas operations, where certain tax concessions or incentives may be available to the company operating or owning a hotel. The intent may also be to avoid taxation of other earnings of the chain by maintaining separate corporate structures for each operation. For example, were a hotel chain to operate two hotels in two different countries under the same corporate structure, it is quite possible that both countries might attempt to tax the earnings of both hotels.

Sometimes the need to maintain a separate corporation for a particular hotel results from agreements made with a landlord or partner, in terms of either a rent calculation or profit participation. Where such agreements exist, the operating results of the specific property must be isolated.

Following is an examination of the alternatives available for forming an overall corporate structure for the chain.

One Corporation Owning Several Hotels

This is the simplest form of corporate structure, in that it requires the formation of only one company, of which each hotel operates as a branch or subsection. This structure saves money as filing fees, legal costs, registration fees, and other expenditures incurred in forming and maintaining a company are kept to a minimum. On the other hand, it furnishes no protection whatsoever toward limiting the potential loss in the event of a legal action taken against the company. All assets are exposed in such a case. Furthermore, all earnings are thrown into the same pot, so little maneuvering or structuring can be done to obtain income tax relief or incentives.

Parent Company with Individual Subsidiary Owning Each Hotel

This arrangement, as mentioned earlier, provides maximum benefits in protection of the assets of the chain from lawsuits or legal action brought against a particular property. Furthermore, it has all the advantages in income taxes, grants, or incentives that are available to individual corporate entities. Although additional costs are incurred by having a multitude of individual companies, these costs are in the nature of filing fees, legal fees, audit fees, and the like, and are minor when compared with the advantages.

In such an arrangement, the parent company functions as a holding company whose principal asset is the shares of the subsidiaries, each of which owns the assets of an individual hotel. Earnings or profits flow from the subsidiaries to the parent company by means of dividends paid.

Limited Partnership with a General Partner and a Group of Limited Partners

Because of changes in the income tax laws, this structure has lost a great deal of its attraction.

The concept is essentially one where a partnership is formed in which there can be a substantial number of limited partners (the number is usually restricted only by the degree to which the administration of the partnership can be effectively carried out) whose investment, and the return thereon, is related to the tax advantages and the degree of risk.

The partnership agreement determines the amount invested by the limited partners, usually in terms of dollars-per-unit owned, and the amount invested by the general partner. The amount of investment required from the limited partners is in fact "limited" to a specific amount while the general partner's investment can increase as additional investment is required to fund capital expenditures or operating deficits. The limited partners' investment, although predetermined, may be phased in over a set period of time rather than fully at inception.

Profits or losses are divided between the general partner and the limited partners in a ratio prescribed by the partnership agreement rather than directly in proportion to investment by the two categories of partners. Furthermore, the ratio usually varies in amount from earlier years to later years.

Since the earlier years frequently produce substantial losses for tax purposes, losses that are more advantageous to the limited partners, a larger share of profits or losses are ascribed to them in these years while the general partner receives a larger share in later years.

The tax advantages were particularly important when these early losses were magnified by maximizing depreciation expense. Now, however, changes in the tax laws have severely restricted the deductibility of such losses.

REITs (real estate investment trusts) are similar to a limited-partnership concept in that they represent investment by the public in which multiple real estate investments quite frequently are in hotels as well as other forms of real estate.

Lease Arrangement between Parent Company and Subsidiaries

In this structure, the same advantages are obtained as in the parent company/individually owned *subsidiary* structure—protection against lawsuits or legal actions, and full utilization of tax advantages, concessions, or grants. But there is also additional protection, inasmuch as the real property—the land, the building, and possibly even the furniture and equipment—is owned by the parent company and therefore is also protected from losses incurred by the subsidiaries. Under such an arrangement, the subsidiary pays rent to the parent company for the property. Such a rent could be a fixed amount, or could vary according to various formulas, discussed later in this chapter.

Management Arrangement between Parent Company and Subsidiaries

The advantages here are the same as in a lease agreement in terms of taxes, incentives, and protection against lawsuits; however, the real property is exposed, since the land, buildings, furniture, and equipment are owned by the individual subsidiaries. The parent company is a management company, providing services to the subsidiaries for which it receives payment. Such fees are determined in various ways, and possible methods of calculating them are discussed later in the chapter.

Joint Venture between the Chain and an Outside Party

The joint venture form of structure has been used in the area of motel development, although its use in major hotel projects has been somewhat limited. A joint venture is a partnership between two companies, a company and an individual, or two individuals, for the purpose of developing and operating a specific project rather than a series of projects. The division of ownership and the participation in profits can be on any basis agreed upon by the two parties; there does not have to be equal participation by each partner. The joint venture arrangement in business is most often used where one party is providing the basic investment capital and the other is furnishing management and development expertise, in addition to possibly a more limited amount of capital.

In the motel field, joint ventures have been formed between an individual proprietor or developer and an established motel chain. The developer is responsible for providing the site and financing the major portion of the construction, possibly even the complete building. The motel chain provides a more limited amount of financing, probably covering the furniture and equipment, inventories, preopening expenses, and the *working capital* required for the operation. In addition, the chain supplies the development and management expertise, together with the advantages derived from identification and participation as a part of the chain. The ratio of participation in the joint venture or of the division of profits is agreed upon between the two parties and depends partly on the ratio in which capital or financing is contributed.

Where the individual developer personally invests, the potential liability is similar to that of a partner in a partnership, that is, liability to the full extent of his or her own personal assets. Obviously, this liability could be limited by forming a corporation to enter into the joint venture with the motel chain. Then, the assets of that corporation would be the only liability. The motel chain, on the other hand, as a partner in the joint venture, is liable up to the extent of the assets of the company entering into the agreement on behalf of the chain. This could be the parent company of the chain, but in many instances it would be a subsidiary created for the sole purpose of entering into this joint venture, or various joint ventures.

Most joint ventures in the motel field consist of an individual who makes a large initial investment, and a motel chain that contributes a smaller portion of initial capital, together with management and development expertise, but is generally called upon to provide additional working funds if the business is not successful within a reasonable period of time.

CONTRACT FORMS

The preceding sections have described the various corporate structures that exist in the hotel industry and the fact that within these structures many hotels operate under lease and management contract arrangements. These arrangements will now be discussed in detail, under four main headings: straight lease, profit-sharing lease, sale-and-leaseback agreement, and management contract.

Straight Lease

A *straight lease* on a hotel differs very little in legal format from a lease on any other kind of structure. It is, in effect, an agreement under which a tenant pays a fixed monthly amount to a landlord for the complete use of a specific hotel or hotels.

In some instances, hotel leases cover only the land and building, but it is not unusual for the owner of the building to own the furniture and equipment in it, and lease these also to the tenant. Under such an arrangement, the lease will contain some provision for the replacement of furniture and equipment. This replacement can be the full responsibility of the landlord or tenant, or there may be an agreement to divide the responsibility according to a predetermined format.

The lease should specify with whom the responsibility lies for the payment of certain *fixed charges* related to the property. The two principal items in this category are property taxes and fire insurance. Other minor items such as sewer, rent, water, garbage disposal, and items of like nature may also be covered in the lease. It is normally in the landlord's interest to have the tenant pay the property tax and fire insurance, so that the rent received is in fact a net rent. In any case, procedures for prompt payment of these items, as well as stipulations as to insurance levels, must be outlined in the lease in order to protect the landlord.

When a hotel is built and owned on land that is leased for the proper and successful operation of the hotel on a continuing basis, a hotel lease should be written for a period of at least 20 years.

Profit-Sharing Lease

Profit-sharing leases are perhaps more frequently found in the hotel and motel field than in any other area of real estate. The general intent is that although the hotel is, in legal terms, leased to an operator, the owner will participate in its profits. Not only is the desire of the landlord to enter into a profit-sharing lease profit-motivated, it also evolves from the fact that a profit-sharing lease eliminates the need for the insertion of clauses or conditions related to inflation. Normally, increases in profits resulting principally from inflation will result in a higher level of participation by the landlord, thus providing built-in inflation protection.

Profit-sharing leases in the hotel industry usually provide for payment of the property taxes and fire insurance by the landlord out of profits received (rent). This is not always the case, but it appears logical since the owner has control over the amounts of real estate taxes and insurance premiums and, since rent is based on the profit figure achieved, these items should therefore be excluded from the calculation of that figure.

Although the determination and compilation of hotel profits will be discussed in later chapters, at this juncture the basic structure of the hotel's income statement must be reviewed in order to understand the rent formulas. The income statement lists first the revenues of the hotel, then reduces them by the amounts of direct operating expenses of each revenue-producing department to yield the departmental profits of the operation. These are then reduced by the combined total of the overhead expenses to arrive at the house profit. The house profit is reduced by property taxes and fire insurance to arrive at the gross operating profit, which is then reduced by interest and depreciation to arrive at the net profit of the hotel. Table 3-1 gives an example of a hotel income statement down to house profit.

Table 3-1   Hotel Graylig Statement of Income for the Year Ended December 31, 2000

Revenue

Rooms	$2,000,000	
Food	1,200,000	
Beverage	600,000	
Telephone	150,000	
Laundry and valet	50,000	
Rents and other income	100,000	
Total revenue		$4,100,000

Department Profits

Rooms	$1,600,000	
Food and beverage	240,000	
Telephone	(15,000)	
Laundry and valet	10,000	
Rent and other income	100,000	
Total departmental profits		$1,935,000

Overhead Expenses

Administrative and general	$250,000	
Advertising and sales promotion	120,000	
Heat, light, and power	200,000	
Repairs and maintenance	210,000	
Total overhead expenses		−780,000

House Profit		*$1,155,000*

The house profit or the gross operating profit are most frequently used to determine the rent to be paid under a profit-sharing lease. However, there are many formulas used in such leases; the more common are:

1. Rent can be computed as a percentage of total revenue; for example, 20% of total revenue. Applying this formula to the figures in Table 3-1, the rent would be 20% of $4,100,000, or $820,000.

2. Rent can be computed as a percentage of gross operating profit, for example, 80% of gross operating profit. Applying this formula to the figures in Table 3-1, the rent would be 80% of $1,155,000, or $924,000.

3. Rent can be computed as a percentage of total revenue plus a percentage of gross operating profit; for example, 5% of total revenue and 60% of gross operating profit. Applying this formula to the figures in Table 3-1, the rent would be 5% of $4,100,000, or $205,000, plus 60% of $1,155,000, or $693,000, for a total rent of $898,000.

4. Rent can be computed by any of the formulas above but with the stipulation of a guaranteed minimum rent. On this basis, if the calculated rent is

higher than the guaranteed minimum rent, the calculated rent must be paid, but if the calculated rent is less than the guaranteed minimum amount, the guaranteed amount would have to be paid.

Obviously, in these formulas, certain calculations are more favorable to the landlord and others to the tenant. Rent that is determined only as a percentage of revenue is dangerous from the point of view of the operator. Inflation will cause revenue to increase even though occupancy stays constant and, meanwhile, payroll and other costs could increase at a faster rate than revenue. In these circumstances, the operator would be faced with higher rent even though the gross operating profit is decreasing.

Such a situation is, at the same time, obviously more advantageous to the landlord. On the other hand, if the rent is calculated as a percentage of gross operating profit, the landlord might suffer. A hotel could be extremely successful in attracting business and developing sales but, as a result of poor management, have a low gross operating profit and therefore a low rent. Clearly, a combination of both methods provides certain safeguards for both the tenant and the landlord, although the landlord usually obtains the required protection through a guaranteed minimum rent. Even though property taxes and fire insurance can be a substantial cash burden for the landlord, the landlord's primary consideration is to receive an amount of rent adequate to cover the debt service—interest and principal payments on the mortgage. The amount of guaranteed rent stipulated in profit-sharing leases is usually, therefore, set at a figure that will provide the necessary funds for the debt service.

The guaranteeing of a specified amount of rent provides a certain element of risk for the operator should the gross operating profit not be enough to meet the guarantee. The operating company would have to pay the additional amount needed out of its own *cash reserves,* with the result that it would have a loss equal to the excess of rent over gross operating profit. Under a lease where rent is a percentage of the gross operating profit without a minimum guarantee, the operator can still incur a loss if, in fact, the gross operating profit is a negative figure. Under these circumstances, it is a gross operating loss, one that the operator must absorb.

Sale-and-Leaseback Agreement

The sale-and-leaseback agreement is basically a financing arrangement designed to afford certain advantages in cash flow to a hotel operator while providing certain income tax advantages to the buyer of the property.

Many hotel chains own properties that they no longer feel it is advantageous to own. Perhaps these properties were acquired long ago and there is a current need to convert such assets into cash. Or the chain no longer wants to be a combination of hotel operating company and real estate company and for this reason wants to dispose of the hotels it owns. Or if a hotel was recently constructed by the chain, it may find the debt burdensome, particularly as it affects the balance sheet. At the same time, the chain wishes to continue operating the hotel, and therefore it makes an agreement with a buyer whereby the hotel is sold to the buyer and leased back by the chain, which continues to operate it. (We should mention, however, that in some countries accounting standards require that such a lease be treated as a purchase.)

Management Contract

There are many similarities between a hotel operated under a profit-sharing lease and one operated under a management contract, but there are certain major differences in the basic principles under which these two types of operations are carried on. Despite the complicated formulas that have been developed to ascertain the rent payable under a profit-sharing lease, the legal status of the operator is the same as that of an operator with a straight lease. The hotel is operated by a company that is legally completely independent of the owner. It is this company that employs the staff, bears the liability for any lawsuits brought against the hotel operator, and incurs the losses that result from the payment of a rent higher than gross operating profits.

A management contract, on the other hand, stipulates that the operator is acting fully and completely as an agent of the owner and for the account of the owner. The employees of the hotel are employees of the owner, and losses resulting from lawsuits of judgments against the hotel must be absorbed by the owner. Similarly, the final financial result of the operation, be it a profit or a loss, is a result for the owner's account and not that of the operator. The operator, in acting as a manager of the hotel on behalf of the owner, receives certain fees for managerial services. These fees may be an agreed-upon flat sum paid each year. More commonly, however, the fees are variable and related to the success of the operation. The more common bases for the calculation of these fees are the following:

1. A fee based on the total revenue of the hotel; for example, 5% of total revenue. In the example in Table 3-1, these fees would amount to 5% of $4,100,000, or $205,000.
2. A fee based on the gross operating profit of the hotel; for example, 20% of gross operating profits. From the figures in Table 3-1, this would amount to 20% of $1,155,000, or $231,000.
3. A combination of 1 and 2 above; for example, 3% of total revenue and 10% of gross operating profit. From the figures in Table 3-1, this would amount to 3% of $4,100,000, or $123,000, plus 10% of $1,155,000, or $115,500, for a total of $238,500.

As with profit-sharing leases, the method of calculation of management fees can be advantageous to either the operator or the owner. Where the fee is based solely on total revenue, the operator can spend money almost at will, particularly in advertising, so that a high revenue and therefore a high fee is achieved even though the hotel is not actually being operated profitably. Of course, calculation of the fee only on the basis of the gross operating profit places the strongest obligation on the operator to manage the hotel profitably. However, when results are poor, possibly owing to conditions beyond the operator's control, he or she could well discover that operating costs are not even being met. A combination fee based both on total revenue and gross operating profit is therefore probably the most equitable to both the operator and the owner.

In addition to stating the method of determination of the fee and clarifying the position of the operator as agent for the owner, management contracts usually contain certain other clauses, such as:

1. A definition of the type and quality of the hotel and of those items that are to be furnished by the owner.
2. The term of the agreement.
3. A requirement that the mortgage commitment provide for a nondisturbance clause in the event of a default by the owner. This ensures that the operator will continue to manage the hotel in case it changes hands due to a default on the mortgage.
4. A definition of the technical services to be performed by the operator and the fee to be received for such services. The fee usually consists of a dollar amount per room, say $1,500 to $2,000. These technical services are generally:
    a. A review of architectural and engineering designs prepared by the owner's architects, contractors, engineers, specialists, and consultants, including the preliminary and final plans and specifications.
    b. Advice and technical recommendations on interior design and decorating, with the owner's decorator.
    c. A review of the owner's mechanical and electrical engineering designs: heating, ventilating, air-conditioning, plumbing, electrical supply, elevators and escalators, telephones, and so on.
    d. A review of the owner and the owner's consultants of plans, specifications, and layouts for kitchen, bar, laundry, and valet equipment.
    e. Assistance and advice in purchasing and installing furniture, fixtures, and equipment; chinaware, glassware, linens, silverware, uniforms, utensils, and the like; paper supplies, cleaning materials, and other consumable and expendable items; and food and beverages.
    f. On-site visits to assist in scheduling installation of various facilities.
5. A definition of the preopening services to be performed by the operator and an agreement as to the costs of these services, which are amortized against the operating results of the early years and deducted in computing gross operating profit. Preopening budgets vary greatly, depending largely on the labor market and its effect on the preopening staff. Preopening services may include:

      a. Recruitments, training, and direction of the initial staff.

      b. Promotion and publicity to attract guests to the hotel on and after the opening date.

      c. Negotiation of leases, licenses, and concession agreements for stores, office space and lobby space, and employment and supply contracts.

      d. Procurement of the licenses and permits required for the operation of the hotel and its related facilities, including liquor and restaurant licenses.

      e. Any other services reasonably necessary for the proper opening of the hotel, including suitable inaugural ceremonies.

6. A description of the operator's duties. These normally include:

      a. Operation and maintenance of the hotel in a first-class manner.

      b. Hiring, promotion, discharge, and supervision of all operating and service employees.

      c. Establishment and supervision of an accounting department to perform bookkeeping, accounting, and clerical services, including the maintenance of payroll records.

      d. Handling of the complaints of tenants, guests, or other patrons of the hotel's services and facilities.

      e. Obtaining and maintenance of contracts for services to the hotel.

      f. Purchase of all materials and supplies required for proper operation.

      g. Maintenance and repair of the premises.

      h. Services in collection of receivables due the hotel.

      i. Inclusion of the name of the hotel in the operator's group hotel advertising.

7. A provision for the setting aside of an agreed-upon reserve fund for the purpose of making replacements, substitutions, and additions to furniture, fixtures, and equipment.

Franchise Agreement

In addition to the contract formats described in this chapter, an important form is the franchise agreement, under which the owner operates as a member of the chain, utilizing the name and for a fee obtaining certain services of a marketing and operational nature. Not only are the formats of franchise agreements very lengthy and varied, but there are many legal complications and ramifications related to them. Therefore, in order to do proper justice to the description and analysis of the franchise field, a full chapter must be devoted to the topic. You will find franchising covered in detail in Chapter 24.

CHAPTER SUMMARY

Hotels are operated under many corporate structures and arrangements.

Where the structures involve a landlord and tenant or a management agreement, the structure may be beneficial to either party.

Common structures are the following:

1. One corporation owning several hotels.
2. Parent company with individual subsidiary owning each hotel.
3. Limited partnership with a general partner and a group of limited partners.
4. Lease arrangement between parent company and subsidiaries.
5. Management arrangement between parent company and subsidiaries.
6. Joint venture between the chain and an outside party. Various contract forms used include:
   a. Straight lease
   b. Profit-sharing lease
   c. Sale-and-leaseback agreement
   d. Management contract
   e. Franchise agreement

Major consideration in determining the structure are financial exposure and income tax considerations.

REVIEW QUESTIONS

1. List the advantages and disadvantages of having one corporation owning several hotels.
2. What are the advantages of individual subsidiaries for each hotel?
3. Describe the operation of a limited partnership.
4. Describe a joint venture.
5. What are the advantages to an owner of a profit-sharing lease over a straight lease?
6. Describe various methods of calculating a management fee. Indicate which are more advantageous to the owner or operator.
7. List normal preopening services provided by a management company.
8. Give a description of an operator's duties under a management contract.

4

Feasibility Determination

Determining the feasibility of a hotel entails covering three major areas in detail: (1) the preparation of a feasibility study for the project, (2) the estimation of costs for all elements of the project, and (3) sources of financing. Within these areas, many individual factors must be examined.

After studying this chapter, the student should be able to:

1. Understand the importance of a feasibility study.
2. Understand the various elements that make up a feasibility study.

THE FEASIBILITY STUDY

There are several major firms of hotel consultants—notably Pannell Kerr Forster Consulting—that are experienced in preparing feasibility studies for proposed hotels. Of course, it is not absolutely necessary to hire an outside consultant for this purpose; in fact, extremely detailed studies are prepared internally by many of the major hotel companies. Nevertheless, the same companies usually also employ the services of hotel consultants, in part to obtain confirmation of the feasibility of their projections from outside sources. At the same time, financing institutions to whom project developers apply for the necessary funds will normally request a feasibility study prepared by an outside consultant.

The feasibility study itself can be broken down into several segments, each of which has an impact on the potential success of the project.

Site Selection

Without a doubt, the most important factor in the success or failure of a proposed hotel is the site location. The economic environment of the area must be considered; zoning laws must be researched; and, of course, the size of the site is very important. There is no cut-and-dry formula for the number of rooms that can be built on a given area of land. In city projects, height restrictions and parking requirements are determining factors in the amount of land required. For example, the Loew's New York, a 794-room hotel in New York City, sits on approximately 32,000 square feet—less than an acre of land. However, it has 19 floors and limited food and beverage facilities. On the other hand, the Paradise Island Hotel and Villas, a 503-room resort hotel with 9 floors, is situated on about 12 acres, offering a beach, tennis courts, pool, and other facilities common to resort properties. The physical location of the site is probably more important in many ways than the size itself, inasmuch as the proper approach is to determine from the size of the area the size of hotel that can be built to conform with all legal requirements.

The access of the site to the necessary utilities, such as water and electricity, is vital. If water and electricity are not already available, the provision of power lines, water pipes, and so on from the nearest source of supply to the site can be a major cost. Similarly, if it is necessary for the hotel to build a generating plant to provide its own electricity, or to dig wells for adequate water, again construction costs rise. The lack of nearby sewer lines can also contribute to an increase in costs.

The selection of a site is important relative to the impact on the cost of utilities. The site must be reviewed in relation to existing access to roads by which guests can arrive at and depart from the hotel. If the site does not have proper access roads, they must be built, resulting in further cost increases.

The natural advantages of the site must be considered, particularly as they provide additional incentives for guests to stay at the hotel. Nearby beaches, ski slopes, and similar natural attractions are very desirable. And the geographic contours of the site are important as they relate to the accessibility of such attractions. A smooth stroll from the hotel room to the beach is obviously much more desirable than a climb down 80 or 100 feet of rock. Many guests also like to view the sunset, but it is sometimes difficult to satisfy everyone's desires.

In considering natural attractions, the direction in which they face can often determine to what degree they will be used by guests. A beach facing east will provide a combination of morning sunshine and afternoon shade, which will probably be more desirable than a beach that faces west.

It follows, therefore, that the first step in any study of a potential project should be a careful, detailed examination of the site.

The Market

In order to ascertain whether there is demand for a hotel in the area where the site is located, certain very important factors must be considered. Of great importance is the existing tourist or business demand for hotel rooms in the area.

To analyze this demand, it is necessary to examine statistics on visitor arrivals, not only in the particular area but in the city and, indeed, in the country. Expected changes in the local economy should be considered, as this can impact the market. Such statistics are usually available from local tourist boards and chambers of commerce. The average length of stay of visitors in that location can also help to determine the demand for hotel rooms.

A hotel's location in relation to the city can be a positive or negative factor in creating demand. Proximity to the airport, shopping, golf, and historical and natural attractions are all factors that may increase or decrease the demand for accommodations. The relationship of the site to the airport should always be evaluated in terms of not only distance but also convenience. For example, a site could be located very close to the airport but on the opposite side from the city, town, or main shopping area and thus lose any advantage from its proximity. A site located at a point on a direct line between the airport and the downtown area likely to be most frequently visited would be much more desirable.

Supply of Rooms

It is of extreme importance to ascertain not only the existing supply of rooms but also the future supply.

The existing supply should be charted by first setting down the names of the current properties, chains, or other affiliations and the number of rooms they have available, then forming an opinion as to whether the overall location is good or bad. Facilities should be examined and charted as to type and size. In particular, present facilities for convention or group business should be analyzed and a determination made as to their quality.

Similarly, an investigation should be made of all proposed future hotels, their affiliations, and the number of rooms. Their facilities, too, must be charted and graded.

Labor Situation

One of the greatest problems in recent years in successfully developing new hotel projects has been the lack of an adequate labor supply. In many areas, the rapid development of the hotel industry has resulted in a labor demand exceeding the supply, especially at the middle-management or supervisory level. Before a project is undertaken, the source of staff must be determined.

Even if there is an adequate source of labor available, it may very well be that wages and benefit costs, because of conditions either in the industry or in the country, will result in abnormally high payroll. Such a high cost may render the project unfeasible.

Wage trends must also be examined. Even if current wage levels are acceptable, the recent rate of increase may indicate a trend that would cause excessively high wage levels within a short period of time.

The union situation should be studied to find out whether labor demands are reasonable. In some cities, for example, New York, the combination of high wages and the lack of flexibility in the work that can be performed has forced hotels to lease out their restaurant operations. This will require obtaining and reviewing existing *labor contracts* as indicative of the trends in labor negotiations. Optimally, the record of the unions should indicate that they are reasonable, flexible, and prepared to bargain in good faith.

Finally, the quality of labor that is available must be considered, not only because poor quality will have an adverse effect on business but also because unexpected costs may be incurred to properly train the staff. These training costs may be an important factor in determining the overall cost of the project.

Room Demand

At this juncture in the preparation of the feasibility study, the site has been evaluated to determine suitability for a hotel, the market has been analyzed to determine potential demand for a hotel in this location, and the supply of existing and future rooms—that is, the competition—has been evaluated. Based on the analysis made of statistics on arrivals and room nights, a projection should now be made of future demand for accommodations. It should be measured in numbers of future room nights, which can be set down and matched against the combination of currently available rooms and future rooms to be constructed. The comparisons will indicate the number of rooms for which there will probably be a future market.

An example of this type of projection of market demand is shown in Table 4-1. This assumes a tourist destination where visitors arrive by air and room night demand is based on airport arrivals, actual for years 1–5 and projected for years 6–8. The continued shortfall in first- class rooms available indicates that the addition of a 200-room hotel (73,000 available rooms) is entirely feasible.

Facilities

Concurrently, the analysis of the market should provide information as to the types of guests that may be anticipated—ethnic background, cultural preferences, income level, and, of course, country of origin. It will also include information as to whether the guests will be principally business travelers, tourists, or a mixture of both. Such data must be fully analyzed and considered in deciding the type of facilities to be constructed. Ethnic backgrounds may indicate the type of restaurant that would be most preferred; annual income levels could provide guidance as to whether there would be a demand for lavish floor shows requiring nightclub facilities, or whether the beverage facilities should be limited to bars and cocktail lounges.

The propensities of the anticipated tourist business would relate to the degree to which tourism-related facilities should be provided—particularly

Table 4-1 Estimated Capacity and Average Occupancy for Five-Star Hotels

Year		AIRPORT ARRIVALS		ROOM NIGHTS		Total	5-Star Rooms	Over
		Tourists	Business	Tourist(1)	Business(2)	Room Nights	Available	(Under)
1	Actual	52,000	8,000	312,000	24,000	336,000	292,000	(44,000)
2	"	55,000	8,500	330,000	25,500	355,500	292,000	(63,500)
3	"	61,000	9,000	366,000	27,000	393,000	328,500(3)	(64,500)
4	"	64,000	9,500	384,000	28,500	412,500	365,000(4)	(47,500)
5	"	67,000	10,000	402,000	30,000	432,000	365,000	(67,000)
6	Projection	70,000	10,500	420,000	31,500	451,000	365,000	(86,500)
7	"	73,000	11,000	438,000	33,000	471,000	438,000(5)	(33,000)
8	"	76,000	11,500	456,000	34,500	490,500	438,000	(52,500)

(1) Based on six-night stay
(2) Based on three-night stay
(3) Addition of 100 rooms to inventory (36,500 rooms available)
(4) Addition of 100 rooms to inventory (36,500 rooms available)
(5) Addition to inventory of 200-room hotel under construction

recreational facilities, such as swimming pools, tennis courts, and possibly golf courses. The importance of relating the facilities planned to the market rather than trying to find a market for predetermined facilities cannot be overstated.

Financial Projections

The accumulation of the information outlined in the preceding sections permits the preparation of perhaps the most important part of the feasibility study: the financial projections. The future room demand determined through the market analysis should be related to the number of rooms decided upon when planning the facilities, and this interrelationship should be used to obtain estimated occupancies for the hotel for a period of several years. The comparison of rates charted by existing competition, together with the quality of facilities to be provided, permits the determination of room rates that it is anticipated will be acceptable to future guests. The combination of occupancy figures and average rates permits a calculation of future room sales. Proper consideration must be given to increased demand and inflation in estimating the sales after the first year. A sample of the calculation of projected room sales is set out in Table 4-2.

Analysis of the market and the competition can be used to estimate average checks and volumes for each of the planned food and beverage facilities and ultimately for the total food and beverage sales. Other departmental income can normally be projected directly in proportion to either room sales or food and beverage sales. Once the projected sales have been determined, estimates must be made of cost of sales, payroll and related expenses, and other miscellaneous expenses, in order to arrive at an estimated operating profit. In estimating payroll figures, analyzing the labor situation will furnish guidelines to overall labor costs.

The first step in estimating the payroll is to prepare an expected staffing analysis for the hotel by job category. By multiplying the staffing analysis by the expected work week, weekly totals of hours in each job classification can be projected. Current wage rates can be obtained from either the records of existing hotels or existing union contracts. An inflation factor must be applied to these rates to cover the increase between today's rates and those that will be in force when the hotel opens. Then, by multiplying the project hours in each job classification by the projected rates, a total payroll for the first year of operation can be estimated. With minor modifications and the application of an inflation factor, payroll can be projected over a period of years.

Related expenses, including employee benefits, are projected as a percentage of cash payroll. The fact that this percentage has historically been increasing should be taken into consideration in future projections. Other departmental expenses are usually projected as a percentage of sales or as an amount per room, based on the experience of existing hotels in the area or similar hotels elsewhere.

Table 4-2   Estimated Rooms Sales

It is estimated that a 200-room hotel could be constructed and opened by the end of year 7, as reflected in Table 4-1. Thus the first year of operation will be year 8, which reflects a shortfall of 52,500 rooms. Matching 52,500 room demand against an available of 73,000 provides an occupancy of approximately 72%.

It could be argued that occupancy will be higher as a new hotel will attract business from the existing hotels. On the other hand, it is possible that some of these visitors who had to settle for less than first-class rooms in prior years will continue to do so. Therefore, we will use an occupancy of 72% increasing 2% per year in the second through fifth years.

A survey of the competition suggests that rates in year 8 will be in the range of $150, increasing at 4% per year. Projected room sales for the first five years are therefore as follows:

Year	Occupancy	Occupied Rooms	Average Rate	Room Sales (1)
1	72%	52,560	$150.00	$7,884,000
2	74%	54,020	156.02	8,427,000
3	76%	55,480	162.24	9,001,000
4	78%	56,940	168.74	9,570,000
5	80%	58,400	175.45	10,249,000

(1) Rounded to nearest $1,000

As can be seen, a feasibility study is, in fact, the development of the operating income to be derived from the project, starting with the very basic examination of the proposed site. The ability of the operating income to cover the fixed costs is the determining factor in the feasibility of a project.

COST ELEMENTS OF THE PROJECT

As in any construction project or any real estate development, there are certain elements of cost that make up the total package. In a hotel project, these elements can be broken down into the following:

1. Land
2. Construction
3. Interest during construction
4. Furniture, fixtures, and equipment
5. Operating equipment
6. Inventories
7. Preopening expenses
8. Working capital

In the following sections, each of these elements are discussed.

Land

Land is not necessarily an element of cost in a hotel project, as many hotels are constructed on land leased from the owner. However, where the land is actually purchased or owned, it becomes the most variable cost of all. In some instances, the land may have been owned by the developer for many years, in which case the historical cost may be relatively low; on the other hand, the developer may very well be acquiring a land site in a city such as London, New York, or Chicago. The cost of land, therefore, measured in terms of a per-room figure, may vary from as low as $500 per room to as high as $30,000 or $40,000. In most instances, a land cost exceeding $20,000 per room will make the project unfeasible. In considering low land costs in certain locations, the cost of necessary improvements in the infrastructure must be taken into account. Of course, a very deluxe hotel that gets a high average rate and a satisfactory occupancy could carry a higher land cost per room.

It should be remembered that, in determining the cost of land, taxes during construction and costs of clearing the land to make it suitable for building must be considered part of the overall cost.

Construction

The cost of construction is, of course, the biggest element of cost in any hotel project. Therefore, it is important to evaluate various types and quality of construction techniques and materials available in order to keep the construction cost within a practical figure. Currently, a per-room cost of construction of around $60,000 is considered to be satisfactory.

Cost of construction is most easily controlled if a fixed-price contract can be obtained from a contractor but, because of the inflation prevalent both in labor and in construction materials, this is not often feasible. So most hotels today are built under a cost-plus contract. Cost-plus means that the contractor's profits are a percentage of the costs. However, most of the advantages of a fixed-price contract can be obtained if a maximum ceiling on cost can be written into the contract.

Both fixed-price contracts and cost-plus contracts with a ceiling frequently contain provisions that permit increases in the price or the ceiling that are tied to changes in various government-established indexes, such as the consumer price index, the cost-of-living index, or some form of a cost-of-labor index. The inflation provisions may relate to materials, cost of labor, or both.

Many hotels, especially the budget hotels, are being constructed using prefabricated rooms, which are then placed side by side.

Interest during Construction

During the period when the hotel is under construction, this construction is usually financed with borrowed funds. The interest that must be paid on such a loan must be considered part of the cost of the project. Where the construction cost is the aforementioned $60,000 per room, an interest cost during construction of $6,000 per room would be reasonable.

Furniture, Fixtures, and Equipment

Various methods are used by hotel developers to purchase furniture, fixtures, and equipment. In some instances, the developer pays a fee to a supplier who plans and purchases all items in this category; in others, the purchases are made on an individual basis directly by the developer. A combination of these methods is feasible when a certain segment of the furniture, fixtures, and equipment—for example, the kitchen equipment—is purchased in total from one supplier.

Furniture, fixtures, and equipment can be subdivided into what is visible to the guest and back-of-the-house equipment. The first category would be guest-room furniture, lobby furniture, and furniture and equipment in the restaurants and bars. The second category includes those items not visible to the guests, such as kitchen and laundry equipment. Building equipment, such as air-conditioning or heating, is considered to be part of the construction cost.

A suitable figure per room for furniture, fixtures, and equipment is approximately $12,000.

Operating Equipment

Operating equipment in a hotel is a term used to cover linen, silver, china, glassware, and, in some instances, uniforms. In addition to the operating equipment that is immediately put into service in a hotel, a certain amount of back-up inventories, known as reserve stocks, must be acquired. A cost for operating equipment of $8,000 per room is acceptable.

Inventories

In order to open a hotel, various operating inventories must be acquired in addition to the reserve stocks mentioned. These inventories can be broken down into the following categories:

1. Food
2. Beverages
3. Cleaning supplies
4. Paper supplies
5. Guest supplies
6. Stationery
7. Engineering supplies

The quantities of such inventories should be related to the anticipated consumption. Although it is desirable to have adequate inventories on hand, excessive inventories tie up capital and create additional interest costs. A cost per room of $6,000 for operating inventories should be considered satisfactory.

Preopening Expenses

Prior to the opening of a hotel, expenses are incurred for such items as preopening payroll, training costs, advertising, and sales expenses and travel. The amount that should be allocated for preopening expenses must be determined at the time the overall budget is produced, but it would depend on the preopening philosophies of the operator. These will dictate at what point in advance of opening personnel will be hired, to what degree they will be trained before the hotel opens, and the extent of preopening advertising and sales. Some chains feel that it is in their interest to spend substantially prior to opening so that the hotel will open smoothly. Others, because of either different thinking or lack of adequate preopening funds, do not agree. In our opinion, preopening expenses should be at least $3,000 per room.

Working Capital

In addition to having adequate inventories on hand, it is obviously necessary to have a certain amount of money in the bank when a hotel is opened. Such funds must be sufficient to meet the early payrolls and to finance the operation before a normal level of cash flow is reached. It should be anticipated that, in the early days of operation, accounts receivable will accumulate without any material amounts of cash income being collected. It is to cover this period that adequate working capital must be provided. It should amount to at least $2,000 per room.

Summary

In recapping the elements of cost outlined, an overall figure for cost per room can be arrived at as follows:

Land	$10,000
Construction	60,000
Interest during construction	6,000
Furniture, fixtures, and equipment	12,000
Operating equipment	8,000
Inventories	6,000
Preopening expenses	3,000
Working capital	2,000
Total	$107,000

These cost figures are estimates for an average first-class hotel in the United States, based on prices and costs for a 1999 completion date. Economy hotels can still be built for $50,000 to $60,000 per room, while deluxe hotels, because of all the facilities, can cost $300,000 to $500,000 per room. Estimates for future hotels should incorporate a reasonable inflation factor. Naturally, deluxe hotels will require a higher cost per room, and lower-grade hotels and motor inns should have a considerably lower figure. Where the amount of public space in relation to the space occupied by the rooms is reduced, a considerable reduction can be obtained in the cost per room.

SOURCES OF FINANCING

In many instances, the sources of financing available to hotel developers are similar to those available to real estate developers of other kinds of projects. However, there may be specialized financing available for tourist development. The sources of financing are principally the following:

1. A certain amount of financing in North America is still obtained from the traditional lenders, that is, banks, mortgage lenders, and insurance companies. However, the amount of funds available from these sources has dropped considerably in the late 1900s.
2. The largest source of funding presently available for hotel development is from private groups of investors in various types of structures . Low interest rates has encouraged investors to look for investments, where, even if a better return is not guaranteed, a participation in the project is available.
3. Loans provided by such organizations as the World Bank or the Export–Import Bank for hotel and tourism development in various areas.
4. Loans provided by governmental or tourism bodies in an effort to promote tourism in a specific country.
5. Funds provided by various governmental bodies in the United States. Federal agencies, such as HUD, and state developmental agencies will provide financing.
6. Low-cost loans in the United States by state or city to assist in area development.

In each of these instances, it may be necessary to secure a separate source of financing during the construction period, which would then be replaced by the *permanent financing* when the hotel is opened. When funding is obtained, that is repayable in a foreign currency, the investor must be alerted to the possible impact of currency fluctuations.

CONCLUSION

This chapter has illustrated the steps that must be taken in the planning and development of a hotel project. The commencement of such a project without consideration of each of these steps is not only dangerous but foolish. With them, its financial success should be at least probable if not ensured.

CHAPTER SUMMARY

A feasibility study is essential in evaluating a project. Also, it is often required in order to obtain financing.

The various elements of a feasibility study are:

1. Site selection
2. Analysis of the market
3. Analysis of the existing and future supply of rooms
4. Analysis of the labor situation
5. Analysis of the room demand
6. Financial projections
7. Cost elements of the project
8. Sources of financing

REVIEW QUESTIONS

1. What are the elements of a feasibility study?
2. What are the factors to consider in site selection?
3. What are the sources of information used in estimating room demand?
4. What factors relate to labor should be evaluated?
5. What factors are considered in deciding upon the facilities?
6. What are the elements of the financial projections?
7. Describe briefly each element of the project cost.
8. What are the sources of financing available for a hotel project in United States?

5

Hotel Structure and Staff

After studying this chapter, the student should be able to:

1. Understand the overall structure of a hotel organization.
2. Understand the responsibilities of each area.
3. Understand the responsibilities of the general manager.

Regardless of whether a hotel is a simple rooming house or encompasses within its four walls all the facilities of a small city, it is truly a "people" business—not only in that it exists to serve people, but in that it requires the services of people to exist. Automation may help, but only human beings can furnish the bulk of the services needed for the well-being of the guests.

All hotels rent rooms, and most also offer food and beverages for sale. The successful ones add an extra ingredient: good service. This is the only product that cannot be purchased. Fine furniture, gourmet food, and vintage wines are available in many hotels, but service in each depends entirely upon its staff. Human behavior in a free society cannot be standardized; it can only be guided, a process that requires constant supervision, attention, and training.

This chapter will define the duties of the general manager, chart the chain of command, and describe the interdependence of the staff and the cooperation needed for the efficient and successful operation of a hotel. Specific duties and areas of responsibility for each department head will be covered in subsequent chapters.

In these discussions of both general and specific areas of duties and responsibilities, it is important to understand that the organization chart does not imply that a person is required for each function. The concept is that the function exists, and the duties relative to it must be performed. In a small hotel, all the functions may be combined and the duties performed by one person, be it the owner or an employee. The larger the hotel and the greater the volume, the more staff is needed to service the guests properly. The major convention hotels, with 1,000 or more employees, require more supervisors, thus creating more departments and, as a result, assigning more specific duties to each employee.

Hotels vary not only in size but in character, in type of clientele, and in scope of activities. Every function exists, but priorities differ from hotel to hotel. The management of each must determine the departments, and the number of employees in each, needed for its own operation. Assigning an individual to each function in this text is done merely to highlight it, thereby making the function easier to describe and to understand.

As in any business, there must be one person responsible for the overall operation. That person is the general manager, sometimes, particularly in the larger hotels, called the managing director.

In the past, possibly into the 1930s, the hotel manager was primarily a genial host, personally greeting the guests and seeing to it that they were properly cared for. But as the banks (through bankruptcies and foreclosures), corporations, conglomerates, and other business organizations began acquiring hotels, this image began to disappear. The first concern of executives and stockholders of these companies was that the property show a profit. As a result, a new type of innkeeper emerged, and today the successful general manager is a highly trained person, capable of directing a complex business enterprise.

HOTEL POLICY

Although the general manager has the responsibility of running the hotel and is usually held accountable for its financial success or failure, he or she does not always have the authority to establish the overall policy for its operation. This function is the prerogative of the owner or owners. In an individually owned hotel, or even in a small chain, it is not only possible but probable that the owner will delegate this authority to the general manager. But large chains want uniformity in the operation of each of their properties, so the central corporate office will formulate broad management policies and assign home-office executives to see to it that they are properly implemented at each property. The more successful groups have learned, sometimes through a costly experience, that such standardization is not always possible. State and local laws and regulations, customs, unions, availability of qualified personnel, and even environmental considerations may mandate modification and sometimes complete reversal of certain policies. This decision becomes the responsibility of the general manager, bolstered by the aid and consent of the assigned home-office executive.

Major areas that could be, and usually are, covered by broad management policies will be summarized in the remainder of this section.

Labor

Since salaries and wages are the largest single expense in a hotel's budget, it follows that most owners or operators reserve the prerogative to formulate the employment policy. The initial staffing of a new hotel requires a top-management decision. Once the hotel is operating, the permanent staff must also be finalized, subject to changes necessitated by the volume of business. Fringe benefits, hospitalization, major medical, insurance, pensions, savings plans, and the like for eligible employees are normally uniform throughout the chain and therefore subject to overall corporate policy. Uniform salary and wage guidelines may also be formulated for the chain, although they must be flexible enough to fit the different needs of each hotel. Obviously, the salary of the general manager, and possibly that of the sales manager, director of human resources, and controller, can be predetermined, since these positions are usually filled by people interviewed and hired by some home-office executive. Salaries of other department heads, their assistants, and other nonunion personnel must be flexible and depend to a great extent on the availability of trained, experienced people. The remaining staff, far greater in number and usually unionized, is mostly unskilled. Their salaries depend on many more factors; among the most important are state minimum-wage laws and regulations, local customs, union contracts (if any) and, naturally, the availability of labor.

Rate Structure

In a new hotel, the original room-rate schedule is set up before the opening. In a sense, it is predetermined by the owner in the initial planning stage of the building, since the style and type of hotel to be built, the appointments and facilities to be provided, and the class of guest to be serviced all affect the rates that can and should be charged.

Using the original guidelines developed in the feasibility study regarding the location, availability of rooms, and potential volume of business, the rates are established. The schedule can be set up either by the general manager and submitted to the assigned home-office executive for approval, or by the home-office staff with the assistance of the general manager. Subsequent changes are normally made by the general manager with the knowledge and consent of the home-office supervisor. The same comments apply to the original food and beverage menu prices and subsequent changes in them. Guidelines must also be established for the type and length of lease and the rent to be charged for any stores and concessions available for rental.

Purchasing

Some chains have a central purchasing department. Others establish a separate corporation that does all the buying, then resells the merchandise to the individual hotel at a small markup. Food and beverages are rarely centrally purchased, except where more than one hotel is operated in the same city; food is too perishable to store, repackage, and reship.

Beverages are subject to different regulations and licensing requirements in each state. Most states require direct shipment by the distributor or wholesaler to the licensee. The home office will establish the brand of liquor that is to be used in the bars when the guest does not specify a brand when ordering. For example, if the guest orders a scotch and soda, the bartender will use the "house scotch" decided upon for that hotel.

There are two principal reasons for centralizing the purchasing of all but the small items needed for a hotel's operation. The first, and possible the most important, is financial. Bulk buying usually lowers cost, either directly or through quantity discounts. Certain items, such as furniture, carpets, linen, china, and glassware, can be purchased directly from the manufacturer, thus reducing the cost even further. The second reason is quality control. The executive office can determine which merchandise to standardize in which hotels and retains the option to raise or lower the quality as conditions warrant.

Insurance

Insurance, like other merchandise, is cheaper to purchase and easier to standardize and control through centralization. As a result, most chains maintain an insurance department headed by a licensed broker. Coverage of the type and in the amount determined by the home-office executive is purchased for each hotel, and premiums can be reduced through negotiation with different companies.

Advertising

Hilton, Sheraton, Loews, Holiday Inn, Ramada Inn, Howard Johnson, and the other major chains have one thing in common: the bulk of their advertising is directed toward popularizing their name. The theory is that most travelers will stay, or stop to eat, at a hotel with a familiar name. Rooms, food, and beverages are no different from any nationally advertised product. Constant repetition is the only way to ensure that the public will recognize and purchase a product when they are in the market for it. Hence the need for a central advertising department.

The cost of this type of advertising would be prohibitive for a single hotel, whether owned or franchised by one of the chains. However, some local advertising is necessary for each property—not only for its banquet facilities, specialty restaurants, cocktail lounges, and bars, but for the rental of the hotel rooms themselves. Thus, a provision should be made in each individual hotel budget for local advertising. The home-office executive in charge of operations will probably have to approve the dollar amount, the central advertising director, the copy, and the media to be used.

All advertising, national or local, seeks to project an image—in this case, the hotel's. The general manager is the person who has the responsibility to develop and maintain this image. Therefore, regardless of the type of ownership, he or she should be, and usually is, consulted before any copy is finally approved for publication. On the local level, the general manager is the logical and most qualified person to establish personal contacts with political leaders, influential citizens, members of civic and charitable organizations, and the press and other media. He or she is invaluable in securing publicity for the hotel and for building and projecting the desired image. Add a working knowledge of and familiarity with regional customs, and the general manager is in a position to initiate, recommend, supervise, and assume full responsibility for placing and following through on all local advertising and publicity.

Accounting

The one standardization really necessary is in accounting. Most hotels are required to forward forecasts, reports, statistics, and operating results to the main office. Unless these are uniform in content and in the methods used to assemble the information, comparisons are meaningless, and top management is deprived of a valuable tool with which to judge the operation of each property.

The chief accountant or controller is one of the major department heads and a very important member of the management team. However, since he or she is usually hired by the corporate or financial vice president, the position carries with it a dual responsibility to the home-office executive and to the general manager.

Credit

Most major chains have an overall credit policy. Except in one area, acceptance of national credit cards, this policy should be flexible enough to conform to local customs. All hotels in the group are usually required to honor certain credit cards, principally for financial reasons: the discount rate charged by the national credit card companies and banks depends to a great extent on the volume of business generated by their clients.

Another important consideration is publicity. All major credit card companies advertise extensively to solicit new members and popularize the use of their cards. Such objectives can best be achieved by the frequent mention of the names of companies honoring the card. In addition, the credit card companies often include in the monthly billing to cardholders literature supplied by the establishments honoring the card. The timing and number of mailings is negotiable and is usually established at the original signing of the agreement. No individual hotel could possibly negotiate from the same position of strength as a chain speaking for a whole group of hotels.

Miscellaneous

It would be almost impossible to list all the functions capable of being centralized in any one chain of hotels. However, most lists would also include both legal and reservation divisions. Aside from the fact that it would be financially prohibitive to maintain a separate legal department in each hotel, the executive officers need attorneys to guide them in their conduct of the corporate business and in the acquisition or sale of properties. A central reservation office is needed to complement the individual hotels' reservation departments. It processes requests for information or rooms generated by chain advertising and channels them to the proper location. Also, the central reservation manager can more effectively negotiate package deals and special or group rates with corporations, associations, clubs, or travel agents.

Finally, the list would probably include a construction or engineering department to supervise the building or acquisition of new hotels and to direct and be responsible for any major improvements or alterations in the existing properties.

THE GENERAL MANAGER

After reading about all the operations of a hotel that may be centralized at the home office, you may very well be wondering what, if anything, a general manager does. Is he or she merely an intermediary between an absentee owner or home-office executive and the department heads, hired only to relay orders? Definitely not. Running a hotel is a full-time, 24-hours-a-day, 7-days-a-week operation. The hotel is never closed—there can be no time off, no holidays. Someone representing management, and some members of the operating staff, must be on duty every hour and every day of the year. No broad policy could possibly cope with the many diverse situations that occur daily in any given hotel or for that matter even cover all the variations in the very circumstances to which it was designed to apply.

The general manager is the person responsible for defining and interpreting the policies established by top management. In addition, the successful manager must implement and improve them and, on occasion, may be forced to completely disregard them. To perform these duties properly requires a working knowledge of all phases of hotel operation. No one can properly give or explain an order without some idea of what is involved. The quickest and easiest way for an executive to lose the respect of the employees is to give instructions without understanding their implications or the amount of time necessary to carry them out. In fact, we believe it is impossible to properly and intelligently supervise anyone without having at least a general idea of that person's duties and responsibilities.

THE STAFF: MAJOR DEPARTMENTS

A hotel, except a very small one, is like any other business enterprise in that it is physically impossible for one person to personally supervise all the different phases of the operation. Thus, one of the primary responsibilities of a manager is to assemble a team to assist in running the hotel. For the purpose of this discussion, the staff is grouped into four main categories:

1. The management policymaking and implementing team—the general manager and his or her primary department heads
2. Subdepartment heads
3. Assistant department heads
4. General staff and operating personnel

This grouping is best illustrated in Figure 5-1, an organizational chart. It charts the chain of command, identifying the primary department heads (those reporting directly to the general manager), the subdepartment heads under them, their assistants, and the general staff. Note that the number of employees in a department is not related to the classification of its department head. The executive housekeeper has the largest staff to supervise, yet reports to the general manager. The director of human resources has the smallest, yet reports to the general manager and is an important member of the management policymaking team.

The chart reflects the generally accepted chain of authority. It can be varied, by any owner, organization, or general manager, to conform to any given policy or concept of operation. For instance, operators of some hotels that have large banquet facilities producing a substantial share of the total income have upgraded the position of banquet manager. This is easily accomplished by removing the department from the control of the food and beverage manager and requiring the banquet manager to report directly to the general manager. In effect, it creates another member of the management team.

To discuss the general manager's areas of responsibility, we need only analyze the organizational chart and highlight the duties of the major department heads. Although these duties and responsibilities differ, since those of each department are restricted to one general area, there is one common denominator in all their functions—the guest. Since no hotel can exist without the patronage of its guests, it follows that the only reason for the existence of a staff is to provide for their comfort and convenience. Thus, a general manager must not only assemble a team, but mold them into a coordinated, cooperative group of people capable of working together for a common goal: creating a satisfied guest.

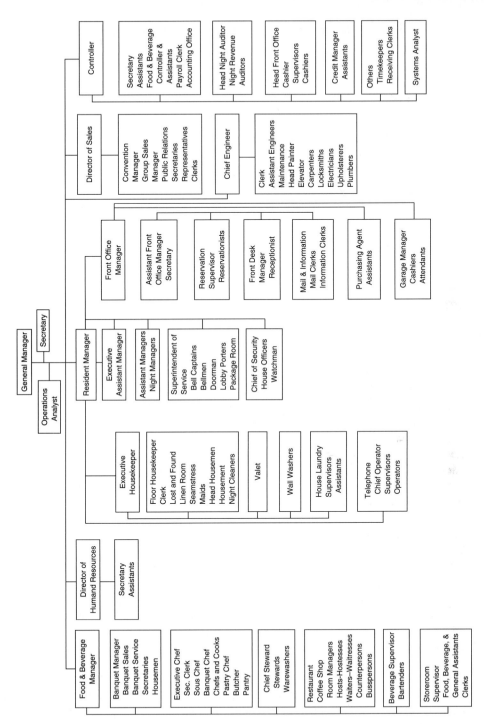

Figure 5-1 Hotel Organizational Chart

In the following narrative, and for that matter in the chart itself, no attempt has been made to emphasize the importance of any one department head. Each performs a function that would be handled personally by the general manager if it were feasible. Therefore, they are all members of the management team and, in that sense, equally important.

Rooms

The primary responsibility for the well-being of the guests is delegated to the head of the rooms department, known as the resident manager. He or she heads the numerically largest department in the hotel, many of whose members come into direct contact with the guests. In fact, it can be said that from the moment of the guests' arrival to their departure, someone in this department is performing a direct service for them. Training, a must for all hotel employees, takes on an added significance for the members of this staff. Frequently, employees coming into personal contact with the guests not only must be trained in the functions and duties of their positions, but must be told how to interact with guests.

The resident manager carries out what may be the most important responsibility of the general manager—the day-to-day operation of the guestrooms. Subsequent chapters will describe in detail the duties of the various subdepartment heads, such as the executive housekeeper, executive assistant manager, front-office manager, chief telephone operator, and the garage manager. It is sufficient to say here that they register, maintain, and clean the room, and provide information on the facilities of the hotel and the local points of interest—cultural, recreational, or amusement. They also handle all guest complaints.

The purchasing agent was not included in the list of subdepartmental heads for two reasons. The first and perhaps obvious one is that he or she performs no service directly affecting the guest. The other is that the position varies in importance with the size, type, and ownership of the hotel. In a small- to medium-sized individually owned hotel, the position may be little more than clerical, involving the typing of purchase orders for items previously requested, priced by the department heads, and approved by the general manager. In a large hotel that is not part of a chain, and excluding for the moment food and beverages, the position may require obtaining price quotations and possibly setting specifications for the merchandise needed. In any size hotel that is part of a group, the position, again excluding food and beverages, often entails little more than the processing of requisitions to the central office for merchandise ordered by department heads. Thus, all requisitions and purchase orders should require the approval of the general manager or a designated representative.

The purchasing of food and beverages is a field in itself, and the procedure will be fully reviewed in a subsequent chapter. In many hotels, this purchasing is done by a person under the control and direction of the food and beverage manager. Personally, we are strongly opposed to such an arrangement because it seriously affects accounting controls. The food and beverage manager supervises the preparation of the food and the service, recommends or actually sets the specifications, and determines the quantities needed. He or she should not have the added authority to select the purveyor and the price to be paid for the food.

The organizational chart shows the purchasing agent reporting to the resident manager, acting, of course, as the designated representative of the general manager.

Food and Beverages

The food and beverage manager heads a department that also involves guest relations. The service staff in the restaurants, coffee shop, bars, and banquet rooms come into direct contact not only with resident guests but with members of the general public who use the hotel facilities other than its sleeping rooms—equally important in the overall operation.

This is the department that perhaps most clearly demonstrates the old hotelier's famous saying: "Service is our most important product." A meal of good food, well cooked and beautifully presented, can be easily spoiled by a careless or sloppy waiter or waitress. Proper attention to the table setup—silverware, china, glasses, and so on—plus proper attention to guests' needs for such items as bread, water, and liquor, are just as important as the food itself. How often we hear the complaint: "We wanted another round of drinks, but we could never get the waiter's attention." The attention given to the guests while they are eating can be as important as the prompt taking of the initial order. No one likes to be rushed, but most people need to feel that there is someone near to help them in case they want something. It has been said that more food and beverage repeat business has been lost by poor service than by poor or badly cooked food. Moreover, repeat business in the restaurants, banquet rooms, and sleeping rooms is the single most important factor in the success or failure of the hotel as a profit-making enterprise.

In the final analysis, all that advertising can accomplish is the attraction of new guests. Only the concerted efforts of the staff can create a satisfied guest—the repeater, the person who spreads the word among friends and business associates of the "wonderful hotel we stopped at." Word-of-mouth advertising is the most powerful medium in the service industry, for both good and bad. Many hotel owners have discovered that it is very difficult to build a good reputation and very easy to ruin one, again emphasizing the need for organization, training, and supervision.

Engineering

The chief engineer is concerned with the appearance and physical condition of the building. Having limited personnel, the chief engineer depends on others, primarily the rooms department staff, to detect and report bad physical conditions and out-of-order appliances in the guestrooms. This is one small example of the teamwork needed to successfully operate a hotel.

Human Resources

The prime responsibility of the director of human resources is to staff the hotel. It is the employees who take care of the guests, and good service is the most important ingredient for the success of the operation. Need we say more? We do, in the next chapter.

Sales

There is very little need to dwell on the importance of a good sales department. Large hotels, those with convention and banquet facilities, could not exist without the business generated by their sales and convention staffs. This department is further discussed later in this chapter and in detail in Chapter 8.

Accounting

As previously mentioned, the controller or chief accountant in multiple operations has a dual responsibility—to the general manager and to the chief financial officer in the home office.

The corporate responsibility serves as a definite aid in the performance of a controller's duties. The title suggests one who controls, not merely records, the income and expenses of the hotel. In respect to the income, the position involves checking the accuracy of the amounts reported, thus ensuring that the hotel receives 100% of the money spent by the guests. Checking expenses requires more than the mere verification of the mathematical accuracy of the creditors' bills. The legitimacy of the charges, as to both quantity received and price charged, must be checked.

Since all purchases should be approved by the general manager or designated representative, the controller is in effect checking the general manager. It is easier, and the results more meaningful, to check the work of a person who does not have the sole authority to hire or fire you. However, this does not in any way alter the primary function of the controller—to fully cooperate with the general manager and provide all the reports and statistics requested and needed to properly evaluate and operate the property.

Most hotels operate on a budget, the preparation of which is the responsibility of the controller. Despite the many elements that are taken into consideration in assembling the figures, a budget is ultimately only an estimate, an educated guess, of the income and expenses for a given period in the future. The primary department heads, with the aid of their assistants and subdepartment heads, are the best qualified to make these forecasts. With their figures as a guide, the controller prepares the budget and presents it to top management, the general manager, and, in multiple operations, the designated corporate officer, for final approval. Once this has been obtained, each member of the management team is obligated to abide by the budget and hold his or her department's expenses to the allocated amount.

Summary

These six departments have been highlighted, because the men and women who head them make up the top-management team. They advise and help the general manager in formulation of the operating policy and see to it that it is carried out. Thus, they supervise and share the responsibility for the daily functions of the entire hotel staff.

The succeeding chapters will set forth in greater detail the teamwork, meetings, and discussions needed among the staff for the successful operation of the hotel. It is the general manager's responsibility not only to assemble this team, but to settle any disputes or jurisdictional conflicts between members. Differences of opinion should be not only tolerated but encouraged. We believe that there is no better way to arrive at the best solution than through a frank, open, and, if necessary, heated discussion.

The head of a very successful hotel chain always welcomed new members of the management team with words to this effect: "At these meetings, everyone is invited—no, expected—to voice his or her opinion. If it is different from mine or everyone else's, fight for what you believe is the correct solution. Give all your reasons, and any facts or figures you have to back them up, but never let me hear the words, 'It has always been done that way.' Keep in mind, however, that when every view has been presented and discussed, we cease to be a democracy and become a dictatorship. Unless we have all agreed on a course of action, I will make the final decision. All of you are expected to accept it, forget all your differences, and work your heads off to make it succeed."

SENSITIVE STAFF FUNCTIONS

Although all departments and functions are important to the overall operation, some are considered particularly sensitive, and executives tend to participate more fully in them. The following have one thing in common: in some way, they directly affect the image of the hotel.

Sales

The sales department has been called the lifeblood of the organization. Few outsiders realize that the director of sales is called upon to make more decisions affecting not only present but future earnings than any other department head.

Hotels—indeed, cities—compete fiercely to attract large groups, companies, or organizations. Conventions are sometimes booked years in advance, and hotels are called upon to guarantee room rates within a certain range, and to give such other inducements as free meeting rooms and possibly discounts on banquets. These are decisions that should be made only with the knowledge and consent of the general manager. Huge national conventions, of such organizations as the American Legion, Shriners, and the two major political parties every four years, are booked by city officials with the aid of all hotels. They work through a city-wide agency, such as the Convention and Visitors Bureau, or the local chamber of commerce. Rates and other inducements may vary on a city-wide basis. Practically the only decision an individual hotel has to make is the number of sleeping rooms to commit and guarantee to the central agency for the convention.

It is the smaller groups, those booked and handled by a single hotel, that require the most top-management decisions and often create interdepartmental problems. Food and beverage and banquet managers rarely take very kindly to free meeting rooms. Public-room rentals are very important to them, particularly since the food and beverage department is usually charged for the labor in setting up and cleaning these rooms. Special food discounts increase food cost and adversely affect the department's profits. Another important consideration is the possible loss of food and beverage business; a banquet cannot be accepted if the room is reserved for a convention group. Many a banquet manager has tried to explain a poor operating result in a given month by citing that reason. There have also been heated discussions regarding accepting conventions during certain months of the year because of the possible loss of banquet functions, particularly repeat business. Sales personnel theorize that local organizations, companies, and groups that hold annual or more frequent functions will not return if they are driven to use another hotel and find it equally or more desirable. A healthy interdepartmental rivalry develops, the solution to which is the sole responsibility of the general manager.

Labor

Labor relations are often the responsibility of the director of human resources, who usually handles the many problems and minor disputes with and among the employees that occur in the daily operation of the hotel. When a union is involved and the employee appeals to it for help, the director of human resources will meet with the union delegate and resolve most of these differences. It is only when a dispute is serious, or cannot be settled at the hotel level and requires arbitration or court action, that the general manager should step in. No general manager likes to lose a case at that level, and too many adverse decisions can seriously affect the morale and discipline of the staff and thus the service to the guests. These are reasons enough to require top-management approval before proceeding with this final step in labor relations.

Stores and Concessions

Although the hotel owner or owners will establish certain rental guidelines, the actual negotiations, particularly on renewal of leases, are handled by the general manager or a designated representative. The store operators, concessionaires, and their staffs are associated by the general public with the hotel, and in some cases even considered employees. Therefore, they directly affect guest relations and must be monitored in the same way as any hotel department whose employees come into contact with the guests. Only the general manager has the status and, in the final analysis, the authority, to do this.

Entertainment

Many hotels offer dinner music in their restaurants or some form of entertainment in the bar or cocktail lounge, and many have nightclubs. The hiring of the musicians and entertainers would normally be the responsibility of the food and beverage manager or, in multiple operations, of a central-office executive assigned to this function. However, we have never known a general manager who did not insist on at least the right of refusal before final approval of entertainment.

There are several very valid reasons for such an attitude. The first is the cost compared with the projected income and all the related factors—for example, possible increases in menu or drink prices; in a nightclub, the imposition of a minimum or cover charge. Another and possibly more important reason is related to the major responsibilities of the position. A general manager should be familiar with the local market; understand and know the preferences of the guests; and build, project, and protect the desired image of the hotel. It follows, then, that he or she must be in the best position to select a musician, entertainer, or type of entertainment that would be popular with the guests and at the same time maintain the hotel's image.

This section has highlighted those functions usually supervised personally by general managers. Not all managers will participate to the same extent in all, or for that matter any, of these sensitive areas. Such decisions depend on the type of hotel, the priorities established, and the background and special interests of the manager.

CHAPTER SUMMARY

Every hotel has certain functions that must be performed. In some hotels one person may perform several functions. In other hotels some functions require some or many people.

In chain operations the head office sets policy in the following areas:

1. Labor
2. Rate structure (mainly for new hotels)
3. Purchasing
4. Insurance
5. Advertising
6. Accounting
7. Credit
8. Reservations

The general manager becomes more involved in certain areas:

1. Sales
2. Labor
3. Stores and concessions
4. Entertainment

Principal departments are:

1. Rooms
2. Food and beverages
3. Engineering
4. Human resources
5. Sales
6. Accounting

REVIEW QUESTIONS

1. Describe the various areas in a hotel operation that may be mandated by an overall chain policy.
2. Describe the various concerns involved in an overall credit policy.
3. In what areas of the operation does the general manager participate?
4. Explain the basic function of the following departments:
   a. Rooms
   b. Food and beverage
   c. Accounting

CASE STUDY 1

As the new general manager of a 200-room resort in South Carolina, John White has been asked by the owners to minimize management payroll by consolidating responsibilities. What consolidations would he make and why?

CASE STUDY 2

Marion Smith has become the director of sales in a major hotel in Chicago. What actions must she initiate to maximize the convention business?

6

The Human Resources Department

After studying this chapter the student should:

1. Understand the function of the human resources department
2. Understand the recruiting process
3. Understand the makeup of the various employe-related programs

The creation of the human resources department and its important position in today's hotels can really be regarded as a modern phenomenon. In early years, the owner, or a general manager directly hired by the owner, selected the department heads, who in turn hired their own staffs. This may still occur in small hotels but for most there has been a significant change. Early management policies were loosely applied and rarely put in writing—a simple, direct approach impossible in today's complex technology.

Absentee management, government labor laws and regulations, unions, the growth of fringe benefits, the upward spiral in wages and related expenses, automation, and the flood of paperwork generated by all these have contributed to the growth of the human resources department. In most hotels, the human resources department does not hire, set labor policies, or define the duties of hotel employees. The final responsibility for hiring is in the hands of the department head. Top management sets policy, and the management team (the general manager and the major department heads) defines the duties of each category of employee. The director of human resources, as a very important member of this team, assists by recommending and finally formalizing these duties. It is then up to the human resources department to administer, interpret, and implement them.

Figure 6-1 shows the organization chart of a typical human resources department. Basically, the duties of this department can be summarized as follows:

1. Recruit
2. Interview and screen applicants
3. Select applicants
4. Verify and check references
5. Refer applicants to the proper department head for final action
6. Process successful applicants for employment and explain company policies regarding work rules, benefits, vacations, etc.
7. Orientation of new employees
8. Set up training programs
9. Set up safety programs
10. Administer benefit programs
11. Negotiate with union officials and represent the hotel in all dealings with them; interpret the union contract
12. Interpret labor laws and ensure adherence to the regulations of the government agencies involved

Figure 6-1   Human Resources Department Chart

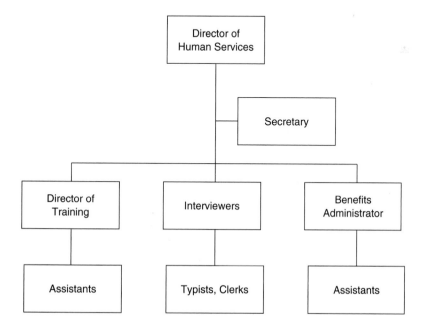

PHASES IN STAFFING

Before examining in detail each of these 12 basic functions, it might be well to discuss the management policies that must be set up before the human resources department can begin to function. Once a hotel is in full operation, these policies are, or should be, well defined. In many cases, they are contained in a pamphlet distributed to new employees.

There are two separate and distinct phases in the staffing of a hotel: 1) initial staffing and 2) replacements for the normal turnover of employees.

Initial Staffing

It is in the first phase that guidelines for the hotel's labor policies must be laid down by top management. In a multiple or chain operation, broad policies are set by the head office and are applied to each property as it is acquired. However, these policies must be flexible enough so that they can be adapted to local conditions. Wages must be competitive. Minimum wages and overtime requirements vary under state laws. If a union is or will be involved, hours, working conditions, and benefits for union employees may be fixed under existing union contracts. Finally, the qualifications set for each job classification must depend to a great extent on the availability of labor.

Depending on the size and type of hotel, defining each position and its duties is fairly routine and follows industry-wide procedures. However, even in these definitions, local customs and union regulations must be considered.

One factor that is not always taken into account, even by the large chains, is the physical layout of offices, working space, and storage facilities in the property. A kitchen that has a poor layout or is too far from restaurants and banquet facilities may require more help to service the guests. Lack of storage space leads to poor security and large losses from theft. Poor or crowded working conditions reduce employee efficiency and increase the possibility of accidents, both resulting in increased costs.

Thus, good labor policy begins in the initial planning of the hotel. Multiple and chain operations have an advantage here; their experienced personnel can assist the architect in planning the layout of the building. Individual owners, unless thoroughly experienced, would do well to hire consultants for this important phase of the work. Once the building is complete, the most important, and possibly only, tool available to management is the feasibility study. Here we find a discussion of the available labor supply, wages paid, and unions, if any, in the surrounding area. The study also projects estimates of income and occupancy, a very important guide in determining the number of employees in each category.

With this study and full knowledge of the applicable federal, state, and local laws and regulations, top management must promulgate the broad labor policies of the hotel and establish the salaries and qualifications for the major department heads. The salaries, numbers, and duties of the general staff are usually set up by the management team. In effect, this means that the director of human resources has to be the first department head to be hired, since he or she must recruit the other department heads.

The timetable for this recruiting and the starting date for both the department heads and the staff must also be fixed by management. These target dates depend on the labor situation (the more experienced help available, the less time required for preopening training sessions) and to a certain extent on the financial position of the owner or operator. For a well-planned and efficient operation, the following timetable is suggested (the periods listed refer to length of time before opening date):

General manager: at least 1 year

Director of human resources department and controller: 1 year

Sales and banquet managers: 6 months to 3 years

Department heads: 4 to 6 months

Human resources department staff: immediately after department heads

General staff: 2 to 8 weeks, depending on amount of preopening training needed

The listing for the sales and banquet managers may seem strange; 6 months to 3 years is quite a difference in time. However, if either or both managers are needed, depending on the facilities and size of the hotel and to a certain extent on the type of ownership (individual owner or chain), then that span of time is accurate. Small- to medium-sized properties, up to 600 rooms, could easily combine the two positions, or possibly eliminate both, but larger properties with sizable banquet facilities need a separate executive to head each department.

Large hotels cannot operate profitably without the extra occupancy, banquet, and food and beverage income generated by conventions and group sales. Arrangements for national conventions and large banquets by local or regional businesses or groups are made far ahead of the function, sometimes as much as 2 to 3 years in advance. Most large cities have a visitors' and convention bureau that is actively supported by the hotels and that, in turn, works with the convention and sales departments of the large hotels to attract national conventions to the city.

An individual owner must therefore start a sales and promotion effort years in advance of the hotel's formal opening and immediately hire the necessary personnel. A chain usually has a central sales and promotion department, which can carry the ball until someone is transferred or hired for the new property, possibly with, or shortly after, appointment of the general manager.

It has been said that a hotel is only as good as its employees, since it really offers only service for sale. Every modern hotel has fully equipped, comfortably furnished rooms and usually purchases the finest-quality food available, has it prepared by the finest chefs available, and presents it appetizingly for the guests' enjoyment. Yet one hotel will enjoy more success than its competitors in the same general area. Why? Advertising? Possibly, to begin with, but repeat business is needed. Advertising alone cannot ensure success. Only people—management, department heads, and staff, working as a team—can fulfill the glowing promises of the advertisements. The human resources department's only responsibility is people, hence its importance. And hence the need for careful planning in the pre-opening schedule.

A good director of human resources must initiate, direct, and, if necessary, conduct training sessions. He or she should actively promote teamwork between departments through department-head meetings and group discussions. The director of human resources is responsible for organizing and, through the department leads, conducting full-scale "dry runs" of the complete process of registering, rooming, feeding, and checking out imaginary guests. Finally, he or she may find it necessary to instruct the department heads in good employee relations—very important in the hotel industry, since a satisfied and happy employee is the most important ingredient for good service.

Replacement Staffing

The foregoing paragraphs set out the available tools and steps to be followed in the initial staffing of a new hotel. The second phase, replacements for turnover of employees, also requires top-level decisions. When opening a new hotel, some organizations find it advisable to overstaff, for two principal reasons: first and foremost, in the first few months of operation, it enables the hotel to service the guests with inexperienced people; second, it gives the department heads the time and flexibility to work with their staffs, weed out undesirable, inefficient, or uncooperative workers, and weld the teamwork that is so necessary for the efficient and successful operation of a hotel.

Thus, there are two separate management decisions that need to be made as to the number of employees to be hired: the number needed for the opening, and the number needed for the permanent staff. The latter, obviously, is always subject to revision, depending mainly on the volume of business. Once these decisions have been made, and policy formulated, the human resources department can begin its work.

FUNCTIONS OF HUMAN RESOURCES

Other than in recruiting and in the referral of applicants to department heads, the duties and functions of the human resources department are much the same in both phases of staffing a hotel. During the preopening period, recruiting is done "wholesale": as many applicants as possible are delivered to each department head until the quota set by management for every job classification has been reached. In the second, or replacement, phase, human resources can act only after notification by the department head. For this purpose, most hotels use an employee requisition form containing the following information:

1. Job classification
2. Special skills or qualifications desired
3. Date that replacement is needed
4. Name, employee number, and salary of person being replaced
5. Reason for termination
6. Management approval

With this difference between the two phases of staffing in mind, a detailed examination of the human resources department's duties, as listed at the beginning of this chapter, are now in order.

Recruitment

Recruitment can take many forms, subject only to a budget set by management, which in turn must take into consideration the availability of qualified people. The most common forms are newspaper and trade-magazine ads; employment agencies, both state and private; unions; personnel contacts of the recruiter or other human resources staff members; and employee incentive plans. This last is a cash or other incentive to a current employee who recommends a qualified friend who is hired for an available position.

Interviewing and Screening of Applicants

This is a very important function of the department. A good interviewer not only must know the special skills and qualifications needed for any job opening, but should be able to match the personality of the applicant to that of the department head. The two must be able to work together if the position is to be filled permanently and satisfactorily. Frequent turnovers or dissatisfied employees are not only bad for morale, but are also costly in time and money spent in new employee training. The cost of turnover can be from $1,000 to $5,000 per employee.

Selection of Applicants

The process of selecting applicants is primarily determining that certain applicants should be considered for the position. This can be achieved by eliminating those applicants who do not meet the minimum job requirements.

Verification of References

This duty, although listed as the third step, is usually performed simultaneously with the fourth, referral to department heads. If time is of the essence, telephone references may be solicited, but an attempt should be made to obtain written references. Written references are preferred because they are not subject to interpretation by the clerk who solicited them, they become a permanent record in the employee's file, and, finally, they serve as proof that references were checked.

Due to a high incidence of lawsuits emanating from the giving out of poor references, many employers now, as a matter of policy, do not give out references without a specific written authorization of the former employee.

Referral to Department Heads

Applicants deemed qualified by the interviewer are sent to the department head for final disposition. The interviewer should forward the application and references, with a personal comment on any experience, skills, or special qualifications considered important, to the department head, who will conduct the final interview and make a decision.

All applicants, whether hired or not, should be sent back to the human resources department. For the successful applicant, the starting date and any other information not recorded on the requisition is filled in. For all other applicants, the reason for rejection should be recorded. This is important, in that it gives the interviewer another indication of the type of employee desired by that particular department head.

Processing of Successful Applicants

Here begins the flood of paperwork required for computerized payroll systems. Some of the more usual forms used, with a brief explanation of each, follow.

Statement of physical condition. With escalating costs, most hotels have discontinued or never instituted preemployment physical checkups. Instead, the applicant, if offered a position, is required to state whether or not they have any physical disabilities that would prevent them from carrying out the duties of the position for which they have applied.

Drug testing. Many hotels now require that where permitted by law an applicant take a test for the presence of drugs.

W-4. This is a government form of facsimile needed by the payroll department as authority to withhold payroll taxes. It contains the employee's name, address, Social Security number, number of dependents, and the date, and must be signed by the employee.

Employee's assignment card. This is a form sent to the payroll department, with the W-4, authorizing it to put the employee on the payroll. It must show the department; the employee's name, address, and Social Security number; the starting date; salary; and other remuneration, such as lodging and meals. Tipped employees must be so designated for the computer to record tip declarations. Therefore, this card must show a tip classification for each employee. It is important for proper reporting to remember that tips fall into two categories: declared and pre-arranged. The first are tips voluntarily given by the guest at the time the service is performed, such as to a waiter or waitress at the end of a meal. The second refers to gratuities arranged for in advance, either in a fixed amount—say, a group paying a stipulated amount to the bellman for each suitcase carried at arrival and departure—or as a percentage of the total charges, which is the usual arrangement when booking a banquet or other function (see Chapter 20).

Deduction authorization cards. No deductions other than payroll taxes may be made from an employees's salary except by specific authorization from the employee, or by a court order in the case of garnishes. Thus, human resources must get the employee's signature on cards authorizing the hotel to make such deductions as union dues and fees, U.S. savings bonds, and charitable contributions. If the hotel offers fringe benefits—hospitalization, major medical, life insurance, a savings plan, or a pension—that require employee participation, then individual authorizations for each must be obtained from the employee. Since most of these fringe benefits usually require a waiting period before becoming effective, the human resources clerk will get the employee's signature immediately but will not process the card (send it to the payroll department) until the effective date.

Immigration requirements. Applicants who are not U.S. citizens must submit documents proving that they are permitted to work in the United States—usually an alien registration card commonly known as a "green card." The employer must complete an I-9 form for all employees verifying that they have examined the documents.

Employee bond application. Most hotels cover employee losses (theft) with a blanket position bond covering all employees up to a specified sum. Management employees and those handling cash (general cashier and front-office and restaurant cashiers) are usually insured for a higher sum than other staff members. Many hotels require these employees to fill in a bond application supplied by a bonding company. Human resources forwards these applications to the bonding company for investigation and the hotel has in effect a double-check on these employees. In the event that an application is denied, the hotel has one of two choices: One is to dismiss the employee; the other is to apply for an individual bond covering only the rejected employee. This latter option is much more expensive and obviously involves a certain amount of risk. It should never be taken without the knowledge and written approval of top management.

Employee ID cards. These may be used to identify the employee for security purposes or may be required by a bank for payroll-check cashing if employees are paid by check. Some ID cards bear a laminated picture of the employee, but most have only the employee's signature, verified by the signature of the human resources manager or department head.

Department record card. This is a card sent to the department head with the new employee's name, address, Social Security number, position, salary, and starting date. The department head is required to keep this information current by recording changes in position, salary, address, and so on. The card in effect gives the department head a brief employment history for each member of the staff. When employment is terminated, the card, with the reason for the termination, is returned to human resources and becomes a part of the employee's permanent file.

Miscellaneous. If the employee is entitled to meals, a uniform, or a locker, some hotels require the human resources department to complete and forward to the department heads a properly approved form, as authorization to provide these items.

For purposes of control, it is important that no change in an employee's status—job classification, salary, or even address—be permitted on the payroll without the approval of the director of human resources or a designated representative. For this purpose a change form may be used. Originated by the department head, it can provide for any change in the employee's status, including termination. It is usually processed through the manager's office for approval and then sent to human resources. There it is incorporated into the employee's permanent file, approved, and a copy is forwarded to the payroll department for processing.

Other forms that are forwarded to or initiated by human resources are warning notices sent to employees for constant or major infractions of the rules (particularly important where a union is involved); awards or special commendations from management or guests; and accident reports. Copies of all these are added to the employee's permanent file.

Orientation of New Employees

Proper orientation of new employees not only contributes to employee satisfaction and resulting performance but also has a profound impact on guest service. Hotel guests frequently request information from the staff on various aspects of the hotel's operation. Failure to receive a satisfactory answer results in customer dissatisfaction. All new employees should therefore be familiarized with various aspects of the operation, including:

1. Knowledge of the complete physical layout of the hotel or resort, both indoor and outdoor.
2. A tour of the guestrooms to understand the features of the various types.

3. Knowledge of the food and beverage offerings of the various outlets.
4. Knowledge of various amenities and activities available to the guest.
5. Knowledge of entertainment available not only in the hotel but in the surrounding areas.
6. Introductions to all department heads and other key employees.

Training Programs

The preopening training mentioned earlier is only the first program to be set up, and probably the simplest. Service is a hotel's most important product, and good service does not just happen. It is a team effort, requiring constant attention, training, and supervision. The director of human resources is the coordinator, the team captain, making sure that the department heads work together and devote enough time and effort to the on-the-job training of their staffs. Where full-time training sessions are needed or desirable, the human resources department may take over and conduct them.

From the moment the guests make their first contact with the limousine driver or doorman until they check out at the cashier's desk, their comfort, happiness, and well-being are in the hands of every employee with whom they come in contact.

A pleasant greeting by the doorman, fast and courteous service by the registration clerk, and a friendly greeting by the bellman are very important in creating the proper image of the hotel. The bellman should not only carry the guests' bags, but should make sure the room is properly made up, see that the bathroom has the required linen and supplies, check that equipment, such as television and lamps, are in good working condition, and, finally, solicit and answer questions. The bell staff also points out hotel features. This is covered in more detail in later chapters. Room attendants, houseworkers, and engineering-department employees will meet the guests and should greet them courteously. The chef can contribute to the guests' well-being by making sure that the kitchen staff cooks and prepares the food properly for presentation. The dining-room and bar managers are responsible for, and must train their staffs to give, efficient, pleasant, courteous, and proper service. When guests check out, the front-office cashier is the last employee with whom they come in contact. Just as many a good meal has been ruined by a bad cup of coffee or a poor dessert, so also can a guest's stay be spoiled by a rude, discourteous, and inattentive cashier.

Training, then, is a constant, never-ending function, that shows the employees not only what to do and how to do it, but also what to say and how to say it.

Safety Programs

Safety also entails a training program requiring teamwork by department heads, cooperation of every employee of the hotel, and the active interest and support of top management.

A good safety program is important for both humanitarian and financial reasons. Injuries can be very painful, leave employees with permanent disabilities, and even result in death. If an accident causes serious injuries and loss of time, the employees and their families may suffer financial hardship. Finally, premiums for accident insurance (compensation for employees, public liability for guests) are very expensive and directly affected by the accident rate (see Chapter 15).

Since this program involves all the employees and cannot be departmentalized, it is usually administered by the director of human resources or a designated representative. The broker or the insurance company will help set up a safety program and provide speakers, posters, and films showing the correct way to perform various tasks, such as making beds, emptying wastebaskets, lifting heavy objects, and the like. The posters should be conspicuously displayed around the hotel where employees with jobs that involve such tasks can see them, and the films, accompanied by explanations from the speakers, should be shown to them.

However, the impetus for a successful safety program can come only from an active, well-trained safety committee. The committee should consist only of staff employees, with at least one member from each department. The chairman may be the designated representative of the director of human resources. And because the continued success of the program requires the interest and cooperation of top management, its representative (possibly a different department head) may be present at each committee meeting.

Management must not only be present but must follow through on the committee's recommendations. Nothing discourages people more than being ignored. If the employees have enough enthusiasm and interest in safety to make recommendations, then the least management can do is act on them, or else give the committee an explanation as to why the recommendation cannot be put into effect. Only in this way can the momentum of the group be maintained and the savings in human suffering and improvements in the net earnings of the hotel be realized.

Benefit Programs

In this area, human resources needs the cooperation and close collaboration of the accounting department. For hospitalization, major medical, group insurance, and savings or pension plans, lists of the employees with the required supporting data must be initially submitted and frequently updated, usually monthly. If employees' contributions are required, then schedules of these amounts are also needed. As new employees are hired or old ones replaced, the insurance company, fiscal agent, or bank administering the program must be notified. Required also are schedules of changes in employees' status—position, salary, address, number of dependents, and so on. Depending on the program, any one of these can affect the cost or amount of the benefit. Employees who are eligible for retirement must be informed of their rights and options, if any, and in many cases assisted in making relevant decisions. Also, retirees may be given benefits other than pensions, such as prepaid life insurance or major medical, which require contact with the employer and continued updating of the former employee's file.

The duties, therefore, of the benefit administrator are to set up the program initially and to continually update the information required for its administration.

Union Relations

Most union contracts are negotiated by the hotels through their local trade associations. Nonmember hotels usually wait for a settlement and then agree to similar terms. After a contract has been signed, the interpretation of its terms as applied to union employees' problems becomes one of the more important functions of the director of human resources. Many of the questions raised call for nothing more than a simple decision, but others may require a meeting with the employee (always accompanied by a union delegate), and with the department head if this is deemed advisable or necessary by the personnel representative. Finally, for major disputes or problems that cannot be settled at these informal meetings, the hotel and the union must submit to arbitration or whatever other formal settlement procedure is provided for in the contract. At these formal hearings, the director of human resources or department representative will present the hotel's viewpoint and should have the authority to arrange for whatever assistance may be needed, including, in extreme cases, legal counsel.

Labor Laws and Regulations

Labor laws vary from state to state, so specific statements covering a hotel's obligation under the law cannot be made here. The federal government has a minimum-wage law that includes the number of hours to be paid at straight time and overtime requirements for nonadministrative employees. However, federal law states only absolute minimums, intended as guidelines for the states. The states can, and most do, pass legislation exceeding these limits.

States have laws covering the hiring, hours, and minimum wages of minors, and special rules relating to the hiring of women and minorities. Some even require a minimum number of hours off each week for nonadministrative employees. Bureaus established by state and local governments—for example, alcoholic beverage control boards and health departments—each have their special rules, and issue regulations directly affecting the hiring and working conditions of some hotel employees.

Labor laws at all levels of government, and the rules and regulations of the many government bureaus involved, are constantly updated and changed to meet current social and political requirements. Only a labor specialist, the director of human resources, can keep abreast of these changing conditions of employment and work rules. It is therefore the human resources department's responsibility to see that local, state, and federal labor laws and the bureau rules and regulations are not violated by the hotel.

Appraisals and Evaluations

All properly operated hotels should have a formal system of employee performance appraisals and evaluations. These appraisals are used to evaluate performance for possible pay increases, promotions, and at the end of an employee's probationary period in order to make a determination as to whether the employee will be given permanent employment status.

Appraisals should be performed on a predetermined basis, at least once per year. Most employees want to know how they are doing, good or bad. Lack of an appraisal leaves them in limbo. While the appraisals will be completed by the department head or supervisor, the format should be established by the human resources department, who should also be responsible for documentation of the results and actions taken.

Motivation

Service industries, because of their dependence on work performance, to achieve success are particularly impacted by the problem of motivation.

Certain hotel departments, notably housekeeping, employ large numbers of employees with low skill levels whose earnings are low compared to some of the other departments. Motivating these employees to perform at desired skill levels usually requires some form of recognition of achievement and related rewards.

Devising the best methods of motivation is a task for all management, not only human resources. However, because it is a hotel-wide problem impacting many departments to varying degrees, the human resources department must be deeply involved. They should also be responsible for the administration of any reward programs put in place. Such rewards can be in the form of cash, additional benefits, time off, paid trips or vacations, and so on.

CHAPTER SUMMARY

The final decision to hire an employee is made by the department head.

The duties of the human resources department are:

1. Recruit
2. Interview and screen applicants
3. Select applicants
4. Verify and check references
5. Refer applicants to the proper department head for final action

6. Process successful applicants for employment and explain company policies regarding work rules, benefits, vacations, etc.
7. Orientation of new employees
8. Set up training programs
9. Set up safety programs
10. Administer benefit programs
11. Negotiate with union officials and represent the hotel in all dealings with them; interpret the union contract
12. Interpret labor laws and ensure adherence to the regulations of the government agencies involved

Recruiting can be either for a new hotel or replacements or additions for an existing hotel.

The department is also responsible for the processing of appraisals and evaluations. Motivation is also a major responsibility.

REVIEW QUESTIONS

1. List the responsibilities of the human resources department.
2. Suggest a timetable for hiring staff for a new independent hotel.
3. What information is usually required on an employee requisition form?
4. What are the steps taken in hiring a new employee?
5. What are the steps in an employee orientation program?

7

Reservations: Systems and Operations

After studying this chapter the student should:

1. Understand the various types of central reservation offices and how they function.
2. Understand how to take a reservation.
3. Understand the operation of a hotel reservation office.

There have been some major developments in computerized reservation systems and these will be discussed in various sections of this chapter. Although computerization has provided certain advantages, it has not changed the principles by which reservation systems operate.

The principal function of a reservation system is to furnish those hotels serviced by it with a maximum number of reservations at a minimum cost to the system and therefore to the hotels themselves.

While in recent years some independent organizations have developed reservation systems, the real advances in the systems have been made by the chains. Such companies as Holiday Inn and Sheraton have not only developed their own systems but have used them as a selling tool to further expand the scope and size of their chains, particularly in franchising. Both through direct control and through the structure of their franchise agreements, the chains have been able to exercise the proper discipline over participants in their reservation systems. At the same time, they have been able to achieve in the areas of billing and collection—the principal sources of the problems encountered by the independents—the success necessary to operate on a sound financial footing.

Where the owners and management of the participating hotels are varied and widespread, it naturally follows that the operating procedures used in the hotels are also varied. A reservation system operates on the premise that every hotel in the system will communicate with and use the system in the same fashion. With a vast number of divergent procedures, this is very difficult to achieve or control.

In the long run, however, the billing and collection process has proved to be a much greater obstacle. Charges to an individual hotel using a system are, for the most part, generated by the reservations taken for that specific property. However, most hotels are reluctant to pay for a reservation when the guest does not, in fact, show up, so in many cases billings to the participating hotels permitted the deduction of charges for "no-shows." The validity of such deductions can be verified only by examination of the hotel's records or direct communication with the source of the reservation but verifying the no-show deduction by either of these methods was too costly and cumbersome for most reservation systems. As a result, such deductions were often made by the hotels, validly or otherwise, without question by the reservation system. And even when these deductions were questioned or examined, the hotels had justification for objecting to billings or delaying their settlement. Thus, several attempts to create independent systems ran aground, owing to inability to generate adequate cash flow or exercise proper financial management.

It is not meant that a successful independent reservation system cannot be created; rather, it is the need for proper planning and the disciplining of clients that is being stressed as a requirement for a successful operation. These goals can be at least partially achieved by uniform, financially sound reservation agreements that provide proper protection for the owners of the system. While it is recognized that there are several options open to the systems to achieve these goals, it is strongly recommended that each agreement include a provision for a minimum guaranteed fee, payable in advance by the participating hotels.

Several chain-based systems have successfully extended themselves into the independent reservation area. Not only has the existence of the chain provided the necessary organizational and administrative power, but hotels within the chain have formed a sound financial basis from which the reservation system has been able to expand.

Earlier, it was indicated that the principles involved in the operation of computerized and noncomputerized systems are the same, and it is now time to examine the techniques and features of such operations.

CENTRAL RESERVATION OFFICES

Central reservation offices, commonly known as CROs, are the heart of a reservation system and, more important, the method by which the public has access to the system. A decision must be made first as to whether one CRO will be used for nationwide coverage or several offices will be established. There are advantages and disadvantages to either option. The use of a single, large office provides potential savings in time and payroll costs:

1. Such an office can be located in an area of the country where wage levels are low.
2. Through the use of a *one-number system*—for example, Sheraton's 800-325-3535—reservation calls made from all parts of the country flow into the same office, where they are handled by a large body of reservationists.
3. Having all reservationists in the same location, to which all reservation calls are directed, permits the ultimate in flexibility and staff planning, not available where regional offices with small staffs are servicing specific geographical regions.

Another advantage of a one-number system is the role it can play in the advertising campaigns of a chain. The system provides a constant factor, the telephone number, that can be used as a theme or focal point for all chain advertising. On the other hand, having all reservation calls flow to one destination makes the entire system dependent on the effectiveness of the telephone system in that area. Should the circuits become overloaded or the telephone system fail to work for any reason, the whole reservation-system process simply stops. To some degree this situation has been addressed by the telephone companies, who can reroute incoming calls to designated back-up locations. Nevertheless, considerable time delays with the accompanying loss of business do occur.

Regional offices do provide certain marketing advantages. Many reservation systems offer their clients or participants sales support in addition to reservation processing, and this sales support is much more effective when performed through regional offices.

Regional-office staffs usually consist of an office manager and one or more reservationists performing a dual function: aiding in the reservation process at peak periods, and, at other convenient times, making sales calls to travel agents and other potential customers in the area. Thus, the travel agent has personal contact with the reservation system, often resulting in a good deal of business from that agent. Where a single central reservation office is in use, reservation processing tends to become an extremely impersonal business. Figure 7-1 is a picture of a CRO in operation.

Central reservation offices can access or be accessed by Global Distribution Centers such as Sabre, Galieo International, and Amadeus, which provide a connection to the airline systems.

In addition to the changes, there are several Central Reservation Services (CRS) such as Leading Hotels of the World, Preferred Hotels, and Distinguished Hotels, which provide reservation services to independent hotels.

Figure 7-1   Central Reservations Office

Acceptance of Reservations

The most important element in the handling of reservations is time. The acceptance of a reservation should take up a minimum amount of time on the telephone, thus permitting the handling of a larger volume of reservation calls. For this reason, the techniques involved in handling reservations are very important.

In responding to a telephone call requesting a reservation, the reservationist should first announce that the caller has reached the reservation office and should then identify himself or herself. The reservationist should listen carefully to the caller and be enthusiastic, friendly, and sincere. Addressing the guest by name in the conversation can be a selling point. Most important of all, the sale should not be lost.

The order in which information is requested is very important. This applies to both computerized and noncomputerized reservation systems.

Figure 7-2 is a reservation screen by which the reservationist can input the reservation as the reservation information is provided on the telephone by the customer. Most systems are programmed to prompt the reservationist to take the information in the proper order. It is very important that the initial information be arrival date and length of stay. If rooms are not available, it is a waste of

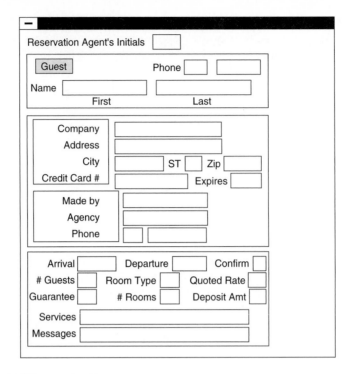

Figure 7-2 Typical Reservation Screen

time to go further, both for the reservationist and the caller. The following is a suggested order for inputting the information:

1. Name of hotel (if the reservation does not go directly to the hotel)
2. Arrival date
3. Departure time
4. Time of arrival
5. Number of rooms
6. Rate (see the discussion that follows on rate)
7. Last name of guest
8. First name of guest
9. Address of guest (if the reservation is made by other than the guest, also obtain the address to which the confirmation should be sent)
10. Credit card number if reservation is guaranteed
11. Amount of deposit required if caller cannot provide credit card number
12. Date by which deposit is required
13. Any special instructions; such as, VIP, cot required, ocean front, etc.

Additionally, if the reservation comes from a travel agent, the information relative thereto must be inputted so that the proper commission can be processed.

The reservationist not only has taken a reservation but has actually performed a sales function; therefore, the manner in which the reservation is taken is important. The following are certain key techniques that should be used in handling a reservation call:

1. The reservationist should never say, "we are booked up," "sold out," or "don't have anything." Instead, the phrases "filled to capacity" or "not available" should be used.
2. The plural "we" should always be used instead of the singular "I."
3. The phrase, "you have to," should never be used in requesting the deposit. Instead, the reservationist should say, "the hotel requires a deposit."
4. If asked why space is not available, the reservationist should never give the impression that the hotel is booked to capacity because of a convention or group. It is not desirable to leave the impression with any prospective guest that the hotel caters primarily to this type of business, leaving no room for regular guests. Instead, the reservationist should indicate only that space is not available because it is heavily in demand.

All reservations should be accepted and completed before the rate is quoted, unless the guest specifically requests the rate first. This reduces the number of lost sales because of resistance to the rate. The minimum rate should never be quoted, nor should the reservationist quote only one rate. The standard and superior rates should be quoted and, unless the customer requests the lower rate, the reservation should be made at the higher rate. In regard to rates, policies, and procedures, explanations should be clear but brief. These techniques will not only result in the taking of a reservation in an orderly fashion, but improve the overall sales ability of the reservation system.

Reservation Status

When a request for a reservation is received in a CRO, the reservationist must be able to advise the caller whether or not the reservation is confirmed. For this reason, each office must at all times know the status of each hotel for which it is accepting reservations.

A hotel's rate structure usually consists of five levels that relate to various qualities of accommodations: *minimum, standard, superior, deluxe,* and *suites.* Each type of accommodation represents a different rate, both for single and double occupancies. Every day, the hotel should analyze the number of reservations it has on hand or projected and make a determination of whether or not to close out reservations at certain rate levels. When high occupancies are projected, a hotel may simply not accept any reservations in one or more of the lower rate categories. In other situations, the decision on acceptable rate levels is made as a result of the buildup of reservations. So, as the reservations for a particular date accumulate, a hotel will close out (no longer accept) reservations starting with minimum, then standard, then superior—perhaps ultimately accepting only suite bookings. The reservation status of a hotel can, therefore, be classified as follows:

Minimum rate: Accepting all reservations

Standard rate: Accepting reservations only at standard rate and up

Superior rate: Accepting reservations only at superior rate and up

Suite only: Only accepting requests for suites

On request: Reservationist required to check with the hotel before confirming or turning down a reservation

No arrivals: No longer accepting any reservations for arrivals on a specific date

No through bookings: Not accepting any reservations where the guest's stay will continue through a specific date

In the "no arrivals" classification, the hotel, because reservations are tight, may determine that it will not accept any further arrivals on a specific date even though it is still prepared to accept reservations for an arrival on an earlier date and going through that date. In "no through bookings," the hotel advises the reservation offices to accept no reservations that go through a specific date, because that date is already too heavily reserved.

Most systems now in use permit the central reservation office to directly access the hotel's property management system, enabling the reservationists to verify the reservation status. Nevertheless, communications between the CRO and the hotel are very important to avoid any confusion or uncertainty, possibly resulting in overbooking or underbooking.

Reservation Confirmations

When a reservation has become confirmed by a reservation office, a confirmation (see Figure 7-3) will normally be sent to the guest, giving the guest the particulars of the reservation, including rate, arrival date, length of stay, and any special request. In addition, it provides the guest with a notice that he or she can present to the front desk upon arrival, indicating that there is a confirmed reservation. However, if the time between the acceptance of the reservation and the arrival date of the guest is so short that a confirmation would not arrive prior to the arrival date, the confirmation is not normally sent unless specifically requested by the client.

Reservation confirmations are usually preprinted forms, printed in four or five copies. The original is sent to the guest, the second and third copies go to the hotel, and the fourth copy is retained in the reservation office's files.

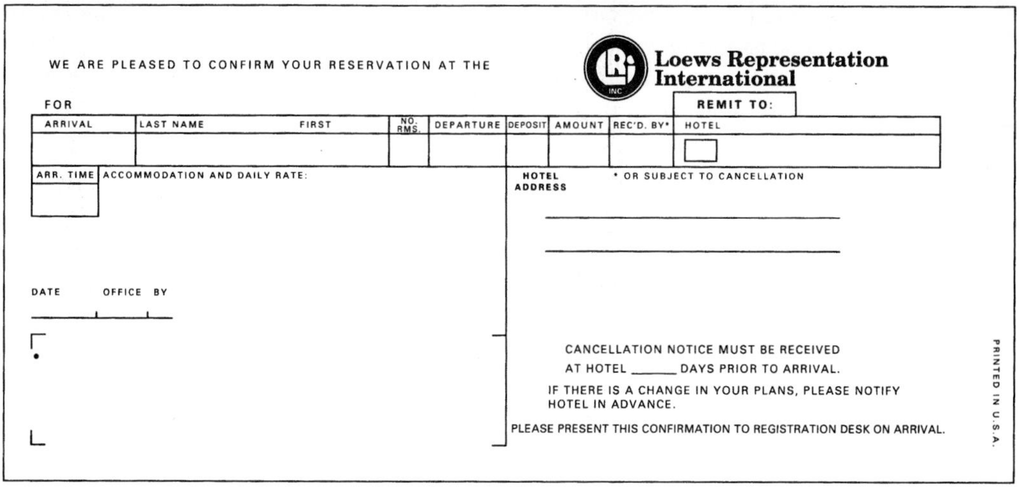

Figure 7-3 Sample of Reservation Confirmation Form

Computerized reservation systems can produce confirmations automatically as a direct product of the information that has previously been entered. To balance the load in computer time, confirmations are usually printed at the end of the day, when the reservation activity of the computer is very low.

The Internet now provides opportunities for the guest to initiate their own reservations by keying directly into the reservation network.

HOTEL RESERVATION OFFICES

Let us now examine the operation of the reservation department within the hotel. In several of the succeeding chapters, we will discuss various functions of property management systems. While they make major contributions in the areas of guest accounting, their roots are deeply centered in the reservation area. The systems store and control the entire reservation status of the hotel. The reservations are initiated by the reservationists, and the information generated at that point flows into other sections of the system to meet other goals, including the development of a history of the sources of reservations. The use of this history is described in Chapter 8, under "Guest History."

The following are the basic principles of the systems as they relate to reservations:

a. The system must contain a complete inventory of rooms available by type and rate for the entire hotel. If there are seasonal variances, these must be reflected.

b. The reservationist will access the computer through a terminal similar to those used in a central reservation office and will input data into a screen set up to accept the reservation information in a standardized manner.

c. Ideally the system will "prompt" the reservationist with key information; for example, most desirable room, type, and rate to sell.

d. The system should apply the reservations inputted against the inventory, reducing the number of rooms remaining available in that type for each day of the reservation.

e. Information on projected occupancy, remaining availability by room type, projected arrival listings, room revenue projections, VIP lists, and so on, should be printed by the computer in report form on a daily basis or as required.

f. The reservation information should be stored in the computer in a fashion that permits easy printing of a registration card and rack slips on the day of arrival, and facilitates overall check-in.

Forecasting

A major function of these systems is to provide various types of forecasts and projections for use not only by the reservation department but by other areas of the hotel. An availability summary (Figure 7-4) is used for a fast picture of the reservation status of the hotel. Reports such as a rooms booked analysis (Figure 7-5) provide information for staffing as well as room availability. Long-range forecasts such as a 6-month forecast (Figure 7-6) are used in budgeting, staffing, and cash flow projections.

Yield Management

Hotels use their reservation systems in a program known as "yield management." The purpose of yield management is to obtain the maximum revenue by changes in the room rates in relation to demand. Thus the highest revenue is obtained when demand is highest and business is not lost by too high a rate when demand is low. The principles followed are explained earlier in the section on reservation status.

Yield management has been practiced—for many years. For example, in New York City during the week, the rate you pay for a particular room may be twice the amount you pay for the same room on the weekend when demand is low. Now, however, the computer has facilitated the use of yield demand by automatically changing rates as demand increases.

Availability Summary

| 120% | 96% | 72% | 48% | 24% | 0% |

```
1  3  5  7  9  11 13 15 17 19 21 23 25 27 29 31
```

Oct 17/99 - Oct 31/99   All Room Types   Total Rms:163

Figure 7-4 Availability Summary

```
10/17/99
10:22                              Rooms Booked Analysis
                                   Oct 17/92 - Oct 31/92
```

Rm Type/Date	17	18	19	20	21	22	23	24	25	26	27	28	29	30	31
DELUXE KING	15	9	7	5	5	7	11	13	0	1	4	4	9	11	13
DELUXE QUEEN	3	1	0	0	0	0	2	2	0	0	0	0	0	0	0
DELUXE DOUBLES	0	0	0	0	0	0	0	0	0	0	0	0	0	0	0
DELUXE QUEENS	11	0	3	1	1	0	20	15	1	1	0	1	11	6	5
SUPERIOR KING	34	25	10	8	10	10	27	31	7	2	3	6	5	16	19
SUPERIOR QUEEN	2	1	1	0	6	1	6	5	0	0	0	1	2	3	2
SUPERIOR DOUBLES	12	7	0	0	3	1	7	8	1	0	0	0	10	5	5
SUPERIOR QUEENS	13	3	5	5	2	0	14	14	0	1	3	1	0	11	15
STANDARD KING	4	1	4	7	3	3	4	3	5	3	2	3	3	5	6
STANDARD QUEEN	5	2	3	2	4	7	5	9	0	0	1	1	0	6	6
STANDARD 2 DOUBLE	0	0	0	0	0	0	0	0	0	0	0	0	0	0	0
STANDARD QUEENS	7	6	4	3	3	6	7	8	1	1	1	1	0	4	6
CUPOLA SUITE	1	0	1	1	0	0	1	1	0	1	1	0	0	0	0
GREEN MOUNTAIN SU	1	1	0	0	0	0	1	1	0	0	0	0	0	1	1
PARLOR	6	1	1	2	2	2	5	6	0	0	2	2	0	0	1
PREMIUM ROOMS	13	5	3	2	2	3	14	14	2	4	4	2	0	2	2
PRESIDENTIAL SUIT	3	1	1	2	2	1	2	3	0	0	0	0	0	0	0
KING SUITE (PARL	3	0	0	0	0	1	3	3	0	0	2	2	0	0	1
TOWNHOUSE #2-QUEE	8	1	1	0	0	0	9	9	3	2	2	2	1	1	1
TOWNHOUSE #3-QUEE	10	1	0	0	0	0	7	8	0	2	2	2	0	2	0
TOWNHOUSE #1-SUIT	8	2	1	1	1	1	7	9	4	3	3	4	3	3	2
Total Booked	159	67	45	39	44	43	152	162	24	21	30	32	44	76	85
Rooms Out of Order	0	0	2	2	2	2	0	0	0	0	0	0	0	0	0
% Occupancy	98	41	28	24	27	27	93	99	15	13	18	20	27	47	52

Figure 7-5   Rooms Booked Analysis

Overbooking and Underbooking

The purpose of all the systems just described is to permit the proper control of the number of reservations. Reservation control can be defined as the attempt to fill the hotel every day at the highest possible rate without refusing business. To achieve this, a certain level of overbooking is necessary. Without it, the hotel would be continually underbooked, resulting in lower revenue and profits. The key is to maintain the proper level of overbooking. Every hotel has a certain percentage of cancellations and people who do not arrive—"no-shows." An experience factor, developed from the historical pattern of cancellations and no-shows, must be used to set the proper level of overbooking.

Underbooking is often caused by the failure of the reservation department to accept telephoned reservations on the assumption that walk-in business—people coming in off the street—can fill the hotels. But this is negative thinking. The telephoned reservations are usually from regular customers who, if refused, may not call in the future; people walking in off the street usually don't care where they stay. Therefore, telephone reservations should be accepted whenever possible, even if they result in some overbooking.

Group Reservations

Although handling individual reservations is the major function of a hotel reservation office, group reservations are important and require certain specific procedures.

Group reservations are made far in advance of the proposed date of arrival. Consequently, the initial reservation is of a preliminary, estimated nature, which must be defined in several steps as the actual date of arrival comes nearer. The initial reservation will provide arrival and departure dates and an estimated number of people and rooms required. On this basis, the hotel will "block" a certain number of rooms for that period; that is, tentatively reserve the rooms for the group. At the same time, a group-reservation file is set up that will establish the dates at which the reservation will be more defined.

Although it is the responsibility of the group-sales department to prepare the original booking sheet and to obtain a signed agreement with the organizers of the group, the reservation department is still responsible for policing the various phases. In particular, this includes the determination of the arrival and departure patterns of a group. The sales department will obtain the principal dates, but some members of the group will arrive earlier than others, and some will leave before others. Only by defining these variations can the group be properly fitted into the overall reservation picture of the hotel.

The agreement with the group should call for a series of advance deposit payments to be made in accordance with the agreement and related to the number of rooms needed. As each deposit is received, the number of rooms required by the group naturally becomes a more firm figure. Should there be a change in those requirements, this will probably be reported to the hotel at the time a deposit is sent. Consequently, it is very important that the deposits be received on the scheduled dates and that any change in the size of the group be reported so that the number of rooms blocked can be revised. This minimum size of groups is usually 20 rooms, but sometimes large groups or conventions will take the whole hotel. In the latter event, the hotel can commit all its facilities to the group. In some cases the convention may utilize several hotels in which convention and visitors bureau reservations are coordinated by the city.

If preregistration of a group requires preassignment of rooms, it is necessary that the rooming list, setting out the name, address, and exact accommodation requirements of each member, be received by the hotel in advance of the arrival date. The person handling group reservations should therefore be in direct communication with the group to make sure that this list is received. He or she will usually have the responsibility for assigning specific rooms to each member of the group.

Six-Month-Forecast
Oct 01/99 to Mar 31/00

Oct 1999	Reg	Guar	Group Res	Tent. Group	Total	%Occ
Oct01/92	-	1	-	-	1	1%
Oct02/92	-	1	-	-	1	1%
Oct03/92	-	1	-	-	1	1%
Oct04/92	-	1	-	-	1	1%
Oct05/92	-	1	-	-	1	1%
Oct06/92	-	1	-	-	1	1%
Oct07/92	-	1	-	-	1	1%
Oct08/92	-	1	-	-	1	1%
Oct09/92	-	1	-	-	1	1%
Oct10/92	-	1	-	-	1	1%
Oct11/92	-	1	-	-	1	1%
Oct12/92	-	2	1	-	3	2%
Oct13/92	1	2	2	-	5	3%
Oct14/92	-	6	15	-	21	13%
Oct15/92	3	23	76	-	102	63%
Oct16/92	7	49	106	-	162	99%
Oct17/92	11	34	32	-	77	47%
Oct18/92	7	40	-	-	47	29%
Oct19/92	12	33	-	-	45	28%
Oct20/92	17	28	-	-	45	28%
Oct21/92	8	35	1	-	44	27%
Oct22/92	11	60	83	-	154	94%
Oct23/92	17	73	71	-	161	99%
Oct24/92	2	17	5	-	24	15%
Oct25/92	-	16	7	-	23	14%
Oct26/92	2	14	15	-	31	19%
Oct27/92	3	13	16	15	47	29%
Oct28/92	1	13	30	-	44	27%
Oct29/92	7	45	3	18	73	45%
Oct30/92	6	51	9	18	84	52%
Oct31/92						

Nov 1999	Reg	Guar	Group Res	Tent. Group	Total	%Occ
Nov01/92	1	18	34	-	53	32%
Nov02/92	-	5	38	-	43	26%
Nov03/92	-	2	30	20	52	32%
Nov04/92	-	4	19	20	43	26%
Nov05/92	-	17	53	-	70	43%
Nov06/92	6	66	63	-	135	83%
Nov07/92	11	85	38	-	134	82%
Nov08/92	2	5	-	-	7	4%
Nov09/92	-	3	-	10	13	8%
Nov10/92	-	6	-	10	16	10%
Nov11/92	1	4	8	8	21	13%
Nov12/92	1	4	12	28	45	28%
Nov13/92	4	24	10	-	38	23%
Nov14/92	5	24	-	-	29	18%
Nov15/92	1	3	-	-	4	2%
Nov16/92	1	1	-	-	2	1%
Nov17/92	1	3	-	20	24	15%
Nov18/92	-	3	-	70	73	45%
Nov19/92	-	1	-	70	71	44%
Nov20/92	4	19	-	-	23	14%
Nov21/92	5	21	-	-	26	16%
Nov22/92	-	15	-	-	15	9%
Nov23/92	-	8	-	-	8	5%
Nov24/92	-	8	-	-	8	5%
Nov25/92	-	38	7	-	45	28%
Nov26/92	-	53	15	-	68	42%
Nov27/92	5	57	15	-	77	47%
Nov28/92	5	39	7	-	51	31%
Nov29/92	4	6	-	-	10	6%
Nov30/92	-	1	-	-	1	1%

Dec 1999	Reg	Guar	Group Res	Tent. Group	Total	%Occ
Dec01/92	-	2	-	-	2	1%
Dec02/92	-	1	-	10	11	7%
Dec03/92	2	4	3	10	19	12%
Dec04/92	6	14	38	-	58	36%
Dec05/92	6	18	48	-	72	44%
Dec06/92	-	3	-	-	3	2%
Dec07/92	1	1	17	-	18	11%
Dec08/92	1	1	17	-	18	11%
Dec09/92	1	1	-	-	1	1%
Dec10/92	-	5	-	-	9	6%
Dec11/92	4	12	30	15	61	37%
Dec12/92	5	14	30	15	64	39%
Dec13/92	1	4	-	-	5	3%
Dec14/92	-	1	25	-	26	16%
Dec15/92	1	1	25	-	26	16%
Dec16/92	1	1	-	-	1	1%
Dec17/92	-	7	-	-	1	1%
Dec18/92	1	7	-	-	8	5%
Dec19/92	1	10	-	-	11	7%
Dec20/92	-	3	-	-	1	1%
Dec21/92	1	3	-	-	4	2%
Dec22/92	1	10	-	-	11	7%
Dec23/92	4	17	-	-	21	13%
Dec24/92	12	24	-	-	36	22%
Dec25/92	12	27	-	-	39	24%
Dec26/92	18	32	-	-	50	31%
Dec27/92	20	30	-	-	50	31%
Dec28/92	21	30	-	-	51	31%
Dec29/92	20	18	-	-	38	23%
Dec30/92	15	19	-	-	34	21%
Dec31/92	11	32	-	-	43	26%

Figure 7-6 Six-Month Forecast

Oct 1999

Oct 1999	Reg	Guar	Group Res	Tent. Group	Total	%Occ
A1K	1	73	42		116	
A1Q	1	3	5		9	
A2D	–	–			–	
A2Q	3	20	66		89	
B1K	34	94	100		228	
B1Q	7	20	12		39	
B2D	2	4	60		66	
B2Q	–	66	29		95	
C1K	4	48	6		58	
C1Q	13	32	7		52	
C2D	–	–			–	
C2Q	3	51	9		63	
CUQ	2	3	2		7	
LOFT	–	7			7	
P	14	14	12		40	
PREM	7	55	21		83	
PSK	7	4	6		17	
SK	4	12	6		22	
TWN2	3	7	37		47	
TWN3	9	10	22		41	
TWNS	1	43	30		74	
Totals	115	566	472		1,153	

Nov 1999

Nov 1999	Reg	Guar	Group Res	Tent. Group	Total	%Occ
A1K	14	73	32		119	
A1Q	–	4	4		8	
A2D	–	–			–	
A2Q	4	44	2		50	
B1K	11	63	163		237	
B1Q	1	9	30		40	
B2D	–	8	37		45	
B2Q	2	58	34		94	
C1K	2	28	–		30	
C1Q	5	27	2		34	
C2D	–	–	–		0	
C2Q	2	52	4		58	
CUQ	–	2	2		4	
LOFT	–	1			1	
P	2	21	3		26	
PREM	10	28	3		41	
PSK	–	5	3		8	
SK	2	16	–		18	
TWN2	–	25	14		39	
TWN3	–	22	–		22	
TWNS	2	57	16		75	
Totals	57	543	349		949	

Dec 1999

Dec 1999	Reg	Guar	Group Res	Tent. Group	Total	%Occ
A1K	16	13	30		59	
A1Q	–	–			–	
A2D	–	–			–	
A2Q	3	14	25		42	
B1K	6	56	87		149	
B1Q	–	7	–		7	
B2D	–	5	31		36	
B2Q	7	58	44		109	
C1K	4	23	6		33	
C1Q	–	25	–		25	
C2D	–	–			–	
C2Q	11	32	–		43	
CUQ	–	2	2		4	
LOFT	–	–			–	
P	24	12	4		40	
PREM	3	7	–		10	
PSK	18	2	4		24	
SK	4	12	–		16	
TWN2	31	6	–		37	
TWN3	28	6	–		34	
TWNS	10	64	–		74	
Totals	165	344	233		742	

Figure 7-6 *(Continued)*

Relations with Other Departments

All activities of the hotel reservation office require its working closely and cooperating with every other department of the hotel. This is particularly important, as it relates to sales. There must be continuous, close communication between the sales and reservation departments to ensure that the records of both in respect to future group business are in agreement. Without such communication, there is always the danger that a group may be sold but not recorded in the reservation records. This can, of course, result in an extremely embarrassing situation, possibly involving major costs to the hotel, if the sales department has signed an agreement with a group but the hotel cannot provide the necessary accommodations.

As previously mentioned, the reservation department must also provide the other departments with a forecast of expected occupancy. This forecast is prepared in cooperation with the sales department in respect to groups. The forecast is extremely important, since it provides housekeeping, food and beverage, and other departments with continuous information on anticipated occupancies, thus permitting the heads of these departments to plan their staff requirements and control their payroll costs. Consequently, proper forecasting by the reservation department is essential to the overall efficiency and profitability of the departments affected by the forecast.

Longer forecasts, such as, the 6-month forecast shown in Figure 7-6, may be used for longer-term staffing and budgeting purposes.

CHAPTER SUMMARY

While there are some independent reservation systems, the more successful are operated by the chains. The main problem for the independents relates to no-shows.

Central reservation offices may be one office for the entire chain or a series of regional offices. There are advantages and disadvantages to both.

The order in which reservation information is obtained is extremely important.

Each hotel has various reservation statuses that determine which reservations can be accepted.

The reservation department in a hotel must provide the other departments with forecasts of occupancy on which they base their staffing.

Yield management is a technique used to obtain the most profitable combination of rate and occupancy.

A certain level of overbooking is necessary to maximize occupancy.

Group reservations require close cooperation between reservations and group sales.

REVIEW QUESTIONS

1. What was the major problem encountered by independent reservation systems?
2. What is a CRO?
3. What are the advantages of a one-number system?
4. What should be the first information obtained by a hotel reservationist?
5. What are the five levels of a hotel's rate structure?
6. When is a reservation confirmation not sent?
7. What is the purpose of yield management?

CASE STUDY 1

William Smith is front office manager of a 500 room hotel. He has been asked to establish a policy relative to overbooking. What factors should he consider?

8

Sales and Marketing

After studying this chapter, the student should:

1. Understand the organization of a hotel sales department.
2. Understand the functions of the department.
3. Know the various techniques used in hotel sales.

Chapter 5 briefly covered the involvement of the general manager in the sales function in a hotel. We mentioned that the general manager participates actively in this area for two basic reasons: first, sales and their development are a long-range activity of the hotel, rather than part of the day-to-day operations; second, the hotel's sales policy is interwoven with the image the hotel has in the eyes of the public, and the general manager wishes to enhance that image.

In addition to the general manager and the individual hotel's sales department, many chains have regional sales organizations whose staffs are directed toward producing business for the chains' hotels. The advantage of having such staffs for this purpose cannot be overstated. At the same time, it must be recognized that the use of such a regional staff may result in the need for fewer sales people on the individual hotel's payroll.

Throughout this chapter, we may from time to time refer to regional sales personnel in regard to additional benefits they give to chain hotels over individual hotels, but the chapter will be primarily directed to a discussion of the structure and functions of a sales department within an individual hotel.

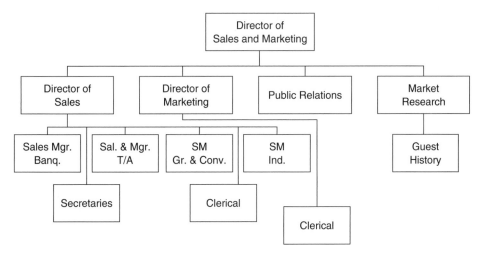

Figure 8-1   Organization Chart of Sales Department

Figure 8-1 is an organizational chart of a hotel sales and marketing department. The department is headed by a director of sales and marketing, who may sometimes be known as vice president-sales, or may bear a lesser title such as sales manager. In any case, the director of sales and marketing is responsible for administering and directing the sales effort within several subareas into which the sales function is normally divided. Note that the dotted line to guest history recognizes that the actual function is managed by the front office but that the data is used in sales and marketing. In smaller hotels many of the functions may be combined but, nonetheless, exist. The governing factor in determining the number of people in the department is the level of group and convention business, as this is where the major part of a hotel sales department's activities are directed. We will examine the activities of each area of the sales department, emphasizing the related factors that dictate their activities and the techniques they employ.

GROUP AND CONVENTION SALES

With the structure of the hotel sales department, group and convention sales is the largest element, not only in terms of time and effort but also in the number of people employed. In a large convention hotel, as many as 8 to 10 people work in group and convention sales; therefore, an examination of the operations of this area will be dealt with first.

Room allocations. Every hotel seeking group business must evaluate the number of rooms it wishes to allot to group sales. The allocation of rooms for this purpose will vary from month to month, depending on the amount of business anticipated from regular transient guests. Therefore, transient business should be estimated first, and the rest of the anticipated available rooms allocated to group sales. The group allocation can be presented in bar-chart form, as shown in Figure 8-2. However, inasmuch as groups tend to drop in numbers as they get closer to the date, an allocation of rooms 10% in excess of those available is reasonable.

Planning. Planning is the most important responsibility of any hotel sales department. It is in group and convention sales that the long-range planning requirements become most essential. Group and convention business does not materialize overnight. Most organizations that have annual or periodic conventions plan many months ahead—indeed, in many cases, 3 to 5 years ahead. Therefore, it is impossible for business of this nature to be generated by the group and convention sales staff without emphasis on planning. There must be continual communication with such organizations to learn of decisions made in respect to dates and geographical areas being considered for future conventions. Even more important is the knowledge of when such decisions are in the review stage and of

Figure 8-2   Bar Chart Showing Allocation of Rooms

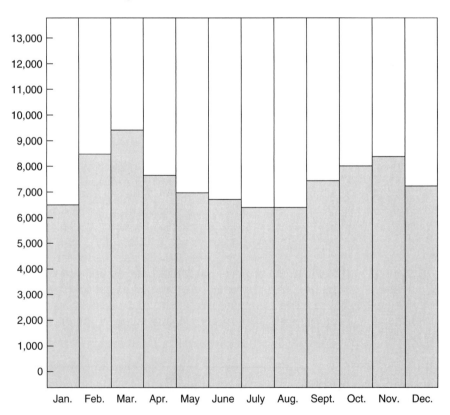

who is responsible for making the decisions. Only then can the proper approach be made to the right people at the right time.

Many organizations create planning committees to either recommend or decide on the location of future conventions. These committees are usually appointed during the course of a current convention. For example, a major organization having its convention in Hawaii in 2000 will appoint a planning committee to research and recommend a destination for the 2005 convention. Approval of this destination is quite often made at the next convention. In order to acquire close contact with these committees and at the same time try to get a jump on the competition, a member of the group and convention sales staff of a hotel may attend major conventions taking place in the current year. Not only does this give the sales staff a competitive sales advantage, it also familiarizes them with the type of function and activities conducted at the convention.

Proper planning involves certain other factors, without which success cannot be achieved.

Research

In order that the greatest possible amount of group and convention business may be obtained, and especially since such business must be booked far in advance of the arrival date, research must be carried out to ascertain and develop the sources of such business. Research is, therefore, a particularly important function of the sales department in regard to group and convention sales.

In addition to knowledge gained through personal contact on inquiry, information about future conventions can be obtained from various travel and convention publications and by contacting the convention bureau or chamber of commerce in likely destinations.

Policies

In all phases of hotel operation, certain policies must be established and adhered to, and this is particularly important in the sales area since the process of selling must be done with certain policies in mind. Sales policies must be established for the following:

1. Rates for future bookings, for groups, and for conventions
2. Size of groups to be accepted at certain times of the year, depending on seasonal factors
3. Amounts of advance deposits to be obtained, and at what intervals
4. Commissions to be paid
5. Requirements such as rooming lists, prelabeling of baggage, preassignment of rooms, and overall handling
6. Numbers of complimentary rooms to be given to groups

The policies established in relation to each of these must be so designed that they will result in the maximum revenue to the hotel.

Department Management

A person with great sales ability, regardless of what the product is, doesn't always make a great administrator. In fact, the drive and enthusiasm desirable in the salesperson may make his or her eagerness to sell overcome the need to adhere to established policies; therefore, the sales staff must receive the proper direction.

Consequently, the person holding the position of director of sales must be an administrator, capable of managing the department in addition to selling.

Interdepartmental Cooperation

Many hotels have problems resulting from a lack of communication or cooperation between the sales department and other departments. Selling a service is like selling a product: in addition to selling it, you must deliver it, and it is pointless to sell services or features that you cannot provide.

There have been many glaring examples of such selling. A salesperson promises a convention 300 ocean-front rooms in a hotel that actually has only 200 rooms that face the ocean; promises to serve 500 full-course breakfasts between 8:00 and 8:30 in the morning; or promises a menu on which there are certain items that are not available at that time of year. These are very simple examples of selling a product that cannot be delivered. Had the sales representative in each instance communicated first with the reservation department or the food and beverage department, he or she would not have placed the hotel in a position where at a later date it had to make excuses or lengthy apologies. And too often, the burden of making these apologies falls upon someone other than the person who made the sale.

Such problems are often the result of sales staff not being fully familiar with the product. This situation can be avoided if every person joining the sales staff is required to work in each department for a limited period of time.

Cooperation between the sales department and other departments of the hotel is fundamental to the proper delivery of services that are sold. In the long run, the reputation for always delivering is the sales department's greatest asset.

Identifying Prospects

A key element of group and convention sales is the identification of prospective customers.

The group may be divided into three segments; association, group, and other (social, religious, etc.). There are certain major differences between the two major segments.

1. Associations are, in general, larger groups than corporate.
2. The lead-time for associations, often in excess of 3 years, is much longer than corporate groups.
3. Numbers of attendees for corporate groups are easily defined, being mandated by the corporation. Association attendance depends on the marketing ability of the organizer.
4. Corporate group rooms are paid by the company while association attendees are usually responsible for their own rooms.

From the above, it can be seen that corporate groups are easier to handle than associations.

The following are several possible sources for identifying prospects.

1. Local organizations and companies who may have periodic group meetings or conventions.
2. Divisions, not previously contacted, of corporations with whom the hotel is already doing business.
3. Referrals from past or present customers.
4. Determining customers who are currently using the competition. This can often be achieved by periodic reviews of competitors' reader boards.
5. As previously mentioned, convention and visitors bureaus and chambers of commerce.

In order to qualify as a prospect, the quality and quantity of potential business must be defined.

Sales Calls and Presentations

While some hotels make extensive use of the telephone to solicit prospects, it is the opinion of the authors that, once identified, a prospect should receive a personal visit from a member of the sales staff. The purpose of the visit is to further define the potential of the prospect in terms of volume, possible dates, and so on. Each visit requires the completion of a call report (Figure 8-3), which provides the information required for further follow-up.

Since most associations are headquartered in Washington, DC, or the state capital, it is desirable to send a sales team to cover them.

If there is a sufficient level of interest by the client to justify a presentation, the various steps to carry out such a presentation must be followed.

A complete package must be prepared describing the property, its facilities (for example, restaurants, bars, and recreational activities), and the various services that it can provide for a successful convention (for example, audiovisual equipment, meeting room capabilities, menus, etc).

```
                        CALL REPORT FORM
TO _____ FROM _____ DATE _____
ORGANIZATION _____ FILE # _____
CONTACT _____ TITLE _____ PHONE # _____
STREET _____ CITY & STATE _____ ZIP _____
MEETING MONTH _____ # ROOMS _____ # PEOPLE _____
TYPE OF CALL: PERSONAL _____ TELEPHONE _____ ON-SITE _____
MAIN MEETING SCHEDULE (Past, Present, Future)
DATES & DAYS OF THE WEEK        CITY        HOTEL
_____
_____
_____
_____
_____

EXHIBITS? _____ PREFER: Cities _____ Resorts _____ Airport _____
WHO MAKES DECISION _____
WHEN & WHERE _____
CONSIDER:        DOMESTIC _____ CANADA _____
(Region/City)    EUROPE _____ RESORTS _____

BOARD MEETING _____ SALES MEETING _____
INCENTIVE TRIPS _____ SEMINARS _____
COMMENTS: _____
_____
_____
_____
_____
_____
_____
_____
_____

AGENCY _____
ADDRESS _____ PHONE _____
   If a Travel Agency or Incentive House handles the account, please note pertinent data:
   H-1929-1-77  No.1 File Copy   No. 2 Follow-Up Copy   No. 3 Follow-Up Copy   No. 4 Regional V.P.
```

Figure 8-3 Call Report

It is important to know and evaluate the competition. If possible, to determine other hotels that are being considered, and to be ready to advance reasons why your property is superior to the others. It is important also to research the potential client, to learn their preferences and philosophy. The presentation team must make use of literature, photographs, and videos to sell the property.

Hopefully the presentation will be successful and initiate the presentation of a group booking sheet, shown in Figure 8-4.

Incentive groups. Much of the group and convention sales business results from incentive programs that are maintained by large companies. For example, a car manufacturer or maker of major appliances will reward the leading retail dealer in each geographical area with a free trip for two to some exotic destination. These trips are not taken individually, but rather as part of a group or convention, which provides the manufacturer with the opportunity of further promoting its particular product.

Within the travel industry there are certain companies—travel agents or tour operators—whose principal business is the handling of these "incentive groups," and others that specialize in other types of group and convention sales. These sources of business are spread around the country, and it is necessary for members of the group and convention sales department of a hotel to be continually traveling to visit them. In this respect, the hotel chains probably have a very definite advantage. It is extremely difficult and expensive for an independent hotel to continuously and completely cover the country. With limited coverage, priorities must be established and some opportunities for future business are missed. The chains, however, can use their regional sales staffs to promote business for all their hotels, giving them a decided advantage in both extent of coverage and ability to spread the cost.

The coordinator. Perhaps the greatest marketing tool in obtaining group and convention business is the proper handling of business that is already booked. Major hotels handling this type of business employ a "group and convention coordinator," a position that is a part of, or extension of, the group and convention sales function. The prime duty of the coordinator is to work closely with the group leader or leaders to ensure that the entire event is handled properly from beginning to end. Although many groups, particularly those from incentive programs, are handled by professional group leaders, others have group leaders who are inexperienced in coordination. Thus the hotel's coordinator is called upon in many instances to resolve problems, soothe angered guests, and meet all emergencies. He or she must be available around the clock when the group is in the hotel.

The following are specific areas in which the coordinator has a major responsibility:

1. The handling of airport arrivals, whether via scheduled or charter flights, requires proper coordination. Arrangements should be made to facilitate

---

HOTEL GRAYLIG

( ) INQUIRY ONLY   ( ) TENTATIVE   ( ) DEFINITE

GROUP NAME _____ AGENCY_____

CONTACT PERSON _____ TITLE_____

Address _____

City & State _____

DATES _____ # of Rooms / people _____ /_____

Telephone, Area Code _____

COMPLIMENTARY   QUOTED   NET_____GROSS_____%

```
                        _____ Twin, EP
                        _____ Single, EP
( ) Welcome rum swizzles _____ Third Person, EP
( ) 1 Room EP per _____  _____ 1 Bedroom Suite, EP
         Rooms paid      _____ 2 Bedrooms Suites, EP
( ) purchasing two cocktail _____ pp, pd, MAP plus 15%
    parties, compliment  _____ pp, pd, FAP plus 15%
    third party.        _____ pp, pd, Gourmet-Dine Around plus 15%
                        _____ pp, Cocktail Party Dry Buffet plus 15%
                        _____ pp, Cocktail Party with H/C plus 15%
                        _____ pp, Banquet/Barbeque surcharge plus 15%
                        _____ Music
                        _____ Native Show
                                     Round Trip Transfers
                        _____ pp, scheduled flight
                        _____ pp, charter flight
```

DECISION DATE:_____ DEPOSIT DUE:_____

ROOMING LIST DUE:_____ OTHER PAYMENTS: (90) (60) (40)

REMARKS:

SALES PERSON_____

FOLLOW UP DATE (1)   (2)   (3)   DATE_____

Copies: (white) R.V.P.   (green) C.O.F.   (green) Agent   (green) Salesman
H-1106-8-76

Figure 8-4 Group Booking Sheet

the clearing of passengers through immigration and customs, to make available proper transportation to the hotel, and to greet the group members upon their arrival.

2. Baggage handling must be supervised and coordinated with the rooming of the guests. The members of the group should, of course, be preregistered. For this purpose, a rooming list setting out their names and addresses should have been obtained by the sales department at least 30 days before the group's arrival. Rooms can then be preassigned and folios and registration cards prepared ahead of time. Distinctive baggage tags of a uniform design should be sent to the group before the members leave home, so that all baggage can be tagged with names and addresses. The entire group's baggage can then be picked up at the airport and delivered to the hotel, and a staff of bellmen under the supervision of the coordinator, equipped with the lists of the guests' names and room numbers, can match names on the baggage tags to the rooming lists and write the proper room numbers on the tags. This permits baggage to be sent directly to the guests' room without need for identification by the guest. Meanwhile, from a desk or desks set up in the lobby, the guest can get an envelope containing a room key, registration card, and any literature the hotel or group may wish to distribute. Since the registration card is pretyped, the guest need only sign it and turn it over to the person staffing the desk, and then go directly to the room. Incidentally, the provision of some kind of refreshment, such as a "welcome drink," will give the baggage handlers additional time to get the luggage into the rooms.

3. Each function must be properly monitored to ensure not only that it is run properly but that the requirements of the group are being met. For example, if entertainment is to be provided, the coordinator should be responsible for its proper production. Or the group leader may want a change in the arrangements or format, such as an extension of a cocktail party beyond the previously agreed-upon time. This can be worked out between the coordinator and the group leader.

4. The coordinator should have responsibility for verifying daily with the group leader all charges to the group master account. In this way, disputes at the end of the convention will be avoided, and problems or misunderstandings will be resolved as they occur and before memories become clouded.

And so the value of a good coordinator cannot be overstated in terms of reputation, and, ultimately, additional group sales.

TRAVEL AGENT SALES

As with group and convention sales, travel-agent sales require substantial travel by the sales staff. Whereas the sources of group and convention business are concentrated in certain geographical areas, travel agents are spread across the width and breadth of the country. Consequently, sales calls must be made even in many small towns, which may have two or three agents who are potentially good sources of business.

There are two types of travel agents that must be visited: wholesalers and retailers. The retail travel agent, like any other retail business, is the agency that sells to the public. But in addition, behind the scenes in the travel business are a number of wholesale agencies, with whom the retail agents make their bookings, rather than making them directly with the hotel.

In most instances, it would be very costly for retail agents to communicate directly with the hotel each time they have a booking. Besides, business booked directly by a retailer requires the sending of a deposit to the hotel. In many instances, particularly during busy periods, the retail agent cannot know immediately whether the hotel will be able to provide the requested accommodations. Finally, many customers have come to desire a travel package, combining hotel accommodations, air travel, group transfers, and tours. Each of these problems can be solved through the retail agent's working with a wholesaler.

Each wholesaler works directly with specific hotels or airlines to develop packages that can be sold to the public. These packages are of different kinds: some are for groups and others for individuals or couples; some call for stays at two or more hotels; some have special themes such as honeymoon packages, golf packages, or ski packages.

In all instances, a brochure must be printed to inform the public of the contents of the package. These brochures are designed, printed, and paid for by the wholesaler. (Although it is considered unethical, there is occasional financial participation by the hotels involved.) With the use of these brochures, the retail agent sells to the public the package the agent can buy from the wholesaler.

Through his relationship with the hotels, the wholesaler obtains allocations of a certain number of rooms that can be sold without checking back with the hotel. Furthermore, the wholesaler, having established credit with the hotel, is not required to make an advance deposit. A coupon is issued by the wholesaler to the retail agent, who in turn gives it to the customer. The guest presents the coupon to the hotel at the time of check-in and it is subsequently used by the hotel as a basis for billing the wholesaler. Then the wholesaler invoices the retail agent. In most instances the retail agent has obtained a cash deposit from the customer, thus giving the agent the use of certain funds for a period of time.

Where business has been booked through a wholesaler, the commission paid by the hotel is higher than that paid directly to a retail agent. It is divided up in a prearranged format between the wholesaler and the retail agency. Some wholesalers, such as American Express, also operate retail agencies, with which they work on the same basis as with nonaffiliated retail agencies.

When the sales representatives personally visit the retail agencies, they can ascertain that brochures and rate sheets for their property or properties are on display there. At the same time, they are familiarizing the staff of the agency with the characteristics of the property and, of course, attempting to motivate the staff to sell the property or recommend it in preference to others. In visiting wholesalers, the principal objective is to persuade them to incorporate the property into their packages. This often involves lengthy negotiations on rates and room allotments.

Most hotels use direct mailings of promotional literature to agents as a means of developing interest and business. Although the results that can be expected cannot be defined at the time of the mailing, of course this does provide an easy method to get the retail agent to focus on the hotel in question.

It is common practice in the hotel industry to offer discounts of various types to travel-agency personnel who wish to visit the hotel. The degree of discount—which may even be a fully complimentary offer—varies depending upon the importance of the agency, its location, and the amount of potential business that may be developed.

Hotels also give cocktail parties in various cities throughout the year for the staffs of the agencies in each city. At such a party, a presentation is made setting out the features the hotel has to offer. At the same time, the parties provide an opportunity for the sales staff to meet many agents on a semi-social basis.

Many hotels use a form of selling called the "sales blitz" to promote sales in a specific area. Blitzes may be directed at travel agents and wholesalers as well as corporations, state associations, and the like. The direction of the blitz will vary from state or city to city, depending on the type of business to be expected from each location.

The blitz may be carried out in telemarketing style using the telephone or by making door-to-door sales calls.

BANQUET SALES

Banquet sales are usually handled by a local banquet-sales manager who is not involved in selling rooms other than for functions. It is necessary to distinguish between this position and that of banquet manager, which is an operational food and beverage function. The source of banquet business is the local community in which the hotel exists, so the successful banquet-sales manager must develop the proper relations within that community.

Close contact must be maintained with major companies in the area, particularly those who have periodic meetings, dinners, and other functions. Although the most important element in developing this business is the creation of a good personal relationship between the banquet-sales manager and the executives of the companies, there are certain techniques that can promote this business:

1. Periodic luncheon and cocktail invitations should be extended to appropriate executives in the companies.
2. The issuance of local credit cards, to be used only at the particular hotel, should be considered. The distribution of such cards among the members

of the business community will encourage them to patronize the property.

3. Consideration should also be given to issuing VIP cards to those people in the companies responsible for choosing the locations for their functions.

In addition to maintaining good relations with the local business community, it is important to keep close contact with fraternal and charitable organizations, such as the Rotary Club or Kiwanis. Such organizations usually have weekly luncheons, and even though the revenue from them is limited, they do familiarize the leading members of the community with the facilities available.

The type of functions the banquet-sales manager may expect to be selling are the following:

1. Weddings
2. Dinners, both business and organizational
3. Dances and other social events
4. Cocktail parties
5. Meetings of business organizations (sometimes including a light meal or coffee break)

For any such function, preestablished menus and prices should be used. It is easier for a potential customer to select an appropriate menu if he or she is provided with several alternatives appropriately priced from which the selection can be made.

GENERAL LOCAL SALES

In addition to function business, much of the room business of a hotel is developed from sources within the business community. Consequently, there is a local sales manager whose responsibility it is to obtain this business. Particular emphasis should be placed upon certain specific areas:

Airlines. Many people looking for accommodations upon arrival in a city inquire at the airline desks at the airport. Good relations with the airlines' staffs will help to promote this business. Furthermore, the airlines themselves are an excellent source of business, for housing crews and passengers on delayed flights. Crews usually involve a contract between the airline and the hotel for rooms at a discounted rate.

Travel and tour operators. Many out-of-town travel agencies, and particularly overseas agencies and tour operators, are affiliated with a local agency or operator through whom reservations are placed. Therefore, close contact should be maintained within the travel field.

Secretaries. In every major company, certain secretaries are responsible for making hotel reservations for visiting executives. In many instances, the selection of the hotel is completely in their hands. So it behooves the hotel to provide an occasional luncheon or cocktail party for these secretaries.

Taxi drivers. Never underestimate the influence of taxi drivers in determining what hotel a traveler will stay at. Not only are they often directly asked to make such a recommendation, but remarks they drop, favorable or otherwise, may influence the selection of a hotel. Many hotels, therefore, periodically throw a party for the local taxi drivers.

Professional people. Professionals—lawyers, doctors, and so on—frequently have clients or patients who come from out of town. In many instances, these potential guests are affluent and therefore able to pay premium rates. Therefore, this area should be developed as a source of business.

Embassies. In a large city such as New York, there are many foreign embassies whose staffs are continually changing. New arrivals rarely find housing immediately and are often forced to spend an extended period of time in a hotel. Long-staying guests are extremely valuable to a hotel, particularly when paying full rates, and should be courted vigorously.

Car rental firms. Keeping in close contact with car rental firms can produce results. Many travelers arriving in town may ask these firms for recommendations of a hotel to use.

Other areas. None of the material just presented is meant to suggest that the general public should be ignored for the purpose of developing a reputation and potential business. Local packages should be promoted to obtain weekend business. Such business is often generated through an "escape package"—for example, "Escape from Your Children," "Escape from Your House," or "Escape from the Bad Weather."

Local credit cards, as described in the preceding section, should also be used to develop business within the local community. If the hotel is located in a strongly ethnic region, the appropriate entertainment in the lounge and nightclubs and promotion of local fare can improve the food and beverage business.

It is not uncommon in certain countries for lower rates to be offered to residents of the country than to overseas visitors. This is particularly true in resort locations such as Jamaica, where, even though the prime source of business is the tourist, many local businesspeople also desire accommodations, particularly if they are given a favorable rate.

ACTIVITIES AFFECTING ALL AREAS OF SALES

Training

The sales department in a hotel must, like all other departments, be structured on a reasonable economic basis. True, a tremendous sales organization can be developed by hiring a series of highly qualified and highly paid sales executives, but this is rarely practical. Consequently, the average sales department, like most other departments, finds itself staffed with the very experienced, the less experienced, and the rather inexperienced. The successful department is the one that can train the less-experienced sales personnel within a reasonably short time. Proper direction in such training is an important part of the duties of the director of sales.

Budget

No department in a hotel should operate either without a budget or over its budget. Over the years, sales people gained a reputation—justified or not—for failing to realize the need to live within a budget. Here again, we see the need for proper management by the director of sales. An agreed-upon budget must be established, and it is the responsibility of the director of sales to see that the department operates within it.

Incentives

Although incentives are not endorsed by everyone in the business for motivating hotel sales staff, it is recognized that throughout the industry they are used to a certain degree. Where incentives are used, however, it is important that the incentive payment be made only after the business has actually been received, and not at the time of the booking, since it is difficult to justify the payment of commissions on unrealized business. Inasmuch as major group bookings are made 2 or 3 years in advance, the value of incentives thus becomes questionable.

Direct Mail

The sales staff can communicate with possible sources of business by direct mail, through "shotgun"-type mass mailings. This can be accomplished by acquiring lists of potential customers to whom information is mailed. Such lists can be purchased from credit companies (for example, American Express), magazine subscribers, members of associations or clubs, and other sources. Direct mail is valuable, inasmuch as it is targeted at a specifically identified group. Negatives are the ever-increasing cost of postage and the public's perception of such mailings as "junk mail."

Perhaps the most successful mailings result from utilizing guest history.

GUEST HISTORY

"Guest history" is shown on the chart with a dotted line, since this area is maintained by the reservation department rather than by the sales staff. However, the maintenance of proper guest-history records is extremely useful as a sales tool in mailing brochures, rate sheets, and even Christmas cards. Much care should be taken, however, to ensure that the records are accurate. The mailing of a Christmas card to "Mr. and Mrs. John Doe" when Mrs. Doe did not happen to be the lady at the hotel could be very embarrassing for the husband.

But in the matter of good guest relations, nothing can make guests happier, when checking in after a year's absence, than to have the front desk welcome them as long-lost friends.

Achieving the maximum level of success in sales requires close coordination and harmony among all segments of the sales function. Only then can truly intelligent selling take place—the booking of the right business at the right time at the right price.

The computerization of reservations in the form of property management systems has resulted in a greatly expanded use of guest history. The source and type of reservations can be identified and guest lists printed in a variety of classifications. The system can be utilized to print mailing labels for each of the classifications. Thus mailing to former guests has become more segmented and selective. Some of the more common classifications are:

a. Grouping by ZIP code
b. Grouping by length of stay
c. Grouping by date of arrival
d. Grouping by source of business, such as newspaper advertising, radio, and so on
e. Grouping by total expenditure
f. Grouping by travel agent

In addition to classifying former guests, these reports can provide valuable information or marketing and utilization of acquired mailing lists.

Figure 8-5 is an example of grouping by geographic area.

MARKETING

While sales is an actual hotel department, marketing is an encompassing term that includes sales, advertising, and public relations. In Chapter 5 we discussed the advantages in advertising as they related to a hotel chain and the ability of the chain to spread the costs over a group of hotels. This opportunity is not available to the independent hotel, and thus, advertising becomes a major part of the sales

RESERVATIONS BY ZIP CODE

— JULY —

AREA	No. of Reservations	
	Month	Y-T-D
ALABAMA	5	15
CALIFORNIA	12	30
COLORADO	2	4
CONNECTICUT	88	740
FLORIDA	17	182
GEORGIA	5	42
ILLINOIS	11	82
INDIANA	6	26
KENTUCKY	2	32
MAINE	11	77
MARYLAND	0	14
BOSTON	72	812
EASTERN MASS. (508)	61	720
WESTERN MASS.	42	480
MICHIGAN	4	4
NEW HAMPSHIRE	12	38
NO. NEW JERSEY	75	520
SO. NEW JERSEY	30	181
NY - Upper	71	436
NYC	180	922
WESTCHESTER	164	782

Figure 8-5   Grouping by Geographic Area

and marketing department's budget. In some properties, particularly resorts, which are dependent on the individual traveler, advertising may run as high as 4–5% of total sales.

In an independent operation, advertising is the responsibility of the director of sales and marketing. Larger properties may also employ a director of marketing, whose principal task is the advertising program. In such circumstances, the director of sales and marketing can be expected to devote most of his or her time to the sales effort. The other principal players in the advertising picture are the general manager, who must be concerned that the advertising portrays the proper image of the hotel and the outside agency, who is responsible for the production of the ads and usually the eventual placement. The income of advertising agencies is usually derived from the commissions paid to them by the media, although some work on a set fee. In either circumstance, the reality is that the cost is in some way borne by the hotel.

The three principal types of hotel advertising are print advertising, broadcast advertising, and collateral material. In the following paragraphs each type is reviewed as well as other forms of advertising, which find some use.

Print Advertising

Without question, newspaper advertising reaches more readers than any other print form. It is, however, a shotgun approach with no guarantees that the ads will actually be read. For this reason most hotel advertising is run in the Sunday editions, as they are read in more depth than during the week. Also, many newspapers run a vacation or resort section in their Sunday edition, and it can be expected that potential vacation travelers are more likely to read that section.

Criteria in selecting a newspaper are its circulation, for example, number of readers, the rates, and the image that the paper portrays. Newspapers, such as the *New York Times*, have a readership that is more inclined to travel than some other papers. The positioning of an ad to make it highly visible to the reader and the size of the ad are important considerations. These factors do, of course, affect the cost, which is usually measured in dollars and cents per column inch.

The ads are normally designed and written by the agency. Key considerations are that the property is easily identified and the wording is simple but catchy. Artwork or photographs also catch the reader's eye. The most important message in the copy is to deliver and offer or challenge the reader, prompting immediate action. Some ads, known as "advertorials," are written in the form of an editorial, which may incite people to read it.

Magazines are another form of print advertising frequently used by hotels. Magazine advertising can target the readership better than newspapers, inasmuch as many magazines cater to specific groups. Magazines also have a longer life than newspapers, and ads are read by a high percentage of the readers, many of whom read the magazine from beginning to end. Magazine advertising is also of higher quality than newspapers with extensive use of color and special effects.

Unfortunately, magazine advertising is more expensive. Space is sold not by the column, but as a segment of a page, such as, full page, half page, quarter page, and so on. Magazines can be divided into two categories, the consumer magazine, which covers topics of general interest (such as, *Time* or *Life)* and special-interest magazines (such as, *Golf* or *Ski)*. There are also trade magazines related to specific businesses or interests. Similar to newspaper advertising, magazine advertising should be simple, use illustrations, be consistent with the image of the hotel, and solicit a response.

Directory advertising is another form of print advertising not only in telephone directories but in directories such as travel guides.

The effectiveness of your advertising can be measured by asking reservation callers how they heard about the hotel. Another possibility is to include coupons in the ad, which can be redeemed for a specific reward.

The collateral materials that a hotel uses are flyers and brochures and to some degree tent cards and similar pieces. Since the cost of brochures has become quite expensive, most hotels use flyers or mini-brochures in their direct mail, sending full brochures only upon request. While narrative can be important in a brochure, the prime element is the quality of the pictures. Convention hotels also produce specialized brochures intended for the group market, featuring banquet and meeting facilities.

Broadcast Advertising

The most common form of broadcast advertising is radio. In selecting a radio station on which to run commercials, factors to be considered are number of listeners, frequency of spots, and cost per thousand listeners (CPM). However, the most important factor is whether the station reaches your target market. Guidance on this can be obtained from Arbitron, a rating service that monitors radio stations and provides various information related thereto, including demographics of the listeners, which can tell you what market you are reaching.

Radio ads should be directed at specific market segments and designed to get the listener's attention and hopefully promote some action. The driving to and from work periods, morning and evening, are considered prime time for radio advertising. Most ads use a regular radio station announcer, but some hotels use celebrities to promote their property. The cost of the ads varies depending on whether you want the ad always to run at the same time, which is the most expensive, or allow the station to pick times. Weekly and monthly plans are available at reduced rates, again related to the time the ads run. One of the major pluses for radio advertising is its relatively low cost. By providing some kind of a reward to anyone responding, it is possible to measure the effectiveness of the ad, at least to the extent it reaches listeners.

Television advertising is similar to radio advertising in two ways. The number of viewers is measured by national rating services, and results are usually directly related to the number of ads run. However, television varies substantially in content from one program to another, making it more difficult to ascertain the demographics of the viewer and thus target your market. Also, costs are high compared to radio if you advertise nationally. Much lower costs are available for local cable advertising, which runs only in the immediate vicinity. While this provides a method to advertise restaurants and lounges, its effectiveness in selling rooms is limited since it is not reaching the desired market.

Factors that make television expensive are not only the air time but the production costs, including payments to the members of the cast. Ads must be very visual, distinctive but simple, and designed to motivate action on the part of the guests. Several types of ads are available other than the straight announcement, such as, demonstrations, testimonials, and the use of animated characters. It is fair to say that television advertising for hotels is dominated by the chains, who can spread the cost over a number of properties.

Other forms of broadcast advertising are videos and video brochures, which can either be shown to prospects or mailed to them. Video magazines are a form of in-house advertising promoting the facilities of the hotel, either on lobby screens or frequently on designated television channels.

The most exciting new form of broadcast advertising is over the Internet. Hotels have developed Web sites from which an extensive selection of Web pages can be reached that extol the various activities and facilities.

Public Relations and Publicity

Public relations (PR) augments the marketing efforts of a hotel and forms an integral part of the marketing plan. PR can be used both inside and outside the property and should target those markets set out in the marketing plan. Important elements of proper distribution of public relations are identifying the media and the message to be distributed.

Many hotels engage professional PR services. Before contracting with an agency, it is important to evaluate it in terms of experience, effect, and of course, cost. Care should be taken not to hire an agency that already represents one of your competitors.

Publicity is an essential part of public relations. While public relations is geared at enhancing the image of the hotel, publicity can be regarded as an element of advertising. Planned publicity should be distributed to the press at every opportunity. This includes, of course, the hotel opening but also should recognize new facilities or programs, notable personnel hirings, and visits of celebrities. Press kits should be a complete, professional package issued on a timely basis.

Visits from travel writers' staff or freelancers can be opportunities to promote the hotel, but care should be taken not to overdo it and to respect the writer's privacy. Any opportunity to grant interviews should be utilized, and news conferences should be scheduled where deemed appropriate. Unfortunately, there are occasions where a negative situation exists. When dealing with a negative subject, it is always desirable to designate a single speaker for the property.

While it is difficult to evaluate the results of public relations, a possible method is to compare the PR costs to what would have been spent to advertise in the media up to the same level of exposure received.

CHAPTER SUMMARY

The staffing of a hotel sales department depends on the level of group and convention sales.

The operations of a group sales department involve the following:

1. Room allocations
2. Planning
3. Research
4. Policies
5. Department management
6. Interdepartmental cooperation
7. Identifying prospects
8. Sales calls and presentations
9. Incentive groups
10. The group coordinator

Other sales areas are travel-agent sales, banquet sales, and general local sales.
Activities affecting all areas are:

1. Training
2. Budget
3. Incentive
4. Direct mail

Guest histories are very valuable as a source for mailings.

Marketing in an independent hotel must focus heavily on advertising. Types of advertising are:

1. Print (newspaper, magazine, and collateral material)
2. Broadcast (radio, TV, video, and Internet)

Public relations and publicity are also a departmental responsibility.

REVIEW QUESTIONS

1. Explain the purpose of room allocations.
2. Why is long-range planning important in group sales?
3. What policies should be established for group sales?
4. What are the differences between association and corporate groups?
5. Explain incentive groups.
6. What are the duties of a group and convention coordinator?
7. What is the difference between retail travel agents and wholesalers?
8. What are the types of banquet functions?
9. What are good sources of local business?

CASE STUDY 1

John Smith, who has been in Florida, has been appointed Director of Sales for a new resort in New England. His first task is to prepare a chart of group sales allocations. What might John's chart look like?

CASE STUDY 2

Peter White's resort hotel has just acquired a new property management system with a expanded guest history program. Peter must decide on the various types of groupings to be produced. What might he select?

9

The Front Office

After studying this chapter, the student should:

1. Understand the structure and staffing of the front office.
2. Understand the functions of each of the areas.
3. Be knowledgeable of the various reports produced and used in the front office.

The front office is truly the nerve center of a hotel. Members of the front-office staff welcome the guests, carry their luggage, help them register, give them their room keys and mail, answer questions about the activities in the hotel and surrounding area, and, finally, check them out. In fact, the only direct contact most guests have with hotel employees, other than in the restaurants, is with members of the front-office staff.

The sleeping rooms in just about all hotels are comfortable, well equipped, and clean. So the guests must evaluate a hotel and its services by the courtesy and efficiency they find in its employees. The importance of the role played by the front-office staff in promoting good guest relations is self-evident and cannot be overemphasized. Less known, but almost as important to the financial success of a hotel, is the staff's role in credit, payroll, staff planning, and income control. These functions are discussed, under their respective chapters, in Section IV.

The front-office functions can be divided into five general areas:

1. Reception
2. Bell service
3. Mail and information
4. Concierge
5. Cashiers and night auditors

Two major departments are represented in this list. The employees staffing the first four areas are in the rooms department. The fifth is the financial area, where guest charges are accumulated and posted to the bills, and all cash transactions are consummated. These are all accounting-department functions, and so the cashiers and night auditors are in that department.

There is an old adage in the hotel field that says success depends on two Cs: cooperation and communication. Nowhere in the hotel is this more applicable than in the front office, where every mistake is costly, in either dollars or guest relations or both. The need for the two Cs can best be illustrated by outlining the duties and responsibilities of the staff in each of the five functions.

RECEPTION

For most guests, the reception area is the *registration desk.* There, greeted by a receptionist, they receive their first impression of the hotel, its staff, and its service. Guests rely heavily on that first impression and, during their stay, tend to be overcritical if it was bad and more tolerant if it was good.

As far as guests are concerned, the receptionist is the employee who helps them register and assigns them their room. Few realize the work and preparation that precedes this relatively simple but important function. It starts early in the morning, when the employees staffing the first of the three 8-hour shifts on the registration desk report for duty.

Although the occasional small property still manually registers guests, automated systems are now designed for all sizes of properties ranging from the very small to the very large. The systems for use in smaller properties utilize personal computers rather than mainframes and are therefore quite affordable. The systems, large and small, are utilized in much the same fashion as they relate to registration (in later chapters we describe other features of the automated systems, which are commonly referred to as *property management systems*).

At the time of installation, the room inventory of the property becomes a part of the master files of the system. This section of the files stores the following information relative to the room structure of the hotel.

a. Number of rooms of each type available—usually broken down by desirability, location, number, and type of beds, and possibly even size
b. Rates (by time of year, etc.)
c. Availability (by date)

Thus by accessing the computer, either reception or reservations (reviewed in Chapter 7) can readily determine what rooms are available at any point in time.

There are, of course, factors that could result in wrong data, the most common being duplicate reservations or failure of housekeeping to activate a change in room status to indicate that the room is ready for a new occupant. Either of these situations can result in loss of revenue.

Receptionists

Let us examine the daily activities of the reception area. Since very few guests arrive early, the initial activity in the morning is usually to print various reports, which will assist in the daily operation.

1. An arrival list—this lists the expected arrivals for the day by reservation number (Figure 9-1). Arrival lists are also printed for other departments according to their specific need for information, for example, housekeeping, restaurants, bellmen, health spa, etc.
2. A departure list—this is similar to the arrival list, except it lists the expected departures by room number. This report is also distributed to other departments as required.
3. A housekeeping status report—this report lists rooms occupied by area or section of the hotel and is used by the housekeeper to schedule work for the day.
4. A high balance report (if not left by night audit). The high balance report is a listing of the guests and their folio balances when they have exceeded their credit limits. It is reviewed the following day by the individual responsible for administering credit.
5. A forecast of occupancy—can be for varying periods of time up to 6 months. This report is also used by other departments for scheduling purposes.
6. A VIP arrival and a VIP in-house list—used by all departments.

Registration cards should then be preprinted for the day's arrivals.

Other functions performed at the start of the day include checking supplies (registration cards, forms, pens, etc.) and changing dates on time stamps and credit card authorization machines. Also, housekeeping should be advised of any no-shows as it will not be necessary to clean those rooms.

Other than the routine preparations described above, the receptionists' morning activities are mostly related to checkout. While large properties have separate check-out areas staffed by front-office cashiers, the function of the cashier is performed in many hotels by the receptionists. Even though receptionists may perform the front-office cashier function, it is nevertheless an accounting function (the recording of the various transactions is described in detail in

10/17/92
9:50

Today's Expected Arrivals - Oct. 17, 1992

Reser. #	Guest Name	Rate	Guest	Type	#Rms	Nights	Booked
037845	Hillman, Mr. William R.	139.00	TR	C1K	1	1	Guaranteed
038167	Lewis, Mr./Mrs. Joseph P.	0.00	COMP	A2Q	1	1	0344
039142	Madison, Ms. Elizabeth	239.00	TR	PREM	1	1	Guaranteed
040599	Scheck, Mr./Mrs. Nelson T.	159.00	TR	C1Q	1	1	0228
040714	Robertson, Mr. John C.	199.00	TR	A2Q	1	1	Guaranteed
040826	Goodhart, Mr./Mrs. Raymond	248.40	A3SA	B2Q	1	1	0302
041559	Hunter, Ms. Althea	590.00	SPOR	B1K	1	2	0239
041660	Jennings, Mr./Mrs. Randolph	199.00	TR	A1Q	1	1	Guaranteed
042626	LaVecchia, Roderick Dr.	159.00	TR	C2Q	1	2	Guaranteed
043115	Molaski, Mr./Mrs. Henry W.	218.16	A3SA	B1K	1	1	Guaranteed
044247	Hutchins, Mr./Mrs. Robert	218.16	A3SA	TWN3	1	1	0573
044704	Driver	189.00	TR1	A1K	1	3	Guaranteed
045000	Iverson, Ms. Christine	0.00	COMP	TWN3	1	1	Guaranteed
045001	Faller, Mr./Mrs. Jeffrey R.	0.00	COMP	B1K	1	1	0236
045002	Hertig, Mr. Donald	105.00	T2TS	B2D	I	1	Guaranteed
045003	Chioffi, Mr./Mrs. Reginald M.	105.00	T2TS	B2D	0	1	Guaranteed
045004	Ackerman, Ms. Josephine	210.00	T2TS	B1K	1	1	Guaranteed
045005	Peer, Mr./Mrs. Merrill J.	161.00	T2TS	TWN3	1	1	Guaranteed
045006	Whittemore, Mr./Mrs. David	210.00	T2TS	B1K	1	1	Guaranteed
045007	Silverman, Ms. Martha	105.00	T2TS	B2D	1	1	Guaranteed
045008	Silverman, Ms. Linda	105.00	T2TS	B2D	0	1	Guaranteed
045009	Whyte, Ms. Elaine H.	161.00	T2TS	TWN3	1	1	Guaranteed
045010	Godzik, Mr./Mrs.Willard J.	210.00	T2TS	B1K	1	1	Guaranteed
045011	Gebhart, Mr./Mrs. Anthony	210.00	T2TS	B1K	1	1	Guaranteed
045012	Vitagliano, Mr./Mrs. Gregory S.	161.00	T2TS	B1K	1	1	Guaranteed
045013	Bovey,Mr./Mrs.Gordon	105.00	T2TS	B2D	1	1	Guaranteed
045014	Schleibner, Mr. Brian	105.00	T2TS	B2D	0	1	Guaranteed
045015	Ryan, Dr./Mrs. Kenneth P.	210.00	T2TS	B1K	1	1	Guaranteed
045016	Greene, Ms. Kimberly	210.00	T2TS	B1K	1	1	Guaranteed
045017	Frederick, Mr./Mrs. Leonard	210.00	T2TS	B1K	1	1	Guaranteed
045018	Gagnon, Mr./Mrs. William B.	210.00	T2TS	B1K	1	1	Guaranteed
045019	Frost, Mr./Mrs. Daniel	105.00	T2TS	B2D	1	1	Guaranteed
045020	Tuttle, Mr. James	105.00	T2TS	B2D	0	1	Guaranteed
045021	VanGuilder, Mr. Douglas	210.00	T2TS	B1K	1	1	Guaranteed
045022	Brown, Ms. Lillian	210.00	T2TS	B2D	1	1	Guaranteed
045023	Underhill, Mr./Mrs. Raymond	210.00	T2TS	B1K	1	1	Guaranteed
045024	Pelkey, Mr./Mrs. Victor	210.00	T2TS	B1K	1	1	Guaranteed
045025	Sherman, Mr./Mrs. Robert	210.00	T2TS	B1K	1	1	Guaranteed
045131	Shavi, Mr. Hanif	139.00	TR	TWN3	1	1	Guaranteed
045204	Martin, Mr./Mrs. Matthew	275.00	TR	SK	1	1	0231
045205	Pritchard, Mr./Mrs. Thomas	0.00	TR	P	1	1	0229
045286	Goodspeed, Ms. Patricia	139.00	TR	C2Q	1	2	Guaranteed
045325	Combs, Mr./Mrs. Gregory M.	239.00	TR	PREM	1	1	Guaranteed
045356	Lawler, Mr. Scott	105.00	T2TS	B2D	1	1	Guaranteed
045357	Swahn, Mr./Mrs. Donald	161.00	T2TS	C1Q	1	1	Guaranteed
045359	Birmington, Mr./Mrs. Joseph M.	105.00	T2TS	B2D	0	1	Guaranteed
045753	Esposito, Mr./Mrs. Alan	161.00	T2TS	TWN3	1	1	Guaranteed
046012	Alpert, Ms. Margaret	169.00	TR	B2D	1	1	0218

Figure 9-1 Arrival List

Chapter 18). The check-out procedures are described later in this chapter under "Cashiers and Night Auditors."

At checkout, the computer automatically updates room status information. However, reception has the responsibility to monitor the order of checkout and housekeeping activity so that they know which rooms are readily available for rooming new guests. They must keep housekeeping advised of checkouts (unless housekeeping has access to the computer) and must also deal with and advise housekeeping of room changes.

Registration

Barring unusual circumstances, the bulk of the checkouts end early in the afternoon, and the heavy traffic of arrivals starts shortly thereafter. Now begins what is to the guests the receptionist's most important function, the registration procedure. For a better understanding of this process, the incoming guests will be divided into three general categories: group and convention guests; individual guests and small groups with reservations; and walk-ins, or people without a reservation.

Groups and conventions. This category involves a substantial number of guests who may all arrive at or about the same time. To register them individually would create problems for the hotel, both in time and number of receptionists needed, and for the guests, who would be stranded for long periods at the registration desk. To prevent this confusion, most hotels preregister these guests from lists containing the members' names and home addresses, furnished in advance by the person or persons in charge of the group or convention. The list should indicate the type of accommodation required—single or double occupancy—and the names of the people sharing a room. Preregistering involves filling in all information called for on the registration cards, including the assigned room number.

Another reason for preregistering these guests is that, in many cases, the sponsors want to present each member on arrival with a booklet or other material relating to meetings, banquets, or other functions on their itinerary. Most hotels add their own promotional material and give the full package, including the room key, to the guests as they register. To further expedite this process, separate registration desks are often set up in the lobby in designated alphabetical groupings. As the guests arrive, they are referred to the proper desk and asked to check their name and address on the registration card and sign it. They are then given an envelope with the materials mentioned and the room key and are escorted to their room by the bellman. If the sponsors are not paying all charges, the guest may be required to provide a credit card to cover those charges.

Guests with reservations. As guests come to the desk, each should be pleasantly greeted and asked if he or she has a reservation. If the answer is yes, the receptionist should pull up the reservation on the computer and verify that the information reflected therein is accurate, pull the preprinted registration card, and obtain a signature. If there is no reservation in the computer and the person cannot present a written confirmation, the receptionist should inquire how and when the reservation was made. Often it will have been made over the telephone, possibly on the same day. If the reservation manager has no record of a call, then the guest is roomed as a "claimed reservation" and should be considered a walk-in.

When the card is signed, the receptionist should select a room from the availability file (unless a room has been preassigned). The room number should be entered on the card, and the date of departure and method of payment should be verified. When payment is to be made by credit card, the receptionist should ask for the card, imprint it on the appropriate blank credit card charge voucher, and staple that to the registration card.

No person should ever be asked to pay more than the quoted rate for the first day. Such action by an overzealous room clerk can only create resentment; it is one of the leading causes of guest complaints. Even after agreeing to it when they register, many guests will dispute the increase in rate when they return home. Hotel controllers frequently have no alternative but to rebate the overcharge and rebill the guest at the quoted rate.

If the type of accommodations requested is not available, the next higher grade should be assigned at the same rate and the guest informed of this. When the stay is for more than one night, most receptionists are instructed to advise the guest that the room will be changed as soon as the desired type becomes available, generally on the following day. Only if the guest objects to this room change do we recommend that the receptionist quote the higher rate of the available accommodations. The guest is then given a choice: to agree to the room change or to accept the new rate, effective the second day, for the balance of the stay.

Walk-ins. Walk-ins are people who come into the hotel without a reservation and ask for a room. When this happens, the receptionists must exercise some degree of judgment, tact, and salesmanship. Using general guidelines furnished by management as to what type of guest should be discouraged, the receptionists must make this judgment and, in the rare instance when the person at the desk appears likely to cause problems, tactfully turn them away. Fortunately, most of these cases occur late at night, when there are few people nearby to overhear the conversation. An approach favored by many receptionists, particularly if there are others in line waiting to register, is to ascertain the number of days the room is needed and then inform the person that no rooms are available for a stay of that duration. Others will quote their top rate and declare that payment in advance for the full length of the stay is required. If this offer is accepted, an entry should be made in the logbook, asking the assistant managers to alert security to check on this guest.

Renting rooms involves much more than just quoting rack rates. Receptionists will try to sell the higher-priced rooms first without antagonizing or losing the prospective guest. Too many receptionists will quote the maximum rate and, if that meets with the slightest resistance, immediately switch, almost in panic, to the minimum rate. Many people resent this tactic, because they feel it reflects on their ability to pay. Others may hesitate to accept a lower-rate room for fear it will not meet their standards. The receptionist should first ascertain the type and general location of the accommodations desired, and then quote a rate. The preferred quotation is a restricted range of rates, rather than a specific figure. Depending on the prospective guest's reaction, the receptionist can then determine the advisability of trying to sell that person a higher-priced room.

Anyone without confirmed reservations—walk-ins, same-day telephone reservations, or whatever—should be asked for some form of identification before being allowed to register. Most receptionists are instructed to ask for a national credit card as identification and to determine that it will be used to settle the account. Lacking one, the guest is usually required to pay in advance. In addition, all bills should be coded as to the type of reservation or lack of one. This will alert the credit manager to monitor more closely the accounts of all guests without confirmed reservations.

Assistant Managers

The assistant managers are not part of the front-office staff, yet they must be included in the reception area. They are usually stationed in the lobby, near the front office. Their principal responsibility is to ensure the well-being of the guests. Whenever possible, they will personally greet frequent visitors to the hotel. Because of their title and accessibility, most guests will direct to them any questions and complaints regarding accommodations. It is their responsibility to appease the guests and coordinate the hotel staff's efforts to satisfy them. In the absence of the credit manager, they are called upon to settle guests' disputes over charges and to approve their personal checks for cashing. Finally, the executive assistant manager is responsible for the bell service, an important area in guest relations.

BELL SERVICE

The head of this subdepartment is usually aptly titled "superintendent of service." Service, as we have frequently mentioned, is a hotel's principal product, requiring directly or indirectly the participation of every employee in the hotel. In respect to this department, not only is it the principal function, it assumes even greater importance because it is performed while in direct contact with the guests. (No inference to the exclusivity of males in these positions is meant by the terms "doorman" or "bellman.")

Doormen

If the guests arrive in a hotel limousine or van, the driver is the first person they meet. For those guests who arrive by private car or taxi, the first hotel employee they meet is the *doorman*. This employee greets them and sees that their baggage is taken into the hotel—a simple, routine function, yet very significant in the staff's overall efforts to make the guests feel at home and happy with their accommodations. A smile and a pleasant greeting welcoming the guests will go a long way toward helping the receptionists satisfy them, creating the favorable first impression that is so important. During their stay, the doormen are called upon to assist the guests in many ways—to obtain a taxi, help them in and out of cars, give directions to restaurants, theaters, or local points of interest, and so on. Finally, in the case of guests who leave by car or cab when they check out, the doormen help them to load their baggage and thus become the last employees with whom they have direct contact. These reasons are important enough to require that the doormen be pleasant and helpful. In the absence of a doorman, these functions are handled by the bellman.

Bellmen

Once the guests have registered and been assigned a room, they are turned over to the bellmen, whose function it is to carry the guests' baggage and take them to their room. But if that is all they do, then the bellmen have lost an opportunity to be "ambassadors of goodwill," to sell the hotel and its facilities to the guests. A well-trained, experienced bellman can sense the guest's mood; he or she may carry on a conversation on the way to the room or else just briefly mention the facilities available in the hotel—its restaurants (with particular reference to the service and any specialties offered), bars, cocktail lounges, and any music or entertainment offered. Once they are in the room, the bellmen should at least show the guests where the thermostat is and how it works. If there is a television set in the room, he or she should test it and explain what channels are available.

In some hotels, bellmen are also instructed to check the bathrooms (to be sure they are properly made up, with the full complement of linens), the ashtrays, wastebaskets, closets, and all electrical equipment in the room—lights, lamps, switches, and so on. This is not intended as a check on the room attendants; that is the responsibility of the floor supervisors or assistant housekeepers. It is required only to make sure that, in case an engineer, houseman, or other authorized employee has had to perform some work in the room after the room attendant was finished and the room inspected by her supervisor, everything was put back in order. Any disorder in the room or malfunction of equipment should be referred to the housekeeper or engineer for immediate attention.

The bellmen are called upon to assist the guests in many ways during their stay. They deliver messages and packages, and, depending on the policy established by management, may even run errands for the guests. When room service is closed, some hotels have a sandwich maker on duty in the kitchen, so the bellmen can take orders from the guests for sandwiches, cocktail snacks, and beverages from the bar, and deliver them to the room. Other hotels permit their bellmen to buy food and bottled liquor for the guests from outside vendors when the hotels' outlets are closed. Finally, the bellmen assist the guests when they check out by carrying down their baggage. They can also be very helpful to the credit managers, as we will point out in the chapter devoted to that department.

Other Bell-Service Employees

Other members of the bell-service are *valet parking attendants,* and on occasion, *elevator starters* and *lobby porters.* Parking attendants collect arriving vehicles from incoming guests and park them in the prescribed area. They issue receipts to the guest, which are then used to retrieve their vehicles upon department.

Some of the large convention hotels have a starter in front of the elevators on the lobby floor. It is his or her responsibility to direct the guest traffic, which is particularly important during a convention or large banquet, and to speed up the elevator service during the peak hours of use.

Lobby porters are a European phenomena, not found in North American hotels. Their function is to retrieve the guest's luggage from the doorman and deliver it to the guestroom. The bellman is relieved of the responsibility of transporting the luggage and is primarily responsible for the rooming of the guest. If you are arriving in London for the first time, be aware that it is customary to tip the lobby porter as well as the bellman.

MAIL AND INFORMATION

The most important function of the mail and information clerk is the handling of the guest's mail—before they arrive, during the guest's stay, and after they depart. In small- and medium-size hotels the function is handled by the receptionists, but in many large hotels the handling of mail and information is done by a specific employee. All guest mail received is forwarded to the clerk, who checks the guest name against the computer.

Mail for guest residents in the hotel is marked with the room number and placed in the mail rack. Most hotel telephones in the guestrooms have a flashing message light. When the guest returns the call, they are advised that they have mail to retrieve. Mail that can be identified as not belonging to a current guest is checked against future reservations and, if identified, is marked with the date of arrival and filed by arrival date. Theoretically, this should ensure delivery of all mail received before the guest's arrival. However, many people have found that the only way to be certain of this is to mark on the envelope: "Hold for Arrival."

Forwarding mail to guests after they check out is not a normal or automatic procedure. Few hotels will forward mail unless requested to do so, and then only for a limited time. The burden is on the guests to inform the mail and information clerks before they check out that they want to have mail forwarded. The clerks have a card for this purpose on which the guest can write in his or her name and forwarding address.

CONCIERGE

By definition, a *concierge* is a doorkeeper, male or female. In European hotels, he or she is in charge of the bell-service department and is the person most guests turn to for any kind of assistance. The concierge provides directions to points of interest, a recommendation for restaurants or nightclubs outside the hotel, tickets to the theater, a rundown of the tours offered and the tickets for them, the purchase of airline tickets or the confirmation of tickets already purchased, and other services of this kind. He or she will also assist guests with most problems concerning their accommodations, take their keys each time they leave the hotel, and, for a favored few, even handle their mail.

In other words, the concierge is the equivalent of a superintendent of service and performs the functions, insofar as they relate to guest relations, of the assistant managers, mail and information clerks, doormen, and travel agents.

Many hotels are now establishing a concierge floor, particularly to serve the business guests. The concierge is there to answer all questions but the floor also provides various office services such as a fax machine. In many instances refreshments are available in the early evening.

CASHIERS AND NIGHT AUDITORS

Cashiers and night auditors are not truly members of the front-office staff. Their duties are primarily accounting functions and will be fully discussed in a subsequent chapter, under income control. They must, however, work very closely with the receptionists and, like them, are directly involved in guest relations.

The cashiers and, to some extent, the night auditors are in frequent direct contact with guests during their stay. In many ways, they perform the same services as a bank teller, giving the guests change, converting their foreign currency, and cashing their travelers checks and, with proper approval, their personal checks.

The cashier's station is where the guests go to check out and settle their bills. Thus, the cashiers are the last members of the front-office staff to come into direct contact with the guests. As has been repeatedly stressed, first and last impressions carry the most weight. The first, at the registration desk, often affects the guests' attitude during their stay. The last, at the cashier's desk, is probably even more important. That is the impression the guests carry home and are most apt to remember. It probably affects their attitude in later discussions of the services and facilities of the hotel with their friends and business associates. A pleasant greeting when the guests come to settle their bills; fast, efficient service in checking them out; and a cordial farewell—the effect of these should be obvious.

The computerization of the front office and specifically of the guest ledger has made the check-out process relatively simple. The cashier asks the guest for his or her room number and whether or not there have been any recent charges, usually breakfast or telephone use, that might not have been posted to his or her account. While point-of-sale and call-accounting interfaces have resulted in charges being posted promptly to guests' accounts, a heavy volume of activity can result in delays in posting charges in the restaurant. Similarly, call-accounting systems post telephone charges on a delayed batch transmission basis, usually every 20 or 30 minutes.

The cashier checks the account to determine whether any recent charges have been posted and, if necessary, calls the outlet to obtain the amount. Telephone charges can be activated also, if not posted. A copy of the folio is then printed and presented to the guest. If a credit card imprint has been obtained at check-in, the guest should be asked if he or she prefers to charge the card or to pay by an alternate method.

The guest's signature is obtained on the charge voucher and the settlement posted to the guest folio using the proper charge code (charge codes are explained in detail in Chapter 18). If the bill is to be transferred to a city-ledger account, the guest's signature should be obtained and the transfer from the guest ledger made.

If the hotel automatically transmits its credit card charges to the bank, a transmission slip should be printed and the guest's signature obtained. Similarly, a signature should be obtained on any other charge vouchers. The guest should be thanked and given a copy of this or her settled account.

CHAPTER SUMMARY

Front office functions are:

1. Reception
2. Bell service
3. Mail and information
4. Concierge
5. Cashiers and night auditors

Reception has specific procedures that start in the morning and continue through the day. Separate procedures are normal for registering groups and conventions. Different procedures apply to guests with reservations and walk-ins.

Assistant managers perform certain functions in the reception area.

There are certain services that doormen and bellmen perform. The handling of mail and providing information are front-office functions.

The concierge provides many special services to the guest.

While cashiers and night auditors are actually accounting employees, they work in the front-office area.

REVIEW QUESTIONS

1. List the functions performed by:
   a. Reception
   b. Bell service
2. What reports are normally printed early by the front desk?
3. Explain the desirable procedure for registering guests.

4. What is the procedure for handling "walk-ins"?
5. Explain the term *concierge.*

CASE STUDY 1

John Brown has been appointed front-office manager of a new 300-room luxury hotel. His first task is to decide on the required staffing. What would you anticipate would be the results and what factors should be considered?

CASE STUDY 2

Peter Smith is the front-office manager of the Downtown Hotel. The hotel does not have a property management system and all front-desk functions are performed manually. Peter has been telling the owner that he should buy an automated system. The owner has asked Peter to prepare a report to substantiate his request. What would you expect to see in this report?

10

Food and Beverage Preparation and Service

After studying this chapter, the student should:

1. Understand the principles of good nutrition.
2. Understand concepts of menu preparation.
3. Know which appetizers and soups should be served hot and which should be served cold.
4. Understand the variations in cooking meat, fish, poultry, and vegetables.
5. Understand the importance of sanitation.
6. Know the various types of service.

Even though the sleeping rooms provide the major source of income for a hotel, a quality food and beverage operation can often be its best advertisement, directly influencing the results of the rooms operation. A quality food and beverage operation calls for excellence in both preparation and service.

While the traditional hotel dining room format, wherein the restaurant is directly identified with the hotel, can still be found in many locations, there is now a greater emphasis on portraying hotel restaurants as being free-standing operations.

The direct result of this trend is many restaurants that, although physically located within hotel structures, have names that do not reflect the hotel affiliation. In some instances, these restaurants are leased out to independent operators. However, most of the time the name is merely reflective of the hotel's desire to market the restaurant as a free-standing entity rather than as a "hotel" food and beverage outlet.

The principal goal of this approach is to more effectively compete for the nonhotel guest market and to move away from the traditional image of hotel restaurants.

The food and beverage operation consists of four major elements:

a. Preparation
b. Service
c. Purchasing, receiving, storage, and issuing
d. Control

Items (c) and (d) are dealt with in a later chapter. In this chapter we are concerned with (a) and (b).

FOOD PREPARATION

While nutrition is perhaps the most important factor in institutional feeding, that is, schools and hospitals, it is, nevertheless, getting more significance in commercial food operations. The public has developed a greater awareness of their health and the impact of diet thereon.

Principles of good nutrition focus on the six nutrients that supply energy, promote growth or repair, and regulate the body processes.

a. **Proteins**—Amino acids, meat, fish, eggs, milk, and cheese, which build and maintain body tissue.
b. **Carbohydrates**—Starches and sugar, which provide calories to enable the body to perform.
c. **Fats**—concentrated sources of energy.
d. **Vitamins**—Various vitamins assist the body in different manners.
e. **Minerals**—build muscle and bone.
f. **Water**—The solvent for the other nutrients to function and to keep the body's waste removal system operating.

Types of Cuisine

The creation of the "self-standing" image for many hotel restaurants has enabled them to respond to the continuing changes in the style of food and decor currently in favor with the discerning diner.

In the 1990s, there has been a strong emphasis on regional American cuisine (Figure 10-1). Particularly noteworthy in this area has been Mark Miller, who,

A U T U M N

NEW • ENGLAND • FARE

Gingered Apple & Butternut Bisque
with Cinnamon Sippets

♦ ♦ ♦

Salad of Grilled Fall Radicchio
with Pickled Harvest Vegetables

♦ ♦ ♦

Roasted Breast of Vermont Pheasant
with Autumn Cranberries & Persimmons
with Maple Potato Cakes

♦ ♦ ♦

Chestnut Cornbread

♦ ♦ ♦

Pumpkin & Cider Cheesecake

Figure 10-1   Example of Regional Menu

with his "Mark Miller's Coyote Cafe" in Santa Fe, has made Southwestern cuisine, a combination of Mexican and Western food, very popular on the American scene.

In a similar style, with a regional flair, the Trellis Restaurant in Williamsburg features mid-Atlantic cuisine. In New England, Yankee cuisine is having similar success. This emphasis on regional cuisine represents a movement away from the "haute cuisine," which, with its European emphasis, held the premier position for many years.

However, the latest entry in food styles is called "comfort foods" a return in fact to simplicity. Included in this category are the old-style items: stews, liver and onions, meatloaf, lamb shanks, and chilis (Figure 10-2). With these items no one has to worry about what they're ordering.

Figure 10-2   Comfort Foods Menu

EAST ARLINGTON CAFE
East Arlington, VT 05252

Owner/Chef—David M. Ingison

COMFORT FOOD MENU
Comfort foods are common dishes with which customers can easily identify. In many of the dishes new ingredients have been introduced to accent regional ingredients.

Soup and Appetizers
Traditional Green Pea Soup with Cob Smoked Ham (Vermont)
French Onion Soup with Cheese
Oysters on the Half Shell with Texas Hot Sauce

Entries
Fresh Corn Chowder with Maine Crab and Smoked Bacon (Maine)
Pheasant Chili with Vermont Cheddar, Corn Bread with Maple Butter (Vermont)
Venison Pot Pie in Puff Pastry (New England)

Vegetables
Souffle of Winter Squash with Roast Garlic
Maple Baked Beans

Desserts
Apple Fritters with Fruit Relish
Chocolate Bread Pudding with Maple Glaze

Menus

Menus basically come in two styles—*a la carte* and *table d'hote* (also called *prix fixe*).

The original concept of a la carte was a separate charge for each item, each vegetable, and even a bread and butter charge. On the opposite side, the table d'hote menu had one price for everything. While some of the finer restaurants still adhere to the principles of a la carte, most restaurants offer some combination of both. Gone is the bread and butter charge, and some vegetables are usually included with the entree. Soups and salads are separate on some menus but included on others. Most restaurants have a separate charge for a dessert.

Menus can either be fixed or cyclical. Fixed menus can become boring to regulars, but this can be alleviated by offering daily specials. A cyclical menu may mean a cycle of menus from a week to even a month. The effort necessary to change the menu daily can be costly not only in time but in other areas. Varying menus necessitate larger inventories and more difficulty in getting rid of leftovers. On the other hand, the restaurant can take advantage of a particularly good buy on a particular item.

Regardless of the style or ethnic background of the menu, there are certain basic rules that govern all food preparation. Perhaps the most fundamental ingredient of proper food preparation is proper purchasing. There is an old expression: "You can't make a silk purse out of a sow's ear"; and neither can proper cooking methods produce a good meal if the ingredients are of poor quality. Food purchasing must be based on written specifications that determine the quality and type of food required for each menu item. This does not mean that all meals must be cooked from scratch. The proper use of leftovers can provide an acceptable assortment of menu alternatives and, at the same time, help to reduce food costs.

Appetizers

Appetizers can be broadly placed in five categories: cocktails, salads, hors d'oeuvres, canapes, and relishes. Some are served hot, some cold; the most important factor, aside from flavor and appearance, is the temperature. Hot appetizers—small meatballs, chicken livers, hot canapes—must be really hot, and cold ones—shrimp cocktails, olives, fruit juices—really cold.

Soups

This is a course whose preparation is much too often neglected. There are a good many restaurants whose popularity rests to a large degree on the excellence of their homemade soups. Care in soup preparation can pay big dividends.

Meat, Fish, and Poultry

Assuming that these items have been purchased according to the proper specifications, it is vital that they be cooked properly and served promptly.

The more tender cuts of meat should only be roasted, broiled, or fried; braising or stewing should be reserved for the tougher cuts. Overcooking must be avoided.

Overcooking is even more to be avoided with fish. The popularity of fish and seafood has been increasing recently, since they combine high nutrition with low calories, and the proportion of the menu taken up by these items has increased correspondingly. They should always be cooked to order, never in advance.

Poultry offers a great many methods of preparation, chicken in particular can be cooked in almost unlimited ways. And in these days of rapidly rising costs, it is wise to realize that chicken is perhaps the lowest-cost entree available.

Vegetables

An otherwise successful meal can easily fail if the vegetables are not up to the quality of the rest of the food. Fresh vegetables should be used whenever possible; otherwise, the best available ones in another form.

In addition to enhancing the meal by their flavor, vegetables can add greatly to its appeal by their color and the contrast their texture provides. This is a matter that must start at the menu-planning level.

As with other dishes, overcooking of vegetables is a sad mistake. It is much better to undercook them slightly than to allow them to sit in the cooking liquid after they are ready.

Keep in mind, too, the value of raw vegetables, which are becoming more and more popular—not only in salads, but as side dishes.

Desserts

Desserts and pastries have traditionally been high-profit items and, in addition, many reputations for quality food have been a direct result of exciting desserts. Therefore, care and skill should be used in their preparation. Top-rated restaurants often have special pastry cooks for this purpose.

Beverages

A good meal should end with a good beverage. Good coffee requires three key elements: clean equipment, proper brewing temperature, and fresh coffee. A fresh quantity should be started at least hourly. Espresso, demitasse, and decaffeinated coffee should also be available, as well as iced coffee.

The essential ingredient in good tea is the use of fully boiling water to make it, and if individual teapots are used, they should be preheated by rinsing with boiling water.

Sanitation

The first rule of sanitation is clean food, served on clean dishware by clean people.

The importance of sanitation in a food production area cannot be overstated. There must be continued vigilance to protect against food poisoning (illness caused by germ-produced poisons) and food infection (illness caused by germs in food).

The most common form of food poisoning is *botulism,* using caused by improperly processed canned food. Another form of poisoning is *staphylococcal poisoning* (staph), caused by germs from people with colds and sinus infections. *Salmonellosis* is a common form of food infection usually found in ground beef, pork, eggs, and egg products. *Trichinosis* is also an illness caused by undercooked pork, although health authorities now permit pork to be cooked pink. The newest form of food poisoning is *ecoli,* from undercooked beef.

The two elements of good sanitation are cleanliness and good health in employees and proper purchasing. Proper safeguards should be maintained in purchasing and storage and in the preparation area.

Staffing

Kitchen staffing usually consists of the following:

1. Executive chef—essentially an administrative position
2. Sous chefs and banquet chef—participate in and direct the cooking
3. Cooks—have various responsibilities while doing the body of the cooking
4. Assistant cooks—prepare foods and assist in cooking
5. Dishwashers and warewashers
6. Baker or pastry chefs

FOOD SERVICE

For many years, all first-class hotel restaurants and dining rooms featured French service; that is, service at the table. All food is prepared table-side in chafing dishes, and, at the appropriate time, is individually served to the guest by the waiter or captain. Specialty dishes requiring flaming (such as Steak Diane) and are prepared by the captain, as are salads and flaming desserts. But French

Figure 10-3   Waiter Serving Customer in Plate Service Manner

service requires more space and more staff than plate service does, so, owing to economics and a need for higher volume, this service is now available only in a limited number of deluxe hotels.

In Russian service the food is brought to the table on platters and served on plates using fork and spoon service. Plate service usually involves the direct plating of all food in the kitchen (see Figure 10-3). However, some hotels have maintained some elements of French service, preparing certain specialty items at the table, or serving them from a service cart. This may include soups, bread and rolls, and salads, which are relatively easy to handle on a table-service basis.

As service payrolls have increased, more and more hotels have been using buffet service in certain areas. Since the customers mostly serve themselves, it reduces the number of staff required and often speeds up turnover, resulting in a greater number of covers.

Buffet service is particularly adaptable to breakfast service, where the number of hot dishes is limited and the cover count can be easily controlled. Buffet luncheons have also become increasingly popular. However, in lunch buffets, customers often return for second helpings, so the composition of the buffet should be carefully planned to prevent the cost of customer excess and wastage from exceeding the payroll savings.

Service Personnel

Typical staffing for a restaurant in the service area is:

a. Restaurant managers—manages the restaurant, supervises the staff, ensures guest satisfaction, and prepares reports.
b. Captains or maitre d's—direct all service staff, may help seat, and take orders.
c. Servers—serve food and beverages
d. Buspersons—set up tables and remove dirty dishes
e. Cashiers—collect payments (*Note:* Many establishments now use server banking, eliminating the need for cashiers.)

In the matter of food service, great emphasis must be placed on coordination—not only between the various service-staff members but also between them and the kitchen. Such coordination requires the proper layout of the kitchen so that the pickup of food by the waiters or waitresses can be made systematically. Entrances and exits should be laid out to prevent criss-crossing and collisions and to establish a standard format for traffic flow. Pickup areas should be clearly defined to prevent confusion, particularly for new employees. Rather than having confusing orders screamed at the kitchen staff, many hotels find it better to have the *slideman,* or *expediter,* often the chef, transmit all orders to the cooks, thus providing a buffer zone between the service and preparation staffs.

Room Service

In examining the service area, it would be remiss to bypass room service. Room service is the most unprofitable area of food and beverage operations. It involves the service to the guestrooms of both food and beverages. The peak period for room service is during the morning hours, when many guests prefer having breakfast delivered to their rooms rather than going into the restaurant. In an effort to plan and more efficiently service the breakfast demand, hotels have been placing advance-breakfast-order forms in the rooms. The form, which indicates not only the order but the time at which it is to be served, can be completed by the guest prior to retiring, and hung on the doorknob, from which it is collected in the early hours of the morning. Nevertheless, many orders are still telephoned to room service in the morning; thus, an order taker and often a cashier are required, as well as supervisory and service personnel.

It is anticipated that within the next decade room service, with the possible exception of breakfast, will be eliminated in many hotels. It requires the maintenance of a number of service staff to handle what can be a greatly fluctuating amount of service. In high-demand periods, the staff may not be adequate, resulting in criticism of the hotel. At other times, the staff may be excessive, resulting in unproductive payroll costs. And in addition, removal of dirty dishes is a problem; they may be left in the hallways, giving a negative, often unsanitary, appearance, and removing them makes extra work for the room attendants.

BEVERAGE PREPARATION

Although the beverage-service personnel fall within the jurisdiction of the maitre d'hotel, the overall beverage operation is usually under the supervision of a bar manager, or possibly a head bartender.

The bar manager is responsible for scheduling the shifts of the bartenders and any other necessary personnel or payroll functions. He or she is also responsible for ensuring that the bars are properly stocked and that ice, bar napkins, coasters, swizzle sticks, and the like are in proper supply.

The bar will serve the customer a requested brand if it is stocked, but selected bar brands should be established not only for drinks where a brand is not specified, but also for use in mixed drinks. Bartenders should know the recipes for the standard cocktails and have a recipe guide available for the unusual. Standard measurements, which may vary depending on customs in the areas, should be prescribed. Bar porters may be employed to assist bartenders with ice handling, glass washing, and so on, but this is another position that has often been successfully eliminated.

Wine stewards are employed in the more elegant hotel dining rooms to handle the sale of wine to diners. The actual physical control of the wine may be in the hands of the bartender, but more frequently it is handled by a head wine steward. Red wines will be readily available in racks, while white wines and roses will be stored in a chilled compartment, the keys of which are in the possession of the wine steward. As with all food and beverages, the ultimate key to success is proper sales ability on the part of the service staff. A wine steward well versed in the product can greatly improve the results of the department through good selling.

It is not feasible in writing to fully explain service and preparation. Practical experience in both areas is the key to learning this phase of the hotel industry.

CHAPTER SUMMARY

Nutrition is very important in institutional feeding, but public awareness has increased the significance in commercial operations.

Certain types of cuisine such as regional and most recently comfort foods have become popular.

Menus can be a la carte, table d'hote, or combination thereof. They can be fixed or cyclical.

Categories of food are appetizers, soups, meat, fish, and poultry entrees, vegetables, and desserts prepared in various manners.

Sanitation is extremely important.

There are various types of food service.

Both kitchen and service personnel are fairly standard in the industry.

Room service is being gradually phased out.

Beverage service is an important element of the operations.

REVIEW QUESTIONS

1. What are the six nutrients in good nutrition?
2. What is regional cuisine?
3. What are comfort foods?
4. What are a la carte menus?
5. What are table d'hote menus?
6. Which appetizers should be served hot and which should be served cold?
7. How should tender cuts of meat be cooked, and how should tougher cuts be cooked?
8. Name the various forms of food poisoning.
9. What are the various types of food service?
10. What is typical staffing in the kitchen and with service personnel?

11

Telecommunications

Earlier editions of this book addressed this chapter as "The Telephone Department." In this era of communication technology, "Telecommunications" is a more appropriate title.

After studying this chapter, the student should:

1. Understand the changes that the telephone industry has undergone since 1968.
2. Understand how a call accounting system operates.
3. Understand the changes in telecommunications.

HISTORY

Before examining the complexities of today, it is appropriate to review a brief overview of the changes that evolved in the second half of the twentieth century.

Until 1968, there were basically two companies dominating the field—American Telephone and Telegraph (AT&T), by far the major company, and General Telephone and Electronics (GTE), the number two company. Both enjoyed complete monopoly in their respective areas. In 1968, as a result of a historic court decision in Texas, the Carter Fone Decision, private companies were permitted to manufacture, sell, and service all the equipment needed for the internal operation of a telephone system. The government-regulated companies were restricted to charging only for the trunk lines needed to connect these installations to the central system. One major effect of this new competition was a change in the marketing procedures of the telephone companies; from mere order-takers for new telephones into aggressive sellers of their products and services.

The hotel industry, as one of the major users of telephone equipment and services, obviously rated special attention. Both companies assigned marketing managers or other executives to work exclusively with the hotels. The Bell System also instituted for its account representatives special training programs to give them a basic understanding of hotel operations.

The court ruling did not affect the cost of calls. The matter was still under the jurisdiction of the regulatory agencies. The only change was to allow users to lease or purchase their telephone equipment from private companies. Since most of the companies were subsidiaries of well-established electronics firms, they could offer the latest electronic equipment, full service (24 hours a day, seven days a week), and the possibility of substantial savings over the equipment rentals paid to the utility company. Hotel operators had the option of purchasing their equipment, leasing it, or accepting one of the many variations of the two offered by each company.

There is no doubt that the private companies made serious inroads into the hotel field. Yet the vast majority of hotels, old and new, still rented their equipment from the telephone companies. There were undoubtedly many reasons for this, but they can probably be summed up in three words: fear of change. Telephones are vital to the operation of a hotel. Any interruption in service can adversely affect guest relations. Service is a hotel's most valuable commodity, its principal product, thus dollar savings alone cannot sell most hotel managements. Apparently they were not convinced that private companies could deliver the full service major corporations offered.

That was only the first step in the loss of the government-protected monopoly that the telephone companies had enjoyed for almost 100 years. Under new regulations from the Federal Communications Commission (FCC), and from a United States District Court Order announced in August 1982, a new national telecommunications policy emerged. It encouraged unregulated competition in the telecommunications industry wherever possible. To give the telephone companies time to adjust to the new regulations, they did not go into effect until January 1, 1984. On that date, the Bell System (AT&T, Western Electric, Bell Laboratories, long lines, and the 22 Bell operating companies) was restructured into new entities with new functions and responsibilities. As part of these changes, the 22 Bell operating telephone companies were divested by AT&T and regrouped into seven independent regional organizations. Each of these seven regional companies are regulated entities, subject to tariffs approved by the Public Service Commissions of each state, and the Federal Communications Commission. They were responsible only for the local calls in their area and any long-distance calls within that restricted area. They must offer their customers the right to use whatever long-distance company they desire to handle their calls out of the areas assigned to each of the companies. They do not rent out any of the equipment or telephone sets used by their customers; those customers that rented AT&T equipment continued to pay rent to AT&T. Those that brought new equipment would continue using their own equipment and make whatever arrangements needed for the repair and upkeep of their equipment. General Telephone was not large enough to be broken up but it, too, was restricted to selling only local calls and long-distance calls within the area that they had previously serviced. It was also required to give its customers the right to select any long-distance company they desired. Thus, the telecommunications industry came full cycle, from a protected monopoly to a totally unregulated one. The FCC retained only the right to monitor charges and markups on long-distance calls.

PRESENT DAY

Deregulations brought about a drastic change in the operation of telephone departments within hotels. Perhaps the most significant change in the telephone operation was the advent of direct-dial, permitting the guests to direct-dial their outgoing calls. Guests can, of course, call the hotel operator and ask them to place their calls, but, at most hotels, the operators are not permitted to place such calls except in emergency situations and so will inform the guests. Thus the role of an operator is reduced to handling incoming calls, operator-assisted calls, and collect calls. Manual equipment is still available, but it is used mainly in the smaller, older hotels and in small, usually individually owned roadside motels.

Dial systems, originally introduced to cut payroll costs, are now generally accepted and used in major hotels all over the world. Switchboards have been periodically improved. Competition, as a result of the 1968 decision, greatly speeded up this process. Adding to the need for a faster, more efficient, and more sophisticated switchboard was an FCC public notice dated June 26, 1981, allowing hotels to collect a surcharge on the guests' long-distance interstate calls. Hotels, however, had to wait until the Public Service Commission in their state issued the same ruling before they could add the surcharge to the cost of interstate toll calls. Some state commissions were slow in doing so, and it was not until well into 1982 that it was generally permitted.

By 1982, electronic systems had so improved that the computerized switchboard could determine the room number of the guest making the call. Until then, the utility company's operator had to cut into all long-distance calls and ask the guest for a room number. The call was then considered to be an operator-assisted call, and the utility company added a surcharge for this service. The total cost of the call plus the surcharge was teletyped to the hotel so that the charge could be posted to the guest's bill. With the new switchboard, the outside operator's assistance was no longer needed, and the hotels were permitted to add and retain this surcharge. That truly marked the beginning of a new concept in the operation of the telephone department. The modern, computerized system completely eliminates the human factor and provides all the necessary accounting controls.

Deregulation brought many companies into the field. However, the investment needed to finance new telephone lines required for long-distance calls has limited most companies to resell operations, buying time on a discounted basis and reselling to consumers.

Two major competitors, MCI and US Sprint, emerged to provide serious competition to AT&T. Since those two companies merged in the late 1900s, they have waged a major marketing campaign against the latter offering the same full range of services including overseas calling and "800" number service. Judging by the reaction of AT&T, they made serious inroads into AT&T's market, causing both sides to offer discounted packages and other pricing alternatives to attract customers. At the same time, some of the regional Bell companies, for example, Bell Atlantic, are starting to compete for both intrastate and interstate long distance.

Basically there are three types of calls that a guest can make: a long-distance call that can be dialed directly and paid to the hotel, a long-distance call that can be dialed but charged on a credit card (or charges reversed to the party they are calling); and lastly a local call. At this point, it might be well to point out that computer programming to properly recognize the three types of calls and compute the necessary charges would be very expensive and difficult, if not entirely impossible, for each hotel to produce on its own. However, there are companies that offer a package program that can easily be converted to the individual needs of each hotel.

With this in mind, the electronic miracles that the modern switchboard, using a system known as "call accounting," performs will be noted. It adds the cost of the call, the taxes, the operator-assistance charge, and a reasonable hotel service charge, and shows the total amount that is to be charged to the guest. The amount of the hotel service charge varies from hotel to hotel. Most hotels add a percentage (usually around 35%) to the cost of the call. Many hotels use AT&T rates and add the percentage to that. To the extent that their own telephone service charges less than AT&T, the hotel picks up an additional profit. For the next category of long-distance calls, the credit card or reversed charge calls that require the guest to dial "0" before the area code, there is obviously no need to compute any charges except a reasonable service charge that the hotel can make for the use of its facilities. On local calls, it times and accumulates the total charges, which can be posted by the day, upon checkout of the guest, or at any time period desired and programmed. Some hotels charge $1 to $2 for each local call. All three types of charges can be sent to the front office in the form of a voucher. However, in most modern hotels having a Property Management System, a direct charge is made by the computer onto the guest bill, charging the guest a single amount for each long-distance call. By direct communication from the front office, telephone service in each room can be discontinued upon checkout of the guest and reinstated when a new guest checks in to the same room. The computer will also accumulate, by department, the cost of local and long-distance calls made by executives and employees of the hotel. To prevent the unauthorized use of the instrument for long-distance calls, each employee can be assigned a code number that must be dialed before dialing the long-distance number. As an additional control, it is recommended that the equipment be programmed to issue a detailed list of long-distance calls at periodic intervals, daily or certainly no longer than weekly, which would then be sent to the authorized employee for inspection. At the end of the month, the computer is programmed to charge the exact costs of these calls to the proper departmental expense account. There is one problem that was prevalent in the older systems, many of which are still in use. The system cannot tell exactly when the party called answered the telephone. Studies have shown that most people will hang up if the party called does not answer within seven or eight rings, which is to say about 40 seconds after the first ring. Thus, the equipment is programmed to start timing and accumulating the charges on each call at the end of the waiting period. Hotel controllers contacted by the authors stated that a waiting period of anywhere from 37 to 43 seconds works well, and they have relatively few complaints from the guests that they were charged for calls when their party did not answer. Naturally, when a guest complains, and the charge is minimal, cashiers are instructed to cancel the telephone charge without question.

Newer systems have a "ring-back" ability, which activates the charge mechanism only when the call is answered. However, upgrading to these systems is expensive and many hotels have opted not to do so.

In the early days of these systems, telephone companies and call equipment companies frequently blamed each other for problems. Arguments between service providers and telephone equipment vendors were also common.

COSTS

Until 1980, with very few exceptions, hotels in the United States operated the telephone department at a loss. The losses ranged from thousands to hundreds of thousands of dollars per year. Unlike most operations, volume adversely affected the net results; thus, the greatest departmental losses were recorded in the very large convention hotels.

The principal reason was that the hotels were not selling their own product. In fact, insofar as guest calls were concerned, they acted only as, so to speak, "agents" of the telephone company. The Public Service Commission in each state, which has jurisdiction over local and intrastate toll calls, allowed the hotels a small markup on the cost of local calls and, in some states, permitted hotels to add a service charge onto the cost of intrastate toll calls. In other states, the Public Service Commission issued the same regulations as the FCC, which required the hotels to charge the guests the costs of long-distance calls as billed by the telephone company, and then the telephone companies were obligated to pay a commission of 15% to the hotels on the total amount of toll calls made each month. Unfortunately, this relatively small, controlled income, which was discontinued on January 1, 1983, was in no way sufficient to offset the costs of the rental equipment, payroll, and other related expenses. Decontrol and modern technology, which permits the hotels to dispense with the aid of the telephone company's operators in designating the room number of the guest, or in making long-distance calls for the guest, effectively reversed the operating results of the telephone department. The additional income generated by charging for operator assistance completely eradicated the losses suffered by most hotels in their telephone department. Guests were in no way affected by this change. They had always paid for operator-assisted calls, and the only change was that instead of the money they paid going to the telephone company, it stayed with the hotel. The only change as far as they (the guests) are concerned is that hotels are now permitted to add a reasonable service charge to the cost of each long-distance call.

CHANGES IN TELECOMMUNICATIONS

When the fax came into use as a method of communication, it was, for the hotels, merely a replacement for the old Western Union telex. After all, it is nothing more than a message going out over telephone lines.

Other innovations and changes have had a more serious impact on the industry, sometimes reducing the profits of the hotel's telephone department: Many travelers now use calling cards to access 800 numbers reaching a carrier's network. The usage has a twofold impact on the hotel; it increases the traffic on the local telephone company's network, causing congestion, and reduces the commission add-ons of the hotel.

Another area that completely bypasses the hotels in terms of revenue is the use of cellular phones. Cellular phone revenues, according to industry statistics, have tripled in the last six years. Hotels see none of it. The use of computers, whether email or via the Internet, to communicate has also affected the hotels' revenues. Ironically, most hotels have added computer access to their guest services in order to avoid losing business to competitors.

Since many travelers have reached the conclusion that hotel charges for telephone service are excessive, the hotels find it difficult to react to the loss of revenue from the preceding changes.

Possible options include putting charges for 800-number calls on a timing basis rather than a fixed access charge, currently the normal procedure. By using one of the discount service providers to handle 800 traffic, a hotel can earn additional commissions. However, this may be a negative if not monitored carefully, as some of the discount carriers have been involved in the exorbitant overcharging. It may be advantageous to a hotel to use a communications consultant to review all their options and make recommendations.

CHAPTER SUMMARY

Certain dates are important in the history of the hotel industry:

1. In 1968, the Carter Fone Decision permitted private companies to sell telephone equipment.
2. In 1981, the hotels were permitted to add a surcharge to long-distance interstate calls.
3. In 1982 (in effect January 1, 1984), the Bell system broke up.

The merger of MCI and US Sprint provided major competition to AT&T.

Call accounting recognizes the three types of calls; long distance dialed directly, long distance charged on a credit card, and local calls. The appropriate charge is made to the guest.

Telephone operations are now profitable to a hotel. However, cellular phones bypass the hotel in terms of revenue.

REVIEW QUESTIONS

1. What is the signification of the following dates in the telephone industry?
   a. 1968
   b. August 1982
   c. January 1, 1984
   d. June 26, 1981
2. Explain how a call accounting system operates.
3. Do hotels charge for:
   a. local calls—if so, how much?
   b. 800-number calls—if so, how much?
4. What were the reasons that a hotel's telephone department was transformed from a losing operation to a profitable one?

12

Engineering

After studying this chapter, the student should:

1. Know the primary fuels in use.
2. Understand the HVAC, electricity, and water systems, and how they are monitored.
3. Know the elements of a preventive maintenance program.

The responsibilities of the engineering department in a hotel fall within two principal areas.

1. Utilities
   a. Energy and energy management and control
   b. Heating, ventilation, and air-conditioning
   c. Electricity
   d. Water

2. Property maintenance
   a. Building and building equipment
   b. Swimming pools
   c. Grounds

ENERGY AND ENERGY MANAGEMENT AND CONTROL

The most important uses of energy in a hotel are to provide heat and hot water, which is usually an extension of the production of heat.

The three primary fuels used in the production of heat in North America are coal, natural gas and oil.

Coal

While coal is abundant and the cheapest of the three, it is the least used and will remain so unless the available supply of oil and gas drops significantly or unless a way is found to use coal efficiently and without damage to the environment. Coal is, by nature, a dirty fuel producing sulphur dioxide, an air pollutant that is a health hazard when inhaled by humans and that is the cause of acid rain, which destroys tree and plant life. Since, at present, the supplies of oil and natural gas are adequate and available at an acceptable cost, the research on cleaner methods of coal utilization is limited. A material reduction in the availability of the other two fuels at reasonable prices would obviously stimulate efforts to find solutions to the pollution problem.

Natural Gas

Natural gas would appear to be the ideal fuel. In the United States the gas produced is either domestic or imported from Canada or Mexico. It is a very clean fuel that burns efficiently without any pollutants, and the gas-burning plants can be constructed at a relatively low cost.

While it is believed that a large supply exists, the exact extent of the supply is unknown. At present the cost of natural gas is very competitive, but as the presently accessible supply diminishes, it will become necessary to tap gas at lower depths, creating an unknown increase in the cost, which will be forthcoming. Since, at present, gas and oil compete for the market, it is difficult to estimate the impact on demand that increased prices would cause.

The supply of natural gas is very regionable, with some areas of the country being producers and other areas being strictly consumers. This also causes variances in price from one part of the country to the other. In the northeast it is cheaper to pipe the gas from Canada than from other parts of the United States.

Oil

Oil is the most widely used fuel in the hotel industry at present. While it is primarily used for heating and indirectly producing hot water, it is also the primary fuel used for travel, both by automobile and airplane. An increase in travel costs can have a major impact on hotel occupancies, particularly resorts to which vacation travel is discretionary.

While a large supply of oil is produced domestically, the level of consumption in the United States is such that it must import large quantities, primarily from the Middle East. Thus the price and supply of oil can be impacted by political upheaval. There was a period during the 1970s when available supplies dropped, and a mild form of rationing accompanied by price increases took place. Current unrest in the Middle East coupled with reduced quotas by OPEC has again pushed up oil prices.

Like natural gas, there are untapped oil reserves in North America, particularly offshore and in Mexico and Alaska, but the costs to obtain it would require higher prices than presently demanded for imported oil. Furthermore, it is felt that some of that oil would be poorer in quality, emitting higher levels of pollution. Government regulations to restrict usage of heavier grades of oil, which have high levels of sulphur released into the air, are on the increase.

Other Energy Sources

Nuclear power is considered by many to be the energy source of the future. A process, known as fission, uses uranium to produce electricity in nuclear plants. Thus, from the hospitality industry's point of view, the interest is strictly in low-cost electricity, which could be used as a substitute for oil. However, uncertainties as to the safety of nuclear plants have caused a high level of public opposition to nuclear energy, indeed causing the closure of some plants and freezing the construction of others.

Because of its cost, electricity is not used as a heating source in hotels, except where the existing heat system is inadequate, requiring the use of baseboard heating at certain times of the year.

In Canada there is a higher level of electricity usage, where waterfalls and rivers are used to produce hydroelectric power at a lower cost.

In Florida and in the southwest United States, the need for air-conditioning results in high electricity usage.

Solar energy, the use of heat from the sun's rays, finds very little usage at present, primarily as a supplementary source of energy. It is dependent on the weather, a large amount of sunlight, and no obstructions to block the rays of the sun. However, as costs of other energy fuels increase, the interest in development of solar energy will similarly increase.

Energy Management and Control

Increases in the cost of energy have resulted in increased focus by hotel management on energy management. This was particularly evident in the 1970s when increased oil prices resulted in a heavy increase in energy costs. Unfortunately, a period starting in the mid-1980s up to the present time has produced increases in energy costs no higher than other costs (and probably less than labor), resulting in less focus on energy conservation.

Also, energy management usually requires a large investment of capital to put a system in place. Hotels can only make a certain amount of capital expenditure each year, and each project must be justified in terms of higher earnings or cost savings. Stable energy costs have reduced the level of priority for energy management expenditure, and projects producing increased revenues tend to be the first to get approvals. Nevertheless, energy management is still receiving a fair level of interest.

Early efforts to produce energy savings were simply training employees to be energy conscious, starting with the housekeeping department. Room attendants were instructed in such practices as minimizing the use of electric light in the rooms, turning lights off when not necessary, and resetting thermostats in vacant rooms to a prescribed level. Similarly, kitchen employees were instructed to turn off appliances not in use. Such efforts require a reasonable amount of monitoring to be effective.

Initial capital expenditures during the construction of the building can result in major energy savings. This primarily relates to various types of insulation. Placing desired levels of insulating materials within the walls is effective in conserving heat. Similarly, wrapping pipes and ducts in the plumbing and HVAC systems is also effective in reducing heat loss, as is the use of thermopane glass in the windows. Energy savings during construction should not be restricted to insulation. The building's design frequently impacts energy costs for heating or air-conditioning. Therefore, the design must take into consideration the proper balancing of aesthetic appeal and energy conservation.

More recently, computerized energy control systems have been put in place to reduce energy costs. While such systems are desirably installed during construction, many older hotels have been retrofitted with such systems. Some of the systems use sensors to initiate actions to create energy savings. For example, photoelectric sensors can detect undesired levels of lighting and trigger the turning off of lights. Similarly, sensors can measure the outside temperature and accordingly adjust the levels of heat or air-conditioning in use in the building.

Other devices are simply timers that turn off lights, heating, and air-conditioning in public areas, including banquet rooms when they are not normally in use. Heating and lighting in the guestrooms are frequently controlled by systems activated by guest check-in and check-out. The property management system activates or deactivates the room based on a change in room status in the computer. Such systems are fairly expensive if installed after construction, as they require hardwiring of each room to the computer. If done during the initial construction, the wiring can be done concurrently with the main electrical system.

In some systems a change in levels of guestroom heating and lighting is triggered by insertion of the key (usually a plastic card) being inserted in the electronic lock.

Most public utilities bill for electricity or natural gas are based on a combination of actual consumption and what is known as the "demand charge." The electric company charges for consumption in terms of total kilowatt hours (KWH) and the demand charge is based on the highest level of consumption of any two 5-minute periods in a month. The logic to justify the demand charge is that it compensates the utility for the cost of the additional equipment required to have the ability to provide the highest level of consumption demanded by the customer.

In a hotel the highest demand usually occurs when guests return to their rooms and turn on lights while the kitchen and restaurants are gearing up for the evening meal. To minimize the demand charge (which sometimes is as much as the charge for consumption), hotels use a system known as "shedding" to reduce demand. A computer is used to monitor the hotel's demand for electricity, and when the demand reaches a certain level, the computer automatically shuts off power to certain areas for limited periods of time. The most common load shedding involves shutting off heating or air-conditioning in public areas for a short period of time. It could also involve reducing the level of lighting, shutting off music, or even reducing the number of elevators in service.

Many hotels that have such systems have installed interfaces with their Property Management Systems to monitor the electrical systems and print out daily reports, usually as part of the night audit function.

HEATING, VENTILATION, AND AIR-CONDITIONING

The heating, ventilation, and air-conditioning systems in a hotel interact so much with each other that they are usually regarded as subelements of the HVAC system. The purpose of this system is to provide air and increase or decrease heat levels to provide the guest with a desirable level of comfort. At the same time, it must be recognized that individuals have varying comfort levels, and while in-room controls permit the guests to adjust heat levels to their own preference, not everyone will find the same comfort level in the public areas.

Ventilation

Ventilation is the part of the HVAC system that provides the guest with clean, fresh air. The most simple manner of doing this is to replace the stale air inside with clean air from the outside. Unfortunately, this has an impact on heating and cooling costs, as the air from outside must be brought to the level of the inside temperature. Filtering the air inside the building can be effective in reducing the need for outside air. Also, it is known that humid air is warming to the human body while dry air has the opposite effect. Therefore, in cold weather the air is frequently humidified by circulating it through sprays of water. Fresh air is distributed through a series of ducts with fans being used to control the speed of the flow. The air then enters the area to be ventilated through grills with dampers behind the grill to control the airflow.

Most large hotels have independent ventilation systems in the kitchen and bathrooms to combat odor problems.

Heating and Air-Conditioning

Heating and cooling systems may utilize air, water, or steam. Although steam is an efficient carrier of heat, it cannot be used for cooling. Therefore, steam is used only in hotels in locations where there is no need for air-conditioning.

It would initially appear that air would be the most desirable, since in the final stage heat carried by water must, on delivery, be transferred into air. However, water can hold much more heat energy than air, and therefore the air ducts for an air system will occupy a much larger area than the pipes required to deliver water with a corresponding level of heat energy. Furthermore, larger amounts of energy must be expended to force the air through the system. Most hotels, therefore, use water-delivered heating and cooling systems.

The earlier HVAC systems were two-pipe systems, meaning that there was one pipe carrying water to the room and the second returning it. The problem with this type of system is that it can only be used for heating or air-conditioning at a specific time, giving the guests no opportunity for individual preference. The more desirable system is a four-pipe system, which has two sets of pipes, allowing the hotel to provide heating and air-conditioning to the guest.

The heat delivery system is relatively simple to understand. Water is heated in the boiler and flows into a water tank from which the hot water is pumped through the pipes. The combustion chamber or firebox in which the fuel burns must have a continuous supply of air, as combustion will not take place without the presence of air. A chimney equipped with flues is also necessary to dispose of gases. The flues may be used to transfer the heat from the gases to the heat transmission system so that a minimum amount of heat is lost up the chimney. With high chimneys a fan may be required to force the gases upward.

Understanding air-conditioning is more difficult, and it is necessary to understand the scientific basics on which the systems are based. It is helpful to think of the system in terms of heat removal instead of air-conditioning. The basic principle is that when a liquid boils, it soaks up or absorbs heat. Furthermore, under pressure the boiling point of a liquid changes; the higher the pressure, the higher the boiling point. However, those substances that have lower boiling points are found normally in a gaseous state but under pressure can be converted to a liquid state. When the liquid is released, it quickly boils and as it does, it draws the heat from the surrounding air, thus cooling it.

Using this principle, a gas known as a "refrigerant" is sealed in tubes and circulates through two phases. In one phase the refrigerant is in liquid form, which is the "evaporator," where it boils and in the process draws the heat from the rooms. In the second phase the refrigerant cools, returning to a liquid form.

During this phase, heat is emitted so this process must be conducted in an area completely separate from the areas to be cooled. In large hotels it may be necessary to have a cooling tower to dispose of the heat from the condensation process. Individual controls in the guestrooms permit the guests to access either the heating or air-conditioning systems.

ELECTRICITY

As mentioned earlier in this chapter, electricity is used for heating in hotels only when the primary heat is inadequate and it is necessary to use electricity for baseboard heating in those situations. However, hotels are extremely dependent on electricity for other purposes.
These include:

1. Electric lighting
2. Electric motors used for various purposes
3. Kitchen appliances
4. Television, radios, and telephones
5. Computers

Lighting

Lighting is produced in three forms: incandescent, fluorescent, or vapor. Incandescent lighting is commonly recognized by the public in the form of light bulbs. Light bulbs are sealed glass containers holding a metal filament, which produces light when heated by electricity. The glass containers are filled with a gas mixture, usually nitrogen and argon, which extend the life of the filament. Although not as efficient as fluorescent lighting, they are used extensively in guestrooms and even in public areas for decorative reasons.

Fluorescent lighting produces a much higher degree of light while using essentially the same amount of electricity. Fluorescent lighting is created by filling glass tubes with mercury vapor and argon gas. The tube is sealed at both ends. Electricity is passed through the tube traveling backward and forward from one end to the other. At each end of the tube there is a filament-cathode, which when heated emits small particles that are carried by the electricity through the tube. The glow from the particles traveling back and forth in the tube produces the light. Fluorescent lighting is used extensively in banquet rooms and other public areas.

Vapor lamps are used principally for decoration rather than functional lighting. They are glass tubes filled with neon or helium, or a mixture of both, or sometimes mercury vapor. The most common use of vapor lamps for other than decorative purposes is in the yellowish lights often seen in streets and parking areas; the lamps are very efficient and have a long life, so they are ideal for this purpose. When they are used as decoration, various combinations of the helium and neon gases can be used to provide different-colored effects.

Electric Motors

Electric motors have a variety of uses in the hotel industry. They are used to operate various elements of the HVAC system such as fans and pumps. The use of electricity in the air-conditioning phase of the HVAC system is much higher than in the heating phase. As a result, hotels that are required to provide air-conditioning extensively incur much higher electrical costs.

Electric motors are also used to run freezers and refrigerators as well as elevators and escalators.

Kitchen Appliances

There is a limited usage of resistance heat in grills, fryers, and ovens for cooking. However, where available, natural gas provides a cheaper alternative in most areas. In areas where natural gas is not available, some hotels use propane gas for cooking. However, propane gas is more volatile and also requires storage tanks.

Television, Radios, Telephones, and Computers

While the usage of electricity in those categories has increased, particularly in the area of computers, the amount of electricity consumed in each category is small in relation to other usage.

Most hotels and motels purchase their electricity from the local utility. However, in some remote locations electricity is not available and hotels are forced to generate their own. Most hotels have a backup generator so that in the event of a loss of power they will be able to provide essential lighting, maintain fire alarm systems, and possibly run elevators and selected kitchen equipment.

Water

There are three essential uses of water in a hotel: consumption, bathing, and sewage disposal.

Water consumption is not limited to water drank by guests and staff. It is an essential element of certain foods and beverages produced in the kitchen and used to boil other foods, where, although the water is not consumed, it is essential to the process.

Water is required by the guests for purposes of personal cleanliness. It is also used to wash dishes, utensils, and glassware. Furthermore, it is needed to wash floors and walls, toilets, and other areas where cleanliness is essential to the appearance and operation of the hotel.

Water is also necessary for the disposal of sewage, both human waste and waste from the kitchen. In the disposal procedure sewage is usually treated with chemicals to remove bacteria.

The most important aspect of water is its system of distribution. As with electricity, water in most areas is purchased from the local utility. However, in remote areas, where hookups to the local utility are not available, the facility may have to sink a single well or several wells in order to obtain water. In such locations it is essential during the feasibility stage to ensure that an adequate supply of water exists. The capacity of the wells mentioned in terms of available gallons per minute or hour may be governed by zoning code requirements and local regulations. It should be noted that where a water hookup is not available, a sewer hookup will also not exist, and it will be necessary to install a septic system to dispose of sewage. The capacity of the septic system may also be subject to local zoning. Where water is obtained from wells it may have to be filtered and chemicals added to purify the water. Normally, water purchased from a local utility will have already been treated.

Even when purchased from a utility, a problem that may be encountered is "hard water." Hard water is water that contains high levels of magnesium and calcium. Problems caused by hard water are primarily related to laundry and dishwashing operations. Detergents are less effective in hard water, creating a need for larger quantities of chemicals, which in turn impacts the life of the linens. Also, hard water can result in a chemical buildup in pipes, contributing to blockage and eventually creating a need for pipe replacement. The problem of hard water can be solved by using a water softener, which adds sodium to the water supply to correct the problem. Properties with landscaping must maintain a source of untreated water, as sodium is detrimental to plant growth.

Water is distributed throughout the building by a network of pipes. Piping materials can be made out of iron, steel, cast iron, brass, lead, copper, or plastic. The type of pipe has a direct effect on the cost of the water distribution system. Certain types of pipe have lower costs but require greater maintenance. Copper pipe is most commonly used for both water supply and waste disposal, although in some properties plastic pipe is used as a substitute in certain specialized areas, principally waste removal.

An important factor in the selection of pipe is a minimum amount of friction so that minimum pressure is required to move the water through the pipe.

The flow of water within the system is controlled by valves, used to set the rate of flow, to maintain proper direction of the flow, and for various safety purposes. Valve maintenance is very important and occupies a substantial portion of the time of the hotel's plumbing staff.

Whether the water is supplied from the local utility or pumped from a private source, the water distribution system in a hotel is the same. The water is carried through a series of pipes to locations within the hotel. The "upfeed" system is used when the water enters the building at a lower level and is carried to the distribution point through a pipe known as a "riser." The water may feed directly from the pipes coming into the building or via a storage tank. Hot water passes through a heater and storage tank before being carried upward to the hot water distribution plant. Circulating pumps are used to increase the pressure and thus lift the water more easily to the higher levels. The use of constant-pressure pumps permits better balancing of the supply of hot and cold water, so that a person stepping into a shower will not have the discomfort of getting either mostly cold or mostly hot water.

A "downfeed" water distribution system operates on most of the same principles as an upfeed system in that it uses risers, distribution pipes, and a hot-water heater. The principal difference is that the water is pumped directly from the entry point into the building to a gravity storage tank, which is higher than the highest distribution point in the building. The hot-water heater is on the same level as the storage tank. Water flows downward either directly if cold or via the heater if hot, through simple gravity to the distribution points. Upfeed and downfeed systems can be combined in a building to provide a more efficient supply of water.

Water is heated in a similar manner to its use as primary heating for the building. Chilled or ice water systems operate much the same as hot-water systems in an upfeed system, except, of course, that the water is chilled rather than being heated before being fed to the distribution point.

Maintenance of distribution systems is directed toward ensuring that sediment and rust are periodically removed from the pipes by means of traps and strainers. Proper insulation of the hot-water pipes will result in substantial reduction in heat loss and therefore much greater efficiency of the system. Insulation must also be used on pipes that are exposed to temperatures below the freezing point, to prevent freezing.

Plumbing

In addition to the maintenance of a water-distribution system, proper plumbing fixtures are very important to ensure that the water supply can be made use of. In the bathroom, several types of fixtures are used:

1. Water closets made of solid vitrified china are used to control the flush of the toilets. Maintenance problems usually relate to the failure of the flush tank to control the proper volume of water, resulting in leaks into the water closet. Malfunctioning of pressure valves and the proper cleaning of the water-closet bowls can also be a problem.
2. Urinals are similarly made out of solid vitrified china, and, as with the water closets, the problems relate to improper flushing due to faulty pressure valves and the need to keep the urinals clean.
3. Sinks are used for the washing of hands and face. In this area, the major problem is the failure of the faucets to supply hot and cold water properly.
4. Bathtubs, like sinks, may have the problem of a proper supply of water. Additionally, however, they should be properly finished with a nonskid surface to prevent the guest from slipping.

5. Shower stalls have exactly the same maintenance problems as bathtubs. Many hotels are now using various forms of prefabricated bathtubs and shower stalls. These are fabricated from a fiberglass material and shipped to the hotel in a completed state. Once inserted in place, the walls are then finished and the fixtures hooked up.

Within the kitchen area, plumbing fixtures provide supplies of hot and cold water for various purposes. In addition to the proper supply of water, there should be proper drainage in the kitchen for waste materials and disposal of excessively spilled water.

Overall, major maintenance problems in plumbing are the result of the failure of the sewage or drainage system to dispose of the wastes discharged into it. These systems require continuous maintenance to ensure that the sewage flows properly without creating any sanitary problems. The venting system must provide proper pressure and circulation to prevent corrosion, organic matter sticking in the pipes, and bad odors. Where plumbing fixtures are below the sewage line of the building, gravity alone will not give the proper flow of sewage, and sump pumps, or sewage ejectors, must be used to transport it into the sewer line.

Where sewage does not get discharged into a public system, the hotel must have its own sewage-disposal system—a septic tank in which solids or semi-solids are decomposed and converted to a liquid form. The liquid can then be purified by passage through a seeping pit, a drain tile field, or a filter system.

Problems in a drainage system result principally from clogged pipes and traps. Using the proper chemicals on a continuing basis can greatly reduce the risk of such problems. When they do arise, mechanical means must be used to clear the clogged materials and keep the system in functioning order.

Public utilities charge for water based on the total volume used with a basic connection charge and decreasing per-gallon rates as consumption increases. The utilities have, in most locations, distained from measuring the sewage, electing instead to use the water consumption as a basis for arriving at the volume of sewage, although at a different rate. Obviously arguments can be raised to refute this method of measuring the volume of sewage and the authors have attempted to do so on several occasions but with little success. While water consumed either in the drinking or cooking process probably ends up in the sewers, water used in landscaping is absorbed in the soil. On the other hand, rainwater falling within the property's boundaries is not included in the water consumption but does end up in the sewers.

MAINTENANCE OF BUILDING AND BUILDING EQUIPMENT

The importance of an effective preventive maintenance program cannot be stressed too much. Unfortunately, many hotels, principally for financial reasons, choose instead to adopt a "break and fix" philosophy. While it is recognized that preventive maintenance will not avoid every breakdown, the program substantially reduces the risk of such an event.

There are eight steps that constitute a preventive maintenance program.

1. **Lubrication.** Any equipment with moving parts should, like an automobile, be lubricated on a scheduled basis.
2. **Cleaning.** Equipment must be cleaned periodically to maximize efficiency and reduce the possibility of breakdowns.
3. **Repair leaks.** Leaks are not only important to avoid damage to equipment but leaks in walls, roofs, windows, and doors result in loss of heat or, in hot days, permit heat to enter more easily. Preventive maintenance is therefore an important part of energy conservation.
4. **Removal of residue.** This is very similar to cleaning. Residue such as soot or buildup of mineral deposits reduces the effectiveness of equipment.
5. **Scheduled replacement of parts.** Most parts have an expected life cycle, beyond which they may fail at inopportune times. A program of scheduled replacement can avoid unexpected problems. Many hotels extend this philosophy to light bulbs, replacing them on a scheduled basis rather than only when they burn out.
6. **Protective coating renewal.** Many areas have protective coatings that prevent leaks or other problems. This is particularly important with electrical wiring. All protective coatings should be renewed periodically.
7. **Adjusting, tightening, balancing, or aligning.** Again, a comparison to an automobile is applicable. Failure to check these areas on a scheduled basis can result in loss or unbalanced equipment, resulting in a breakdown.
8. **Testing equipment.** Certain types of equipment, such as fire alarms, are not used on a regular basis. They should be tested periodically to ensure that they are properly functioning.

The key to an effective preventive maintenance program is diligent supervision and proper documentation. Utilization of a computer program to control and record various actions can be very beneficial.

Building maintenance in many areas is scheduled according to the time of year. While it is obvious that failure to equipment essential to the operation requires immediate action, for other maintenance there is a time of the year when it is more appropriate to do the work. For example, a major painting or redecorating project should be carried out when occupancy is low, as closing guestrooms or other outlets during a busy period can result in lost revenue. Such projects as roof repairs or window washing are best carried out when the weather is cooperative. Projects involving digging in outside areas are also impacted by the weather. It should be recognized in budget that maintenance expenses may be higher in slow periods, as may the engineering payroll.

Another decision that hotels face is what maintenance should be done in-house and what should be done by outside contractors. Plumbing and electrical problems occur on a regular basis and professionals in these areas must be on staff. Painting, however, is very seasonal and it must be evaluated as to whether it is advisable to carry high-paid painters on the staff when, at certain times of the year, they are relegated to cutting grass or shoveling. Such decisions are subject to climactic conditions and occupancy levels.

SWIMMING POOLS

The best pools are made out of concrete containing water-resistant plastic. Fiberglass and steel are also used with lower construction costs.

Pool decks are usually made of concrete, ceramic tile, or outdoor carpeting. Whatever the surface, it must be skidproof. In locations where the temperature drops below freezing during winter, the pool must be drained and covered to prevent cracking.

Beneath the pool is a series of pipes to provide the water supply for the pool. Pumps are required to keep the water continually circulating. This system involves the use of filters, sand, or gravel, through which the water is pumped to remove undesirable materials suspended in the water. These filters must be cleaned on a regular basis to keep them functioning properly. Providing a heated pool involves additional energy costs.

Swimming pools are subject to regulation by health authorities, not only to ensure noncontaminated water but also to meet required safety standards. Unfortunately, pools are frequently the location for guest accidents with resultant lawsuits. Skidproof surfaces around the pool can help to avoid accidents. Depths must be properly posted and lifesaving equipment must be available. Many hotels have eliminated diving boards and water slides, as they can be prime hazards resulting in accidents.

Cleaning the pool is a major responsibility of the engineering department. Leaves, insects, and sediment must be continually removed to maintain good visual effects. More important, chemicals must be added to control algae and bacteria. Records must be maintained on chemicals added and available for inspection by the health department. The department will also periodically test the pH levels.

GROUNDS

Landscaping is another area where decisions must be made as to whether it should be handled in-house or by an outside contractor. Obviously, if the areas are limited to lawns that must be mowed and shrubs that must be trimmed, these can easily be handled in-house. However, if there is extensive landscaping involving exotic flowers and plants, it may be advisable to use a landscaping contractor. This becomes a major consideration if the hotel is located in a region where weather conditions prohibit year-round landscaping. In such situations a hotel must decide whether it is desirable to have landscaping professionals on the payroll when, in winter, they can end up shoveling snow at high hourly rates. If the hotel has a golf course, there may be more flexibility in staffing.

CHAPTER SUMMARY

Responsibilities of engineering fall into two categories:

1. Provision of utilities: energy and energy management; heating, ventilation, and air-conditioning; electricity; and water.
2. Property maintenance of building and building equipment, furniture and equipment, swimming pools, and grounds.

Energy is required to provide heat and hot water. Primary fuels are coal, oil, and natural gas. Other sources are nuclear plants, hydroelectric, and solar energy.

Computerized systems are now being used to control energy. Shedding is a process used to reduce the demand charge.

Ventilation is the provision of fresh air. Heating and cooling systems use air, water, or steam.

Electricity is used for lighting, powering motors, kitchen appliances, televisions, radios, telephones, and computers.

Lighting can be incandescent fluorescent or vapor. Motors are used for refrigeration, elevators, and escalators.

Water is used for consumption, bathing, and sewage disposal. The system of distribution can be upfeed or downfeed. Upfeed uses pumps to get the water to the rooms while downfeed uses gravity. The pipes for water distribution are known as risers. Chemicals and sediment may have a negative effect on your plumbing. The major reason for problems with plumbing is improper sewage flow.

An effective preventive maintenance problem can reduce repairs. Various steps such as lubrication should be done on a regularly scheduled basis.

Certain major maintenance projects such as painting can only be done when business is slow. Maintenance that is seasonal can often be done more economically by an outside contractor.

The cleaning of swimming pools is a major responsibility subject to inspection by the health department.

Landscaping in hotels where it is only required on a seasonal basis may also be done by outside contractors.

REVIEW QUESTIONS

1. What are the primary fuels used in the production of heat? What are the positives and the negatives in the use of each?
2. What are other sources of energy?
3. What systems are used in energy management?
4. Describe the operation of a heat delivery system.
5. Describe the operation of a air-conditioning system.
6. What are the three types of lighting? Explain their characteristics.
7. Discuss water distribution systems.
8. What are the major types of plumbing problems?
9. What are the elements of a preventive maintenance program?

13
Housekeeping

After studying this chapter, the student should:

1. Be familiar with the daily routines and subroutines in housekeeping.
2. Understand all the paperwork involved in operating the housekeeping department.
3. Be knowledgeable of the responsibilities of the executive housekeeper in the areas of furnishing and decor.

AREAS OF RESPONSIBILITY

The dictionary defines *housekeeper* as "one who does or oversees the work of keeping house." This simple explanation states the principal function of all housekeepers, whether they are responsible for a one-room apartment or a thousand-room hotel—with one minor exception. In private family homes, "keeping house" includes taking care of the kitchen. In a hotel, the housekeeper's responsibility rarely includes the kitchen, pantries, refrigerators, storage rooms for groceries, kitchen-cleaning and related supplies, and the dish- and ware-washing areas. The maintenance, cleaning, and daily operation of these are under the supervision of the chef and chief steward.

The rest of the hotel, all under the direct supervision of the executive housekeeper, can be divided into eight general areas:

1. Guestrooms
2. Halls and corridors
3. Lobby
4. Public rooms and restaurants
5. Offices (hotel personnel)
6. Stairways
7. Windows
8. Stores, concessions, and other leased areas

Figure 13-1 is an organization chart of the typical housekeeping department in a large hotel.

Figure 13-1   Housekeeping Department Organization Chart

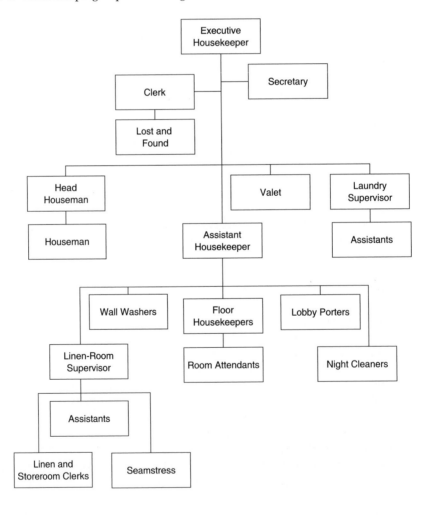

FUNCTIONS OF THE HOUSEKEEPING DEPARTMENT

A hotel housekeeping department has four main functions:

1. Cleaning and maintenance
2. Training and its personnel
3. Requisition and control of necessary supplies and equipment
4. Paperwork—schedules and reports

These four principal functions are so intermingled that it is almost impossible to describe one without including the others, as they overlap to a great degree.

Cleaning and Maintenance

The primary function of the housekeeping department is, of course, the cleaning and daily maintenance of the areas under its supervision. However, many hotels have found it feasible to have this function, in at least some of these areas, performed by an outside contractor rather than by their own staffs. Areas generally included are the lobby, public rooms and restaurants, offices used by the hotel personnel, and window cleaning. The expense is listed under "Contract cleaning" in the hotel's operating statement.

Contract cleaning is a top-management decision, and may be made for several reasons. The first and most important is cost. Many studies have been made by hotel controllers, as well as by accounting firms, on this phase of hotel operation, and most have found that an outside contractor can perform this function at a lower cost to the hotel than the sum of the payroll, taxes, and related expenses of its own employees. Cleaning in all these areas except the last, windows, must be done at night or very early in the morning, when there are few guests in the lobby and the public rooms and restaurants are closed, and before the majority of the hotel's personnel report for duty. It is not only very difficult to recruit a staff for these hours, but almost impossible to properly supervise them. The housekeeper, the principal assistants, and the department supervisors must all be on duty during the daytime hours, and thus they are unable to check on the night staff. The hiring of only one night supervisor is insufficient and therefore unsatisfactory; hiring several adds too much to the cost. Outside firms, with many such contracts, can better afford enough roving supervisors to properly check on and control their employees.

Window cleaning presents another problem. It is a very hazardous occupation; accidents are costly and insurance is expensive. It cannot be delegated as a part-time job to any hotel employee. It requires the skill and knowledge of a full-time, professional window cleaner, who obviously commands a much higher salary than any other member of the housekeeper's cleaning staff. Again, the outside firm is in a better position to hire such people and provide their services at a lower cost than the hotel would incur with its own employees. Such a contract also eliminates the risk of an accident and a possible costly increase in the premium for compensation insurance as a result of serious injuries to a hotel employee. The fact that these areas are serviced by outside contractors in no way affects the responsibility of the executive housekeeper to supervise the staff and to inspect and approve the results. Windows are a very visible part of the hotel, and their maintenance, cleanliness, and general appearance are vitally important to the comfort and well-being of the guests.

Stores, concessions, and offices differ only in that they are not usually the responsibility of the hotel to clean and maintain. Most agreements and leases call for these functions to be performed by the concessionaire or lessee. Nevertheless, as far as the guests are concerned, they are a part of the hotel, so their appearance is just as important to the image of the hotel as that of the lobby or other public areas. The housekeeper or a designated representative must periodically inspect these premises and refer any problems to the resident manager; in some cases, they are handled personally by the general manager. After all, even though concessionaires and lessees are not employees of the hotel, they and their employees are in direct contact with the guests, and commissions and rentals paid by them are very important to the profitability of the property. Many managers, to lessen the effect of criticism and to preserve harmony with the operators, will instruct the housekeeper to refer all complaints to them and then take whatever action is deemed necessary. This approach usually promotes cooperation and goodwill between the parties.

Of all the areas in the hotel that are the housekeeper's responsibility, the one that often appears to the public to be the simplest is the *guestrooms*—simplest because all it seems to entail is cleaning the room, changing the linens, and making up the bed. Since they believe that it is so easy, the guests are more annoyed by—indeed, will not tolerate—an imperfectly made-up room. Such an attitude helps to make this function one of the most difficult in the hotel, and it is performed by a comparatively unskilled employee: the room attendant. Thus the room attendant has a major role in establishing good guest relations.

Historically, there are three categories of room attendants—day, bath, and night. Their daily duties are almost self-evident. The day attendant services and cleans the guestroom while the bath attendant thoroughly cleans the bathroom, washing the wall tiles and floor fixtures. The night attendant services the rooms in the case of late checkouts, is on call for extra supplies or other requests by the guest, and, in luxury hotels still offering the service, "turns down" the beds.

But because of constant increases in payroll and other operating costs, bath attendants have been phased out and their work assumed by the day attendants and housemen. The attendants give the bathrooms a daily light cleaning, particularly tubs, walls, and fixtures. A thorough cleaning is done periodically by the housemen, during the *general cleaning*, which will be covered later in this chapter. Thus, the daily servicing of the guestrooms falls on the day attendants, and we can best learn what it entails by describing their duties and the training needed before they can properly perform this function.

In many hotel suites, particularly in extended-stay facilities, the room attendant is required to clean pots and pans, dishware, cutlery, and the kitchen itself.

First, each attendant is given a linen cart to carry supplies. Since these carts are left in the halls, in front of the door behind which the attendant is working or where the attendant's card is on the door handle, they are visible to every guest. Each morning they must be thoroughly cleaned before being equipped with linens and other supplies. In most high-rise hotels, carts and supplies are kept in an attendant's closet on every floor, the supplies being replenished each evening by a houseman. Most people are aware of the different kinds of linens required—sheets, pillow cases, bath towels, washcloths, and bathmats. In addition, each floor closet should contain a reserve of mattress pads, bedspreads, blankets, and shower curtains to replace any that have been stained, badly soiled, or otherwise damaged; and a great number of other items are also needed to properly equip a room in a first-class hotel. Here is a list of the most common:

Glasses	Postcards
Toilet tissue	Pens
Facial tissue	Telephone memo pads
Shoeshine cloths	Laundry lists
Soap	Guest laundry bags
Ashtrays	Room-service menus
Matches	"Do not disturb" cards
Guest stationery	Clothes hangers
Shampoo	Body lotion

The attendant is also required to inspect each room in the assigned section for vacancies in the morning and afternoon and prepare a room report. This report will be examined later in the discussion of housekeeping paperwork. The detail involved in these preliminary steps gives an inkling of the training needed for the position. In fact, it can be said that an attendant's period of training never ends.

Good housekeeping procedures require that checkouts (vacant rooms occupied the preceding night) be serviced first unless a guest requires early service. Many hotels now have a system where, upon inspection, the floor supervisor can update the room status via the telephone. Let us follow an experienced and thoroughly trained attendant while making up a room. First, the attendant turns off all unnecessary lights and the air-conditioner, or, in winter, lowers the thermostat to the temperature suggested by management. Next, an inspection is made of closets, dresser drawers, and the back of the bathroom door for any articles that might have been left behind by the guest. If any are found, they are immediately turned over to the floor housekeeper, who sends them to the lost-and-found clerk. They are marked with the room number and the name of the employee who turned them in.

Removing soiled linens from the bathroom does not require much care or training, but stripping a bed does. Spreads and blankets are carefully removed, inspected for stains, burns, or tears, and neatly folded. If in poor condition, they are taken to the floor housekeeper for possible replacement. Sheets and pillow-cases are then removed and shaken before being thrown into the soiled linen bag or cart. Guests have been known to store cash and other valuables overnight in their beds, particularly in pillowcases, forgetting to remove them the next day.

Our attendant will never empty a wastebasket by removing the contents by hand. There may be broken glass or a loose razor blade in it. Instead, it will be emptied onto sheets of newspaper and checked for any article belonging to the guest that might have been lost in the rubbish. Ashtrays are also emptied into a noncombustible container, to guard against a lighted cigarette. In recent years attendants have to contend with hypodermic needles and other drug paraphernalia.

The room is then cleaned and vacuumed, but the attendant will never move a heavy piece of furniture to do this. When making the bed in the prescribed way, the mattress will be turned when necessary only if it is a single or twin size. If the room has a double bed, a houseman will be called to help turn the mattress. Some housekeepers allow only housemen to turn mattresses regardless of size.

The attendant knows the value of safety and how to avoid injuries. When cleaning the bathroom, fixtures and faucets are automatically checked, not only to make sure that they are operating properly but to inspect for sharp or broken edges that might cause injury. After setting up the bathroom linen, she or he will test all lamps, replacing any burned out bulbs if this is permitted (in most union hotels, this is a function of the engineering staff), turn off all lights, and lock the door.

Our little trip clearly demonstrates the need and importance for a comprehensive training program. The room attendant can play a significant role in energy conservation by turning out lights and setting thermostats at the proper reading. However, the attendant's training does not end when she or he has learned the proper way to perform assigned duties. The attendant, like all other members of the housekeeping staff, must be instructed in guest relations: how to enter a room and what to say if the guest is still there; how to answer guest requests; when to help and when to refer the guest to a supervisor. Many guests forget to pick up their keys at the front desk and will ask an attendant or house-man on the floor to open the door to their room. Unfortunately, the same request can be made by a petty thief. In most hotels, the employee is instructed never to open a door for anyone but to courteously refer the person to a supervisor, or back to the front desk.

Housemen are also directly involved in servicing the guestrooms. They are the employees who give each room a general cleaning periodically, ranging from every 3 to 8 weeks, depending on the established hotel policy. This is a thorough and complete cleaning of the room and everything in it. It includes high wall dusting, cleaning the tile in the bathroom, washing pictures, and vacuuming the drapes, blinds, sofas, cushions, and mattresses, as well as the carpet. This, of course, entails moving heavy pieces of furniture. Housemen also carry furniture to and from storerooms and from one guestroom to another. In the smaller banquet hotels, they also help in setting up a banquet room for dinners, dances, meetings, and the like, and stripping the room after the affair is over. Larger banquet and convention hotels have a separate department for this task, with their own head housemen directly responsible to the catering manager. A task formerly handled exclusively by the housemen is shampooing of the rugs in guestrooms, halls, and other public places. Again, because of the constant increase in wages and related expenses, many hotels have reduced the number of housemen and given this job to an outside contractor.

The final responsibility for the condition of the guestrooms rests with the *floor supervisor.* Formerly, a large first-class hotel had one on each floor. Today that is no longer economically feasible, and most are assigned three or more floors. In a union hotel, the union contract may limit the number of rooms that can be assigned to each floor supervisor. Some hotels have even changed their title and now hire them as "assistant housekeepers."

The floor supervisors give the attendants their room assignments and floor master keys, which are returned at the end of each day. They supervise, check, and approve the attendants' work and make periodic inspections of the physical condition of all rooms on their floors for serious damage or deterioration requiring redecorating or refurbishing. Any damage—for instance, leaking or broken faucets, out-of-order lamps, broken toilet seats, improper operation of air-conditioning units—whether reported by the attendant or discovered on periodic inspections, is referred to the executive housekeeper or designated representative for transmittal to the chief engineer for appropriate action. Redecoration and refurbishing usually require top management decisions. The housekeeper, since he or she bears the primary responsibility for the condition of the guestrooms, makes the request, and, unless an interior decorator is hired, supervises the redecorations, choosing the colors of the paint, upholstery, and so on. When a painting schedule is set up, the housemen are responsible for stripping the room and preparing it for the painters. Close cooperation and coordination between the housekeeper and chief engineer is necessary to keep to a minimum the amount of time that the room is out of order. In between paintings, the wall washers, who are members of the housekeeping staff, are assigned to keep the rooms clean and attractive.

The *lobby attendant's* sole duty is to keep the lobby reasonably clean and in order during the day. As it is the most used public area in a hotel, this can be a constant problem.

In a large city hotel, thousands of people—room guests; restaurant, bar, banquet, and convention guests; shop and concession customers; employees; visitors;

and the general public—all congregate in or pass through the lobby. Without the constant attention of the attendant in picking up loose papers, cigarette stubs, and other litter, and cleaning the ashtrays and sand jars, the lobby would be in deplorable condition before the night cleaners came in to clean it thoroughly.

Linens. As we have said, the housekeeper's areas of responsibility overlap considerably. Maintenance and control of the *linen supply* might be thought of as part of the "supplies and equipment" function. Here, however, it shall be discussed under the concept of maintenance, since it ties in so closely with making up the guestrooms as well as other rooms. We will confine the later discussion of supplies to those needed for cleaning.

The linen room has often been called the heart of the housekeeping department. The executive housekeeper's office is either a part of or adjacent to it, as are the storerooms for reserve linen and guestroom cleaning and other supplies. All are received and issued by linen-room personnel. The day linen-room person counts and sorts the soiled linen, preparing it for the laundry. The night person counts and distributes the clean linen and all supplies to the maids' storerooms on each floor. Overstocking can lead to waste and unnecessary expense, understocking to loss of time and even guest complaints. Washable uniforms for any employee of the hotel are issued from the linen room, and minor repairs are made on them by the seamstress, who also repairs drapes, curtains, and other linen products. Many employees wash their own uniforms. Uniforms requiring dry cleaning, although under the control of the housekeeper, are usually cleaned, stored, and repaired by the house valet, whether it be a concessionaire or an employee of the hotel.

Linen inventory control and laundering are among the housekeeper's major responsibilities. Top management must establish an operating *par stock*. In respect to room linen, it is ideally five times the daily amount in use, as determined by the number of beds and bathrooms in the hotel. This allows one set in the rooms and one each in the laundry, the floor closet, the linen room, and in transit. Hotels with their own laundry must have, at minimum, a three par.

Circulating par stock for restaurant linens, also the housekeeper's responsibility, is more difficult to set up and maintain. The dining rooms are not the problem. The highest turnover of guests during any one meal is usually in the coffee shop, and most do not use linen tablecloths or napkins. The daily requirements for the regular dining rooms can be estimated and a par established. Banquets pose the real problem. Functions vary greatly in size and requirements, not only in the table setups but in the color of the linens requested. Hotels must therefore have in stock a sufficient quantity of tablecloths and matching napkins, in at least three or four basic colors, to properly service the number of people that can be accommodated at any one time in their largest banquet room. The alternative is to rent them from a linen-supply company as needed. Because of the uncertainty of the requirements and the initial investment, many hotels use a combination of the two methods, purchasing a smaller quantity of colored linens and renting when more are needed.

Most hotels, however, do not keep their own colored linens in circulation; rather, they are returned to the permanent storeroom after each use. This storeroom will also hold all guestroom and restaurant linens purchased but not yet put into use. Because linens represent a major operating expense, bulk buying reduces the unit cost, and since immediate deliveries are almost impossible to obtain, it is normal hotel procedure for the executive housekeeper and the food and beverage manager to estimate their annual requirements in advance and present them to the general manager for approval. When the decision has been made, an order is issued for the full quantity, with partial shipments arranged at convenient intervals.

Control of the reserve linen is very important. The storeroom must be securely locked, with access given to only authorized personnel; no items must be removed without a requisition approved by the housekeeper, and a perpetual inventory must be kept reflecting purchases, issues, and balance on hand. Frequent spot checks should be made by the linen-room supervisor to verify the balance shown. Semiannually if possible, but not less than once a year, a physical count of every item in stock should be taken and compared with a perpetual inventory. A representative of the accounting department should be present to assist in and supervise the count. Accounting should also test-check the mathematical accuracy of the calculations in the perpetual-inventory book, verifying opening balances and comparing purchases to vendors' bills and issues to approved requisitions.

Although reference has been made to the ideal quantity of five times the daily complement, few hotels have—or for that matter, can afford to have—that much linen in circulation. A factor of three to three-and-a-half, or even two to two-and-a-half, if the hotel has its own in-house laundry, is more common. Operating at these levels presents no problem, except during the peak periods of occupancy, particularly over weekends and holidays. Commercial laundries usually provide 24-hour service with pickup and delivery every day except Sundays and holidays. When a holiday falls on a Monday, as most do, there will be no deliveries of clean linens for two days. If the hotel is fortunate enough to have 100% occupancy over that weekend, the housekeeper will have three complete changes of soiled room linens come Tuesday morning. Hotels with in-house laundry facilities can arrange for coverage on these holidays but only on a costly overtime basis. Few housekeepers can truthfully say that their room attendants never had to leave a bathroom without its full supply of linens, or a bed unmade, until the clean linens were delivered after a busy weekend or holiday. To avoid the outlay of funds needed for the initial setup and annual replacements, some hotels rent all their linens. Many that have their own bed, bath, and restaurant linens will still rent uniforms, particularly uniforms for the room attendants, shirts and pants for housemen, and maintenance staff, and most items used by kitchen personnel, such as aprons, caps, and dresses.

Keeping track of the circulating linen is difficult, and many (we hesitate to say most) housekeepers make very little effort to do so. The fault lies not with them but with the chief accountant, who has the sole responsibility for setting up all controls. The department heads merely follow through and provide the personnel to implement them.

There are four ways in which linen can be taken out of circulation:

1. Normal wear and tear
2. Improper use or carelessness in handling
3. Losses in the laundry
4. Theft

The following paragraphs will outline procedures that should be part of the normal operating routine involved in controlling the supply of linen in circulation. If serious shortages are uncovered through spot checks or periodic physical counts, then these procedures must be reviewed and strengthened, if only by improvement of training programs for the employees and more active participation by supervisors in the daily routines.

Ideally, linens should be replaced only as they are discarded, owing to normal wear and tear. If a figure for this is determined, any additional replacements needed are theoretically avoidable, and an attempt can be made to control these losses. A reasonably accurate figure may be established by use of the standard or average wash-use life expectancy of each article—the number of washes linens can be put through before wearing out. The number may vary according to the quality of the linens and the commercial laundry used, and in the final analysis can only be determined accurately by the experience of the hotel itself, but meaningful estimates are obtainable. The American Hotel and Motel Association, many local hotel associations, laundry consultant firms, and the commercial laundries themselves have studied the problem and can furnish these figures. With this standard, the replacements required for any given period are calculated by dividing the total washes for the period by the wash-use expectancy figure. The total washes can easily be extracted from the creditor's invoices by the accounts-payable clerk, who should review all bills and at least check the extensions. On a simple worksheet, the major items of linens are listed, and the number laundered is extracted from the invoices and totaled for the desired period. Assume that a standard of 120 washes was established for twin-size sheets and that 2,400 were washed during a given period. Then 20 would be the number of replacements needed (2,400 divided by 120). If this calculation is done for major items every month and replacements are made as computed, the number in circulation should remain constant at the established par stock.

The second way to lose linens is through improper use or carelessness in handling. Improper use takes many forms, but they all boil down to employee carelessness and lax supervision—supervisors who cannot or will not take steps to stop the improper action or prevent its recurrence. Some of the more common misuses are the use of linen napkins in the kitchen to clean utensils, countertops, greasy stoves, and floor spills; in the dining room to pick up and wrap broken glasses or dishes; to clean floor spills and wipe ashtrays containing lit cigarettes or burning ashes; and to shine shoes. Rags and kitchen towels are normally available for these purposes. Napkins so used must be discarded, because they are too badly stained for regular use. In addition, if the linen napkins are not removed before the dirty dishes are brought to the dishwashing area, they may be discarded with leftover food.

A test check and review of procedures in a medium-sized New York hotel revealed that the attendants were using face towels instead of rags to dust and clean the guestrooms. Further questioning disclosed that they had been out of rags for two days, but the requisition for an additional supply had only been processed by the housekeeper on the day before the surprise inspection, with a notation, "Please rush." Sheets can catch on springs in sofa beds or folding cots and tear if the attendant pulls them off without first checking to see if they are free. Articles can catch and tear on the sharp edges of the soiled-linen chutes if the attendant tries to pack too many in at one time. Training is a never-ending task, requiring constant repetition of proper procedures for both the staff and the supervisors.

It would appear that losses in the laundry should be the easiest to ascertain. Unfortunately, this is not so, even in hotels where a serious effort is made to do so. Here are two cardinal sins that the authors have personally observed in many hotels. To check against the number of pieces charged for on the laundry bill, most housekeepers instruct their linen-room personnel to carefully count and record the clean linen as it comes from the laundry; however, many make no effort to count the dirty linen before it is sent out. The second and possibly greater sin is to have the dirty and clean linens counted and listed on a daily worksheet, and then carefully file it away each month. Here, the fault lies with the controller or chief accountant for not following through on this very important control function.

An examination of the correct procedures, and a review of some reasons why perfect control is almost impossible, is now in order. Before dirty linen can be counted, it must be sorted by type, a tedious and even a difficult job. Linens with minor tears, if these are observed, should be removed and turned over to the seamstress for repair. Minor tears that are not discovered can develop into major ones in the wash, and the articles may have to be discarded by the laundry.

Commercial laundries will rarely return on the following day all the linens received in one shipment. Some may be held back for rewashing or proper folding or merely because they were not finished in time. The hotel will, on occasion, return batches for rewashing. Also, the hotel employees' count and record of these linens must be kept, both for control of shortages and to avoid double billing.

To record the count requires only a simple worksheet. Across the top, a listing is made of all the sizes and types of linens to be controlled. Two columns are needed for each item, one for soiled linens and the other for clean linens. Each day the linen supervisor enters the number of items sent out and the number returned. At the end of each month, the worksheet is sent to the accounting department to be totaled and reviewed by the controller and the housekeeper—and, if serious shortages are shown, by the general manager. The laundry should also be notified of any shortages and an attempt made to collect for them. In our experience, the actual settlement is always a negotiated amount, possibly 20 to 50% of the total claimed by the hotel, usually covering a period of 6 months to 1 year.

In the daily operation, however, control of the quality of the service is of primary importance. This is the responsibility of the housekeeper, who must of necessity work very closely with the commercial laundries and the linen-rental firms. For many housekeepers, getting good and prompt service is a never-ending battle. Torn, badly stained, or poorly ironed pieces are all too often part of many clean-linen deliveries. Many housekeepers have had a guest complain that the bed has been slept in, because of the poorly ironed sheets used to make it up. Timely deliveries are also important, particularly for a hotel operating with a limited par-circulating linen inventory. Unfortunately, laundry employees are no different from hotel employees; they need the same constant training and supervision. And this is out of the hands of the housekeeper, who can only make the laundry's top management aware of the deficiencies in the quality of the service rendered, and keep doing so until the desired results are obtained.

Losses due to theft are generally accepted as a normal operating expense in many businesses, and hotels are no exception. All that can be done is to set up controls and surveillance to minimize these losses. Many guests like to return home with souvenirs, which can be anything not nailed down in the guestrooms, public areas, or restaurants. In theory, stopping the souvenir hunter is easy: just inspect the room after the guest checks out before he or she leaves the hotel. But this is virtually impossible in most hotels, and the cure—additional staff—costs much more than the expense of replacing the articles taken. (On conducted tours, however, particularly in Europe, the authors have witnessed the embarrassment of fellow travelers called back for an examination of their baggage because of towels, blankets, or other items missing from the room they just vacated. The hotels were small, less than 200 rooms, with labor costs obviously lower and replacement costs probably higher than in most cities in the United States.) Very little can be done except to train the attendants to report to their floor housekeeper any major items (blankets, spreads, pictures) missing and any unusual appearance of, or damage to, the guestroom. If the loss or damage is serious, it should also be reported to the general manager, who can then take whatever action is deemed necessary.

Guests are not the only ones who steal from hotels, and employee theft is almost as difficult to stop. However, definite steps can be taken to control, or at least minimize, these losses. The most effective are the use of timecards, employee package passes, and inspection of the contents of all packages brought into or taken out of the hotel by employees; requiring all employees to enter and leave the premises through the timekeeper's office; and prohibiting loitering in the hotel before or after working hours. Because of the number of employees involved, most large hotels require the housekeeping staff to punch two timecards, one at the timekeeper's station as they enter and leave the hotel, and the other in or near the linen room, as they start and finish their shifts.

It has been said that the vast majority of employees are basically honest and could be discouraged from stealing by strict enforcement of the employment policies. But in too many hotels, the department heads become so engrossed in their daily routine that they fail to exercise the supervision necessary to control the employees, except in the strict performance of their job functions. Unless emphasized by the controller, whose responsibility it is to see that these policies are enforced, the controls fall apart, the opportunities to steal increase, and the possibilities of getting caught diminish, a combination that only the morally strong can resist.

Employee Training

Numerically, the housekeeping department is the largest in the hotel; in hotels or motels with little or no food service, it will comprise 75% or more of the total permanent staff. In large convention hotels, if banquet waiters are excluded, the percentage is closer to one-third of the total. They work and are paid only for each function they serve and can be laid off during slack periods, which can range anywhere from 2 days to 2 weeks before and between holidays, to as much as 2 months in the slow banquet season, usually during the summer. In addition, the number employed varies greatly from week to week, depending entirely on the volume of business.

Since the majority of the workers in housekeeping, principally room attendants and housemen, are entry-level positions, training of these employees is a major responsibility of the housekeeper. At one time or another, all come in contact with the guests, and all are directly involved in a very important phase of guest relations: servicing the guestrooms. These employees must be trained not only in their duties but in their relationships with each other, with staff members in other departments, and with the guests.

Supplies and Equipment

The third major function of a housekeeper is the requisitioning, storage, and control of the many operating supplies required for the daily routine of the department. Any person who has ever been responsible for upkeep of a home can appreciate the difficulty of maintaining on hand an adequate supply of the many items—paper, cleaning, and guest supplies—needed for the efficient operation of a multiroom hotel. The items in the guestrooms must be replenished each day to maintain the par, or standard, set by management. The attendants and housemen need adequate supplies and proper equipment (rags, pails, carpet sweepers, hand and floor vacuums, and so on) in good working order to clean and service the guestrooms, corridors, and other public areas of the hotel. Procedures must be established to reorder any item that falls below the established par, the quantity the housekeeper feels is sufficient to meet the needs of the operation. To ensure adequate inventories of all items, frequent repetition of these procedures is necessary as part of the constant training of the staff, reinforced by good supervision and even spot checks by a supervisor.

Controls, excluding those for equipment, are almost impossible to set up. There are too many employees, not to mention guests, handling and using these supplies. Housekeepers, with the assistance of the controller, can establish a pattern of consumption, a ratio between the volume of business and usage. However, it is not feasible to calculate these ratios or all items used; the time, effort, and expense could never be offset by reduction of losses. The total expense can be judged only as a percentage of income. Ratios can be established for major items, particularly the more expensive ones—guest stationery, soap, shampoo, facial tissues, and postcards. Since all items should be reordered when the storeroom inventory reaches a certain level, it is reasonable to assume that the quantity offered represents the actual number used. Thus, by keeping a record of each order (a simple worksheet showing the date, quantity, and price is sufficient), any variation from the established pattern can be spotted and an investigation to ascertain the cause immediately begun.

An item that particularly requires tight control, because of the cost, is the bathroom amenities provided to the guest. The amenities, usually shampoo, hand lotion, and bath lotion, are frequently designer products and can cost over $5 for three small bottles.

Effective control of the equipment is easier to set up and maintain. It, too, should be limited to selected items, such as the attendant's carts, carpet sweepers, and hand and floor vacuum cleaners. All should be carefully inventoried, kept under lock and key when not in use, and wherever possible assigned to a specific employee, who assumes the responsibility for the safety and condition of the appliance.

Paperwork

The final major area of the housekeeper's responsibilities is the volume of paperwork associated with the department. Record keeping for the proper control of payroll, vital in all departments, is more voluminous and probably even more important in the housekeeping department.

There are many reasons for this emphasis on payroll records. The principal ones are the number of employees involved; the area they cover—the whole hotel; the necessity of scheduling the number needed each day (primarily the room attendants) in direct relation to the percentage of occupancy; and finally, the limitation placed on the number of rooms, whether by a union contract or through a voluntary agreement, that an attendant can service each day. All these reasons emphasize the difficulty and importance of proper scheduling to get maximum productivity at minimum cost.

Also borne in mind should be the fact that although each individual salary is far from the highest in the hotel, the total payroll cost, through sheer numbers, represents a substantial percentage of the rooms department expenses. Most employees are now entitled to paid holidays, and those that are required to report for work on those days receive a minimum of double pay—holiday pay plus regular wages. This is reason enough for the housekeeper to schedule as few employees as possible on such days. The limitation on the number of rooms an attendant can service must be regarded not only as a maximum but, in order to achieve total productivity, as a minimum as well. This requires a very close working relationship between the housekeeper and the front-office manager.

As described in Chapter 7, reservations provides the housekeeper daily with computer forecasts, either 10-day or 31-day. This enables the housekeeper to closely estimate the number of attendants required on a daily basis and to schedule them accordingly. In most hotels, the housekeeping office has a terminal by which they can access the property management system and update the status of each room, indicating whether it has been serviced, is in order, and can be resold. Without a terminal, there must be continuous telephone communication between housekeeping and the front desk. Assigning each attendant the maximum number of rooms to make up is very difficult. Not every room needs to be serviced each day. Out-of-order rooms, vacant rooms (those not occupied since the preceding day), and some sleep-outs (occupied rooms with guests away for the night since last serviced) do not require service. Thus a permanent assignment of rooms cannot be made, except possibly in an apartment hotel where the guests rent by the month or have leases. Keeping all rooms assigned to an attendant on the same floor saves traveling time and is desirable but not always possible.

Each day the property management system produces a floor-by-floor room assignment report, a listing of each room and its status according to the computer. The responsibility for printing the report is normally assigned to the night auditor inasmuch as it usually is included in the report menu. An assistant housekeeper is usually scheduled to start at 6:00 A.M. to coordinate the overall process. This report is used by the floor housekeeper to make the actual assignment of rooms for his or her section. Before starting work, each attendant takes the section assigned to her or him, verifies the status, and reports back to the floor housekeeper (see Figure 13-2). This report not only provides the basis of the assignment of rooms to the attendants but also provides the basis for the housekeeper's morning report. The length of the housekeeper's report depends on the size of the hotel; it ranges from a single sheet, listing every room in the hotel, to separate sheets for each floor. It is usually prepared in duplicate.

The original of the morning report is sent to the accounting department, where it is used to check the preceding night's rooms income. The process is

Graylig Hotel			
ROOM ASSIGNMENT / STATUS REPORT			
Room	Status Per Computer*	Actual Status*	Assigned To
101			
102			
103			
104			
105			
106			
107			
108			
109			
110			
111			
112			
113			
114			
115			
116			
117			
118			
119			
120			

*CODES:
    OOO - Out of Order
    O   - Occupied
    V   - Vacant
    CO - Check Out
    SO - Sleep Out
    DL - Double Locked

Figure 13-2   Housekeeper's Room Assignment Report

ATTENDANT'S ROOM REPORT

Regular*

1 _____   2 _____
3 _____   4 _____
5 _____   6 _____
7 _____   8 _____
9 _____   10 _____
11 _____   12 _____

Extra Rooms

_____   _____
_____   _____
_____   _____

Cots

_____   _____
_____   _____

_____
Attendant's Signature

_____
Date

                              Number   Extra Pay
Rooms: Regular $
        Extra Cots   _____   _____
        Total   _____ $ _____

_____
Supervisor's Signature

*As many lines as needed are used to cover quota in each property

Figure 13-3   Attendant's Room Report

repeated and the same reports prepared each afternoon, before the end of the attendant's shift, but here the original is sent not to accounting but to the front office, where it is used to check the rooms occupied. Copies of both the morning and afternoon reports are retained by the housekeeper. In some hotels, particularly in large cities, the housekeeper's report is made in triplicate and, in a very few, in quadruplicate. The front office and accounting then receive copies of each, and the fourth copy, where prepared, goes to the credit department.

The housekeeper's morning report is sometimes used as the source for the preparation of the payroll. However, it is recommended that a separate report, shown in Figure 13-3, be prepared for this purpose, since it would reduce the possibility of errors and provide better control for the housekeeper. At the end of each shift, the attendant enters the requested information and the floor

NIGHT ATTENDANT'S REPORT

STATUS

Vacant	V
Occupied	O
Checkout	CO
Out of Order	OOO

WORK DONE

Turndown	(1 or 2)*
Refused Service	RS
Do Not Disturb	DD
Douoble-locked	DL

Floor _____

Checkout	Made Up	Cots In	Cots Out	Room No.	Status	Turned Down	Room No.	Status	Turned Down

Number

Makeups _____
Turndowns _____
Cots _____
Total _____
_____

Night Attendant's Signature _____

Date _____

Supervisor's Signature _____

*Number of beds

Figure 13-4   Night Attendant's Report

housekeeper summarizes, signs, and forwards the report to the housekeeping payroll clerk, who uses it in preparing the time sheets.

Night attendants, by the very nature of their duties, cannot be assigned specific rooms. The number of rooms or floors they service varies with the size of the hotel and, if a union is involved, with any restrictions in the contract. In most large convention hotels, and in the so-called luxury hotels, there is an assistant housekeeper on duty during their shift, which is usually 3:00 to 11:00 P.M. However, most hotels have no night supervisors on duty, and the night attendants respond directly to guest requests. Reports prepared by the night supervisors range from a simple entry in a logbook of every call received from a guest and the action taken, to a very detailed and elaborate report, such as Figure 13-4. This type of report is usually prepared with multiple copies and, since it in effect gives the status of every room in the hotel, one copy is dropped off at the front desk so that the receptionist on duty can make a final check of the rooms rack.

Many other forms, too numerous to illustrate, are prepared by the housekeeping staff to meet the requirements of management or the desires of the housekeeper. Some of the more frequently used are signature sheets for pass keys issued daily to the room attendants; houseman's daily room-assignment sheets for general cleaning and miscellaneous duties; houseman's work orders, turned in to the housekeeping office when work is completed; traveling attendant's assignment sheet (attendants sent to another floor); and, of course, overall schedules for the departments (reflecting days off for each employee), timesheets, and in many hotels, a weekly forecast of payroll costs. The schedule is usually prepared for the coming week and is turned in with the timesheet for the week just ended.

CHAPTER SUMMARY

Areas rarely cleaned by housekeeping are the food and beverage areas and tenant space. All other areas are their responsibility.

The four main functions are cleaning and maintenance, training of personnel, requisition and control of supplies and equipment, and paperwork related to schedules and reports.

Some hotels have problem areas, for example, windows, cleaned by outside contractors.

Day and night attendants have different duties. The day attendant is responsible for the cleaning of rooms. Supplies are carried on a linen cart. Rooms are, dependent on status, cleaned in a particular sequence. Procedures for room cleaning are very important. General cleaning is carried out periodically by housemen.

Floor supervisors give room assignments, give out keys, and inspect completed rooms. A lobby attendant cleans the lobby.

Maintenance and control of linens is very important. A par stock should be established for linens. Banquet linens are sometimes rented from a linen service. The supply of linens in circulation should be carefully controlled and reasons for losses analyzed.

Because of the number of people in the department results in voluminous paperwork, varying levels of occupancy impact scheduling and payroll.

REVIEW QUESTIONS

1. Which areas of a hotel are not normally cleaned by housekeeping?
2. Which areas are frequently cleaned by an outside contractor?
3. What is the desirable and what is the minimum linen par?
4. What guest supplies are normally found in a room?
5. What is the housekeeper's morning report and how is it used?
6. What is the housekeeper's afternoon report and how is it used?
7. What is the housekeeper's reason for the difficulty of scheduling?

CASE STUDY 1

Sarah Jones is the executive housekeeper of the 600-room Shoreline Resort. She has asked the general manager for a second assistant because of the extensive paperwork. The general manager has asked her to prepare a report on all paperwork required in the department. What would you expect to find in Sarah's report?

CASE STUDY 2

Jean White has been appointed executive housekeeper of the new 1,200-room highrise City Hotel in downtown Chicago. She has been asked to recommend what cleaning would best be done by outside contractors and why. How would you expect Jean to respond?

14
Other Departments and Sources of Income

After studying this chapter, the student should:

1. Be knowledgeable of the areas where a hotel may obtain additional income.
2. Understand the operation and income control of a parking facility.
3. Understand the factors involved in leasing out of stores and concessions by a hotel.

Rising costs, the need for additional revenue, competition, and the desire to capture as much as possible the guests' dollars all contribute to the tremendous increase in services and facilities being offered in today's modern hotels. The services are provided by the hotel staff, members of the so-called minor operated departments, or employees of the concessionaires and store tenants.

MINOR OPERATED DEPARTMENTS

These departments were created as a source of additional income, to reduce operating costs or to provide better and more efficient service to the guests.

Garage Facilities

Before the automobile became the common method of transportation for the business traveler, city hotels were generally located near the railway station, the usual arrival point for their guests. However, with the advent of the automobile, a new form of competition arrived for the downtown hotel: the motel.

Since their origin as small cabins along the highways, motels have catered to the traveling public. They needed no garages; people parked their own automobiles next to their cabins. The cabins were slowly replaced by one-story buildings with adjoining rooms, then, as land became more expensive, multistory buildings. Parking was free, and guests still parked their own automobiles. Then motels began spreading into cities, where land was scarce and very expensive. Builders had to replace outdoor parking areas with in-house garages. In addition, in order to justify land costs, buildings had to be taller and have more rooms. As a result, guests could no longer drive to their assigned rooms and park nearby. Instead, they drove into the garage, and the garage attendants parked their cars.

It soon became apparent that the name "motel" was no longer appropriate. In addition to garage attendants, the operators provided bellmen, telephone operators, a complete front-office staff, and practically all services normally associated with hotels. Thus, they became known as *motor hotels,* because the owners still wanted to attract the traveling public and never abandoned the concept of free parking for their guests.

Faced with this competition in nearby properties, hotel owners had no choice but to include garages in their buildings. However, they offered the convenience of in-house parking only for an additional charge, probably on the theory that they offered the guests more services, better facilities, and more luxurious accommodations than did their neighboring motor hotels. With the newer motor hotels, however, their theory is no longer valid. The only difference is that while one charges, the other includes parking in the room rent.

For a period of time most hotels advertised free parking for their guests, even when in fact the hotel had no parking but had to rent parking spaces in a nearby garage for their guests. Many hotels continue to offer free parking, but in some large cities, for example, New York, the cost of parking has become so prohibitive that the hotels now charge their guests, sometimes at a lower rate. Otherwise the situation might have developed to the point where it would be more economical for an individual to pay for a hotel room to get the free parking rather than pay parking fees. In some instances, hotels will charge in and out fees in addition to a daily fee.

Except during periods of peak occupancy, all hotels with in-house garages offer parking to the general public at the prevailing rates for their locality. Controlling garage revenue is difficult at all times. In a motor hotel, it is further complicated by the need to differentiate between the guests' cars, parked free, and those of the paying public. (Where a hotel garage is operated by an outside firm, the firm will thoroughly check the daily revenue as part of its normal operating procedure, but this does not relieve the hotel controller from the responsibility to check all revenue generated in any department of the hotel.)

To control the income properly requires two separate and entirely different procedures: (1) the verification of revenue and (2) an actual inspection of the parked cars. Revenue (cash sales and charges) is shown on the garage cashier's daily report. This report is merely a listing, in numerical sequence, of all issued and outstanding tickets with the amount charged or collected that day next to each ticket. A garage ticket should be printed in at least three parts: one for the guest, another for the car, and the third filed in numerical order in a rack at the cashier's station. All three parts should be time-stamped to indicate when the car was brought in. The guest's and rack's segments should be stamped when the car is taken out. In addition, the garage attendant should record, on the back of the rack portion of the ticket, the license number, color, make, and location of the parked car. For a hotel guest, the name and room number should also be recorded.

The garage tickets are issued in numerical sequence, but they can only be canceled by a second time stamp when the guests check out. To assist the accounting clerks in controlling the tickets, garage cashiers are usually required to list first on a tally sheet the unused tickets from prior days, and then the tickets issued on that day. Any checkouts from prior days would be indicated by entering the amount charged or designated code next to the ticket number.

Except where free parking is offered, the clerks can only check the amount charged by calculating, on as many tickets as possible each day, the total number of hours the cars were parked. Where free parking is offered, additional steps must be taken. Hotel guests should be required to present their garage tickets to the front-office cashiers for validation when they check out. The cashiers should time-stamp the tickets, enter the room number, and initial each one. Time-stamping and initialing the ticket serves a dual purpose: first, as the authorization for the garage attendants to release the car without a charge; and second, to prevent overtime parking by the guest.

The regulations in most motor hotels call for a charge to be assessed if guests do not remove their cars within a specified time after checking out or after a certain hour of the day. All cars parked in the garage, or, on a more frequent test-check basis, the cars parked on a particular floor or section of the garage, should be checked. All cars inspected should be ticketed and the ticket time-stamped. Particular notice should be taken of the date stamped on the ticket, and any car parked for a period of more than, say, three days or a week, should be noted. The checker should record the ticket number, license number, make, and color of the car and turn this information over to the garage manager or the chief of security for investigation. As a final test, the information above, on at least 25% of the cars inspected, should be recorded and compared with the entries on the tickets filed in the cashiers's racks.

Garage operations, unfortunately, lend themselves to employee theft. Frequent surprise inspections are the only tool available to minimize these losses.

In-House Laundry

In the discussion of the housekeeping department, it was mentioned that the problems many housekeepers are experiencing with outside laundries are causing some hotels to consider installing their own in-house laundries. In a way, this represents a return to the original concept of hotel operations. During the early years of the twentieth century and through the building boom of the 1920s, most hotels operated their own on-premises laundries. This was a wise policy. It enabled the hotels to service their guests better and was economically feasible. Labor was plentiful, wage scales low, and the linen losses more easily controlled against both wear and theft.

These favorable conditions lasted through the depression years of the 1930s, but toward the end of that decade labor and materials costs began to rise, and during the war years, they soared. In addition, many hotel employees left to go to work in factories, shipyards, and other defense-related industries, attracted by the much higher wages they offered. Replacements were difficult to obtain, and those that were available required constant supervision—supervision that many housekeepers, with depleted staffs, could not give. In-house laundries ceased to be economically feasible. Management in most hotels actually reduced operating expenses by shutting them down and sending their linens to commercial laundries.

In the late 1960s and early 1970s the situation reversed itself. Commercial laundries began to experience the same difficulties with their employees that the hotels had had in the 1940s. And despite the higher prices they now charged, housekeepers could not rely on them for adequate, on-time deliveries or high-quality work. Managements began to set up in-house laundries, aided in this decision by the growing competition for the guests' dollars (see Figure 14-1). Guest relations and good service became once again the principal elements of a successful hotel operation.

Figure 14-1   House Laundry in Operation (Courtesy of Gideon Putnam Hotel)

Today, most new hotels include an in-house laundry in the designed facilities. Hotels have become more encouraged by major technological improvements in laundry equipment. A recent hotel show featured a machine that picked up the sheets or pillowcases from the laundry chutes at one end of the room, did a complete wash cycle, and deposited the cleaned linens in batches at the other end of the room, ready to be picked up by the housekeeping staff. The only human part of the operation is an operator to press the on or off button when necessary and this task can easily be performed by a handicapped worker.

Guest Laundry and Valet

In most hotels, even those with in-house laundries, guest laundry and cleaning services are provided by a concessionaire. In larger hotels, the concessionaire is given space in the building, allowed to install any necessary equipment, and usually restricted to only the hotel guests as customers. Control of the gross receipts is normally easy to establish. Most of the agreements prohibit the concessionaire from accepting payment directly from the guests. On the rare occasions that a guest insists on such payment, the concessionaire is required to turn over the money and the charge to the front-office cashiers, who handle the transaction as a cash sale. Thus, all charges are processed through the front office, and the total daily readings in the front-office machine represent the gross laundry and valet sales for that day.

Smaller hotels cannot generate enough volume from their guests to warrant such an agreement. Their only alternative is to deal with an outside valet. Most of these agreements follow a standard pattern: in return for the exclusive right to handle the guests' laundry and dry-cleaning requirements, the outside firm pays the hotel a commission, usually a fixed percentage of the total guest charges. Both parties must agree on a price list, which is printed by the valet and placed in each room by the hotel maids. Who furnishes the laundry bags, charge slips, or any other supplies needed depends entirely upon the individual agreement.

Whichever system is used, control over gross sales is obtained in the same manner as in the larger hotels, since all sales are posted on the guest bills, but there is a major difference in the handling of the items themselves. The concessionaire operating within the hotel maintains a staff to pick up and deliver the guests' packages. If the guests are out, particularly at the time the finished work is being delivered, these employees are entrusted with passkeys so they can enter the room and leave the clothing. Not so with the outside valets. Their employees are usually not allowed to enter the guestrooms. Pickup and delivery are handled by the bellmen or housekeeping-department employees. The items are gathered in one place, and the outside-valet employees pick them up and deliver them there.

Swimming Pools

At one time, a swimming pool was luxury to be enjoyed only at resort areas during a vacation. Then came the automobile. Highway motels built outdoor swimming pools and used them to attract guests. In the colder regions, the larger motels also included an indoor pool as an added attraction. During this period, few hotels in metropolitan areas had on-premise pools. Where they did, the pools usually served as a major attraction, not only for their guests but for the general public.

When motel owners invaded the cities, they brought in two features long associated with their operations: free parking for guest cars and swimming pools. Most also included saunas and massage rooms. These facilities, except for massages, are available to the guests at no charge. The general public is often invited to join a "pool club," in which, for a specific fee, they have unrestricted use of the pool during the period covered by the fee. Otherwise, the facilities are available to the general public on a daily admission charge. Masseurs and masseuses can be either concessionaires, collecting their fees directly from the guests and paying the hotel a fixed rental or a percentage of the gross, or hotel employees. If they are hotel employees, the usual practice is to pay them a salary plus a commission of a percentage of their sales.

The normal personnel complement, to service both the guests and general public, should include a pool manager, lifeguards, and pool attendants. Depending on the size of the operation, cash for daily admissions is handled by the manager or by one of the pool attendants hired primarily as a cashier. The club memberships are usually sold by the salespeople, and the fees for new members and renewals are collected by the accounting personnel.

An important consideration in deciding whether or not to operate a pool club for nonguests is the capacity of the pool facilities. The hotel guest is the primary concern, and the facilities should not be overloaded by club members to the detriment of the guests. For this reason some hotels restrict their memberships to weekdays. It should be noted that a pool club membership usually increases food and beverage sales.

Other Recreational Facilities

There is almost no end to the number of recreational facilities that are offered by hotels. What is offered depends entirely on the type and location of the hotel. Golf, tennis, horseback riding, and other similar activities can be offered only by resort hotels; usually not by those on oceanfronts or heavily built up and congested beach areas. Game rooms, often including pool and billiard tables, movies, and other free entertainment, are available in most resort hotels. Many employ a social director whose only function is to keep the guests occupied in pleasurable activities.

Many recreational facilities appear in newly built hotels, whether in the large cities or in the surrounding suburbs, which of course includes many smaller cities. Game rooms, gymnasiums or exercise rooms, even walking and running tracks, are often provided for guests. The track is obviously an attempt by the hotel operators to give their guests the option to exercise, walk, or jog, in total safety, rather than in the unfamiliar streets surrounding the premises.

When a charge is levied for the use of these recreational facilities, it is treated as another sale. Adequate procedures should be devised to control this revenue, including frequent on-the-spot checks and surprise audits, because controls on this type of sales are difficult to administer. The procedure should be frequently reviewed and updated.

STORES AND CONCESSIONS

In many hotels, rentals from store tenants and concessionaires are a substantial and reliable source of income—reliable in that the fixed or minimum rentals can be accurately projected for every month of the year. However, finding the right tenants requires a certain amount of expertise in both the real estate and hotel fields. Large organizations operating a number of hotels usually have real estate brokers and attorneys on their staff. When opening a new hotel, executives of smaller organizations would be well advised to consult with such a person. Consideration should be given to the kind of tenants or concessionaires, the fair rental value of the premises, and the type of leases to offer.

Kind of Tenant

The kind of tenant to solicit depends to a certain extent on the location of the hotel, the facilities and shops already available in the area, and those in nearby, competing hotels. But the primary consideration should be the convenience of the guests. Reputable, reliable tenants who can provide the goods and services required by the guests will contribute more in the long run to the financial success of the hotel than the immediate increase in income realized by just renting to the highest bidders.

Fair Rental

Fair market value obviously depends on the rentals charged in the surrounding area and the demand for space there. However, hotels do offer a bit more to their tenants than most landlords do. If the tenants provide goods or services needed by the guests, they are almost guaranteed a reasonable return on their investment, provided the hotel itself is successful and enjoys a high percentage of occupancy. For the convenience of the guests, all stores should have an entrance providing direct access to and from the hotel. Stores that also have a street entrance normally command a higher rental since they can more easily cater to the general public.

The final consideration in arriving at a fair rental value should be the unique status of the hotel operators. As landlords, they have very little control over the actions and day-to-day operation of the tenants, the concessionaires, and their employees, aside from the rules and restrictions enumerated in the leases.

Yet the hotel's reputation can be directly affected by the success or failure of the tenant's business. Success inspires confidence in the hotel's operation, and that usually results in better guest relations. The tenants and their employees are inclined to give the guests more attention and better service. Marginal operations have the opposite effect. Most tenants will put the blame on the hotel's operating policies for their inability to succeed, reflecting this dissatisfaction in their attitude toward the guests. Outright failures have a demoralizing effect on the other tenants, and make it more difficult for management to rerent the vacated premises.

Leases—Tenants' Responsibilities

Hotel leases should define the responsibilities of the tenants in at least the following areas:

Cleanliness. To the guest, as well as to the general public, the stores are part of the hotel. Any unfavorable conditions will adversely affect their opinions of the hotel.

Hours. Since the shops are there primarily for the convenience of the guests, the hours that they remain open should be of prime importance to the hotel operator.

Signs. Every lease should spell out the exact type and size of signs that the tenants can erect or display in their windows. In addition, it should contain a clause requiring the tenant to submit plans or proofs to the hotel manager and obtain written approval before erecting or displaying any signs. Offensive signs, particularly those favored by some storekeepers to advertise sales, should not be tolerated in a hotel.

Prices. This applies to concessionaires such as valets, operators of barber shops, beauty parlors, and others who provide a service rather than sell a product. The original price list should be incorporated in the lease. In addition, the lease should contain a clause prohibiting the concessionaire from making any changes in these guest charges without the prior written approval of the landlord.

Control over personnel. This is probably the most important and most difficult clause to incorporate in any tenant's lease. Yet guest relations are vital to a hotel's success, so discourtesy, inattention, or any attitude that results in poor service to the guests cannot be tolerated. Therefore, the lease should at least require the tenant to enforce some of the rules and regulations promulgated by management as a guide for the hotel's own employees in their relations with the guests.

Leases—Rental Agreements

The kind of tenants, the products they sell, the services they perform, and the size of the space available for rent are all factors that should be taken into consideration by management before making the decision as to what type of rental agreement should be offered to prospective tenants. As with all management decisions involving individual judgments for a single hotel or a group of hotels operated by one company, there can be no set rules to follow in relation to the terms or the kind of tenant to whom they are offered. However, most hotel operators use one of three types of rental agreements in their leases and follow a fairly well-established policy in offering them to their prospective tenants. The terms and the principal considerations for using them follow:

Straight rental. This consists of fixed monthly payments for the full term of the lease. It is best suited for a tenant whose gross receipts are difficult to verify or whose potential volume is limited because of the nature of the business or the size of the space to be occupied. Often included in this category are checkroom concessionaires and individual proprietors operating small newsstands with a very limited selling area in or off the main lobby.

This type of lease is also used for any office spaces available in the hotel and for lobby display cases. Many hotel executives have found these showcases are more than just an additional source of revenue. If they are attractive and well maintained, they can transform a lobby that might otherwise be dull into a very interesting section of the hotel. In a few instances, however, the desire or need for this additional revenue has ruined, rather than enhanced, the appearance of the lobby. Too many showcases may give the impression that management is trying to cover every available inch of space.

Minimum rental plus a percentage of the gross receipts over a specified amount. Most store tenants are offered leases with this type of rental agreement. If proper records are kept, enabling the hotel controller to verify the gross receipts with reasonable accuracy, then it is the best type of arrangement for both parties. The tenants, because the minimum rental is usually low, can function properly and stay solvent even during a protracted period of poor sales. When business is good and the gross revenue high, they can easily afford the additional rent. The hotel operators benefit, because they are ensured of a steady, dependable income, since the minimum rentals are not subject to fluctuations and the possibility of tenant failures is lessened.

Straight percentage of the gross sales. This type of rental agreement is usually offered only to concessionaires, such as the valet whose gross receipts are entirely derived from the guests and charged on their bills. This ensures complete control by the hotel's accounting staff of the gross receipts. Where the hotel does not provide in-house facilities, a similar percentage agreement should be negotiated with outside valets, car-rental agencies, florists, and the like.

Control of Revenue

The tenants and concessionaires should routinely permit guests to charge their purchases or fees for services to their hotel bills. This is expected, and the leases should provide for it. The hotel operators on their part must agree to accept the charges and, subject to some restrictions, reimburse the tenants in full for them. The most common restriction is the amount they will accept without prior credit approval.

These charges, like all other charges incurred by the guests, are then processed through the hotel's normal accounting and collection system, at no cost to the tenants or concessionaires. But problems can and do arise. Guests will occasionally dispute the charges, often as they are checking out, when there is no time to investigate the complaints. The hotel will incur collection expenses over and above their employees' salaries and other normal operating expenses. They may have to pay commissions to credit card companies, collection agencies, or attorneys, and legal fees and court costs for any lawsuits deemed necessary to collect some accounts. And some guest accounts will not be paid at all, and will have to be written off as bad debts. Serious disputes between tenants and the hotel executives cannot be avoided unless agreement is reached in the initial negotiations as to the procedures to be followed, financial responsibility for any additional expenses or losses is clearly established, and the agreement is incorporated in the leases. Such disputes will unquestionably adversely affect guest relations and future earnings of both parties.

The problems and some available options follow. Solutions can be reached only in direct negotiations between the two parties.

Disputes over charges. Guest disputes of any charge should, if time permits, be referred to the credit or assistant managers for whatever action is deemed necessary. An immediate settlement of these questions is the only way to satisfy the guests and keep their goodwill. However, few guests have the time of checkout to wait for their complaints to be investigated. Often, the front-office cashiers have no alternative but to deduct the amount of the disputed charge from the total due and have the guest settle the remaining net balance. The disputed amount is left as an open balance on the bill, transferred to the city ledger, and investigated on the following day by the clerk in the accounting department.

Any disputes involving tenant or concessionaire charges must obviously be reviewed with them. It is at this point that guidelines or adjustments and collections are needed. Disputes involving the amount charged are relatively simple to settle and can be handled by the investigation clerks as part of their daily routine. But if a guest refuses to pay the original or adjusted amount, certified as being correct by the tenant or concessionaire, special collection efforts are called for.

Who determines if they are worth making, who absorbs any unusual expenses, and who takes the loss if they are deemed to be uncollectible? These questions must be settled as part of the original agreement.

Credit cards. A substantial number of guests settle their bills at departure by charging the total amount due on an acceptable credit card. Obviously, many of these accounts include charges by a tenant or concessionaire. The credit card company's discount is based on the total charges submitted. Does the hotel absorb the total expense, or does it charge the tenants and concessionaires their pro-rated share?

Sound credit procedures mandate that all guest accounts that are unpaid after a specified period of time be turned over to a collection agency or attorney for collection, usually for a fee consisting of a percentage of the amount collected. Again, these amounts will undoubtedly include some charges by the tenants and concessionaires. Who is responsible for the collection fees on these charges? The same question arises in those cases where legal action is required, but it is further complicated by the fact that court costs and legal fees are sometimes incurred for lawsuits that do not recover the amount due. Finally, the same problem exists on collectibles and are written off as bad debts.

Solutions are difficult after the fact. Hotel operators would be well advised to discuss these problems with all prospective tenants, resolve them, and include the agreements in the leases.

Check on gross income. Of the three types of rental agreements described earlier, only the second, calling for a minimum rental plus a percentage, requires any control or verification of gross income. This function is the responsibility of the hotel controller. However, the leases should clearly outline the obligations of the tenants regarding reporting requirements, records to be kept, hours they must be available to the hotel's accounting staff, and so on. Finally, the leases should be very specific as to the exact method of calculating the additional rent. Unfortunately, too many are not, creating another area of potential disagreement between the two parties.

These poorly worded leases call for a minimum rental, payable monthly, and a percentage of the gross sales over a specified annual amount. Tenants often interpret such a clause to mean that the additional rent is due only at the end of each year. Management, on the other hand, usually insists on a monthly calculation, based on one-twelfth of the gross sales figures called for in the leases. Some regard each month's calculations as final. Others accumulate the monthly sales figures, calculate the exact additional rent due at the end of the year, and make an adjustment at that time for any difference between the actual amount and the total paid to date. Serious disputes have arisen because of these different interpretations.

Reporting requirements vary. However, most leases obligate the tenants to report their gross sales monthly. In addition, they are usually required to submit a statement from a certified public accountant, at the very least once a year, of the audited gross receipts.

Hotel controllers can verify the reported gross income only through an audit of the tenant's books and records. Cash-register readings and available tapes should be checked against the daily sales as entered in the sales journal. If sales are subject to a sales tax, the records, forms, and returns required by the state, city, or local authorities imposing the tax should be examined during the audit. The gross sales on the returns should be compared with the reported amount, and payment of the tax called for on the return confirmed by the canceled checks issued to and endorsed by the taxing authority.

MISCELLANEOUS INCOME

Discounts

There are two types of discounts: cash and trade. Cash discounts are considered to be a separate item of income, and the total earned is so shown on the profit-and-loss statement under "Other" or "Miscellaneous income." Creditors offer cash discounts only as an inducement to hotels to pay their bills within a specified period of time. If the hotel does not, or cannot because of a weak cash flow, pay its bills within the discount period, payment in full is required and the discount is lost. Thus, cash discounts bear no relation to the type or quantity of merchandise purchased. Excluding errors, they depend entirely on the cash position of the hotel. In the section covering the accounts-payable functions, the controls needed in both purchasing and accounting to ensure that discounts are not lost will be covered.

Trade discounts, on the other hand, depend solely on the type or quantity of merchandise purchased. They are deducted from the gross prices, and the net is the amount due whether or not any cash discount is offered or taken. Net amounts, gross prices less trade discounts, become the actual cost of the merchandise purchased and are so recorded. Trade discounts are never shown as a separate item of income in the profit-and-loss statement.

Commissions

Commissions, included under "Miscellaneous income," represent amounts received from companies or individuals who are not tenants or concessionaires occupying space in the hotel. Thus, commissions included in this category depend to a certain extent on the facilities and services available in the hotel.

Agreements with the neighboring retailers may obligate them to pay a commission to the hotel of a fixed percentage of their gross sales to the hotel's registered guests. In return, they are given the right to extend charge privileges to the guests and are exclusively recommended by the hotel staff on any inquiries for the type of merchandise they offer for sale. However, the agreements usually require prior credit approval on all guest charges.

For retail merchants to be interested in making such an agreement, they must be convinced that most commissionable sales are made as a result of the hotel staff's recommendations. And since these are usually for products that the guests would need in an emergency or for a special occasion, the two kinds of merchants that are most often parties to these agreements are druggists and florists. Controlling the gross sales to the guests, unless most of them are charged, is rather difficult. Obviously, since the commissionable sales represent only a small percentage of the total receipts, the merchants will not agree to any audit or inspection of their records. However, the products they offer—prescriptions, drugs, and flowers—are often ordered by the guests by telephone or through a member of the hotel's staff. These and other charge sales for items personally picked by the guests can at least give the hotel controller an indication of what the total commissionable sales should be.

Many hotels, particularly resorts, collect commissions from various companies whose customers are primarily hotel guests. Falling into this category are car rental firms, sightseeing tour operators, water sports concessionaires, photographers, and vending machine operators. Of particular significance can be the commissions received from companies providing in-room movies for which the guests are charged.

In some of these areas the hotel may not have enough facts available to verify the actual commission due and has no alternative but to accept the amount received. On these accounts, worksheets should be kept showing the amounts and frequency of payments. In this way, any unusually small or missing payments can at least be detected and immediately questioned and investigated.

Food and Beverage Operations/Banquet Facilities

Miscellaneous income is also realized in the food and beverage operations of a hotel. These earnings, however, are not included in the "Other income" section of the profit-and-loss statements. They affect the food and beverage department results only, and are shown as "Miscellaneous income" or applied against the related-expense category for that department. This income is derived principally from two sources: the markup or discount on items specifically purchased for resale to the individuals, groups, or companies sponsoring banquet functions; and the sale of specialty items in coffee shops, restaurants, or bars.

Special items requested by the sponsors of banquet functions—particularly weddings, anniversaries, birthdays, bar mitzvahs, and similar celebrations—are so varied that it would be impossible to list them all. Some representative items are flowers, candles, cigars, cigarettes, wedding or other special-purpose cakes, printed napkins and matchbooks, and party favors. Some sponsors will even request elaborate temporary decorations, often requiring the services of an outside decorator, to change the character of the assigned banquet room so that it will depict a particular locality, event, or date.

Whether the miscellaneous income is realized from a markup of the cost or a discount is entirely a management decision, discounts are usually restricted to printed matter and fees for services rendered by outside contractors, since the charges to the guests are often quoted as "the hotel's cost," and photocopies of the vendors' invoices are attached to their bills. Wherever possible, instructions to the person placing the orders with the suppliers should be in writing and, for better control, should include both the cost and selling price, in various price ranges, for the items most frequently sold. Naturally, this list should be periodically updated.

At this point, it should be mentioned that the leases of tenants or concessionaires of the hotel usually contain a clause giving them the exclusive privilege of supplying any item requested by a banquet guest if it is carried as part of their normal stock in trade. Since most of the leases call for a minimum rental plus a percentage of sales over a specified amount, a hotel's operation can benefit in two ways from such a requirement: first, management may at its discretion mark up the cost, and second, the sale of these items, by increasing the tenants' receipts, may very well increase the gross rental due the hotel.

Adequate control is relatively simple. All that is needed is a worksheet, kept by the banquet auditor, and an absolute requirement that no vendor's bill for any item purchased for resale to a banquet guest be paid without the banquet auditor's approval. The worksheet should indicate at least the date of the function, the room in which it was held, the name of the sponsor, the name or description of the item, the number of units sold, the unit price, and the total sale. This information should be recorded as soon as possible after the function is held, preferably on the following day when the banquet auditor is checking the total guest bills. When the vendor's invoice is received for approval, the banquet auditor should record next to the original entry the date of the invoice, name of the vendor, number of units purchased, unit price, total cost, and the date approved for payment.

Approval of the invoices for payment carries with it the responsibility of verifying the accuracy of the amounts billed. If properly instructed, the banquet auditor can check not only the vendors' invoices but also the charges to the guests. On items subject to discount, he or she should indicate the percentage allowed on the invoice and compute the discount, deducting it from the gross amount, and showing the net amount due. The net is the figure that the accounts-payable clerk processes for payment. Detailed worksheets should prevent duplicate payments to vendors. They also serve as an excellent medium by which the hotel can check on this rather substantial source of income. Needless to say, any differences in the number of units, or between the cost and the guest charges, should be immediately investigated.

Although petty-cash purchases for any of these items are usually discouraged they must occasionally be used, since some vendors will insist upon immediate payment on delivery. When this occurs, the general cashier should be instructed to remove the invoice attached to the petty-cash voucher (without which the voucher should not have been accepted), mark it paid, make a photocopy for his or her records, and forward the original to the banquet auditor. The auditor should then enter the required information on the worksheet, check the banquet charges and, if they are correct, return the invoice to the general cashier.

The income from the markup or discount on these banquet items is usually applied to a food and beverage department expense. That means that the income is picked up as a credit to the expense—for example, flower sales to "Food expense—Decorations." The vendors' invoices are then charged to the same account. The profit or net difference result in a reduction of the hotel's expense for decorations in that department.

A final check should be made on all invoices for items purchased for resale in their original form is of sales taxes where they are required. In some states, these taxes are payable only by the final consumer; however, the laws assessing the taxes usually require vendors to charge them on all invoices unless their customers have filed a sales-tax exempt number or a copy of a resale certificate, if one is issued by the taxing authorities. The controllers in hotels so affected should instruct all concerned—banquet auditors, accounts-payable clerks, and general cashiers in particular—to correct these invoices by crossing off the tax, and to notify the creditors and file information as required by the local statutes.

Speciality Items and Souvenirs

Specialty items sold in coffee shops, restaurants, or bars fall into two general categories. The food-type items are primarily used by hotels for promotional purposes, or as a form of advertising. They usually have the hotel's name or insignia on them and are the same as those used to service the guests. They would include such items as coffee mugs, attractive plates with a small stand for the guest to display them on, unusually shaped glasses, and the like. All other souvenirs, including almost any item offered for sale in a souvenir shop, fall into the second category.

Few metropolitan hotels offer any general souvenirs for sale in their own operated food and beverage outlets. Most of them cannot, because of the restrictions imposed on management by the terms of their tenants' or concessionaires' leases, which, as we have said, may contain a clause giving the lessees exclusive rights to the sale of specific types of merchandise. Souvenirs are often sold at newsstands, in drugstores, or in specialty shops.

The profit on the sale of these items is rarely used to reduce an expense. Rather, the sales and cost of sales for each item are separately shown in the food and beverage accounts in the income-and-expense ledger. On the departmental profit-and-loss statements, the net differences are added together and shown as "Miscellaneous food and beverage income."

Effective control of these specialty sales depends to a great extent on the number of items offered for sale. Where there are many items involved, the time and effort needed to accurately control them is simply not feasible. Most of the outlets where they are offered for sale need a minimum of two shifts to staff them during the hours they are open for business, and for proper control, each cashier should be required to take a complete inventory of all unsold articles twice a day, the first when reporting for duty and the second at the end of his or her shift, making at least four complete inventories each day. In addition, the differences between the opening and closing inventories must be priced and extended, and their totals added and compared to the miscellaneous sales recorded. Any differences between the closing and opening inventories taken by succeeding cashiers should also be reconciled.

This is obviously a very time-consuming procedure, and one that can only be effectively employed in hotels where only one or two items are offered for sale in any outlet. As a result, where many souvenirs are offered for sale, few hotels require cashiers at any time to take an inventory of the unsold items. They usually assign a member of the accounting staff to take periodic inventories and compute the actual cost of sales. This figure is then compared with a potential cost established for that period. Unless the percentage of markup is the same on all items sold, which is rather unlikely, the potential sales should be calculated for each item. Whether the total income from these sales justifies the cost of keeping detailed records is a determination that must be made by each hotel. The alternative is to estimate the average percentage markup and apply it to the actual cost of sales. A more advisable, and cerainly more accurate, method is to calculate the actual average percentage markup at specified intervals, and use that figure for all periods in between.

Sale of Discards

Hotels cannot maintain a competitive position unless their guest and public rooms are clean and attractive, and the furnishings, carpets, and appliances are in good condition. The volume of business, the heavy traffic in public areas, and the careless treatment of hotel property by some guests all combine to make the up-keep and replacement of these items a part of the normal operating procedures.

However, such items are rarely discarded in such poor condition as to be unusable or beyond repair. Thus, management has a choice: to donate them to recognized charity or to offer them for sale. To do either with each individual item as it is replaced would not be feasible, so they should be accumulated and stored until it is convenient to dispose of them in quantity.

Management will often donate to charity those articles of furniture accidentally or otherwise damaged and requiring rather extensive repairs. Most charitable organizations have volunteer workers to repair them. Other items are often offered to the hotel employees at a nominal cost. Any remaining carpets or articles of furniture are then sold to a secondhand-furniture dealer. The housekeepers usually handle these sales. When many articles are being disposed of, as would be the case after an extensive refurbishing program, a cashier or other accounting-department representative should be present. All money received should be immediately deposited; it is usually included with miscellaneous income as "Salvage sales."

Few hotels make any attempt to control this source of income until the articles are taken away by their buyers. That is to say housekeepers are rarely, if ever, required to maintain a perpetual inventory of all items replaced, or for that matter to keep track of them until they are disposed of. Complete control is actually not worth the cost in wages and related expense required to enforce it. But some control over this income should be exercised at the time of sale. The alternative is to accept without question whatever money is turned in by the housekeepers. The following procedures, properly enforced, should ensure adequate control.

Any employee purchasing such articles should receive an itemized statement clearly describing, and indicating the cost of, each item purchased. The statement should be prepared in duplicate, with both copies signed by the housekeeper or person receiving the payments, and by the employee making the purchase. The original is then given to the buyer, as authority to take the merchandise out of the hotel via a designated exit. There the items are checked against the statement by a timekeeper or loading-platform attendant, who records the name of and amount paid by the employee. At the end of the day, this sheet is sent to the controller or designated accounting clerk, who should check, on the following day, the totals listed against the actual deposit. The duplicate statements are retained by the housekeepers and forwarded each day, with all money received, to the general cashier. Secondhand-furniture dealers should be required to send their payments for all purchases directly to the general cashier. The other procedures—itemized statements in duplicate, designated exit, and so on—remain the same.

SECURITY

In the last 30 years, the security department has been the fastest-growing department in most hotels. While theft of property from guestrooms has always been a problem for hotels, the growing concern has evolved from a major increase in the level of violence in the industry. In 1976, a Federal District Court upheld an award of $2.5 million to an entertainer, Connie Francis, for injuries incurred when she was raped in her hotel room on Long Island while performing at a major theater venue.

This award, together with a series of other awards of major amounts, alerted the hotel industry to the need to provide adequate security to protect their guests. The most commonly occurring crimes were rape, assault and battery, and robbery with violence. Despite a higher level of consciousness of the problem, there has been incidents where a test of a hotel's security has revealed major inadequacies. An investigative report shown on a major television station in the early 1990s was extremely embarrassing to some major New York hotels whose security procedures were found to be lacking. In the summer of 1995, students in a hotel, restaurant, and tourism program in a major university conducted a survey in a major city. An example of the results was that in 19 of 24 hotels surveyed, a student was able to obtain an extra room key from the front desk after 11:00 P.M. without being asked for identification.

The Security Staff

The number of permanent employees needed to properly staff this department is a management decision that depends to a great extent upon the size and type of hotel. Temporary guards for special functions or conventions requiring additional security are usually obtained from an outside agency. In most large convention hotels, the department is headed by a former FBI agent or retired high-ranking police officer, a professional thoroughly experienced in criminal investigations and interrogations. Such qualifications are essential for the proper performance of the duties.

The primary function of the security staff is to protect the guests and their personal belongings. This is done by patrolling the lobbies, corridors, and other public areas, as well as staircases and side exits. Hotel employees should answer all guests' calls for assistance, investigate any suspicious actions reported, and, in the event of loss, notify the police and cooperate with them in their investigation.

Almost as important is their responsibility to protect the building, personal property, and reputation of the hotel, and to do so without incurring any legal liability for themselves or the operators or owners of the property—a difficult task, requiring extreme caution, knowledge, and tact. This is particularly true when they are called upon to peacefully silence or eject, and sometimes cause the arrest of, someone who is creating a disturbance in the guestrooms, restaurants, bars, or other public areas. Their expertise in handling people is also utilized by the credit-department staff in its efforts to collect doubtful accounts in city ledger.

Cooperation with Other Departments

Management should establish a definite rule that when a credit-department employee must enter a guestroom—to review the guest's account, demand payment, or request additional identification to warrant the extension of further credit—such entry should be made only when accompanied by a security officer. If it becomes necessary to lock out guests for nonpayment of their accounts, a security officer should activate double locks. When any such guests return to the hotel, they are usually referred to the credit office, where they are questioned regarding payment of their accounts. A security officer should always be present and assist the credit manager in the questioning of the guest. While the guests can be questioned, by law they cannot be forced to respond. Some hotels make it a practice to have all "deadbeats," people with no funds who nevertheless incur substantial charges, arrested. This is subject to state laws. Whether the credit department or security files the complaint is a management decision. In either case, a security officer should make all the necessary arrangements for the arrest and give the police whatever assistance they require.

Security's final major responsibility is to minimize the theft of hotel property. This necessitates a very close working relationship with the controllers and their staffs, particularly the timekeepers, receiving clerks, and loading-platform employees. The timekeepers are responsible for checking all packages brought into or taken out of the hotel by its employees. The receiving clerks accept delivery of all goods ordered for the hotel. Larger properties, particularly in metropolitan areas where street parking is restricted, have an off-street loading platform accessible to a few delivery trucks at a time. In addition, laundry, articles being returned to a vendor, garbage, furniture or equipment sold for salvage, and so on are taken out of the hotel via this platform, under the supervision of the employees stationed there. Needless to say, these exits can also be used to remove stolen hotel property.

Full advantage should be taken of the security chief's expertise in setting up the procedures to check employee packages and all other goods entering or leaving the hotel. Instructions should emphasize the importance of immediately calling for a security officer if employees encounter problems in the performance of their duties, or if they observe any suspicious acts by other employees or delivery people.

Cooperation between accounting and security is extremely important in investigating employee thefts. The controller must pinpoint the areas of suspicion and the employees that could be involved. Security should employ surveillance and whatever other actions are deemed necessary to try to apprehend thieves.

Any culprit apprehended should be interrogated immediately by the chief or other designated security officer in the presence of a witness—if possible, the controller. Immediate questioning often results in a full confession, valuable where the theft is reported to the bonding company and a claim made for restitution. If the employee is a member of a hotel union and is fired, a signed confession will prevent an appeal to the union for reinstatement or for vacation or severance pay. A witness should always be present, not only to testify that there was no violence or undue harassment against the employee in the event such a claim is made, but, almost equally important, to make sure that no such acts are committed. Finally, all arrangements for the arrests and prosecution of dishonest employees and contact with the police should be handled by security officers.

Technology in Use in Security Enforcement

The real advances in the field of hotel security have resulted from increased use of technology rather than increases in numbers of staff.

The most notable of these advances is the development of electronic locking systems, which are triggered by plastic cards issued to guests. These "keys" can be programmed to expire at checkout, providing tracking information on entrances and exits from rooms by having an online connection and permit codings of various levels of access for use by the hotel staff. The newest of these systems permits a guest's credit card to be coded for use as a key.

Many hotels are now installing in-room safes, but the acceptance and use by the public has not been universal. Such questions as where they should be located and whether the guest should be charged for their use are among the concerns. Perhaps the most serious criticism is that they are not a deterrent to illegal entry to the room, as there is no way that an intruder can tell in advance whether an in-room safe is being used.

Closed-circuit television finds some use in hotel corridors and lobbies. The concern with their usage is that they must be monitored at all times. Otherwise the guest might derive a false sense of security from their presence and an unmonitored incident could trigger a major lawsuit against the hotel. In the use of closed-circuit television, the privacy of the guests must be respected.

Exit warning devices are frequently used on doors, but their usage is primarily for the detection of employee theft rather than guest safety concerns.

CHAPTER SUMMARY

There are various areas where a hotel may obtain additional income.

1. Garage facilities (guest and nonguest rentals)—control over revenue is very important.
2. Guest laundry and valet
3. Swimming pools—pool club membership
4. Game rooms
5. Stores and concessions—proper leases are very important
6. Cash discounts
7. Commissions
8. Miscellaneous food and beverage income
9. Specialty items and souvenirs
10. Sale of discards

Security has become a major problem for hotels.

REVIEW QUESTIONS

1. What form should a garage ticket take and how is it used?
2. Who handles the pickup and delivery of garments sent to an outside valet?
3. What is the primary consideration when deciding whether or not to operate a pool club?

4. What tenant responsibilities should be included in a shop lease in a hotel?
5. What is the most desirable form of rent calculation in a shop lease?
6. What is the difference between a cash discount and a trade discount?
7. List five of the more common specialty items requested by an organization or group having a function.
8. What are some of the specialty items sold in a hotel coffee shop?
9. What is the procedure to control the sale of discards?
10. What are electronic locking systems?

CASE STUDY 1

The Smith Hotel has decided to initiate charging guests for parking in the hotel garage. Jim Clark, the controller, has been asked to devise a system for controlling revenue. What are the features of the system that Jim might put in place?

CASE STUDY 2

Sam White, the general manager of the Sunshine Resort, has decided to lease out the hotel gift shop, but must come up with a formula for the rent. What are the formulas that Sam might consider?

15
Insurance

After studying this chapter, the student should:

1. Understand how chains can reduce the cost of coverage.
2. Know what constitutes an insurance program.
3. Understand the impact of employee training in this area.

The person entrusted with purchasing insurance for a hotel should be thoroughly familiar with the product, the market, and the hotel's requirements. Rates and types of coverage included in policies by the different insurance companies frequently vary. Market conditions fluctuate.

In the period from 1970 to 1990, there were several major hotel fires, which resulted in heavy claims and settlements. As a result, insurance companies became more selective in issuing policies and rates increased. Since 1990, the incidence of hotel fires has decreased, due partly to tightening of fire codes but also to an increased awareness of the dangers by the hotel industry, resulting in a higher emphasis on fire prevention and safety. However, any savings achieved by the industry in the area of fire insurance have been offset by increases in public liability insurance resulting from higher judgments by courts in the areas of inadequate protection of guests from criminal activity and the ongoing problem of guest safety.

COVERAGE

Hotel chains have a definite advantage in the area of insurance, inasmuch as they can afford to maintain a staff of insurance professionals, while the independents delegate the responsibility to the general manager or the controller, neither of whom can be expected to have the same level of expertise. Furthermore, chains receive a substantial savings in premium costs by purchasing a policy covering a group of hotels, thus minimizing the overall impact on the insurance company of a major disaster in one location.

Both the chains and independent hotels have developed insurance programs to reduce premiums by combining various types of coverage on the same policy. This is similar in philosophy to homeowners receiving a lower rate on automobile insurance by combining it with the coverage on their house. Most frequently found is all liability insurance coverage in the same policy as coverage for fire and other damage to the property and contents. However, it is not unusual to find crime insurance and coverage on vehicles in the same policy.

Insurance costs represent a major item of expense, yet few hotel executives can properly evaluate the insurance requirements for their hotels. Thus, they must rely on and accept the recommendations of an insurance buyer, an outside broker, or a member of the hotel's staff. Entrusting this function to an otherwise qualified person who has no hotel experience can lead to the complaint by top executives that "We spend thousands of dollars for insurance, yet whenever we incur a somewhat unusual loss, we are not covered."

To entirely avoid this situation is almost impossible. No broker can, or would try to, cover every conceivable risk. In the last few decades, premiums for full coverage have risen so rapidly as to be almost prohibitive. As a result, many hotel operators have become self-insurers, by participating in any losses through the use of deductibles. Some major hotel chains have even discontinued coverage on certain risks and assumed full liability for claims arising from them. Deductibles, depending on the size of the property and the financial status of the owners, range from $1,000 to over $1 million. Under these plans, hotel operators assume full responsibility for any claim settled for less than the amount of the deductible. On settlements exceeding that amount, the insurance company pays only the excess, with the operators paying or absorbing the full amount of the deductible. Obviously, the larger the deductible, the smaller the premium.

A well-planned insurance program can substantially reduce expenses. The first step is to list the major classifications and amount of insurance required for proper coverage. Then the various options offered with each type of insurance should be carefully analyzed, the risks evaluated, and the possible losses compared with the premiums. The recommendations to management should be accompanied by a detailed explanation of how the amounts listed for both total coverage and deductions, if any, were arrived at. The report should also list any known uninsured risks and, of course, the reason for not insuring against them—for instance, that coverage was not available, or costs were considered excessive.

Only with all the facts can management make an intelligent decision and avoid being surprised by the expense resulting from a claim or loss.

THE INSURANCE PROGRAM

Here are the principal ingredients of a well-planned insurance program. The first phase covers the period from the time the architect's plans are being drawn to the day the hotel is opened for business. At the completion of construction, all builder's risk policies expire and must be replaced by permanent insurance policies. The second phase begins with these permanent policies and continues as long as the hotel is in operation. Basically, the insurance requirements are the same as in the first phase. However, the amount of coverage must be reevaluated, the optional insurance broadened, and additional coverage taken out for the interests and property of the guests.

During Construction

The building represents the major part of an owner's investment. Outside financing is usually needed, and the amount is directly related to the cost of the structure. Therefore, it is very important to carry fire insurance at, or very close to, the value of the building, even during the construction period. Because of the amount of coverage required, fire insurance is costly, being based on an individual rate established for each property. Often a lower rate can be obtained—not to mention a more fireproof and therefore a safer building—by presenting the architect's plans to the rating bureau for examination and recommendation before they are finalized. This service by the insurance industry is available without charge.

Before construction actually starts, a study should be made of the comprehensive *multiple-line protection* policies offered by the many insurance companies in this field. They usually include coverage for loss to buildings and personal property on a named-peril basis against fire, lightning, and the extended-coverage perils. Some of the optional coverages that can be included by separate endorsements are for sprinkler leaks; blanket crime coverage, including employee dishonesty, vandalism, and malicious mischief; time-element coverage; and public liability. Building insurance covers all permanent fixtures, such as machinery used in the service of a building, air-conditioning systems, boilers, elevators, and signs that are attached to the building. Most brokers recommend an inland marine neon-sign policy to insure expensive electrical and neon signs against all risks. Finally, the builder's risk policy should provide for periodic automatic increases in the building insurance as construction progresses.

Fire Insurance: Building and Contents

When the same individual or company both owns and operates the hotel, both the building and its contents are usually included under one fire insurance policy. If the owner and operator are not the same, each should insure their own property. Tenants owning contents usually have an insurable interest in any improvements made to the property, and this interest may be covered in the same policy as the contents.

Optional coverage that may be added to the building and/or contents policies include the following:

1. Extended coverage is available to cover property against all direct loss or damage due to windstorms, hail, explosions, riots, aircraft, vehicles, and smoke.

2. Vandalism and malicious mischief may be included, with extended coverage on losses caused by either.

3. Glass insurance covers replacements of plate-glass windows and structural glass accidentally or maliciously broken, including frames and bars. Costs of lettering or other ornamentation may also be included at an additional cost.

4. Sprinkler leakage insurance covers losses due to leakage, freezing, or breaking of sprinkler installations. Both buildings and contents should be covered.

5. A consequential-loss clause is important only to hotels operating their own restaurants and bars. This insures stocks of food and beverages against loss due to a change in temperature caused by damage to the cooling system. However, the damage must be caused by an insured hazard.

6. Boiler and machinery insurance covers damage to property (the insurer's as well as that of others) caused by explosion of covered boilers or breakdown of covered machinery. Bodily injury to persons other than employees may also be included. Policies usually call for periodic inspections of the insured items, which are very valuable in preventing accidents.

7. Flood insurance is available only in areas declared eligible by the Federal Insurance Administrator. It insures the building and contents against financial loss from catastrophic floods and inundation from any resulting mudslides. It is administered in each location by a member company of the National Flood Insurers Association.

8. Earthquake insurance is important in areas where earthquakes occasionally occur. On the West Coast, coverage is available as an endorsement to the fire insurance policy.

9. Tornado and hurricane insurance should be obtained in areas prone to such events.

Liability Insurance

Hotels are particularly susceptible to claims for alleged injuries. The lobbies, corridors, guestrooms, and bathrooms are all potential danger spots. It is impossible to monitor every action of the many people—general public, guests, and employees—who pass through these areas every day. Obstructions on the floor, carpets cut or frayed, and chipped fixtures are just a few of the many hazards that can and do cause accidents. Thus, a hotel should buy the broadcast liability coverage that is available, a comprehensive general liability policy. In addition, most hotel operators add by endorsement some of the optional coverages offered by the insurance companies.

The comprehensive policy insures a hotel against all claims for injuries sustained on the premises or resulting from the hotel's business activities by any person other than an employee performing his or her duties. When a hotel owns and operates automobiles, either for the convenience of its guests or for business purposes, it is advisable to purchase the automobile insurance from the same company to provide overlapping coverage. Some of the usually insured optional risks are these:

1. Product liability protects against claims for bodily injury or property damage caused by the consumption of food, beverage, or other product processed or sold by the hotel operator.
2. Personal injury, commonly called "false-arrest insurance," covers against alleged injury due to false arrest or imprisonment, malicious prosecution, and libel, slander, or defamation of character.
3. Garage coverage is necessary where a hotel maintains a garage or parking lot for the convenience of guests and the general public. Two specific types of coverage are necessary.
   a. Automobile garage liability protects against any liability or bodily injury and property damage to others caused by an accident on the premises.
   b. Garage keeper's legal liability covers liability for fire or theft of stored vehicles.
4. Automobile insurance should be carried for any motor vehicle owned by a hotel and operated for the convenience of the guests or as part of the hotel operation. All available coverage should be obtained, including:
   a. Liability insurance against claims from guests or the general public for bodily injury or property damage resulting from the operation of the business automobiles, trucks, or buses.
   b. Comprehensive insurance against loss by fire, theft, or other physical damage hazards, including glass breakage.
   c. Medical payments to guests or others, except employees, who are injured while riding in hotel-owned vehicles.
   d. Nonownership (contingent) liability coverage can be included by endorsement. This covers the liability of a hotel whenever an employee's

car is used on hotel business. If the hotel occasionally hires cars to transport guests or for any other business purpose, coverage for any liability arising from that use may also be included under this endorsement.

5. Umbrella liability insurance is now commonly used, for several reasons. Settlements, and particularly awards by juries in cases involving personal injuries, have become exceedingly generous, almost unreasonably so. As a result, umbrella insurance is almost essential for complete protection. It provides excess limits and protects the hotel from all exclusions and gaps in its primary liability policy or policies. This coverage becomes effective only when the limits in the primary liability policies, including workers' compensation, have been exhausted or a claim develops from a risk that was not covered. This is the most economical way to obtain high-limit and broadened liability coverage and virtually eliminates any danger of "catastrophic" losses.

6. Workers' compensation insures employees against loss due to personal injury or death suffered in the course of their employment. It is mandatory in most states and provides compensation in amounts as prescribed by law.

Crime Insurance

In order to properly service their guests, hotels must keep large sums of cash on hand at all times. Cashiers in many locations—front office, restaurants, bars, garages, and so on—need sufficient funds to meet the normal requirements of the guests; in addition, the general cashier must keep a substantial cash reserve to replenish these funds. Thus, the hotel is susceptible not only to employee theft, but to armed robbery as well. Many insurance companies offer blanket crime policies that offer complete coverage on a package basis. Individual policies are also available. Total coverage for the full amount of these losses has become almost nonexistent since premiums would have to be too high, so most policies include a deductible.

The following are the principal risks and types of coverage required to insure against them. They are listed separately to describe them more easily, not to imply the need for individual policies.

1. Fidelity bonds insure against losses due to embezzlement or misappropriation of cash or other hotel property by employees. This coverage is usually written as a blanket bond covering all employees. However, most hotels insure for higher limits their executives and those employees handling or with access to cash. This is usually done through a schedule showing the positions and amounts of the coverage. Bonds may also be purchased for individual employees.

2. Money and securities insurance covers losses in or away from the premises caused by destruction, mysterious disappearance, or theft, other than by an employee, of any money and securities belonging to the hotel. Coverage can also be broadened to include damage done to premises and equipment, loss of securities in safe-deposit boxes, or forgery of outgoing instruments.

3. Innkeeper's liability insures against loss due to any damage or destruction of guest property within the premises or in the custody of the hotel. The legal liability of the hotel as defined by the statutes is usually posted in the front office, next to the elevator door on each floor, on the back of guestroom doors, in the lobby, and on registration cards. Liability limits are set by the individual states.

4. Miscellaneous coverage is also available for money orders and counterfeit paper currency, depositors' forgery, and legal liability over the statutory amount for property deposited by guests in the safe-deposit boxes.

General Insurance

Insurance policies are available to cover practically every conceivable type of loss. Only through a careful study of the requirements of each property can proper coverage be ensured. Some hotels, particularly older ones, have valuable paintings, etchings, or tapestries hanging in their lobbies or other public areas. Others may display statues or other works of fine art. These hotels should consider a "fine arts" policy, which would insure them against all risks with minor exclusions. There is also available a musical-instrument floater to cover any such items owned by the hotel. Losses due to damage or destruction of valuable papers and records, caused by an insured hazard, may also be covered. Hotels insuring against these risks usually include losses from accounts-receivable that become uncollectible, owing to damage or destruction of records.

A type of coverage that should be included in every well-planned insurance program is *business interruption* or *use-and-occupancy* insurance. Serious fires or other catastrophies resulting from insured hazards can partially or even completely halt the operation of a hotel. With this type of coverage, a hotel is reimbursed for the loss of earnings, continuing charges, and expenses, including payroll, until the premises are restored and business resumes. Payroll may be completely covered, covered for a specified number of days, or excluded.

OTHER INSURANCE INFORMATION

Reducing Insurance Costs

Insurance planning does not end with the purchase of the needed coverage. Purchasing agents are continually updating their requirements, reviewing operations, and canvassing the market for new and improved products at the lowest possible cost. Can the insurance planner do less? Definitely not, particularly during a period of inflation. Replacement costs may rise so rapidly that what is deemed to be sufficient coverage this year may be totally inadequate next year. Any changes in the method of operation necessitated by a change in clientele may very well affect insurance requirements.

Up to this point, only grouping and deductibles as means of reducing insurance costs have been mentioned. However, deductibles inevitably involve losses, since the hotel assumes a certain portion of the cost of the settlement. There is another much less costly way to reduce premiums on certain types of coverages, so-called *experience-rated policies.* Possibly the best known of these is automobile insurance. The premiums charged to all drivers within a specified area are calculated at the same base rate. All "safe drivers," those that have had no reportable accidents within the previous three years, receive a discount or credit, reducing the base premium; drivers who have had reportable accidents in the same period are charged an additional amount over the base premium. The charge is based on the losses incurred by the insurance company as a result of these accidents. The cost of each accident is included in this calculation for a certain period after the date of it, adversely affecting the premiums for that length of time.

There are four experience-rated policies that all hotels are required to have: workers' compensation, public liability, employee bond, and money and securities. Unfortunately, accidents and thefts cannot be completely prevented, so the same credit cannot be applied to all policies. The percentage of credit or charges depends solely on the actual experience of each insured property. In effect, this means that the insurance companies maintain a separate account for every policyholder, ascertaining their actual losses on each.

Many factors enter into the calculation of base premiums. Simply stated, base premiums are intended to cover average losses plus overhead and provide the insurance companies with a reasonable profit. Individual accounts enable the companies to establish, by policy, the premium that should have been charged to accomplish this. Again, to simplify a rather complicated process, the companies add their overhead and profit to the actual losses on an individual-policy basis. This total is then compared with the premiums charged to that policyholder. If the calculated total is less than the premium, the insured gets a credit on the following year's premium. Conversely, if the premium is smaller, the insured receives an additional charge.

Although experience rating is important in all four categories, it affects most the cost of compensation insurance. Assume that the standard rate in a particular locality is low—say, $2 per $100 of payroll. Few hotels, except very small ones, have a payroll cost of less than $20,000 per week; larger convention hotels average well over $200,000. At $2 per $100 of payroll, compensation insurance is definitely a major item of expense. The difference between a credit and a charge rating, even on a modest payroll of $2 million per year, can amount to $20,000 or more. The standard premium on that amount at the standard rate is $40,000. A 20% credit would reduce it to $32,000, and the same percentage of charge would increase it to $48,000, a difference of $16,000. Obviously, management should be very interested in reducing accidents and thus minimizing the individual-loss factor.

Few accident claims can be settled immediately. Employees with a job-related disability are awarded a weekly settlement plus medical expenses for the length of the disability. The total cost is unknown and must be estimated. Death claims often require court action, again a lengthy process. Similar reasoning applies to accident claims from guests or members of the general public covered under the public liability policy. The total cost of the settlement on all these claims must also be estimated and charged to the individual account of each insured hotel, creating a reserve against which any future settlements are charged. After the final payments have been made, any excesses in the amounts reserved are applied as a charge or credit to the individual accounts. Few hotel executives or insurance buyers are aware of their right to review these reserves and to attempt to have them lowered if, in light of past experience, they deem them to be excessive. But such actions are sometimes successful in reducing the cost of their liability insurance.

The Importance of Job Training

Losses due to armed robbery, employee theft, mysterious disappearance of money or securities, and the like are normally immediately ascertainable and therefore require no estimate of further settlements. However, all policies related to liability or theft share a common denominator. Losses, and therefore premiums, can be reduced at very little additional cost. Employee training programs are the answer, and only management participation and active interest are needed to ensure their success.

Most accidents are caused by human error and are avoidable. Carelessness, failure to remove obstructions or report hazards because of lack of interest or inability to recognize them, and improper work habits in lifting or carrying heavy objects can all cause accidents. In discussing each, the obligation of department heads to properly train their employees has been stressed, and the overall responsibility of the human resources manager to initiate, coordinate, and supervise these training programs is important. Well-trained employees are less accident-prone and contribute more to public safety than do poorly trained workers.

Teaching room attendants how to make a bed, lift a mattress, and empty a wastebasket reduces the possibility of injury in the performance of their duties. They should also be taught to recognize and report hazards that might cause injuries to the guests—loose wires, broken chairs, splintered furniture, worn carpeting, cracked faucets or other sharp edges in bathrooms, and so on. Furthermore, making the attendants aware of the dangers present in these hazards also helps them to avoid injuring themselves.

This example was chosen because it best demonstrates the interrelation of the employee's and the guest's well-being. Many of the areas that the employees work in or pass through are shared with guests and the general public. Thus, proper job training, which should include and emphasize safety, helps to prevent accidents and thus reduces the premiums of both workers' compensation and general liability insurance.

The Important of Safety

Job training is only the first step in setting up a successful safety program; however, it can be a vitally important one if it succeeds in implanting the idea that safety is everyone's business.

In the review of the duties of the human resources department, creating a safety committee whose membership is confined to staff employees only, with at least one member from each department so as to involve all employees in the program, was suggested. Employees should find it easier to discuss safety problems with and report hazards to a coworker. Conversely, the committee members can more readily report back the corrective measures, if any, taken to eliminate the problems. And it is on this last point that the success of a safety program depends.

Few employees will persist in reporting potential danger spots or suggesting corrective measures if no action is taken by management. Of course, not all suggestions are practical or feasible; some may require major building alterations involving great expense, and some may even be impossible to implement. Yet if they were made in good faith by an employee or committee member, they are deserving of an answer. Management, which stands to gain the most from these ideas, can do no less than show an interest by reviewing each suggestion and informing the committee of its decisions—if remedial action will be taken and when, and if not, the reasons. Most employees will be pleased with such attention and satisfied with a reasonable explanation, and they will continue to take an interest in participating in a safety program.

The safety committee should meet regularly, at least once or twice a month, with special meetings called if management thinks they are necessary. Minutes should be kept and distributed not only to the members but to all department heads and other designated representatives of top management. At these meetings, reports of all accidents and injuries since the last meeting should be reviewed, to try to ascertain probable causes and discuss what action can be taken to prevent similar accidents in the future. The management representatives at these meetings should present the discussion and the actions taken by management since the last meeting on all employee suggestions and recommendations.

The examination of all accidents by the committee is important. It can be made more effective by an immediate review of each accident by the head of the department in whose jurisdiction it occurred, with the committee member from that department present. Such a review with the employee involved, or with all witnesses if the injured person was someone other than an employee, is the best way to gather all the facts. Obviously, the presence of a committee member is recommended so that he or she can better explain the circumstances to the other members.

Injury

The extent of personal injuries is difficult to ascertain immediately after an accident. What appears to be a minor injury too often results in the filing of a substantial claim for alleged serious aftereffects. It is important, therefore, that the hotel record and report every accident resulting in personal injury. Federal laws require the insured to submit reports of accidents involving various degrees of personal injury. The reports need not necessarily be forwarded to the insurance company for reimbursement of any expenses involved. It is, however, good policy to notify the insurance company of all accidents since what may appear to be inconsequential sometimes turns out to be major. Because all losses are included in the rating calculation for 3 years, the savings in premium costs will usually more than offset any minor expenses.

The final step in a well-planned safety program is to try to obtain immediate medical aid for all injured persons. Written policies should be posted relative to guest, employee, and vehicular injuries. In many hotels, the "house" doctors maintain offices on the premises, and except for very minor cuts or bruises, all injured persons should be referred to them. Employees cannot refuse, even though they have the right to subsequently consult and be treated by their own doctors. Others can refuse, but every attempt should be made to convince them to at least receive immediate first aid by the house doctor. An excellent precaution is to arrange the doctor take an x-ray of the injury. X-rays taken immediately after an accident have helped hotels avoid costly settlements of claims for alleged injuries. Waivers should be obtained from any person refusing medical attention.

Theft and Money Management

Losses due to theft require a somewhat different approach, because they are basically accounting problems. Employee theft can best be minimized through effective and strictly enforced controls. Theft of money and securities, including armed robbery, can be reduced through employee training in what could be called money management.

Most employees are basically honest, but many cannot resist temptation. This is particularly applicable in the hotel industry, where cash and goods are plentiful and easily accessible. Employee thefts can be broadly separated into two types: the first involves the withholding of income, an area where controls are particularly effective; the second is the outright theft of hotel property, be it money or goods.

Controls are thoroughly reviewed in Section 4. At this point, we will only emphasize the fact that controls are not set up to eliminate all thefts. At best, they can only reduce the temptation to steal by instilling in potentially dishonest employees the fear of being caught and punished. This is why, to be effective, controls must be strictly enforced. Almost as a by-product, good controls will also uncover some thefts and lead to the apprehension of dishonest employees. However, lost income is rarely recoverable from insurance companies, since the individual amounts stolen are usually small, well under the deductible in most policies. To prove that a particular employee withheld a substantial amount of income over an extended period of time is, in most cases, difficult or impossible. Dismissal and, in a few instances, arrest, are usually the only options available.

Controls involved in money management are also discussed in great detail in Section 4, particularly in the chapter dealing with the duties of controllers and general cashiers. These duties include training the cashiers in the management and handling of their floats (house banks), frequent surprise counts of their funds, verification of the daily deposit, reconciliation of bank statements, and so on. But accounting controls can only reduce the incidence of employee theft and, through prompt disclosure, prevent repeated offenses by any one employee. They cannot by themselves reduce losses caused by cashiers absconding with their floats or daily receipts; these losses can be lowered only by reducing the amount of cash in circulation and making full use of whatever security forces are available in the hotel.

Most hotels provide a safe or safe-deposit box, usually behind the front office, with a slot through which the cashiers drop their daily reports. The envelopes are then removed the following day by the general cashiers. An excellent way to reduce the available cash, particularly during peak business periods, is to instruct all cashiers to make one or more cash drops during their shifts. For reconciliation purposes, earlier drops can be recorded on the final envelope dropped at the end of the shift. These extra drops should be required any time cash receipts are unusually heavy. At night, when staffing is at a minimum, some hotels instruct the cashiers to make frequent drops of all cash received.

Security staff can be utilized in several ways: first, as escorts for the cashiers or other employees carrying cash from their stations to the drop box and to and from the safe where the cashiers keep their house funds when off duty; second, in frequent visits to the various cashiers' stations, on a random basis rather than a fixed time schedule. By inquiring about the receipts and the possible need for extra cash drops, the security officer will encourage compliance with the rules.

In summary, the principal ingredients of a successful money-management program (not necessarily in order of importance) are well-trained employees, strictly enforced accounting controls, and alert, prudent, and cautious management, continually conscious of the many dangers inherent in the handling of large sums of money.

CHAPTER SUMMARY

Hotel chains can get lower premiums by covering all their hotels with the same policy. Some hotels now self-insure (with umbrella coverage) or have high deductibles.

During construction, builders' risk insurance must be carried.

Many hotels combine different coverage on one policy. Types of coverage are:

1. Fire insurance—building and contents
2. Liability
3. Crime
4. General
5. Business interruption

Experience rated policies can reduce costs.

Job training and safety programs are very important.

REVIEW QUESTIONS

1. Why can chains have a reduced cost per hotel on insurance?
2. What is self-insurance?
3. What is builders' risk insurance?
4. Make a list of optional insurance thay may be added to the fire insurance policy.
5. Make a list of optional insurance that may be added to the liability policy.
6. Give the various types of coverage in crime policies.
7. Explain business interruption insurance.
8. What are experience rated policies?
9. What is a safety program?
10. Explain the function of a safety committee.

CASE STUDY

Jim Green, the manager of the 300-room Brown Beach Resort in Florida, has been asked to prepare a list of recommended insurance coverage. What would you expect to see on the list?

16

The Organization of Accounting and the Uniform System

After studying this chapter, the student should:

1. Understand the organization of a hotel's accounting department.
2. Be knowledgeable of the uniform system and its various uses in a hotel.

Back in Chapter 5 we presented a chart showing the organization of a hotel. In Figure 16-1 we provide an in-depth organization chart of a hotel's accounting department. By reference to this chart we explain the functions and relationships of the individual subsections of the accounting area, their goals, and the type of support they provide for the other departments. Also, in this chapter we explain how the *Uniform System of Accounts* for the lodging industry provides the industry with consistency and rules for organization, not only in the accounting area, but in the overall hotel.

While a hotel's accounting department will be headed up by the controller, the overall staffing can vary, even in hotels with the same number of rooms. We feel that the chart in Figure 16-1 suits a hotel of around 600 rooms but must emphasize that each block represents a function and dependent on the particular hotel, one person may carry out more than one function while in another hotel a function may require several people..

The number of rooms does not, by itself, determine the size and complexity of the accounting department. This is impacted also by the number of food and beverage outlets and by the existence of other large revenue-producing departments, for example, casinos, golf courses, spas, and so on. In smaller operations

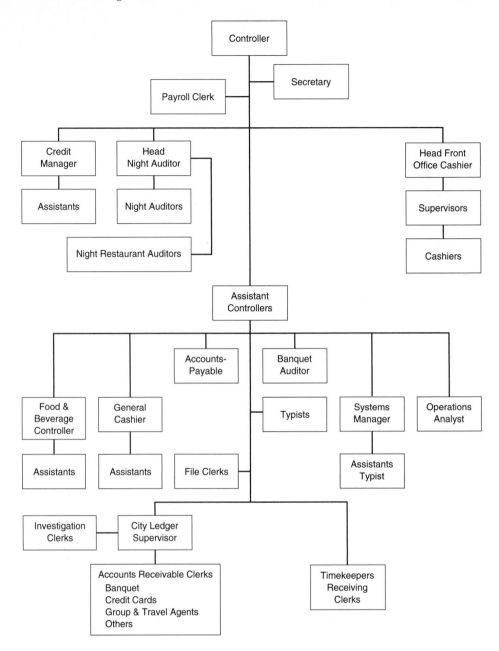

Figure 16-1   Organization Chart—Accounting Department

two or more functions may be combined, but the individual functions always exist and must be performed. However, their magnitude may be such that it does not justify the need for a particular employee. Furthermore, the structure may be modified because of the desires of management or the preference of the individual controller. The order in which the individual subsections are reviewed is based, not on their respective sizes, but rather the degree to which they must be continually involved with the operating departments.

FRONT-OFFICE CASHIERS

The separation of duties between operations and accounting is one of the most fundamental principles of internal control in all businesses. However, in a hotel we commonly find the operational position of receptionist combined with an accounting function, that of the front-office cashier. Except in very large hotels, there are times of the day or periods of the year when two people at the front desk cannot be economically justified. The receptionist greets and registers the incoming guest; the cashier checks out and obtains settlement from the departing guest. Both functions must be performed in the same area: the front desk. Therefore, combining the two roles can be easily accomplished.

NIGHT AUDIT

A similar situation occurs with the night auditor when the cost of a night receptionist cannot be justified, and the night reception function is covered by the night auditor. The principle difference is that during the day you find the cashiering function performed by a receptionist, an employee whose line of reporting is to the front desk manager, a part of operations (see Figure 5-1), while at night the night auditor carries out an operational function—reception but always reports to accounting. However, the night auditor has a dotted-line responsibility to the front office manager for the operational activities carried out. The responsibilities of the night auditor, and the front office cashiers, are explained in detail in Chapter 18.

CREDIT

While a medium-sized or larger hotel generally has, if not a credit department, at least a credit manager, in a smaller hotel the function is frequently performed in part by either the front-office manager or an assistant manager and in part by the city ledger department. The granting of credit and the monitoring of in-house credit often requires direct contact by the guest and can be delegated to rooms department management while the follow-up and collection of overdue accounts is delegated to city ledger employees. Again, the function exists, but the volume cannot support or justify an employee to carry it out. The credit function is covered in detail in Chapter 22.

ASSISTANT CONTROLLERS

While small properties frequently have no assistant controller, a very large property may have two or more assistants; it is strictly a function of size and volume. The functions and areas within the accounting department are divided up between the assistants on an arbitrary basis. However, when there are two assistants, the most common practice is to delegate the day-to-day bookkeeping and accounting including the month-end closing to one assistant while the other is responsible for reports, systems, budgeting, and special projects. In a larger property the latter functions would be handled by the systems manager.

BANQUET AUDITOR

The banquet auditor can be considered an extension of the night audit inasmuch as the function involves the verification of revenue. However, as explained in Chapter 18, it necessitates working closely with both accounts payable and the banquet sales and service staff. Consequently, it is much easier to perform the banquet audit during normal working hours rather than at night.

ACCOUNTS PAYABLE

Chapter 21 is devoted exclusively to the accounts payable function. Accounts payable is a key area in the accounting process, as it is the mechanism that audits and controls most of the operating costs and expenditures and determines to which department expenses should be charged. The responsible individual or individuals must deal with both management and vendors on a friendly but firm basis; always alert to the possibility of error or impropriety.

Accounts payable works extremely closely with purchasing and receiving, as incorrect vendor billings usually result from incorrect pricing or the failure to deliver the proper quantity or quality. Delivery of an incorrect item resulting in it being returned for credit also involves these two areas. However, the frequent need for management approvals requires interfacing with all departments of the hotel.

FOOD AND BEVERAGE CONTROLLER

Whereas we have previously discussed positions where for cost and productivity reasons an individual performs work both of an operational and accounting/control nature, the food and beverage controller's normal activities fall into the scope of both food and beverage operations and accounting. Operationally the food and beverage controller is the analytical arm of the food and beverage director. As such, the diversified duties may include:

1. Test menu items for quality and taste.
2. Obtain samples from purveyors of both ingredients and supplies in order to complete a survey on quality and price.
3. Work with the chef on menu yields.
4. Eat and drink in competitive restaurants or lounges—known as *competitive shopping.*
5. Prepare comparisons of the productivity of individual servers or kitchen personnel.
6. Analyze sales to determine the popularity and profitability of various items—called *abstracting the menu.*

The responsibilities related to accounting involving the preparation of various reports on inventory consumption and costs are explained in detail in Chapter 19.

GENERAL CASHIER

General cashier is a purely accounting function that is principally related to revenue control and accounts receivable. A detailed description of the duties related to revenue control is found in Chapter 18, while the other elements of the function are described in Chapter 16. In terms of necessary communication with other departments, this occurs with both the front desk and the food and beverage outlets on a daily basis. Within the accounting department, communication with accounts receivable personnel is also very important.

CITY LEDGER

In a large hotel you may find more employees in city ledger than there are in the entire accounting department in a small property. Volume in terms of numbers of accounts and transactions is the determining factor in establishing the requisite staffing for this area.

The supervisor must be very well organized and possess excellent communicative skills, as there is daily contact, both by mail and on the telephone, with former and potentially future guests. It is quite possible for the responsibilities to reach a level where the supervisor of the department acquires the title of assistant controller.

Internally inaccurate billings result from mistakes at the front desk or in the food and beverage department. Good communication with them is therefore essential. Differences on group billings between numbers or amounts charged and the contractual agreements also requires a close working relationship with both the sales and banquet staffs. Chapter 17 describes the function and responsibilities in detail.

SYSTEMS MANAGER

As previously mentioned, systems management is frequently the responsibility of an assistant controller. While the major function of computer systems in hotels involves servicing the accounting area, various operating departments also have computer requirements. The need to place all computer system decisions in the hands of one individual cannot be overemphasized. Without it the proper integration of the various systems in use cannot be attained. In Chapter 18 property management systems are described. In addition to accounting, these systems serve reservations, front desk, bell staff, and, provided they contain a guest history segment, sales and marketing.

Other systems-serving operations are telephone and communications, purchasing, utility consumption and environmental control, sales and marketing information, banquet booking, recipe and menu specifications, and, as described in Chapter 19, various segments of the point of sales systems.

OPERATIONS ANALYST

This position should, perhaps, be shown on the organization chart with a dotted line, as the role of the operations analyst is to provide operations with any form of analysis requested in the interests of improving operations or making changes to specific areas. However, as many hotels cannot justify the cost of a full-time operations analyst, the function is frequently delegated to the controller and his or her assistants. Additionally, when a full-time analyst is employed, the necessary research for the assigned project usually requires information or numbers, the source of which is the accounting department.

PAYROLL

In Chapter 20, it is emphasized that for most hotels payroll preparation is done by a payroll service company, and the hotel accounting function is one of verification and input of hours and periodic audit of master file information normally provided to the computer service by the human resources department. Support is sometimes provided by timekeepers, but the timekeeping duties are primarily surveillance of the time clocks and have frequently been delegated to security or receiving.

However, good relationships with the other departments are essential, as an employee who feels that the hours for which he or she was paid are incorrect usually heads for the accounting department first. However, the final resolution usually involves the employee's direct supervisor.

SUMMARY

On the organization chart typists and clerks are indicated in various areas. The degree to which they are required or necessary depends on the volume of work with proper consideration as to whether time-consuming tasks should be performed at a lower labor cost.

Ultimately, it must be remembered that a major function of the accounting department is to provide support for all areas of operations. When called upon for that support, the staff must always be ready and willing to provide it.

THE UNIFORM SYSTEM OF ACCOUNTS FOR THE LODGING INDUSTRY

History

The first edition of the *Uniform System of Accounts for Hotels* was prepared in 1925/1926 by a group of accountants at the request of the Hotel Association of New York City. In March 1926, it was formally accepted and copyrighted by that organization. In September of that year, the American Hotel and Motel Association, then operating as the American Hotel Association of the United States and Canada, at the recommendation of the local association, passed a resolution adopting The Uniform System of Accounts for Hotels.

Another important accomplishment of the accounting committee was the organization of the Hotel Accountants Association of New York City. Through the years, the accounting committee of the organization has periodically updated and revised the manual.

In October 1996, the ninth edition was released. It featured a name change to the *Ninth Revised Edition of The Uniform System of Accounts for the Lodging*

(USAL) Industry. The significant other changes are reviewed later in this chapter. However, it continues to be the bible for the hotel industry.

In a similar manner the Uniform System format has been used to create systems for use in restaurants and clubs. Specifically, the *Uniform System of Accounts for Restaurants* has been developed by the National Restaurant Association and the *Uniform System of Accounts for Clubs* by the Club Managers of America. The uses and advantages subsequently described in this chapter equally apply to the other two systems. Their form is similar but with fewer departments and complexities.

The *Expense and Payroll Dictionary*

A companion booklet published by the American Hotel and Motel Association is the *Expense and Payroll Dictionary.* The dictionary was originally created by a firm of hotel accountants for their staff to use in classifying expense and payroll items in conformity with the Uniform System of Accounts and has been updated and revised by the American Hotel and Motel Association to conform with each revision of the Uniform System.

The dictionary is divided into two parts. Part One lists just about every conceivable item or product that can be purchased, or service contracted for, in the operation of a hotel. (Excluded are items purchased for resale, such as food and beverages, since their costs are charged against sales in the affected department.) Opposite each item is listed the expense department and subclassification to which it should be charged. Here are some examples:

Baggage tags	Rooms	Printing and stationary
Boiler repairs	Repairs and maintenance	Plumbing and heating
Napkins—linen	Food and beverage	Linens
Napkins—paper	Food and beverage	Paper supplies

Similarly, Part Two lists the various job classifications, opposite each, the department and subclassification. All wages for each department are normally shown in one amount; the subclassifications are used only for comparison purposes when analyzing or preparing special payroll reports. Examples are:

Bellmen	Rooms	Service front
Cashiers—restaurant	Food and beverage	General cashiers
Cashiers—front office	Administrative and general	Front office—accounting
Painters	Repairs and maintenance	Painters and paperhangers

Despite its name, the dictionary does not define any of these items or job classifications; it merely lists them alphabetically. Nevertheless, there is no question that it has contributed to the universal acceptance and success of the Uniform System of Accounts.

Concept of the System

The Uniform System is not merely a recommended accounting system for hotels. It formalizes the entire structure and departmentalization now commonly in use in the industry. The Uniform System provides for a series of departments into which the organization of the hotels is structured. These departments can be divided into two broad categories—revenue-producing departments or, as they are called, operated departments, and overhead departments. Operated departments exist for each type of revenue derived by the hotel operation. Obviously, this can vary from hotel to hotel, but the most common are Rooms, Food, Beverages, Telecommunications, Guest Laundry, and Garage. Where there are individual shops within the hotel that the hotel actually operates, these require individual departments. Such other sources such as golf courses and swimming pools would, if they were revenue producing, similarly become operated departments. Hotels have had the option of operating the food and beverage department as a combined entity or as two separate departments. However, the ninth edition dictates that they be two separate departments.

While the logic for mandating two departments is the ability to use new technology to separate costs, the authors feel that the allocation of service payroll between the two areas is quite arbitrary.

The overhead departments, as contained in the ninth edition of the *Uniform System,* are the following: Administrative and General; Human Resources, Information Systems, Security, Marketing, Utility Costs; Franchise Fees; Transportation; and Property Operation and Maintenance. The overhead departments are also referred to as "support" departments. However, it should be recognized that some of these departments will, in certain hotels, be nonexistent or too minor to justify separation of costs.

The Uniform System seeks not only to define the organization of each department in terms of classification of the employees but also to define the expenses that must be charged against the department. The defining of individual positions or their assignment to a specific department serves not only to provide a payroll breakdown by department for cost purposes, but also to determine the reporting responsibility for each job classification. For example, all employees whose job classification falls within the rooms department in the Uniform System should be reporting either directly or indirectly to the person who is responsible for managing that department. Table 16-1 is an example of a chart of accounts for a hotel operation using the Uniform System format, based on the ninth edition of the book. As with all hotels, it has been customized.

Table 16-1 Chart of Accounts, Uniform-System Format

Account Title	Account Number
Cash	
House Banks	11-1000
Payroll Acct.	11-1005
Operating Acct.	11-1006
Escrow Acct.	11-1007
Accounts Receivable	
Guest Ledger	13-1024
City Ledger	13-1025
Miscellaneous	13-1026
Allowance for Doubtful Accts.	13-1012
Inventories	
Food	15-1062
Beverage	15-1063
Miscellaneous	15-1068
Prepaid Expenses	
General Insurance	23-1101
Maintenance Contracts	23-1102
Workers' Compensation	23-1105
Licenses	23-1106
Miscellaneous	23-1108
Fixed Assets and Depreciation	
Building	18-1210
Furniture, Fixtures, and Equipment	19-1282
Automotive Equipment	19-1272
Land	17-1220
Accumulated Depreciation	22-1300
Other Assets	
Security Deposits	23-1405
Investments	23-1410
Accounts Payable—Trade and Concessions	
Trade Creditors	37-1500
Tenant Lease Security Deposits	37-1501
Unclaimed Wages	37-1518
Valet	37-1503
Store #1	37-1504
Store #2	37-1505
Store #3	37-1506
Concessions #1	37-1507
Concessions #2	37-1508
Concessions #3	37-1509
Banquet Miscellaneous	37-1510
Safe Deposit Box Deposits	37-1515
Others	37-1520
Accounts Payable—Banquet	
Banquet Payable—Florist	37-1581
Banquet Payable—Newsstand	37-1582
Banquet Payable—Musicians	37-1583
Banquet Payable—Checkroom	37-1584
Banquet Payable—Other	37-1585

Account Title	Account Number
Taxes Payable and Accrued	
Federal Income Tax	38-1601
State Unemployment Insurance	39-1602
Federal Unemployment Insurance	39-1603
FICA Tax	39-1604
State Sales Tax	37-1605
Occupancy Tax	37-1606
State Use Tax	37-1607
Deferred Federal Income Tax	45-1608
Beverage Tax	37-1609
Entertainment Tax	37-1610
Accrued Expenses	
Salaries and Wages	37-1625
Vacations	37-1626
Electricity	37-1627
Water and Sewer	37-1628
Gas	37-1629
Telephone	37-1630
Audit Fees	37-1631
Group Insurance	37-1632
Savings Plan	37-1633
Workers' Compensation	37-1634
Retirement Plan	37-1635
Sundry	37-1636
Debt, Capital Stock, and Surplus	
Mortgage Payable	52-1650
Paid-in Surplus	54-1675
Retained Earnings	55-1676
Rooms	
Sales—Transient (Individual)	310-1801
—Golf (Individual)	310-1802
—Corporate (Individual)	310-1803
—Group (Corporation)	310-1804
—Group (Tour and Travel)	310-1805
—Group (Association)	310-1806
—Group (Sports)	310-1807
Sales Allowances	310-1808
Salaries and Wages	
Salaries and Wages—Front Office	310-2021
Salaries and Wages—Housekeeping	310-2022
Salaries and Wages—Bell Staff	310-2033
Holiday and Vacation Pay	310-2060
Employee Payroll Taxes and Benefits	310-2065
Employee Meals	310-2070
Expenses	
Cable TV	310-5008
China and Glassware	310-5009
Cleaning Supplies	310-5010
Commissions	310-5011
Contract Cleaning	310-5012

(*continued*)

Account Title	Account Number
Decorations	310-5013
Dry Cleaning	310-5016
Equipment Rental	310-5017
Guest Entertainment	310-5023
Guest Supplies	310-5027
Guest Parking and Transportation	310-5028
Laundry	310-5040
Linen	310-5042
Office Supplies and Postage	310-5050
Printing and Stationary	310-5056
Reservation Expense	310-5060
Telephone	310-5067
Travel Expenses	310-5068
Uniforms	310-5072
Miscellaneous	310-5099
Food	
Food Sales	
Sales—Outlet 1	320-1825
—Outlet 2	320-1826
—Room Service	320-1827
—Banquets	320-1828
Sales Allowances	320-1829
Other Income	
Cover Charges	320-1875
Public Room Rentals	320-1876
Banquet Miscellaneous	320-1877
Banquet Service Charges	320-1878
Cost of Sales	
Food	320-3001
Cost of Employee Meals	320-3003
Salaries and Wages—Kitchen	320-2121
—Service	320-2122
—Administration	320-2123
Holiday and Vacation Pay	320-2060
Employee Payroll Taxes and Benefits	320-2065
Employee Meals	320-2070
Expenses	
Banquet Expenses	320-5003
China and Glassware	320-5009
Cleaning Supplies	320-5010
Commissions	320-5011
Contract Cleaning	320-5012
Contract Labor	320-5013
Decorations	320-5016
Dry Cleaning	320-5017
Dues and Subscriptions	320-6015
Entertainment	320-7010
Equipment Rental	320-5023
Guest Supplies	320-5027
Ice	320-5032

Account Title	Account Number
Kitchen Fuel	320-5036
Laundry	320-5040
Licenses and Permits	320-5041
Linen	320-5042
Menus	320-5045
Music and Entertainment	320-5046
Office Supplies	320-5050
Paper Supplies	320-5054
Postage and Telegrams	320-5055
Printing and Stationary	320-5056
Silver	320-5064
Telecommunications	320-5067
Travel	320-5068
Uniforms	320-5072
Utensils	320-5073
Miscellaneous	320-5099
Beverages	
Sales—Outlet 1	330-1851
—Outlet 2	330-1852
—Bar	330-1853
—Room Service	330-1854
—Banquet	330-1855
Sales Allowances	330-1856
Banquet Service Charges	330-1878
Cost of Sales	
Beverage	330-3002
Salaries and Wages	330-2221
Holiday and Vacation Pay	330-2060
Employee Payroll Taxes and Benefits	330-2065
Employee Meals	330-2070
Expenses	
Bar Expense	330-5004
Glassware	330-5009
Cleaning Supplies	330-5010
Decorations	330-5016
Dry Cleaning	330-5017
Dues and Subscriptions	330-6015
Entertainment	330-7010
Equipment Rental	330-5023
Guest Supplies	330-5027
Ice	330-5032
Laundry	330-5040
Licenses and Permits	330-5041
Wine Lists	330-5045
Music and Entertainment	330-5046
Office Supplies	330-5050
Paper Supplies	330-5054
Printing and Stationery	330-5056
Telecommunications	330-5067
Travel	330-5068

(*continued*)

Account Title	Account Number
Uniforms	330-5072
Miscellaneous	330-5099
Telecommunications	
Revenue—Local	350-1901
—Long Distance	350-1902
—Pay Phone Commissions	350-1903
Allowances	350-1905
Cost of Calls—Local	350-3006
—Long Distance	350-3007
Rental of Equipment	350-3008
Salaries and Wages	350-2321
Holiday and Vacation Pay	350-2060
Employee Payroll Taxes and Benefits	350-2065
Employee Meals	350-2070
Equipment Changes	350-5024
Printing and Stationery	350-5056
Uniforms	350-5072
Miscellaneous	350-5099
Guest Laundry	
Sales	600-1925
Cost of Sales	600-3009
Salaries and Wages	600-2421
Holiday and Vacation Pay	600-2060
Employee Payroll Taxes and Benefits	600-2065
Employee Meals	600-2070
Contract Cleaning	600-5012
Printing and Stationery	600-5056
Supplies	600-5099
Miscellaneous	600-5099
Store Rentals and Other Income	
Store Rentals—#1	450-1951
—#2	450-1952
—#3	450-1953
Concessions—#1	450-1954
—#2	450-1955
—#3	450-1956
Commissions—#1	450-1957
—#2	450-1958
—#3	450-1959
Other Income—Forfeit Deposits	450-1960
—Cash Discounts	450-1961
—Salvage Sales	450-1962
—Miscellaneous	450-1963
Administrative and General	
Salaries and Wages—Accounting	500-2521
—Administrative	500-2522
Holiday and Vacation Pay	500-2060
Employee Payroll Taxes and Benefits	500-2065
Employee Meals	500-2070
Audit Fees	500-6002

Account Title	*Account Number*
Bank Charges	500-6004
Cashier's Short (and Over)	500-6006
Contract Services	500-5013
Credit Card Commissions	500-6009
Credit and Collection Expenses	500-6010
Data Processing Expenses	500-6013
Donations and Contributions	500-6014
Dues and Subscriptions	500-6015
Entertainment	500-7010
Equipment Rental	500-5023
Guest Loss and Damage	500-6018
Legal Fees	500-6025
Licenses and Permits	500-6026
Manager's Expenses	500-6030
Office Supplies	500-5050
Postage and Telegrams	500-6034
Printing and Telegrams	500-5056
Provision for Bad Debts	500-6035
Telecommunications	500-5067
Travel Expenses	500-5068
Uniforms	500-5072
Miscellaneous	500-5099
Marketing	
Sales	
Salaries and Wages	520-2621
Holiday and Vacation Pay	520-2060
Employee Payroll Taxes and Benefits	520-2065
Employee Meals	520-2070
Contract Services	520-5013
Dues and Subscriptions	520-6015
Entertainment	520-7010
Equipment Rental	520-5023
Guest History	520-7015
Operating Supplies	520-7020
Photography	520-7025
Postage and Telegrams	520-6034
Telephone	520-5067
Travel	520-5068
Trade Shows	520-7035
Miscellaneous	520-5099
Advertising and Merchandising	
Agency Fees	530-7501
Brochures	530-7504
Direct Mail	530-7507
Hotel Representatives	530-7512
In-House Graphics	530-7515
Local Media	530-7520
Marketing Fees	530-7525
Point of Sales Materials	530-7530
Print—Directories	530-7541

(*continued*)

Account Title	Account Number
Print—Magazines	530-7542
—Newspapers	530-7543
Production	530-7548
Radio and TV	530-7550
Trade Agreements	530-7560
Miscellaneous	530-5099
Utility Costs	
Electric Bulbs	570-8001
Electricity	570-8002
Fuel	570-8005
Sewage	570-8008
Steam	570-8009
Water	570-8012
Property Operation and Maintenance	
Salaries and Wages	580-2721
Holiday and Vacation Pay	580-2060
Employee Payroll Taxes and Benefits	580-2065
Employee Meals	580-2070
Air Conditioning	580-8501
Building	580-8502
Contract Labor	580-5013
Curtains and Drapes	580-8505
Electrical and Mechanical Equipment	580-8508
Elevators	580-8510
Engineering Supplies	580-8512
Equipment Rental	580-5023
Floor Coverings	580-8515
Furniture	580-8516
Grounds and Landscaping	580-8520
Kitchen Equipment	580-8524
Laundry Equipment	580-8528
Office Supplies	580-5050
Painting and Decorating	580-8532
Plumbing and Heating	580-8535
Printing and Stationery	580-5056
Refrigeration	580-8538
Removal of Waste	580-8539
Service Contracts	580-8543
Snow Removal	580-8544
Swimming Pool	580-8545
Television	580-8548
Uniforms	580-5072
Vehicles	580-8553
Miscellaneous	580-5099
Human Resources	
Salaries and Wages	620-2821
Holiday and Vacation Pay	620-2060
Payroll Taxes	
FICA/Medicare	620-2062
Federal Unemployment	620-2063

Account Title	Account Number
State Unemployment	620-2064
Social Insurances	
Health Insurance	620-2067
Workers' Compensation	620-2068
Savings Plan	620-2069
Employee Relations and Other Personnel	
Employee Relations	620-9001
Medical Expenses	620-9004
Personnel Recruitment	620-9006
Postage and Telegrams	620-6034
Printing and Stationery	620-5056
Telephone	620-5067
Miscellaneous	620-5099
Fixed Charges	
Insurance—Liability and General	650-9004
Insurance—Buildings and Contents	650-9005
Taxes—Real Estate	650-9010
—Personal Property	650-9011
Interest—Mortgages	650-9020
—Notes	650-9021
—Other	650-9023
Depreciation—Buildings	650-9030
—Furniture and Equipment	650-9031
Management Fees	650-9050

The first pages of the table set out the balance-sheet accounts by category and the individual asset and liability accounts that fall within each subheading. The detailed description of each account is provided by the Uniform System. However, it should be noted that in the balance sheets certain accounts may be grouped under one heading; the principal change from prior editions is the elimination of Preopening Expenses as an asset. The ninth edition specifies that such expenses should be written off as incurred. On the following pages, those accounts making up the operating statement, both revenue and expenditure, are shown in detail. In this example, there are only five operated departments—Rooms, Food, Beverage, Telephone, and Guest Laundry. An additional income category, "Store Rentals and Other Income," is also listed in the chart of accounts. The overhead departments are the standard five: Administrative and General, Human Resources, Marketing, Utility Costs, and Property Operation and Maintenance. "Fixed Charges" are also included.

Each department is set out in a vertical column, with the applicable revenue and expense classifications listed by department. Note that in both the revenue and expenditure areas, a certain type of revenue or expense may appear in more than one department. For example, "payroll" is shown in all departments, and "printing and stationary" is applicable to six of the seven departments. Many accounts, however, fall only into one specific department; for example, "bad debts" is applicable only in Administrative and General. Again, the Uniform System provides a detailed description of every expense applicable to every department. Within the scope of the Uniform System, there is the opportunity for a hotel to expand the chart of accounts to show material items separately. This has been done in the exhibited chart of accounts with those items most common to hotels.

Other changes in the ninth edition that should be noted are:

1. General insurance has been removed from "Administrative and General" and is now included with the property insurance in "Fixed Charges."
2. "Energy Costs" has been changed to "Utility Costs."
3. Initial purchases of linen, china, glass, and silver are written off over a period of not more than 36 months and all replacements are expensed. Reserve stocks are included in inventories and expensed when put into circulation.
4. Banquet gratuities or service charges are included in income, and the distribution thereof is included in payroll. This may result in sales taxes not otherwise payable.

The advantages of the Uniform System to the hotel industry are substantial. It provides a uniformity of departmentalization and of classification of assets and liabilities, revenue, and expenditures. What this means to the industry is that job classifications do not vary from hotel to hotel, nor are they included in one department in one hotel and elsewhere in another. Thus, formalized guidelines are available consistently for use by management and personnel as well as accounting throughout the industry.

This consistent classification, particularly of revenue and expenditures, permits comparison of one operation to another. Several firms prepare annual studies on hotel operations, not only in the United States but worldwide. These studies provide averages and medians for hotel operations within various forms of classification, for instance, old and new, city and resort, owned and managed; and by geographical location, statistics that are prepared and categorized in the format determined by the Uniform System. Thus, any owner or manager is in a position to readily compare his or her operation to the average. This is particularly useful where a large number of hotels are owned by a company whose headquarters is based some distance away. Similarly, the Uniform System provides the chains with the ability to compare their operations with those of individual hotels. Individual hotel managers can make comparisons among themselves with the knowledge that within any particular area they are talking about the same thing.

The Uniform System is also an excellent tool in aiding staff training and reducing the amount of time required to familiarize a new employee with the system in use. An employee leaving one hotel that uses it requires only a limited amount of training or indoctrination, being already familiar with the overall concepts of the system in use.

Finally, the Uniform System provides the ability to exercise strong budgetary control. By reference to the system, each department head can be conversant with those expenses, both payroll and other, for which the department has a responsibility. He or she can budget with a full understanding of what must be included, and also police those items of expense charged against the department's budget. Thus, management is enabled not only to demand a high level of budgetary control but to effectively provide the department head with the tools to control the department's results.

CHAPTER SUMMARY

While all accounting functions must be performed, the number of people can vary. One person may perform several functions while others may require several people.
Individual functions are:

1. Front-office cashiers
2. Night audit
3. Credit
4. Assistant controllers
5. Banquet auditor
6. Accounts payable
7. Food and beverage controller
8. General cashier
9. City ledger
10. Systems manager
11. Operations manager
12. Payroll

The Uniform System is not only an accounting system. It performs the following:

1. Establishes an organizational structure for hotels.
2. Determines accounting treatment of income and expenses.
3. Aids staff training.
4. Budgetary control.
5. Permits comparisons between hotels.

The *Expense and Payroll Dictionary* defines where each expense or position belongs.

REVIEW QUESTIONS

1. Is one individual always required for each accounting function, regardless of the size of a hotel?

2. Suggest an area where a member of the accounting staff may also carry out an operational function.
3. When is the banquet audit usually performed?
4. List the duties of the food and beverage controller.
5. What is "abstracting the menu"?
6. Where and when did the Uniform System originate?
7. What is the *Expense and Payroll Dictionary?*
8. What are the most common operated departments?
9. What are the most common overhead departments?
10. Give three examples of expenses that can be found in more than one department.

17

Accounts Receivable and City Ledger

After studying this chapter, the student should:

1. Understand the function of the city ledger department.
2. Be knowledgeable of the various types of accounts in city ledger.
3. Understand the function of investigation clerks.

In a hotel accounts receivable falls into two basic classifications—the *guest ledger*, which represents the amounts owed by guests currently in the hotel, and the *city ledger*, which includes all other amounts owed to the hotel. The handling of the guest ledger is described in detail in Chapter 18. In this chapter we address the city ledger.

Figure 16-1 in Chapter 16 showed an organization chart for the accounting department of a major hotel. One of the major branches of that chart was the city ledger area and the various positions reporting to the "city ledger" supervisor. City ledger is referred to as accounts receivable other than amounts owed by guests still in the hotel. At this point, it is appropriate to more clearly define and explain the term.

In a hotel there are only two basic types of accounts: guest ledger and city ledger. The distinction between the two is simple. The guest ledger includes only the amounts due from guests currently occupying a sleeping room; the city ledger includes all other amounts due. Normally the two amounts are shown separately on the balance sheet. The origin of the term "city ledger" probably relates back to when the only nonguest accounts receivable were amounts owed by local, that is, "in the city," patrons of the restaurants and lounges. Having made a very clear distinction, it is deemed advisable to mention that some hotels carry regular local patrons in their guest ledger during the month, transferring their balance to city ledger at the month end. This only occurs if the customer is being billed monthly and is done as a matter of expedience to avoid having to make daily transfers to city ledger. The balancing and control of the guest ledger is a function of the front desk cashiers and night audit. The procedures related thereto are described in Chapter 18. As with all other accounting areas, the final responsibility for the guest ledger rests with the hotel controller.

RESPONSIBILITIES OF THE CITY LEDGER DEPARTMENT

In a large hotel the level of staffing in the city ledger area can be such that it becomes a department within the accounting department. The primary responsibility thereof is to mail bills and statements to guests who, having been granted credit privileges, did not pay their bills, either partly or fully, at time of departure and to others who did not occupy a room but used other hotel facilities and were granted credit. Included in the responsibility is the mailing of charge vouchers and summaries to those credit companies not being handled as direct deposits in the bank account. The procedure involved in accomplishing this is described in Chapter 23. While the assembling of charge slips and the completion of summaries for credit card bank deposits is normally done by the general cashier, many hotels delegate the function to the city ledger department. However, in this circumstance the completed package is then turned over to the general cashier for completion of the deposit slip and delivery to the bank. The alternative procedure is for the general cashier to accomplish the complete process. Because of the problems that result from charges processed on the incorrect charge voucher, we recommend that all credit card processing be done by the same person or persons. The billing process, other than credit cards, can, however, be divided into specific classifications or segments, which are described in the following paragraphs.

INDIVIDUAL BILLINGS

Individual billings were, at one time, the largest single segment, in terms of number of accounts, in city ledger. However, this is also the segment upon which the introduction of credit cards has had the most impact. It is strongly recommended by the authors that billings to individuals be discouraged through strong enforcement of a credit card-only policy. Vigorous enforcement of such a policy should keep the opening of new accounts to an absolute minimum, while over a period of time these accounts, which predate the advent of credit cards, will slowly die out. It is realistic to expect that any business traveler and most vacation travelers will possess at least one of the commonly accepted cards. In fact, without one it becomes increasingly difficult for any individual to make a hotel reservation. Additionally, the lack of a credit card would seriously bring into question the advisability of granting credit to the person. In today's world the main reason for not owning a credit card is the inability to obtain one due to a poor credit history.

There is, however, one circumstance under which such accounts will continue to be opened. Many local patrons of the restaurants and other facilities do not like to have a bunch of small charges placed on their credit cards. They prefer to receive a monthly statement from the hotel listing their charges. This type of business is highly desirable and considerable marketing is done by hotels to acquire it. However, even this type of account can be regulated by issuing some form of numbered card or I.D. that the patron should present when signing his or her restaurant check. It is important that all outlets have on hand an up-to-date listing of these patrons so no embarrassment is caused because of a lost or mislaid card. Fortunately, also, these customers are usually well known to the staff.

In the case of individual guest folios, the initial billing should be sent out within 24 hours of checkout, including a copy of the guest folio. Care should be taken to ensure that the guest signs the folio at checkout.

CORPORATE ACCOUNTS

These accounts are similar in nature to individual billings in that they involve folios or individual stays or individual charges in the outlets. The difference is, of course, that one company or organization is paying the bills for a varying number of individuals who incur charges at various times during the month. Certain precautions should be taken and a defined policy established relative to such accounts.

The company or organization should, upon opening a *corporate account,* provide the hotel with a list of persons authorized to sign room accounts or other charges on their behalf. A new updated listing should be obtained at least annually. On all other individuals, a letter, signed by an officer of the company, should either be forwarded to the hotel at the time of the reservation or hand carried by the guest and presented at check-in. Both the hotel's registration card and the signature section on the folio should clearly state that the guest has the primary liability for payment of the charges and that in the event the company or organization does not pay, the individual guest will be held responsible. It is recommended that the hotel obtain a credit card number and imprint from the individual, not only for identification purposes, but in the event that certain charges are disputed or unpaid, they can be charged back to the individual. Where overnight stays for that company or organization are a significant number, it is normal policy in the hotel industry to grant such customers a special rate usually referred to as a "corporate" rate. However, any such discounts should be set out in a letter of agreement sent by the hotel to the customer. It should be clearly specified that any failure to reach the required levels of volume will result in discontinuance of the special rate. However, monitoring of the volume levels is usually done by the sales or reservations department utilizing the guest history records and is not normally a function of the accounting department.

A determination must be made relative to corporate accounts as to whether charges will only be billed monthly or immediately after the charges are incurred. It avoids confusing the customer when restaurant charges are only billed monthly. A decision on handling room folios should be the subject of an agreement between the hotel and the customer with due consideration to the volume and dollars involved. A high level of volume would certainly justify billing on a weekly basis or even within 24 hours after checkout. In the latter instance, a complete statement of charges for the month should be sent at month end. However, if complete supporting documents and backup has been sent at checkout, it should not be necessary to repeat the process. While in other industries it is common practice to send billings on a cycle basis other than monthly, the hotel industry has usually adhered to a calendar month cycle. Attempts to do otherwise have not been successful, although the lack of acceptance of this concept by hotel patrons may mostly result from the failure of the industry as a whole to make a serious attempt at adopting it.

GROUPS AND TRAVEL AGENTS

These accounts can also involve substantial amounts, but the principal reason for segregating them is that they require special and rather prompt handling. Groups, and especially conventions, usually entail the accumulation of many individual guest bills into one master account. Some groups or companies pay for all their members' charges; others assume responsibility for room and tax only, with the individual paying his or her own sundry charges; and in some, the individual is liable for all charges—room, tax, and sundries. The group leader should be encouraged to review the master folio on a daily basis. A special invoice format (see Figure 17-1 for an example) should be designed for group billings. While it is recognized that the accumulation of the elements of the billing is time-consuming and frequently requires research, a general policy should be established in writing that such billings should be sent out within 48 hours. However, the most important factor of all is accuracy. A small error of $5 in a $25,000 billing may result in settlement being delayed for a month. In preparing the billing, all elements, for example, room rates, number of nights, meal prices, and so on, should be checked back against the original contract. While it is to be hoped that errors in these areas would have been caught by the front desk or night audit, city ledger still has the final responsibility for the accuracy of the billing.

Travel agents' referrals also require a variety of billing procedures. An agent may book a package tour for any number of guests, which can include room, meals, cocktails, and a show if the hotel has a nightclub, plus tax and possibly even gratuities. The plan might also embrace outside activities—theater tickets,

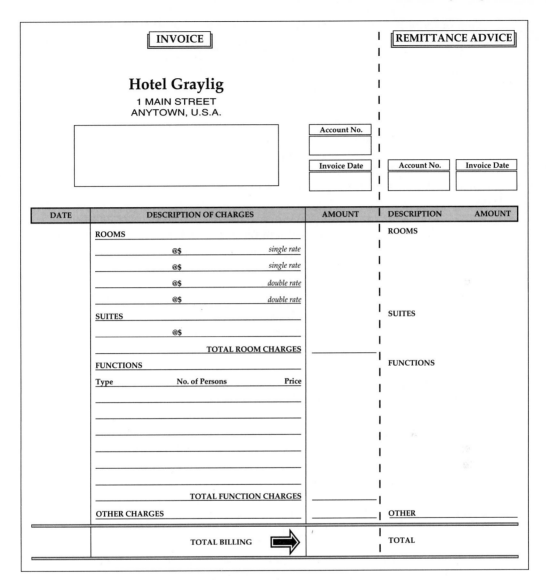

Figure 17-1   Invoice for Group Billing

local sightseeing trips, nightclubs, and so on. The guests pay the travel agent for the complete package and receive a prepaid tour coupon (travel agency voucher) plus, either from the agent or from the hotel at registration, a coupon or ticket for each item included in the itinerary. When using their appropriate coupons in the hotel restaurant, bar, or nightclub, the guest is asked to give them to the person taking the order so that he or she may properly set up the charge to the travel agent. At that time, the guests should be advised of their personal liability for any item ordered that is not included in the package. The same procedure applies to outside restaurants or nightclubs. Sightseeing companies will usually accept a hotel coupon if this has been prearranged, and theatre tickets are normally obtained from a theatre agency, often a concessionaire in the hotel. All these outside firms bill the hotel at an agreed price per person, with the total charge supported by individual coupons, which should be submitted with the invoice. The hotel, in turn, bills the travel agent for the fixed price of the whole plan, enclosing the prepaid tour coupons collected from the guests at registration time to justify the total charges. Obviously, each tour group requires a rather detailed worksheet.

Travel agents also refer individual guests and small groups on a commission basis, which varies. These accounts are normally handled in one of three ways:

1. The travel agent only makes the reservation; the guest is responsible to the hotel for the full amount of his or her charges. The hotel must pay the agent a commission and, to maintain good relations, should do so as soon as the guest checks out, whether the account is paid or not.

2. The travel agent collects the room charges from the guest, either partially or in full, and remits the net amount (total received less commission) to the hotel as a deposit on the reservation. The guest gets a prepaid coupon, which is presented at registration, and receives full credit for the amount paid when checking out.

3. The travel agent collects a deposit from the guest but does not remit any part of it to the hotel. The prepaid voucher, in this instance, serves a dual purpose. It ensures that the guest receives the correct credit at departure, and it substantiates the invoice that the hotel must send to the agent, again for a net amount. Hotels allow this type of settlement only when prior arrangements have been made and the travel agent's credit has been approved.

BANQUET ACCOUNTS

In some hotels banquet accounts may represent a sizable percentage of the total city ledger, whereas in other properties the number of accounts may be insignificant not justifying a separate section in the city ledger. The governing factors are the capacity of the function area and the hotel policy relative to local functions. The determining factor in hotel policy is the degree to which function space must be protected to service group and convention space. The largest type of local banquet business is weddings, which are usually booked well in advance of the event. This requires a major decision on the part of the hotel unless the guest-rooms have already been reserved to near capacity for that date. A hotel cannot afford to lose a group or convention because they cannot provide enough meeting or function space. Therefore, hotels that do a high level of group and convention business must make a policy decision as to how long in advance of a date they will protect function space in order not to lose business, because the space is fully booked with local functions. An exception to this situation would be a hotel that at certain times of the year hosts weddings in outside areas. Normally they can protect against bad weather by use of tents. However, in locations where the temperature in May and June, the heaviest wedding months, is not suited to outdoor functions, a major policy decision must be made. The proper approach is to, within reason, protect the public areas as function business is not good business if it results in empty guestrooms. The ideal situation is, of course, to have a large block of rooms committed to by wedding attendees.

Weddings and other social functions present a higher than average credit risk so advisable procedure is to require a large deposit based on the estimated bill and preferably full settlement on the day of the function. To do otherwise may result in the responsibility for the balance being tossed back and forth from the bride's family to the groom's family.

In Chapter 18, the procedures required to ensure proper billing are described in detail. If those procedures are adhered to vigorously and combined with a stringent credit policy, the volume of banquet city ledger and hence the risk of bad debt loss can be kept to a low level. For those hotels who cater principally to individual transient room business but who have sizable function space, local banquets can be a significant portion of their total volume.

OTHER ACCOUNTS

The final billing responsibility encompasses all other city-ledger balances. Included in this group are *after-departure charges.* As the term indicates, these represent items that were not included on the bill when the guest checked out. If the guest paid the account in full, these guests create an unpaid balance. If the guest charged the account, the amount due increases. Merely billing the guest is not sufficient. An explanation, sometimes an apology, and always a photocopy of the charge, should accompany the statement. This approach not only promotes good guest relations but aids tremendously in the collection of the item. Fortunately, the common practice of requiring a credit card number at the time of the reservation has significantly reduced the volume of after-departure charges.

INVESTIGATION CLERKS

Maintaining good guest relations is the principal—really, the only—responsibility of the *investigation clerks.* Indeed, they are sometimes referred to as members of the customer service department. All their tasks must be directed toward that goal. They are often the final contact the guests have with the hotel and sometimes the only one after they check out—a very important contact, since it occurs only when a guest asks for assistance. There is nothing more infuriating or frustrating than the feeling of being ignored. A prompt reply, whether to comply with the guest's wishes or to ask for additional information, is the only way to ensure the guest's goodwill. The investigation clerks handle all requests, questions, or disputes relating to the guest's account, ranging from a simple request for a duplicate bill to a claim that partial or full payment was made and no credit shown on the statement. They also handle requests from travel agents for unremitted commissions.

Because of voluminous correspondence, most large hotels have set up form letters (see Figure 17-2) to facilitate the handling of these requests. Some go so far as to immediately acknowledge receipt of the request, assign a reference number to it in case additional correspondence is necessary, and advise the guest that the inquiry will be processed as soon as possible. *Caution:* In the attempt to expedite these requests, a hotel may incur unnecessary expenses that in the aggregate can amount to a substantial loss. Two mistakes in judgment are most common, and both can occur on a single transaction—a guest's justifiable complaint of an erroneous charge. To illustrate:

A guest complains that although he or she had no restaurant charges while in the hotel, one appeared on the bill. The investigation clerk pulls out the restaurant check and verifies the fact that it was an erroneous charge. The fastest and easiest way to adjust the error is to write off the charge and send the guest a refund for the amount. The guest is satisfied, but the hotel has incurred a loss, possibly double the amount of the charge. Obviously, the fact that a restaurant check exists indicates that some guest incurred the charge. Thus, the correct procedure is to identify the other guest, obtain a billing address through a folio or registration card, set up a city-ledger account if none exists, and transfer the charge to this account. In this way, the account of the guest who was incorrectly charged is automatically credited, and the hotel suffers no loss of revenue.

The second mistake is to authorize a refund without first verifying that the account was paid in full. If it was not, then the transfer reduced the balance due, and all that need be done is to send a corrected bill with a letter thanking the guest for calling attention to the overcharge. The invoice to the guest who incurred the charge, with a photocopy of the restaurant check, should be enclosed in a letter explaining and apologizing for the delay in billing the item.

The refund of an overcharge to a guest whose account is still open does not necessarily result in a loss to the hotel. In the vast majority of cases, the guest will subsequently pay the full amount, including the overcharge, but some will not. There have been many cases where the guest accepted the refund but still deducted the erroneous charge from the remittance. Collecting this balance is at best time-consuming and expensive, and it is frequently irritating to the guest, who cannot understand why he or she should pay for a charge that was not incurred. The greatest loss results from a refund to someone who never pays the account, which eventually has to be written off as a bad debt. Fortunately, this does not happen very often, but it does happen. Some years ago, the authors encountered

Hotel Graylig
1 MAIN STREET · ANYTOWN, USA

(Insert name and address
of travel agent)

Dear _____

  We acknowledge receipt of your request for commission on the stay of _(name of guest)_ for the period from _(date of arrival)_ to _(date of departure)._

  We will follow up on your request and research our records immediately. Since this process involves searching historical records there may be a short delay before we respond.

  If however you do not receive payment or an explanation within 14 days please contact us immediately.

Yours Sincerely

Janet Smith
Accounts Receivable Supervisor

Figure 17-2 Form Letter to Respond to Commission Requests

a very substantial bad debt write-off that included the account of a bus tour operator in bankruptcy. The itemization of this account showed that the company had erroneously been given a refund by check of over $2,000 for room-rental over-charges on a tour it had booked just two months before declaring bankruptcy.

Such an incident not only demonstrates the need for internal controls, it also shows that the responsibilities of the accounting department extend beyond the universally accepted functions of controlling the income and operating expenses of a hotel.

GENERAL CASHIER

In Chapter 18, the duties of the general cashier, as they relate to the auditing and recording daily front office and food and beverage deposits, are described. Earlier in this chapter a further reference is made to the general cashier's responsibility to assemble and deposit credit card submissions. In addition to the aforementioned, the daily deposit contains two other elements: accounts receivable remittances and miscellaneous other receipts.

Most payments of accounts are received through the mail, and necessary safeguards to protect those receipts must be established. The primary point of control is at the opening of the incoming mail. All mail should be opened by an employee who is neither an accounting department employee nor has any participation in the recording of revenue or receipts. Most commonly the task is delegated to the general manager's secretary. A list of incoming checks should be prepared in triplicate—one copy being retained in the mail openers' file, the second accompanying the checks when they are forwarded to the general cashier for deposit, and the third going to the city ledger department to provide detailed information for posting to the individual accounts. After posting, the city ledger department must verify their total against the total city ledger credit recorded by the general cashier. The copy retained by the mail opener serves two purposes: one, to be available in the event that a problem occurs and the receipt of a check must be verified; and two, to be used by the controller as an internal control mechanism to audit and verify the actual deposit details against the checks received.

Miscellaneous payments, such as telephone commissions, receipts from the sale of waste, and so on, will be received through the mail and should be subjected to the same listing procedure. The nature of these receipts and the accounting treatment thereof becomes a responsibility of the general cashier, who must consult with his or her superior when necessary.

The daily front office and food and beverage receipts, as entered on the general cashiers deposit summary, as shown in Figure 18-6, are automatically recorded in the general ledger through the property management system in the manner described in Chapter 18. A second cash receipts journal entry must be made on a daily basis to record the city ledger payments and the miscellaneous receipts. This can be in the form of a standard journal entry posted daily or the amounts can be recorded in a monthly cash receipts journal and posted at month end.

The general cashier is also responsible for the control and audit of the *house banks*. These are funds in varying amounts issued to front-desk and food and beverage cashiers primarily to make change but also to cash travelers checks and, when approved, personal checks of guests. Other outlets dealing with the public require house banks and even such areas as receiving may need a small bank to handle CODs, freight charges, and so on. The general cashier also has the responsibility for maintaining the hotel petty cash fund, from which authorized cash expenditures are made when required. However, payments in cash should, except for emergencies or extenuating circumstances, be limited to under $25. The general cashier should periodically, at least weekly, prepare a summary of all expenditures together with the supporting vouchers and submit it to accounts payable in order to receive a check that, when cashed, will replenish the petty cash fund. The general cashier is also required to keep on hand a large central cash bank from which to make change for the individual house banks. In total, the house banks in a large hotel can exceed $10,000, and on holiday weekends it may be necessary to temporarily increase the regular amount.

The general cashier should retain the receipts for all house banks issued and together with another accounting employee audit/count all banks monthly. The controller is responsible for counting the funds under the direct control of the general cashier. Since the general cashier, therefore, has access to large amounts in cash, including, of course, the daily deposit, proper procedures are essential to good control. Deposits must be made daily, in consecutive order, and all weekend and holiday deposits must be made on the next banking day. Manipulating the sequence of deposits and misusing the cash included is a method frequently used by dishonest cashiers to cover up their thefts. Checking the consecutive order of the deposits and immediately investigating a missing receipt eliminates this possibility.

ACCOUNTING ENTRIES

The principal reasons for journal entries initiated by the city ledger area are billing errors and disputes. These entries will result in debits to the affected revenue or liability (in the case of incorrect taxes or gratuities) and a credit to accounts receivable. Only in the event that an account is written off purely because it is uncollectible should the debit be made to the bad debt reserve account. Disputes or errors should also be charged back against the revenue accounts. Not only is this proper accounting procedure, but it usually results in saving the sales taxes related to the adjustment. Payments of travel agents' commissions or refunds should be processed through the accounts payable system, as described in Chapter 21.

CHAPTER SUMMARY

Accounts receivable in a hotel are carried either in the guest ledger or in the city ledger. Guest accounts are in the guest ledger. All other receivables are in the city ledger (with the occasional minor exceptions).

The guest ledger is the responsibility of the front-desk cashiers and night audit while the city ledger is the responsibility of the accounting department.

The city ledger is usually segmented as follows:

1. Individual accounts
2. Corporate accounts
3. Groups and travel agents
4. Banquet accounts
5. After-departure charges

Investigation clerks follow up on guest or travel agent inquiries.

The general cashier deposits city ledger payments, miscellaneous payments, and house banks.

Journal entries usually relate to billing errors and disputes.

REVIEW QUESTIONS

1. What type of accounts receivable is not included in the city ledger?
2. What has created a significant reduction in direct billings to individuals?
3. When opening a corporate account for a company's employees, what should the hotel require?
4. In preparing group billings, what should be carefully checked?
5. What credit policy should the hotel adopt on weddings?
6. What are after-departure charges?
7. What should be verified before authorizing a refund?
8. How should incoming payments be handled?
9. What are house banks?
10. What are the principle reasons for journal entries affecting the city ledger?

CASE STUDY

Raquel Marrero is the city ledger supervisor for the San Juan Resort. She has been asked to determine a billing cycle. What would you expect her to recommend?

18

Income Control

After studying this chapter, the student should:

1. Understand the importance of income control.
2. Understand controls over the various income centers.
3. Understand the night audit function.

THE MEANING OF INCOME CONTROL

Simply defined, income control is the attempt to ensure that the hotel obtains full value for its goods and services, and that total revenue is properly recorded and received. Unfortunately, no system has ever been devised to achieve perfect control of income. Human errors cannot be prevented; at best, controls can only discover and correct them. Theft by employees or guests will never be eliminated, and this cost is generally considered a normal operating expense. Controls properly administered and frequently implemented will, however, reduce these losses.

An occupied room for which no rent was charged, food or drinks served but not rung up on a restaurant or bar register, and telephone calls made by guests but not posted on their bills are all examples of income that was never recorded. "Skippers"—guests who check out without paying their bills and have given fictitious names and addresses—represent another kind of income loss. Here, the revenue was properly recorded but will never be received. Such examples show that income control involves more than merely the checking of charges and cash received. It means checking the bartenders, food checkers and cashiers, and waiters and waitresses at their stations while they are working; monitoring all employees who have access to storage areas where uncooked food, beverages, supplies, and other goods are kept; and, in effect, checking on and constantly observing the actions and activities of every employee in the hotel. It also includes inspecting all packages they carry out of the hotel. (This inspection, normally made by the timekeepers, can be effective only if all employees are required to enter and exit through designated areas.) Finally, it means checking the guests' bills, their charges, and even their actions. (For details, see Chapter 22, "Credit.")

Some may disagree with this broad definition. Theft and uncollected guest accounts are not normally associated with income control. But they both result in loss of income—one a loss of what should have been realized from the sale of the stolen goods, the other a loss due to bad debts. Minimizing such losses is important and should certainly be part of the controller's overall responsibility in setting up and administering procedures for proper income control.

It is difficult, if not impossible, for a controller and his or her staff to monitor every location in the hotel where income can be lost or hotel property stolen. To exercise more supervision and to better control the actions of all employees, the controller must obtain the help of all other department heads and their chief assistants. In fact, this cooperation can be so valuable that we believe these executives should be thoroughly briefed by the controller in all possible infractions so that they can more readily recognize them.

Hotel revenue is derived primarily from the so-called operated departments: rooms, food and beverage, telephone, garage, pool, and so on. Other revenue sources are rentals from store tenants and concessionaires, vending machines, display cases, cash discounts, commissions, salvage sales (of furniture, carpets, and equipment), and the like. This chapter will be devoted exclusively to the control of the two principle sources of revenue—rooms and food and beverages. Control of income from the minor operated departments and other sources is covered in their respective chapters in Section III.

ROOMS

Historically, control over room income has come from two sources: the tracking of occupied rooms from the housekeeping report on room status (described in Chapter 13) and the tracking of the registration card signed by the guest at check-in to the revenue record at night audit.

The housekeeping report prepared in the morning continues to be a valuable tool in verifying the validity of room revenue. Each room that is shown as being occupied should be traced to the night audit record of occupied rooms to verify that all occupied rooms were so recorded.

However, the use of the registration card as a method of income control has, except in small properties, ceased to exist. This has aroused very few regrets in the industry, as the tracking of registration cards was cumbersome and lacked substance. It functioned only when registration cards and folios were printed as a prenumbered package. The completed registration card was matched against the folio in order to verify that revenue was recorded for each signed card. However, cards were frequently lost, misplaced, or even voided, severely limiting the effectiveness of the procedure. Furthermore, the receptionist who wished to give a late arrival an unrecorded room and pocket the cash advance payment would usually be smart enough not to complete a registration card.

Automation in the form of sophisticated software packages specifically designed for hotels has reduced the registration card to a signed verification by the guest of precaptured information. The signed card also represents an acknowledgment of the method of settlement, such as American Express or Visa, and can be used to support an unsigned or disputed credit card charge. Additionally, in the United States and many other countries, a signed registration card must, by law, be obtained and retained in a file for an indefinite period. However, the information reflected thereon is recorded at the time of the reservation and retained in the computer. The systems provide that even a walk-in guest is processed in two steps; first by making a reservation, and then by immediately checking that reservation in.

The industry term to describe these software packages is *Property Management Systems* (PMS). The advent of these systems moved the emphasis on front-desk systems from specialized hardware designed for hotels to specialized software using standard computer hardware. The new systems have the flexibility to utilize hardware made by a number of manufacturers, rather than being limited to one specific brand. See Figure 18-1.

The property management systems were designed to perform four primary functions: reservations, check-in and checkout, guest ledger, and night audit. However, most systems also provide the ability to accumulate *guest history*—information on checked-out guests that is not only invaluable in researching information for billing problems or inquiries but can be used in various formats for marketing purposes (see "Guest History" in Chapter 8). Additionally, the use of standard computer equipment provides the ability to interface directly with back-office accounting systems, energy management systems, in-room movies, and other functions not directly related to the recording or control of revenue or guest ledger.

Income recording procedures used in hotels have always followed a format whereby room revenue (and directly related items such as tax or service charges) are posted at the end of the day by the night auditors, while all other charges (food, beverage, telephone, etc.) are posted during the day as close as practical to the time at which the charge was actually incurred. Automation has not changed this policy. However, the use of computer interfaces has dramatically reduced the amount of manual posting by cashiers. The interface programs automatically transmit the room charges from the restaurant registers to the guest accounts. Telephone charges are measured and recorded by an automatic call accounting

Figure 18-1   Computerized Front Office—with Latest Technology

system (discussed in detail in Chapter 11). Manual postings are reduced therefore to miscellaneous items such as laundry or gift shop charges (except in the event that the interface malfunctions).

POSTING OF CHARGES

The principles involved in the posting of charges have changed in the transition to computerization. The act of posting not only accomplishes the debit to the guest folio but also the credit to the revenue, or in certain instances, the liability account. The transaction is directed to the accounts through the use of *charge codes,* which are entered into the computer along with the amount. A listing of common charge codes is shown in Figure 18-2. The codes are identified with general ledger account numbers and account types (1 = balance sheet account; 2 = revenue account). However, hotels with several F & B outlets will have more extensive lists.

The postings are entered by keying in the charge code number and the amount. The charge codes are programmed to reflect a usual entry as a credit or a debit depending on the item, for example, hitting "Front Desk Cash" and $10 will post a $10 credit to a guest's account while hitting "Restaurant Food" and $10 will post a debit. Negative entries or corrections can be entered with a minus (−)

Charge Code	Description	GL Account	Type
10	Front Desk Cash	11-1527	1
11	" " Amex	11-1527	1
12	" " Visa/MC	11-1527	1
13	" " Diners	13-1025	1
14	Restaurant Cash	11-1527	1
15	" Amex	11-1527	1
16	" Visa/MC	11-1527	1
17	" Diners	13-1025	1
18	Bar Cash	11-1527	1
19	" Amex	11-1527	1
20	" Visa/MC	11-1527	1
21	" Diners	13-1025	1
30	Front Desk Paid Outlets	11-1527	1
35	Rooms Transient	310-1005	2
36	" Group - Corporate	310-1105	2
37	" Association	310-1107	2
38	" Tour and Travel	310-1106	2
40	" Adj. - Transient	310-1005	2
41	" " Group - Corporate	310-1105	2
42	" " Association	310-1107	2
43	" " Tour and Travel	310-1106	2
45	Restaurant Food	320-1301	2
46	" Liquor	330-1401	2
47	" Wine	330-1402	2
48	" Adjustment	320-1301	2
50	Bar Food	320-1302	2
51	" Liquor	330-1401	2
52	" Wine	330-1402	2
53	" Adjustment	320-1301	2
55	Rooms Tax	37-7004	1
56	Food and Beverage Tax	37-7003	1
57	Local Telephone	350-1601	2
58	LD Telephone	350-1602	2
59	Laundry	600-1702	2
60	Valet	600-1701	2
61	Telegrams	450-1834	2
62	Fax	450-1834	2
63	Flowers	37-1021	1
64	Shops	37-1024	1
65	Banquet Gratuities	37-2016	

Figure 18-2   Standard Charge Codes

sign. In certain categories, it is common to provide "Adjustment" keys for the front-desk cashier to use to adjust items disputed at checkout.

In order to fully record the revenue for a day, it is necessary to record the revenue that is not charged to a guest account. This is accomplished through the use of a *house folio*. A house folio is an account set up in the guest ledger in the same manner as a room folio, but used for nonguest transactions. The posting to the house folio for cash sales is made by posting the revenue to the house folio on the revenue charge key and recording the settlement by using a settlement charge code, usually "cash" or "credit card." Thus the house folio is zeroed out at the end of the day. Figure 18-3 is an example of house folio entries for one day. House folios are also used to record city-ledger charges, that is, charges to other than hotel guests. The charges may be cleared out of the guest ledger to the city ledger at the end of the day or the end of the period. House folios are also used for adjustments and corrections in addition to recording cash sales and other sales to nonguests. It is important to note that postings to house accounts are normally done by the night auditors rather than the cashiers.

Night Auditor

The property management system has materially reduced the workload of the night auditor, with the emphasis shifting from the recording of charges and revenue to the running and review of reports.

The recording function is limited to the balancing of food and beverage revenue (described later in the chapter) and the recording of all revenue not automatically posted directly to the guest accounts. House account entries, as described earlier in the chapter, must be made for cash sales, allowances, adjustments, and corrections. Long-distance telephone revenue, usually posted automatically, should also be balanced.

Perhaps the most important function of the night auditor is the review of the "preliminary" night audit—a review of various reports on activity for the day. The preliminary night audit usually involves the following:

1. A review of the *end-of-shift report* run by each cashier or receptionist at the end of their shift. This is a report showing all entries made by that cashier or receptionist.
2. A review of the room charges report. This report shows on a room-by-room basis all charges, such as room revenue, tax, gratuities, food, or special items included in a package. Care should be taken to identify and correct rate errors and to review rate variances—rates that are other than the normal rate for that room.
3. A review of transfers to the city ledger for the day.
4. A review of the printout by charge code of all transactions for the day.

If the preliminary night audit is done with proper care, the final audit is simply a question of running a final report, which usually takes 40–60 minutes

N/A Journal Entries

Date		Description of Charges	Charges	Credits
Mon	Feb 01	Restaurant Food	$2,412.05	
"	"	Restaurant Liquor	732.86	
"	"	Restaurant Wine	306.00	
"	"	Beverage Tax	103.89	
"	"	Food Tax	205.37	
"	"	Cost of Wine	4.80	
"	"	Cost of Liquor	7.30	
"	"	In-House Entertainment		$18.32
"	"	Rest. Room Charge	1,360.97-	
"	"	Rest. Cash		698.33
"	"	Rest. Amex		972.60
"	"	Rest. Visa/MC		722.05
"	"	Bar Liquor	322.11	
"	"	Bar Wine	108.54	
"	"	Beverage Tax	42.99	
"	"	Bar Room Charge	180.12-	
"	"	Bar Cash		112.72
"	"	Bar Amex		82.60
"	"	Bar Visa/MC		98.20
"	"	Bar Wine Correction	22.00-	
"	"	Bar Liquor Correction	22.00	
			$2,704.82	$2,704.82
		Total Account 0.00		

Figure 18-3   Example of a House Folio

for a medium-sized hotel. The final report is a complete history of hotel activity for the day, including not only a record of guest charges and revenue but also all reservation activity and advance deposit activity.

Advance Deposits

When a reservation is entered, it receives a reservation number, which also functions as a folio number in the advance deposit section of the guest ledger. (In some systems, it is a separate ledger but functioning in the same manner as the guest ledger.)

When an advance deposit is received, it is posted to the folio in the same manner as a cashier posts a payment to an in-house folio. Thus a reservationist posting advance deposits must print a shift report, make a cash drop, and so on, in the same fashion as a cashier. This permits a cashier to also function as a reservationist and post advance deposits during his or her regular shift. This flexibility in the system aids reduced staffing in slow periods.

Accounting Office Review

Prior to computerization, an extensive review of the night audit work was carried out by the income controller. This function has been reduced to a review of the night audit printout and report with an emphasis on those functions performed manually by night audit—principally adjustments made and the manual postings of revenue not automatically recorded. This, however, pertains mostly to food and beverage revenue.

FOOD AND BEVERAGES

In this area also, mechanical cash registers have been replaced by electronic registers, which capture sales analyses and provide ready information for the recording of income. The principle for balancing food and beverage remains unchanged: Food + Beverage + Tax + Tips = Cash Sales + Charges (room, city ledger, and credit card).

Registers can produce balanced readings in report form, which can be readily entered by the night auditor into the property management system, providing sales information for the daily revenue report, which subsequently flows into the general ledger. Many of the new food and beverage systems are fully interfaced with the property management system, providing an automatic flow of information and eliminating the need for reentry. However, in addition to providing the cash and charge breakdown and the revenue analysis required for revenue recording, these systems incorporate control features, which provide detailed analyses of revenue, inventory consumption, and costs. These functions are described in greater detail in Chapter 19. While a certain level of management supervision is still necessary, much of this control has now been transferred to computers. By having various levels of computer access, certain functions can be restricted to management. The more common of these functions are the ability to void charges, post charges to entertainment expenses, and transfer the responsibility for a check from one server to another. The final clearing of the day's information (commonly called the "z" report) still remains a night audit function, but while under the old mechanical systems the information was fully deleted, the new systems retain all information in computer memory subject to printing and purging either weekly or monthly. The purging is, however, controlled by accounting management and should not be done at the individual outlet level.

Deposit Procedures

The procedures for the physical dropping of deposits remains basically unchanged. All cashiers (front office, restaurant, bar, garage, and so on) must compute their own receipts, place them in a deposit envelope (Figure 18-4), and drop the envelope in a slotted safe-deposit box provided for this purpose. The envelope should show a breakdown of cash, checks, and other items included in the deposit. On the following day, the general cashier removes them, checks the contents of each against the figures entered on the outside of the envelope, and makes up the daily deposit. Although the contents are rarely verified until the general cashier opens them, the number of envelopes dropped into and removed from the safe should be controlled by having any other front-office or accounting-department employee witness both acts whenever possible. For this purpose, an

Figure 18-4 Cashier's Deposit Envelope

DEPARTMENT
CASHIER'S REPORT

DATE ____________

CASHIER ____________

DEPT. ____________

WATCH ______ A.M. P.M. TO ______ A.M. P.M.

	AMOUNTS		✓
CURRENCY: – FIFTIES and OVER			
TWENTIES			
TENS			
FIVES			
ONES AND TWOS			
SILVER			
DOLLARS			
HALVES			
QUARTERS			
DIMES			
NICKELS			
PENNIES			
PETTY CASH VOUCHERS			
TOTAL CASH ENCLOSED			
REGULAR CHECKS			
TRAVELLERS CHECKS			
TOTAL DEPOSITS			
NET RECEIPTS			
DUE BACK			
FOR RESTAURANT CASHIERS			
TOTAL CASH CHECKS			
LESS TIPS			
NET DEPOSIT OR (DUE BACK)			

Station	Cashier	Witnessed By	Net Deposit	Cash	Checks	Travelers Checks	Petty Cash Vouchers	Total Deposit	Due Back	Received By	Foreign Currency At Cost
Front Office											
AM			1000.00		900.00	250.00		1150.00	150.00		
AM			1500.00	500.00	600.00	400.00		1500.00	–0–		
PM			750.00		300.00	500.00	50.00	850.00	100.00		
PM			750.00		500.00	500.00	100.00	1100.00	350.00		
Night			100.00					100.00	–0–		
Sub Total			4100.00	100.00							
City Ledger			2000.00		2000.00			2000.00			
Total F.O.			6100.00								
Restaurant*											
Banquets											
Total Restaurant			2000.00	2000.00				2000.00			
Bar*											
Total Bar			1000.00	1000.00				1000.00			
Total Food & Bev.			3000.00								
Grand Totals			9100.00	3600.00	4300.00	1650.00	150.00	9700.00	600.00		

Day _____ — GENERAL CASHIER'S DEPOSIT SUMMARY — Breakdown From Envelopes — Date _____ — Do Not Include as Part of Deposit

"D" Card Recap
Cash 9200.00
Paid Out 100.00
Net Deposit as Above 9100.00

Deposit Recap
Total Deposit 9700.00
Less: Due Back 600.00
Net Deposit 9100.00

Number of Envelopes _____
Witness _____

Figure 18-5 General Cashier's Deposit Summary Form

individual sheet for each day (or a bound book) should be provided, with columns for the date, number of envelopes, and signatures of the cashiers and witnesses. When the drop is made, the witness's signature attests that he or she actually saw and counted the number of envelopes deposited into the safe. The following morning, the general cashier totals the number listed, opens the safe in the presence of a witness, and counts the number of envelopes in it; if the total agrees, both the cashier and the witness initial the total on the sheet. The general cashier prepares a deposit analysis and summary (Figure 18-5), which compares the deposits of the individual cashiers and their respective computer readings and computes the overage/shortage amount by individual and in total. Where the individual server also functions as a cashier (server banking is described in Chapter 17), a large number of deposit drops will be made. Where tips paid out exceeds the cash taken in, the difference must be repaid to the cashier out of other receipts. This is known as a "due back." This occurs most often during the breakfast period, when most guests sign their checks and there may not be enough cash taken in to cover the tips paid out.

Banquet Controls

Banquet revenue must be checked and verified by a night auditor who is experienced in verifying banquet revenue. The bills often include so many items and must be so detailed that the possibility of errors is great, making it almost mandatory to assign this function to a well-trained, banquet-oriented person. Banquet bills are prepared by the banquet manager, head waiter, or a designated assistant as soon as a function is over. It is the responsibility of the banquet auditor not only to check that the items listed were correctly priced and extended, but to determine that no items were omitted.

All banquet functions should be covered by a contract or written confirmation, at the discretion of management. Either should include the full menu and complete details of the agreement. Attendance figures can only be estimated, since most functions are booked months, and even years, in advance. However, the customer should be informed of the hotel's policy on guarantees and be required to submit definite figures, in writing, some time before the day of the function. This information is needed not only for billing and control purposes, but by the banquet manager and chef to prepare for the function. The guarantee determines the number of waiters needed, the number of tables to set, and the amount of food to order and prepare.

Banquets benefit almost every revenue-producing department in the hotel. Guests attending a function very often use some of the other facilities. To alert the other department heads and to keep management informed of all bookings, the banquet managers prepare various reports of actual bookings. The period covered and the information included varies in each hotel to conform to the management's policy. As a minimum, these reports should be issued once a month, listing all functions booked for the next month, and updated at the end of each week for the following week. The contents should include at least the date, name of person or organization holding the function, type of function (dinner, dance, dinner dance, or whatever), number of people expected, and any special requirements that might affect other departments. The number of people guaranteed should also be provided to the banquet auditor. In addition, the banquet manager should prepare a separate sheet for each function, with the full menu and all other pertinent information.

Copies of contracts or confirmations that were sent when the functions were booked, all function sheets, and final guarantees must be sent to the banquet auditor. In addition, the banquet manager should be instructed to send a memo of any last-minute changes on guarantees or other terms of the agreement. The banquet auditor needs and uses all this information to properly control the banquet revenue.

In some hotels, to accurately verify the number of covers, the chefs are required to enter on the menu the number served and send that sheet to the banquet auditor. Each auditor must set up his or her own routine to verify revenue, but it should include the following procedures.

It must be determined that a bill was prepared and processed for each function held. This is easily done by checking each bill received against those listed on the weekly function sheet for that day. If possible, the number of covers charged should be verified with the number served, and the charge per cover, as well as the unit charge of all items included on the bill, verified with the function sheet. The bill should then be compared with the function sheet to determine that all items separately listed on the sheet that call for an additional charge are on the bill. Included in

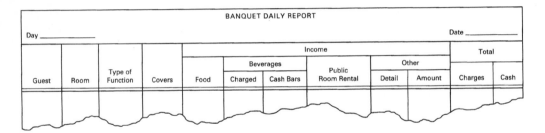

Figure 18-6 Banquet Daily Report

this category are such items as public-room rentals, flowers, music, microphones, photographers, and any extra charge for bartenders. For weddings, extra charges could include wedding cakes, specially printed napkins, matches, and favors.

To verify beverage sales requires an additional step. The function sheet can list only the brands requested by the guest and, if they are to be purchased by the bottle, a minimum quantity and the unit cost. Other methods of charging are by-the-drink or by-the-guest, and in some instances a corkage charge may be added. The bar manager, or a designated assistant, reports the actual number used. This is usually done on a sheet showing the number of bottles issued, the number returned to the storeroom, and the number used. Some will have two additional columns for the unit costs and the total charges. The auditor, after verifying the unit price, can compare the quantities used as shown on this report against the guest's invoice. The final step is to check the extensions, the computations for tax and gratuities, and the total shown on the bill.

What action, if any, the banquet auditor takes for differences between the number of covers charged and the number in the final guarantee depends entirely on the policy established by management. Policies vary between hotels, with guarantees strictly enforced in some while serving only as a guide in others. They may even vary within a hotel, depending on the type of function, sponsor, and so on. All the banquet auditor can do is try to enforce the policy and report any deviation to the hotel controller. Whether to pursue the matter further, by discussing it with the banquet manager or general management, is a decision that only the controller should make.

Finally, the banquet auditor prepares a report (Figure 18-6), which becomes a source document for entering the information into the property management system. Copies of this report are then distributed to designated executives.

ENTRY INTO THE GENERAL LEDGER

The final night audit report includes a total summary of activity for the day shown in a journal entry format. Figure 18-7 is an example of this report using the account numbers shown in Figure 18-2.

A/C No	Account	Debit	Credit
11-1527	Cash	$31,105.20	
13-1025	Accounts Receivable	17,640.05	
37-1021	Flowers		$ 62.00
37-1024	Shops		268.30
37-2016	Banquet Gratuities		1,172.60
37-7003	Food and Beverage Tax		1,705.00
37-7004	Room Tax		1,231.00
310-1005	Rooms Revenue - Transient		16,508.00
310-1105	" " - Group - Corporate		4,702.50
310-1106	" " - " - Tour and Travel		1,520.75
310-1107	" " - " - Association		2,128.60
320-1301	Food Revenue - Restaurant		9,622.70
320-1302	" " - Bar		628.45
330-1401	Liquor Revenue		2,128.40
330-1402	Wine Revenue		4,803.65
350-1601	Local Telephone		240.25
350-1602	Long-Distance Telephone		1,633.20
450-1834	Telegrams and Fax		120.00
600-1701	Valet		109.50
600-1702	Laundry		160.35

Figure 18-7   End of Audit Journal Entry

When the property management system encompasses both front-office and back-office accounting in the same system, the entry is automatically transferred into the general ledger. Even when the two systems differ, an automatic transfer can sometimes be made, provided the two systems are compatible and a software interface can be written. In the event that an automatic transfer is not feasible, the entry must be manually keyed into the general ledger.

DAILY REVENUE REPORT

The last step accomplished by the final night audit run is the printing of a daily revenue report (Figure 18-8). The program normally provides the option of running this report to produce the required number of copies. The format of the report can be customized to meet the informational needs of management. Usually this involves presenting the daily revenue on a grouping basis with subtotals for the various types of revenue and a grand total for the day. Key statistics, available from the information collected by the property management system, are also

DATE: March 11, 2000
DAY: Tuesday

GRAYLIG

DAILY REVENUE REPORT

ROOM REVENUE	Today	MONTH TO DATE Actual	Budget	Last Year
Transient Room Revenue				
Transient Individual	5,178	241,564	92,525	216,542
Golf/Ski Individual	0	7,730	44,489	0
Corporate Individual	665	7,435	3,677	16,133
Total Transient Revenue	5,843	256,729	140,641	232,675
Group Room Revenue				
Group Corporate	0	53,858	107,768	90,921
Group Tour and Travel	0	61,946	22,677	20,898
Group Association	0	21,965	11,974	0
Total Group Room Revenue	0	137,769	142,419	111,819
Total Room Revenue	5,843	394,498	283,061	344,494
FOOD & BEVERAGE REVENUE				
Food Revenue				
Main Dining Room Food	480	83,671	40,343	59,546
Tavern Food	1,807	79,319	34,059	35,360
Room Service Food	0	92	0	0
Banquet Food	918	52,079	71,470	55,173
Total Food Sales	3,204	215,161	145,872	150,079
Beverage Revenue				
Main Dining Room Liquor	0	2,367	3,675	2,920
Main Dining Room Wine	0	7,262	4,519	2,952
Tavern Liquor	236	23,735	15,037	14,902
Tavern Wine	299	13,213	1,739	6,743
Pool Terrace Liquor	0	0	0	0
Pool Terrace Wine	0	0	0	0
Banquet Liquor	54	7,134	9,116	7,211
Banquet Wine	21	4,606	7,265	4,697
Total Beverage Revenue	610	58,317	41,350	39,425
Misc Food & Beverage Income				
Public Room Rentals	0	1,000	1,368	100
Banquet Miscellaneous Comm.	0	0	0	246
Audio Visual Rentals	0	130	0	1,165
Total Food & Bev Misc Income	0	1,130	1,368	1,511
Total Food & Beverage Income	3,815	274,608	188,590	191,016
TELEPHONE REVENUE				
Local & Long Distance Revenue				
Local Telephone	6	268	175	95
Long Distance Telephone	105	4,189	6,196	4,265
Total Local & Long Distance	111	4,457	6,371	4,360
Telephone Commissions	0	0	516	1,861
Total Telephone Revenue	111	4,457	6,887	6,221
GIFT SHOP REVENUE				
Sales Clothing & Gifts				
Sheppard's Store Clothing	21	2,068	5,037	1,542
Sheppard's Store Gifts	142	10,015	5,037	4,797
Total Sales-Gifts and Clothing	163	12,083	10,075	6,339

	Today	MONTH TO DATE Actual	Budget	Last Year
Sales Other				
Magazines and Paperbacks	28	534	206	437
Newspapers	26	1,260	413	808
Vermont Food Products	16	2,150	413	145
Sundries	3	634	0	537
Gift Shop Commissions	0	2,616	0	463
Total Sales - Other	73	7,194	1,032	2,389
Total Gift Shop Revenue	236	19,277	11,107	8,728
GUEST LAUNDRY & VALET REVENUE				
Sales - Laundry	23	385	0	2
Total Guest Laundry & Valet	23	385	0	2
STORE RENTALS & OTHER INCOME				
Store Rentals #1	0	10,799	5,161	13,065
Concessions - Game Room	0	0	0	0
Concessions Vending Room	0	0	40	116
Concessions #1	0	0	323	0
Concessions #2	5	35	0	0
Concessions #3	0	0	0	0
Forfeit Deposits	0	1,648	281	700
Miscellaneous	0	5,872	400	292
Total Store Rents & Other Income	5	18,355	6,205	14,172
COUNTRY CLUB REVENUE				
Sales - Food & Sodas				
Country Club Food	8	5,683	8,281	0
Total Sales - Food & Sodas	8	5,683	8,281	0
Sales - Liquor & Wine				
Country Club Liquor	172	2,363	5,092	0
Country Club Wine	4	229	454	0
Total Sales - Liquor & Wine	176	2,592	5,545	0
Total Country Club Revenue	184	8,274	13,826	0
SPA REVENUE				
A La Carte Services	107	8,894	5,781	4,951
Facility Charge	400	1,164	0	3,444
Local Programs & Misc Spa	58	3,070	4,645	1,635
Spa Pro Shop	25	1,434	1,032	0
Total Spa Revenue	590	14,562	11,458	10,030
GOLF REVENUE				
Greens Fees	5	55,290	68,952	0
Carts	175	13,462	16,012	0
Pro Shop Sales	58	8,230	10,069	0
Other Golf Income	0	0	0	0
Total Golf Income	238	76,982	95,033	10,030
Total Hotel Income	11,043	811,398	616,167	574,663

Figure 18-8 Daily Revenue Report

provided. Month-to-date and year-to-date numbers are normally included, together with comparisons to budget and prior year.

CHAPTER SUMMARY

Income control should ensure that the hotel obtains full value for its goods and services and that all revenue is properly recorded and received.

The housekeeping report is used in verifying room revenue.

A property management system performs reservations, check-in and checkout, guest ledger, and night audit. Most systems also provide guest history.

The system automatically records room revenue. By use of interfaces, restaurant charges and telephone charges can also be posted automatically.

Posting of charges and payments utilize charge codes, which direct the transactions to the proper general ledger account.

House folios are used to record nonguest transactions, for example, cash and credit card sales, adjustments, and entertainment charges.

The night auditor has the following functions:

1. Post any unrecorded charges
2. Review room charges
3. Review shift reports
4. Review transfers to the city ledger
5. Review a preliminary night audit printout

The physical dropping of all deposits should be witnessed by another employee.

Banquet revenue requires specific procedures to ensure that the billing matches the contracted amounts.

The final procedures by the night auditor are to run the daily revenue report and roll over the computer into the following day after performing backup.

REVIEW QUESTIONS

1. What are the purposes of income control?
2. What part is played in income control by the daily housekeeping report?
3. What is a property management system (PMS)?
4. What is "guest history"?

5. What are the most common interfaces used with a PMS?
6. What is the purpose of charge codes?
7. What is the purpose of a house folio?
8. List the functions of the night auditor.
9. Explain deposit procedures.
10. What are the steps in a banquet audit?

19

Food and Beverage Cost Control

After studying this chapter, the student should:

1. Understand the system used to purchase food and beverage.
2. Understand receiving procedures.
3. Understand storeroom controls.
4. Know how to analyze food and beverage costs.

Chapter 10 reviewed two very important elements of a hotel food and beverage operation: the preparation and the service. Now a third element, the control of food and beverage costs, enters the picture.

PURCHASING

Clearly, the amount paid for food and beverage purchases is a major factor (although not always the deciding factor) in controlling costs. A hotel's purchasing procedures should therefore be designed to provide maximum controls.

Most medium- and large-sized hotels employ a *purchasing agent* through whose office all purchasing should flow. The number of staff in the purchasing department will vary in relation to the size of the hotel and the resulting volume of purchasing. However, inasmuch as a large part of the process is the issuance of purchase orders and receipt of quotations, there should be at least a secretary in addition to the purchasing agent. Some large chains use centralized purchasing for all or many items, thus removing the burden of purchasing from the individual hotel.

Certain characteristics of food purchasing are determinants of the procedures used. Food is, in varying degrees, a perishable commodity. In particular, fresh fruits and vegetables, milk and bread, and fresh meat and fish have a limited life; and even frozen meat and vegetables cannot be stored indefinitely.

Perhaps the most important element of food purchasing is to buy the right product. This requires supplying the vendors with *purchase specifications*, which are detailed descriptions of quantity, size, weight, and quality desired for each item. The U.S. Department of Agriculture standards or specifications issued for all produce and dairy products are commonly used for those items. Meat standards are established by reference to the *Meat Buyers Guide to Standardized Meat Cuts*, published by the National Association of Meat Purveyors.

Storage space is also a determining factor in establishing purchasing procedures. Hotels with limited storage capacity find it necessary to purchase more frequently than do those with large storage areas.

For hotels with a large banquet volume, it is not feasible to buy and store all food items required to service these functions. Consequently, buying for banquets is done on a daily basis according to requirements.

The last, but not least, important factor to be considered are *price fluctuations*. Prices for fresh produce change daily. Meat and fish prices are also volatile, often changing more than once a week.

All this points out the impossibility of having the purchasing agent obtain quotations, issue and mail purchase orders, and wait for vendors to receive the purchase orders and deliver the goods. By necessity, food purchasing becomes a telephone or fax process.

Quotations are obtained daily by the purchasing department from the approved vendors. There may be five or six vendors quoting on certain items, whereas only two or three vendors may be considered suitable for others. The selection of a vendor from whom quotations are to be obtained depends on its established record as a supplier to the industry in general and on the past experience the hotel has had with the vendor in regard to reliability, price, credit terms, and product quality.

Quotations for produce are solicited daily, and meat and fish quotations perhaps twice a week, but vendors are instructed to advise the hotel promptly of any price change in items it regularly purchases. Prices for frozen and canned goods are less subject to fluctuation, and quotations can be obtained less frequently.

The major suppliers now issue quotations on a daily basis, which are forwarded to the hotel by fax on a form that can be completed by the hotel and faxed back to the vendor, a much easier process than calling the vendor on the telephone to obtain quotations and then making a second call to place the order if the quotation is accepted.

For comparison purposes the quotations are entered on a *daily quotation sheet* (also referred to as a *market list*), an example of which is shown in Figure 19-1.

M-1932-4/73

STEWARDS MARKET LIST

HOTEL _____   ORDER DATE _____   DELIVERY DATE _____

ITEMS

BEEF

Bones, Marrow, lb. — Cut
BottomRound, BlessGd., 28/30 lbs. qv/ch #170
Bottom Round, Corned, 32-36 lbs.
Rib-Prime, Rump on, Shank off-30/35 lbs. #160
Brisket Corned, Deckle off. 12/14 lbs. #601
Brisket, Fresh, Deckle off. 12-14 lbs. #120
Chipped Beef, ¼ lb. Pkgs. # 619
Top Butts, B'less, 14-16 lbs., qv/ch # 184
Chuck, Arm, Bless, Choice, 65-100 lbs. # 126
Filets, Stripd., Wedge Fat Out 5-6 lbs. #190
Filets, Long, 8-9 lbs. ¼ open #189
Hamburger Meat, 85% Lean — Fresh – Bulk
Hamburger Patties - 4 oz. Fresh- 85/15
Liver, Steer, Fresh – Frozen 9-11 lbs.
Ox Tails, Fresh – Frozen 1¾ - 2 lbs.
Ribs, Choice, 36-38 lbs., 10"- 7 cut #103
Ribs, Prime, 36- 42 lbs., 10", 7 cut # 103
Ribs, Choice-Oven-Prep/Cut 3x4 22-24lbs #109
Flank Steak — Peeled 2½ - 3½ lbs. #193
Stew Meat, lb., 2" Cubed Trimmed
Shin Meat - Boneless
Corner Pieces - 3 Bone – Lean 1 lb. ea.
Strip Loins, Ch., (10 x 10), 22-24 lbs., #175
Strip Loins Pr., (10 x 10), 22-24 lbs., #175
Strip Loin-Ch. 7" – BNLS 13/15 lbs., #180
Top Round, B'less 20-24 lbs., qv/ch # 168
TopSr, B'less 15-16 lbs Mkt'wt Frzp/Ctm167
Deli Top Rd Pr Deli 16/20 #HD Tied
Skirt Steaks

VEAL

Breast, lb.
Bones – Cut
Legs, 35-45 lbs, Nature/Ch # 334 Bnls
Liver, Fr., 2½ - 3½ lbs. Kosher Style
Loin Saddles, 14-16 lbs. qv/ch #331
Racks, (4 x 4) 12-16 lbs. qv/ch #306
Shoulder, 10-14 lbs. p/Ch
Stew Meat, lb. 2" Cubed Trimmed
Sweetbreads, 16-18 oz., Fresh Trimd.
Patties, Breaded, 4 oz. — Frozen
Leg Cutlets, Unbreaded, 4 oz. – Fresh
Veal Kidneys 4/5 oz.
Veal Shanks
Veal Clods 8/12 #

ITEMS

LAMB

Chucks, 16-18 lbs. pv/ch #206
B'nls, Chuck of Lamb, 1¾" cubes – lean
Legs, 8-10 lbs., pv/ch #233
Legs, Boned and Tied 6-8 lbs., #234
Kidneys, Fresh No Fat
Racks, (4 x 4), 6-9 lbs., pv/ch #204
Loin, 8-12 lbs. pv/ch #231
Breast of Lamb
Slaughter House Lamb Liver, Fresh Kosher
Lamb Kidneys
Lamb Shanks
New Zealand Racks of Lamb #4-69

PROVISIONS

Bacon, Canadian, S/2 Domestic
Bacon, Sliced, 18/20 Ct., Layout
Knockwurst, 4/1, 3/1
Liverwurst, Thin, 6-7 lbs.
Bologna, Thin, 6-8 lbs.
Butts, Smoked, 2, 2¾ lbs.
Fresh-Pork Butts 2½ - 3½ lbs.
Frankfurters, Cocktail, 2" (40 to lb.) - Beef
Frankfurters, 8 to lb., S.C. For Staff
Fxfrts, Kosher, 8 to 1 Griddles All Beef
Bratwurst 3/1 lb.
Cocktail Bratwurst 25-30 to lb.
Italian Style Hot or Sweet Sausage
Hams-Serve Ready, 8/10 lbs., 10/12 lbs., B'less
Hams, Canned, Pear Sh., 8/10 lbs., 10/12 lbs.
Hams, Corned, Pullman 8/10 lbs., 10/12 lbs.
Hams, Prosciutto, 7/9 lbs., Belts
Hams, Prosciutto, 12/14 lbs. – Domestic
Hams, R.T.E., 10/14 lbs., 14/17 lbs., Bone in
Hams, Va., 12-14 lbs., 5 mo. Cure, Bone in
Hams Visking, R.T.E., 10/12 lbs., Belts
Pastrami, 2-3 lbs.
Pigs Knuckles, Fresh/Corned ¾ lb. ea.
Pork, Salt, Fresh, Lean Bellies, 12-14 lbs.
Pork, Larding Fat Back, Salt./Fresh 12/14 lbs.
Bnls Pork Loins 6-8 lbs.
Pork Loins, Fresh/Frozen 10-12 lbs. #410
Pork Loins, Smoked, 9-11 lbs.
Pork Chops, C.C./E to E
Pork Shoulders, Fresh, 10-12 lbs., Bnls
Pork Spareribs, 3 lb. down, 2 lb. down-Fresh
Salami, Hard, B.C., 5-7 lbs.
Salami Kosher Style, All Beef, 5-7 lbs.
Salami, Genoa Style, B.C., 5-7 lbs.
Sausage, Cocktail, 35 to lb., S.C.
Sausage Breakfast, 8, 1, 12"1, 15"1 S.C.
Tongues, Smoked Beef, /#5/3, #1 S, Cut #614
Tripe, Honeycomb, White, Fy/lb.

ITEMS

POULTRY

Chicken Brst., 18-20 or 20-22 oz. with Wings
Chicken Legs, 8 oz. or 10 oz.
Chicken Roasters, 3½ - 4 lbs. Evis.
Chickens, Broilers, 2¼ - 2½, lbs. Evis
L.I.Ducklings, 4, 4½, 5 lbs. Evis w/ Giblets
Fowl, 4½ - 5 lbs., 5, 6 lbs. Evis.
Livers, Chicken, lb. Fresh
Chicken Fat, Rendered
Poussins 1-1¼ lbs. Evis.
Rock Cornish Game Hens, 1 lb., Evis.
Cornish Hen – Part Boned – Stuffed, 12 oz.
Royal Squab, 14 lb. N.Y.D.
Turkeys, Evis., Hen, 14-16 lbs.
Turkeys Evis. & T 7 20+ 22 lbs, 24-26 lbs, Gr A
Turkey Brst – Dbl-No Wing 10-12 lbs.
All White Cooked Bst, Turkey-Dbl-Single
Chicken, Wings, Gizzards, Bones
Pheasants, Dom 1-1½ lbs. Evis.
Quail, Dom 7 oz. Evis. Oven-Ready

Figure 19-1 Supplier's Daily Quotation Sheet

263

These sheets should be maintained on file for at least a year, to permit verification by auditors and others that the lowest prices were obtained. The order is marked on the quotation sheet and then placed with the vendor by fax or telephone. If the order did not go to the lowest quotation, the purchasing agent must be prepared to justify this deviation from policy, which usually results from variance in quality. A copy of the quotation sheet must be supplied to the receiving clerk to permit verification of quantity and price.

Although storage space is a consideration in beverage purchasing, perishability is not a factor (although certain wines can go bad), and prices do not fluctuate erratically. Consequently, there is adequate time to obtain written quotations and to issue purchase orders for beverages. When the inventory of a particular brand drops below a specified level, known as the minimum par, the storekeeper issues a requisition, which, after approval by the bar manager, gives authority to the purchasing agent to go ahead and purchase that item.

Food purchasing is based on requisitions issued from two sources. As with beverages, minimum storeroom levels are established for many items, and purchase requisitions approved by the food and beverage manager are issued to the purchasing agent. However, for all produce and other items normally going directly to the kitchen, the requisition is issued by the chef. This is also true with respect to purchasing for functions or for special menu items.

RECEIVING

Receiving is the natural next step in the control process after purchasing, but the two should be completely separate and under different control. Whereas purchasing is a management function and the purchasing agent reports to the resident manager, receiving is a control function and the receiving clerk should report to the controller. Of course, there will still be many occasions when the receiving clerk must consult the purchasing agent, particularly when there are questions as to the specifications or quality of merchandise (usually food), received.

All food and beverage vendors should be instructed that the corresponding invoice must accompany each delivery, or else the delivery will be refused. This is particularly important with food, since there is no purchase order, only the quotation sheet, against which to check the delivery. The immediate verification of the quantities on the invoice, by counting or weighing, and the prices, by comparison to the quotation sheet, will save a great deal of time. All meat and fish, as well as other items when applicable, should be fully weighed when received. The scale at the receiving dock should be periodically checked for accuracy.

The imprint of a rubber stamp, laid out in the manner shown in Figure 19-2, is made on the back of each invoice. The areas indicating approval of quantity, quality, and price should be initialed by the receiving clerk after the necessary

Record of Receipt of Goods			
Quantities checked		Entered on receiving sheet	
Quality checked		Extensions and additions checked	
Prices verified		Approved for payment	

Figure 19-2   Rubber Stamp for Invoice

verification is completed. The verification of quality should be conducted by ensuring that the product delivered conforms to the specifications issued to the vendor. The remaining areas, covering extensions and final approval for payment, will be subsequently completed.

Each invoice is then entered on a *daily receiving sheet*, shown in Figure 19-3. As you can see, the receiving sheet provides a column for the name of the supplier and four columns that separate the incoming shipments into "Beverage Stores," "Food—Direct," "Food—Stores," and "General Stores."

In each column, the monetary amount of the delivery is entered opposite the name of the vendor. "Food—Direct" represents food purchases delivered directly to the kitchen and placed under the control of the chef, as opposed to "Food—Stores," which is food to be placed in the storeroom. Since all beverage purchases should be delivered to the storeroom, only one column is required; "General Stores" represents purchases other than food and beverage. The separation of the direct food charges from the storeroom deliveries is important in establishing proper control over the storerooms. The total of the beverage and food-stores columns shows the dollar value of goods coming into the storerooms; for complete control, all that is needed is control of the issuance of goods from them.

The daily receiving sheet is completed by totaling each column, attaching all invoices, and forwarding it each day to the accounts-payable department. The totals of the three food and beverage columns are entered by the food and beverage controller on a worksheet that is used in the final reconciliation of food and beverage activity for the month. The daily receiving sheet also provides a basis for reconciling the total food and beverage purchases for the month, as discussed in Chapter 21.

Sheet No. _____

of _____ Sheets

RECEIVING CLERK'S DAILY REPORT   Date __May 2__ 19 _9X_

	Quan.	Unit	Description	√	Unit Price	Amount	Beverage Stores	Food Direct	Food Stores	General Stores
GENERAL BAKERIES	–	–	Bread		–	38|62		38|62		
157710	–	–	Discount		–	(2|31)		(2|31)		
2/5/9X										
Quebec Lait	6	1 LIT	Milk		50	3|00				
299 2298	3	20 LIT	Milk		1035	31|05				
2/5/9X	6	BOX	Mini-pots		225	13|50				
	3	10 LIT	Cream 15%		1200	36|00				
	12	1 LIT	Cream 35%		225	27|00				
								110|55		
Primo	3	C/S	Linguine		585	17|55				
0096624	3	C/S	Linguine Di Pass.		585	17|55				
2/5/9X	3	C/S	Rigatoni		585	17|55				
	3	C/S	Pennine		585	17|55				
									70|20	
Canada Packers	150	LBS	Butter		136	204|00				
228740	2	C/S	Lactantia		3480	69|60				
2/5/9X								273|60		
Anco	14.98	LBS	Cheddar Fort		181	27|11				
140181	15.68	LBS	Gouda Fume		235	36|85				
2/5/9X	15.80	LBS	Cheddar Doux		154	24|33				
								88|29		
Trieste	6	PAIL	Oil		1875	112|50				
2178									112|50	
2/5/9X	54.37	LBS	Parmesan		490	266|41				
								266|41		

Figure 19-3   Daily Receiving Sheet

STOREROOM CONTROLS

Proper controls over purchasing and receiving, although they are essential, serve no purpose if controls cease after the food and beverage purchases are placed in the storerooms.

Food

Inventory control over food is, for practical reasons, more easily maintained on a quantity than on a monetary basis. The preceding discussion on purchasing indicated that many food prices fluctuate almost daily. Thus, to attempt to control

BIN CARD

No. _____   Size _____

Commodity _____

Date	Supplier	Quantity Received	Quantity Issued	Balance On Hand

Figure 19-4   Bin Card *(Courtesy of Whitney Duplicating Check Company)*

food inventories on a monetary basis would involve constant updating of the average price of the individual item.

Consequently, control over most items in the food stores is maintained by utilizing *bin cards.* A bin card (Figure 19-4) shows, either by number or by weight, the quantities received (purchases), outgoing quantities (issues to the kitchen), and the resulting balances on hand. The bin cards should be pinned to shelves or hung up in the area where the food is stored. Periodic physical counts, weekly or semimonthly, should be made and the results compared with the bin cards, with variances immediately investigated.

Since frozen meat and fish are stored in a freezer box or boxes within the storage area, the use of bin cards to control the quantities is not very practical. Instead, control is maintained by using meat tags, similar to that shown in Figure 19-5. The meat tag is in two parts, and can be separated by tearing along the perforated line. When the meat or fish is weighed and placed in the freezer box, both sections of the tag are completed; one section is attached to the meat or fish, and the other is hung on a board set up in the storage area for that purpose. When the meat or fish is issued to the kitchen, the tag is removed from the board and attached to the requisition. Consequently, at any time, the tags hanging on the board will represent the amount of meat or fish in the freezer.

In the food storeroom, minimum quantities should be established for those items that are carried in inventory on a continuing basis. When the quantities drop below these minimum levels, the storekeeper should prepare a requisition.

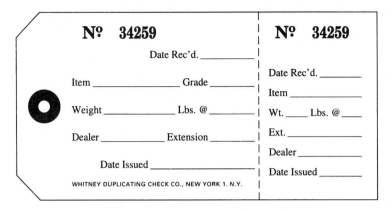

Figure 19-5   Meat Tag *(Courtesy of Whitney Duplicating Check Company)*

Beverages

Whereas control over food is normally maintained on a quantity basis, a complete *perpetual inventory* on a monetary basis is maintained for the beverage stores, usually on cards kept by the storekeeper. When a shipment of beverages is received, the physical quantities, prices, and the total dollar amount of the purchase are entered on a card. When items are issued from the storeroom, entries to this effect are made on the cards, not only for the quantity but for the dollar amount, by multiplying the physical quantity by the average cost of purchases. Therefore, at any given time, each card will reflect not only the physical balance of the item on hand but also its dollar value. At the end of the month, the food and beverage controller and a representative from the accounting department should check the physical quantities against the balances on the cards and make an inventory listing. All variances should, of course, be immediately investigated. Many hotels have replaced the cards with a computer program that permits the storekeeper to enter the activity on a daily basis and at any point in time prints an up-to-date inventory.

ANALYSIS OF FOOD AND BEVERAGE COSTS

All requisitions for storeroom issues, of both food and beverages, are priced and extended daily, then totaled separately for food and beverage by the food and beverage controller's office and entered on daily recap sheets. This can be done manually or by feeding the quantities into a computer program in which the prices are preentered. In this case, a computerized printout of issues will be obtained. The total food issue is then added to the total of *direct* purchases delivered to the kitchen. This figure, after a deduction for food consumed by employees, can be compared with the food sales figure and a daily food cost obtained. Even though such a comparison on a day-by-day basis will show major fluctuations because of changing inventory levels in the kitchen, nevertheless, after two or three days into the month, a comparison of the cumulative issues to sales will give a fairly accurate indication of the *food-cost percentage*—issues as a percentage of sales—for the period covered.

Similarly, a comparison can be made of beverage issues to beverage sales. Since all beverage is controlled in the storeroom and issued on requisitions, there are no direct issues with which to contend. Furthermore, the effect of inventory fluctuations can largely be avoided by having the bars operate with par stocks. This process dictates that at the end of the day a requisition should be prepared to bring the bar inventory back up to the established par quantities. This requisition should be sent to the storeroom, accompanied by the empty bottles being replaced and, for beer and soft drinks, the empty cases. (Liquor bottles must, of course, be stamped with an identifying mark to prevent substitution of bottles.) This is in addition to the state's beverage stamp. Thus, inventory fluctuations in the bars can be caused only by minor variations in the contents of part bottles. The requisition is filled by the storeroom prior to opening the following day, thus bringing the bar inventory back up to par. Accurate daily beverage costs can be obtained by comparing the issues to the prior day's sales.

In order to better refine daily food and beverage costs, certain other adjustments should be made to the issues on a daily basis. In particular, adjustments should be made for food issued to the bar—cream, milk, cherries, olives, and the like—and beverages issued to the kitchen, such as wine and brandy used for cooking. Adjustments are also necessary for supplies issued to the bars for free guest consumption—canapes, pretzels, peanuts, and so on. It may also be necessary to make adjustments for the cost of officers' meal and entertainment checks; however, if these checks are run through as normal sales and only rebated at the end of the month, such adjustments will not be necessary.

The daily costs should be carefully monitored. Unusually high costs for any particular day should be investigated immediately. In some instances it may be caused by unrecorded sales. This most commonly occurs when a banquet check for a function that evening is not given to night audit.

Otherwise it may be evidence of theft, either food taken from the kitchen physically or food served and the sales not recorded by a server. At this point the checks should be analyzed and matched against the food consumed in the kitchen.

At the end of the month, a more complete recap of food and beverage costs should be prepared, reflecting issues, inventory variances, and any special adjustments. An example of such a recap is shown in Figure 19-6.

HOTEL GRAYLIG

RECONCILIATION OF FOOD AND BEVERAGE COSTS

MONTH OF ___Dec. 19___

FOOD

	STOREROOM	BUTCHER SHOP	KITCHEN	RECONCILIATION
Opening Inventory - Physical	6,058.18	1,944.37	4,558.69	12,561.24
Purchases	12,340.59	12,115.21	26,329.92	50,785.72
Total Food Available	18,398.77	14,059.58	30,888.61	63,346.96
Less:				
Closing Inventory - Physical				13,231.32
Cost of Food Consumed				
Add:				
Beverage to Food		12,026.57		180.62
Less:				
Issues	11,833.73			
Grease Sales				39.42
Food to Beverage				867.98
Kosher Catering				
Steward Sales				1,160.25
Cafeteria Sales				3,986.37
Officers Checks and Promotional				1,302.83
Gratis				3,744 —
Employee's Meals–Total				
Food Department				
Beverage Department				
Heat, Light and Power				
Repairs, Maintenance				
Rooms				
Sales				
Administrative and General				
Telephone				
Garage				
House Expense				
Total Credits	6,565.04	2,033.01		11,100.85
Closing Inventory - Book	6,491.92	1,998.22	4,741.18	
Closing Inventory - Physical				
Overage (Shortage)	(73.12)	(34.79)		
Cost of Food Sold - Overall				39,195.41
Total Revenue				136,524.11
Percentage of Sales				28.7%
Inventory Turnover				

BEVERAGE

	WINE CELLAR	BARS	CONTAINER ACCT.	RECONCILIATION
Opening Inventory - Physical	18,248.91	1,268.38	—	19,517.29
Purchases	24,926.04		—	24,976.04
Total Beverage Available	43,174.95	1,268.38	—	44,493.33
Less:				
Closing Inventory - Physical				
Cost of Beverage Consumed				25,607.74
Add:				
Food to Beverage				867.98
Less:				
Issues	18,053.23			
Beverage to Food	180.62			180.62
Steward Sales	61.68			61.68
Promotional Issues	468.33			468.33
Breakage	107.90			107.90
Cooks Beer	203.15			203.15
Promotional and Officers Checks				595.67
Total Credits	1,021.68	1,268.38		1,617.35
Closing Inventory - Book	24,100.04	1,148.13		
Closing Inventory - Physical	24,459.61			
Overage (Shortage)	359.57	(120.25)		
Cost of Beverage Sold - Overall				18,086.72
Total Revenue				72,293.20
Percentage of Sales				25.02%
Inventory Turnover				

Figure 19-6 Recap of Food and Beverage Costs

POINT-OF-SALE SYSTEMS

In the preceding chapter, we refer to point-of-sale systems as the method by which hotels exercise control over food and beverage income. For many years hotels used duplicate orders or duplicate checks in an effort to ensure that what was ordered was recorded on a guest check to be settled in some manner by the customer. Technology, in the form of point-of-sale systems, uses the same theories but eliminates most of the weaknesses of the old manual systems. The earliest point-of-sale systems used basic computer hardware with software designed to provide point-of-sale control. However, system designers now provide hardware designed to more easily perform the goals of a point-of-sale system. In particular the hardware has been specifically designed for easier input by the restaurant staff. The systems focus on three goals:

1. To ensure that the product served is exactly what was ordered.
2. To ensure that each item served is recorded on a sales check.
3. To ensure that each check is settled in a satisfying manner.

One of the earliest companies to develop these systems was Remanco International in 1976. In this chapter we focus on a state-of-the-art system developed in recent years, the Vision Series II illustrated in Figures 19-7 and 19-8. This system not only embodies the finer points of earlier systems but utilizes a recent technological development: the handheld terminal.

Point-of-sale systems utilize a combination of terminals and printers, which function as input and output devices. The Vision Series II utilizes a processor that can support up to three networks, each of which can have up to 30 connected input and output terminals. Several types of input terminals can be used, the most common of which are *touch screen* terminals located at selected locations easily accessible to the servers. The customized screens guide the server through the input process. The essential information inputted is the identity of the server, the location or table number of the customer, the number of people being served, and the menu items being ordered. The input program usually provides the ability to put in preparation instructions, that is, well done for steak, salad dressings, and condiments requested, and so on. Computer cables transmit the orders to the kitchen, where they are printed out at the service line. The sophisticated systems permit transmission to several locations, that is, hot items to the hot preparation area, salads to the salad station, and drinks to the bar. Furthermore, several servers can input simultaneously. The computer queues them in order and prints them out. The Vision Series II's handheld feature permits the server to use an alpha input handheld terminal, really a computerized order pad, with which the orders can be inputted at the table and transmitted to the kitchen. *Handheld terminals* permit the server to spend more time at the tables and less time going to a remote terminal or the kitchen. This speeds up service and permits the server to handle more customers. Another feature of the system permits the server to input

REMANCO VISION Series II System Overview

In the Restaurant

- Remanco Exclusive Low Profile Terminals
- Touch Screen, Full Screen & Alpha Entry Terminals
- Preset and Alphanumeric Support
- Integrated Credit Card Authorization Option

Remanco's Touch Screen Terminal & High–Speed Silent Thermal Printer

Remanco's
Hand Held Terminal

Alpha Entry Terminal, Slip Printer & Cash Drawer

In the Bar

- Remanco Rapid Entry Feature
- Hard Check Support
- Options Include Satellite Displays and Multiple Cash Drawers

Figure 19-7 Vision Series II—Bar and Restaurant

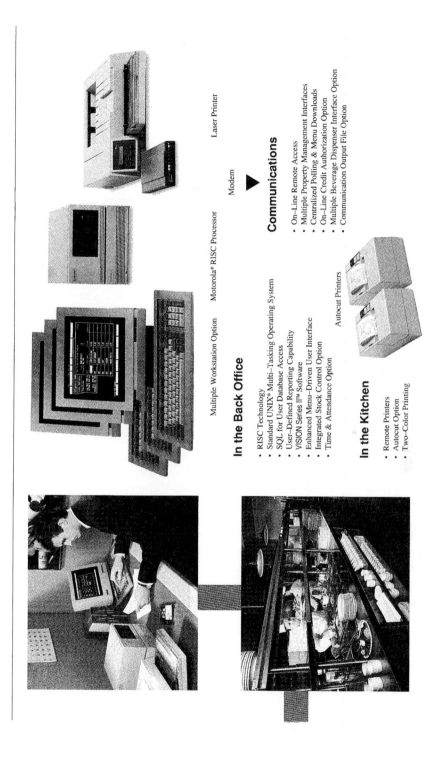

Multiple Workstation Option Motorola® RISC Processor

Laser Printer

Modem

▶

Communications

- On–Line Remote Access
- Multiple Property Management Interfaces
- Centralized Polling & Menu Downloads
- On–Line Credit Authorization Option
- Multiple Beverage Dispenser Interface Option
- Communication Output File Option

In the Back Office

- RISC Technology
- Standard UNIX® Multi–Tasking Operating System
- SQL for User Database Access
- User–Defined Reporting Capability
- VISION Series II™ Software
- Enhanced Menu–Driven User Interface
- Integrated Stock Control Option
- Time & Attendance Option

Autocut Printers

In the Kitchen

- Remote Printers
- Autocut Option
- Two-Color Printing

Figure 19-8 Vision Series II—Back Office

273

the whole order but send parts of it to the kitchen on a delayed basis. Technically the terminals send a computer signal to antennae located in the ceiling of the restaurant, which are connected by cable to the processor.

Prices for all menu items, food and beverage, are stored in memory to be printed on a customer's check. The check is assigned a number at the time of the initial input and can be reprinted on several occasions because of changes or additions to the order. For this reason many restaurants use a soft-copy check with a computerized print design, which is more cost-effective than hard checks. However, the hard-check option is available. Multiple checks can be printed, and items can be transferred from one check to another.

At the time of settlement, the method of settlement (cash, room charge, designated credit card, etc.) is also entered via the terminal. Larger terminals can be equipped with multiple cash drawers. However, common practice is to provide the servers with some form of pouch to hold their cash for a drop in a safe at the end of their shift.

At the end of the shift the server prints a report that indicates which checks are still open (unsettled). After all checks are settled the server can print a settlement report (Figure 19-9), which shows an analysis of his or her total sales and a detailed breakdown of the settlement. This enables the servers to verify their total cash and charges before making their individual drops. The drops should be made in a lock box or drop safe and witnessed by another employee. In some hotels the servers turn over their cash to a supervisor who checks them and makes one drop. Because of the number of servers, this is not practical in many hotels. Employees also use their settlement reports to determine their cash and charge tips. Some hotels provide only the credit sales information to the servers, preferring them to make a "blind," unverified cash drop. While this procedure has merit from a control point of view, it can result in substantially more work for the general cashier in handling and reconciling tips and due backs. This is particularly true where there is a large number of individual servers. Charge tips are "due back" amounts owed by the hotel to the server. Servers will normally recover the due back tips by deducting them from their cash remittance prior to making their drop. However, the cash remittance is sometimes not large enough (this happens frequently at breakfast) to cover the charge tips. When this happens the server is reimbursed for the shortfall by the general cashier, usually on the following day. The tip amounts are also used to meet the tip declaration and other tip reporting requirements of the IRS. A customized report can be designed (Figure 19-10) to provide the requirement information and facilitate payroll preparation and filing requirements.

At the end of the day the system must be cleared by running a "z" report. This clears the day's activity from the active file and also clears out the individual server's files. This does not remove the information completely from the system. All information can be reaccessed through the management terminals. The end-of-day function on the Vision Series II system is very simple, as it utilizes a tape archive system to store the historical information for each recall. The system also

Hotel Graylig

Server: Joan Brown

SETTLEMENT REPORT

Period: 06/03/9_ - 06/03/9_

Printed 06/08/0_ 11:41		Current Database		Rpt# 23 Page 1
Sales Summary	Count	GrossAmt	AdjustAmt	NetAmt

———— SALES SUMMARY ————

	Count	GrossAmt	AdjustAmt	NetAmt
Category Group Sales				
Food	557	2,798.20	0.00	2,798.20
Beverage	404	1,445.35	0.00	1,445.35
Category Group Totals	961	4,243.55	0.00	4,243.55
			Non-Adjusted Sales	4,243.55
Service Charges				
Service Charge Total	0	0.00		
Discounts				
Store Coupon	6	44.17		
Discount Total	6	44.17		
			Net Adjustments	- 44.17
			Net Sales	4,199.38
Taxes				
Sales Tax	180	187.31		
Tax Total	180	187.31		
			Gross Sales	4,386.69
Tips Collected				
Charge Tips	65	431.12		
Serv Charge Tips	7	31.83		
Tips Collected Total	72	462.95		
			Total Revenue	4,849.64

Figure 19-9   Settlement Report *(Courtesy of Ramanco International)*

SETTLEMENT REPORT

Page 2

Revenue Summary	Count	GrossAmt	TipAmt	NetAmt

——— REVENUE SUMMARY ———

	Count	GrossAmt	TipAmt	NetAmt
Payment Media				
Cash	158	1,677.02	0.00	1,677.02
Mastercard	21	950.75	156.93	793.82
Visa	10	700.98	62.74	638.24
American Express	18	730.30	93.85	636.45
Room Charge	18	665.26	117.60	547.66
British Pound	3	22.73	0.00	22.73
(15.00)				
Deutche Mark	1	18.60	0.00	18.60
(30.00)				
Swiss Franc	2	84.00	0.00	84.00
(200.00)				
Payment Media Subtotal	231	4,849.64	431.12	4,418.52
Service Charge Tips			31.83	
Payment Media Total	231	4,849.64	462.95	4,386.69
			Total Revenue	4,849.64

	Gross Cash	Tips	Net Cash
Cash less Tips Collected:	1,677.02	462.95	1,214.07
Cash less Tips Paid:	1,677.02	227.82	1,449.20
Tips Collected less Tips Paid:		227.82	

End of Report

Figure 19-9   Settlement Report *(continued)*

has the ability to recreate individual checks through the back-office terminal and either display or print them.

The Vision Series II back-office system utilizes multiple work station capabilities and has a laser printer for clear, attractive reporting. Updates on menu changes, prices, and so on, are also inputted through a back-office workstation. Menu changes, prices, availability, and kitchen preparation can be scheduled based on time of day or day of week or workstation location. The system is de-

Hotel Graylig - Coffee Shop
Tip Report

Date: April 7, 20—

Server No.	Server Name	Cash Sales	Charge Sales	Charge Tips
2	John Smith	283.45	79.55	16.00
5	Betty Wills	186.45	110.10	20.50
7	Sally Field	274.60	104.20	18.75
8	Peter Pell	194.80	122.00	24.50
10	Ralph Timms	205.20	90.50	15.00
12	Rolf Thor	188.60	78.60	14.25
15	Jackie Kane	172.20	88.40	16.50
17	Molly Gray	191.10	79.50	13.75
22	Tom Brown	164.80	57.20	12.00
28	Jack Cole	179.50	0	0
33	Jim Wells	130.85	120.70	22.00
	Totals	2171.55	930.75	173.25

Figure 19-10   Tip Report

signed to interface with most property management systems; actually, there is a multiple property management system interface capability. The interface provides not only the room charge information to the guest ledger function but also transfers the revenue and city ledger information necessary for the night audit. The system also has a credit card authorization function (optional), which permits the server to swipe the card through the magnetic stripe reader built into the order-entry terminal. The system determines the card type, validity, and expiration date. The credit card vendor is dialed automatically via a modem to obtain an authorization for the amount of the check plus an allowance for probable gratuity. There is a preauthorization feature where an estimated amount can be authorized prior to the customer's order. However, this step would normally only be used at the customer's request or where there is reason for suspicion on the part of management about the customer's ability to pay, perhaps because of prior problems.

The Vision Series II system, like some of its competitors, provides certain other program options. An electronic time clock capacity allows the server to input the time that he or she starts and finishes work. A detailed report then furnishes the information on each employee required for payroll preparation. This is an attractive feature, as it ensures that the employee is actually at his or her station and avoids time lost between punching a time clock and actually starting to work. Inventory control is another option that is frequently utilized.

All functions are subject to management control with different levels of access necessary to control such things as corrections, voids, entertainment charges, changes to hours worked, and so on.

REPORTS

Operational reports can be printed at any time during the day. This can provide instant sales data, information about workload and performance of individual employees, and product usage. In addition to operational reports produced on an interim basis, four major types of management reports are normally generated— income analysis, employee productivity, inventory control, and cost control.

Income analysis is the most direct product of the system. It is the breakdown of sales by type (food, liquor, wine, tax, or gratuities) and by outlet, which is then fed into the property management system, either through an interface or by manual input by night audit, and becomes the data source for entry into the general ledger and for the daily revenue report. This information should also be used to provide a daily food and beverage report, which shows daily and cumulative information on food and beverage revenue, numbers of covers, average check, and so on (see Figure 19-11).

Employee productivity. This report (Figure 19-12) allows management to evaluate the productivity of individual employees with information relative to numbers of covers, average check, total sales, and the ability to promote higher sales with appetizers, desserts, or beverages.

Inventory control. Since the point-of-sale system specifically identifies each item sold, both food and beverage, this information can provide a full analysis of all inventory consumption that has been entered into the system.

The physical ingredients and quantities thereof used in each recipe are fed into the computer. At the end of a day and on a cumulative basis, a report can be produced where the ingredients of each food or beverage menu item are multiplied by the number sold to produce a report showing the total inventory consumption recorded in the system. This report can be produced in dollars as well as quantities by also feeding the unit costs into the program.

A comparison of the consumption reflected by the report against actual physical consumption (opening inventory plus purchases minus closing inventory) will disclose whether all product usage is being properly recorded and whether or not there are physical inventory shortages.

Obviously this report has a higher degree of accuracy in the beverage area than in the food area, as actual product mix used in the cooking process is not as exact as in the mixing of drinks. Nevertheless, the same principles apply. Food numbers become particularly useful if the hotel purchases "portion-controlled" entrees.

Portion control is a term used to describe a process where the purveyor prepares the meat or fish in individual portions, in the weight desired, ready for

DATE: March 11, 20—
DAY: Tuesday

GRAYLIG

FOOD AND BEVERAGE REPORT

	TODAYS			MONTH TO DATE			YEAR TO DATE		
FOOD REVENUE RESTAURANT	Revenue	Covers	Avg. Check	Revenue	Covers	Avg. Check	Revenue	Covers	Avg. Check
— CAFE —									
Breakfast	522.54	39	13.40	8276.54	828	10.00	29876.65	3208	9.31
Lunch	452.35	28	16.19	1433.86	79	18.15	1492.80	92	16.23
Dinner	855.80	41	20.87	6255.65	322	19.43	9065.45	543	16.70
Room Service	76.85	6	12.81	336.00	38	8.84	762.90	130	5.87
Total Cafe	1908.54	114	16.74	16302.05	1267	12.87	41197.88	3973	10.37
— TAVERN —									
Room Service	86.45	21	4.12	906.54	121	7.49	2406.76	312	7.71
Dinner	522.90	34	15.38	7287.65	386	18.88	28172.45	1976	14.26
Total Tavern	609.35	55	11.08	8194.19	507	16.16	30579.21	2288	13.37
Total Restaurant	2517.89	169	14.90	24496.24	1774	13.81	71777.09	6261	11.46
— BANQUET —									
Banq - Breakfast	62.15	10	6.22	422.89	28	15.10	2076.56	222	9.35
Lunch	0	0		587.55	41	14.33	3208.55	286	11.22
Dinner	220.50	36	8.90	5387.62	182	29.60	13087.66	476	27.50
Other	0	0		1302.76	40	32.57	6134.80	328	18.70
Total Banquet	382.65	46	8.32	7700.82	291	26.46	24507.57	1312	18.68
Total Food	2900.54	215	13.49	32197.06	2065	15.59	96284.66	7573	12.71
BANQUET REVENUE									
Cafe	54.20			1244.87			2765.98		
Tavern	240.60			5386.54			21096.54		
Banquet	0.00			3308.72			7634.98		
Total Beverage	294.80			9940.13			31517.50		
TOTAL F&B REVENUE	3195.34			42137.19			127802.16		

Figure 19-11   Daily Food and Beverage Report

Hotel Graylig - Coffee Shop
Servers Productivity Report

Date: April 7, 20—

Server No.	Server Name	Hrs. Worked	Sales	No. of Covers	Avg. Check	No. of Appetizers	No. of Desserts
2	John Smith	5.5	363.00	28	13.96	6	10
5	Betty Wills	4.0	296.55	27	10.98	2	2
7	Sally Field	5.5	378.80	36	10.52	2	1
8	Peter Pell	5.5	316.80	28	11.31	2	5
10	Ralph Timms	5.5	295.70	25	11.82	3	5
12	Rolf Thor	4.0	267.20	27	9.90	0	1
15	Jackie Kane	4.0	260.60	25	10.42	1	1
17	Molly Gray	4.0	270.60	28	9.66	0	2
22	Tom Brown	4.0	222.00	24	9.25	0	0
28	Jack Cole	4.0	179.50	19	9.45	0	1
33	Jim Wells	4.0	251.55	25	10.06	1	1
	Totals	50.0	3102.30	294	10.55	17	29

Highest Average Check	- 2 -	John Smith
Most Appetizers	- 2 -	John Smith
Most Desserts	- 2 -	John Smith

Figure 19-12   Servers Productivity Report

cooking and service to the guest. The number of portions recorded in the point-of-sale system can be matched against the number of portions consumed by the kitchen that day. Portion controlled products are naturally more expensive than meat or fish purchased in bulk and cut in the kitchen, and a periodic evaluation should be made of the cost of the purchased portion-controlled product versus the prepared product.

Cost control. The data utilized to generate inventory control information can similarly be utilized to provide cost control reports.

The beverage consumption recorded by the point-of-sale system represents theoretical usage (at cost) for inventory purposes. The costs reflected in the reports generated can be measured against the sales therefrom to provide a theoretical or potential cost of sales, which can be compared against the actual cost of sales.

Similarly, a potential cost of sales for food can be generated but again this cost will have a lesser degree of accuracy due to variances in preparation methods, recipe mix, and product yield.

BEVERAGE SYSTEMS

This chapter would not be complete without comments related to systems specifically designed to control beverages.

The shot glass is the first "system" devised to specifically measure the size of a drink and still finds a major amount of usage. A more controllable method of measuring is *possi-pourers*, devices that are locked on the tops of bottles and that control the quantity of the liquor poured.

In the early 1960s, several companies manufactured and marketed systems in which the bottles, usually standing on racks, were equipped with **metering devices** that not only measured the size of the drink but actually counted the number of drinks poured. The meters are read on a daily basis and a report is prepared showing the opening and closing readings, the number of drinks poured, the selling prices, and a calculation of the potential sales. This system has proved to have several shortcomings. The time required to read the meters and complete the calculations is considerable, in many instances resulting in a higher payroll cost than the payroll savings. Furthermore, unless every product is metered, the sales of the nonmetered items must be rung on a separate key. Obviously, shortages can be hidden if the bartender simply rings a nonmetered sale, even of soft drinks, on the cash register keys assigned to the metered beverages. The earlier versions of these systems also suffered from high numbers of mechanical problems.

The theory of metering has been improved upon considerably by attaching the meter bottles to point-of-sale systems so that when a drink is poured, not only is it measured, it triggers the production of a sales check. These systems are quite effective and are widely used in banquets and service bars. Their physical appearance does, however, despite efforts to disguise them, usually trigger a negative reaction on the part of the customer. This severely limits their use in bars where they are visible to the customer, except, of course, in those establishments, the management of which are not concerned about image or customer reaction.

CHAPTER SUMMARY

Elements of food and beverage control included purchasing, receiving, storeroom controls, cost analysis, and use of point-of-sales systems to provide various reports.

Purchasing the right product requires the use of specifications. Quantities purchased are dependent on the amount of storage and the life expectancy of the product. Quotations are obtained daily either by telephone or fax, as the price of certain items is volatile. The experience that the hotel has had with a vendor is a factor to be considered.

Price fluctuations are not a factor in beverage purchasing. There, while food purchasing is done by telephone or fax, purchase orders may be used for beverages.

The vendor should be required to send an invoice with each delivery, against which quantity and price should be verified. All deliveries should be inspected. Invoices are recorded on a daily receiving sheet.

Control over food inventories is maintained using bin cards and meat tags. A perpetual record is used to control beverage inventories.

Food and beverage costs are calculated and monitored on a daily basis. A complete month-end recap is the basis for accounting entries.

Point of sale systems are used to ensure the sales are properly recorded and the checks settled.

They are also used to provide settlement reports. Other reports are tip reports, payroll input, sales analysis, productivity analysis, inventory control, and cost control.

Various systems are also available to control beverage sales.

REVIEW QUESTIONS

1. What are "purchase specifications" and where are they obtained?
2. Why is it necessary to purchase food by telephone or fax?
3. What is a daily quotation sheet?
4. What is a daily receiving sheet?
5. What are "bin cards"?
6. What is a "meat tag"?
7. What are direct purchases?
8. Explain the value of par stocks for the bars.
9. What are the three goals of a point-of-sale system?
10. What reports are usually produced by a point-of-sale system?

CASE STUDY 1

James Brown has been appointed food and beverage director for the soon-to-be opened Grand Hotel. He was asked to recommend inventory systems for food and beverages. What would you expect to be in his recommendation?

CASE STUDY 2

Bill White is the systems manager for the Smith Arms. He must write a report setting out specifications for a new point-of-sales system. What are the key points you would expect to find in his report?

20

Payroll

After studying this chapter, the student should:

1. Know the history of payroll withholdings and early payroll systems.
2. Know the various steps involved in payroll preparation.
3. Understand the importance of payroll control.

Payroll has consistently been the largest single item of expense in hotel operations. The ratio of salaries, wages, and related expenses to total sales, exclusive of store rentals, ranges from under 30% in motels with no restaurants to almost 50% in larger transient and resort hotels. Because it is the largest expense, it's also the primary area of management concern and the first choice for possible savings when it becomes necessary to trim costs. Unfortunately, cutting payroll costs through a reduction in staff is sometimes self-defeating. As in all service industries, there is a point beyond which the loss of revenue that is inevitable with any reduction in services will exceed the savings in payroll costs.

The change from the simple "pay-earned-equals-pay-received" concept to the present multi-deduction payroll is a 20-century phenomenon. Payroll deductions started for the vast majority of working men and women in January 1937, when the Social Security tax laws became effective. However, tax withholding was by no means a new concept. The Internal Revenue Act of 1862, taxing personal income for the first time, had such a provision. In many other ways it was also very similar to our present federal income tax laws. It called for individual tax returns, permitted personal exemptions, and provided for graduated tax rates.

This law was repealed in 1872, and a similar law enacted in 1894 was declared unconstitutional by the Supreme Court. No further attempts were made to tax personal income until 1912, when a constitutional amendment was proposed giving Congress the power "to lay and collect taxes on incomes, from whatever sources derived." After having been approved by three-quarters of the states, it became the Sixteenth Amendment to the Constitution on February 25, 1913, and, shortly thereafter, the present income tax laws were enacted.

Both the 1862 and 1914 tax laws were enacted to help finance wars and, in both, personal exemptions ($800 and $3,000 respectively) were high enough to exempt most workers. In addition, enforcement was weak and collections unsatisfactory. Then, again to finance a war, Congress passed the Current Tax Payment Act of 1943. On July 1 of that year, money for federal income taxes began to be withheld from workers' pay. Collecting the bulk of this tax at the source proved so successful that most states and some cities have incorporated similar withholding provisions in their personal income tax laws, of which more than 30 were enacted prior to the 1940s and many more since then.

In the late 1930s, unions made a serious effort to unionize the hotel industry. The large number of employees involved justified the intense efforts required, initially, on a hotel-by-hotel basis. But in the end, they succeeded, and the union leaders became the spokesmen for most hotel employees, particularly in and around the major urban and recreational areas.

Unionization brought with it requirements for new deductions. Not only do union contracts contain a clause requiring deductions for union dues and fees, and for many of the fringe benefits that union leaders fought for and obtained; these benefits indirectly created a whole new area of possible deductions from salaries of nonunion employees. Since most of the fringe benefits enjoyed by union members are entirely financed by hotels, managements felt obliged to give similar benefits to their department heads and other salaried nonunion employees. And because of the scarcity of qualified, experienced people to fill these key positions even in periods of high unemployment, their benefits soon outdistanced those negotiated for the union employees.

Many of these benefits offer options requiring voluntary contributions from the employees: hospitalization, dental and major medical policies, pension and savings plans, and additional life insurance coverage over a specified amount that is issued without cost to every nonunion employee. The list of possible voluntary deductions from both union and nonunion employees' salaries is almost endless. The mandatory deductions are limited mainly to taxed and court-ordered garnishments of wages and child support.

PAYROLL SYSTEMS

Early Systems

Until 1914, when the federal personal income tax laws were enacted, there was very little need in most hotels for detailed payroll records. Around the turn of the century, some large hotels were built in our major cities, but most hotels were relatively small and usually owner-operated. All they needed was a time sheet or book to enter the number of hours worked each day by the employees. Department heads, or even the owners themselves, entered the daily hours worked and totaled them for each pay period. A cashier or other designated employee entered the hourly rates and computed the total wages due. Payment was usually made in cash and, if management so desired, employees signed receipts for their wages, either on the envelopes or on a plain sheet listing only their names and total amounts due.

Larger hotels, because of the greater number of employees involved, required tighter controls and additional records. The controls were achieved principally through the introduction of time cards, the proper use of which will be described later in this chapter in the overall discussion of controls. The records consisted mainly of summary sheets, on which the employees were grouped by positions and by departments. Some hotels also had individual earning cards for their employees, but these were not really necessary, since few employees were interested in a report of their annual earnings.

With the enactment of the law taxing personal income, the era of loose record keeping came to an end. What had been optional became mandatory for compliance with the requirements of the law.

In the early years, the figures on the earnings cards had been entered each payday from summary sheets, a simple but time-consuming process susceptible to errors in transcribing the figures. The obvious next step was to eliminate this duplication of work and minimize the possibility of errors by producing both records simultaneously. The solution was the introduction of a variety of systems all founded on the concept termed one-write systems.

One-write systems were designed to prepare payroll journals and individual employee's earnings records and a check or employee's receipt if payment was made by cash. Carbon paper was placed between the earnings record and the payroll journal while the top line of the check or receipt was carbonized on the back. Thus by placing the check or receipt on top of the other two records the information recorded on the check would be entered in the other two records simultaneously. The earlier versions were referred to as pegboard systems, because the three records were placed on a wooden board and held in place by wooden pegs on each side.

A more sophisticated one-write system is the One-Write Bookkeeping system manufactured by McBee Systems. The board is replaced by a compact (when folded) poster-binder with a firm writing surface and textured vinyl exterior. It employs the same "one-write" principle, recording the check, the employee's earning record, and the payroll journal in one step. A pressure bar on the left-hand side holds the forms securely in place. An example is shown in Figure 20-1. These systems are still used extensively in small restaurants and private clubs and to some degree in small lodging establishments that do not have enough employees to use a computer or do not use a payroll service.

Current Systems

The introduction in the 1920s of electromechanical payroll machines, usually with typewriter attachments, virtually eliminated the use of manual systems in large hotels. Checks and payroll journals were printed mechanically and the machines were programmed to pick up and accumulate deduction totals for the individual employee's records. It should be noted that the only change in the appearance of the final payroll journal from that illustrated in Figure 20-1 is the ever-increasing number of deductions. Not only did the deductions increase in number but the manner in which they are determined has become more and more complex. It was therefore natural that when some companies started to provide computer services to business the first area on which they focused was payroll services. Since, as previously mentioned, the preparation of a hotel payroll is similar to that of other businesses, it was natural that hotels would follow the direction of other businesses in contracting out their payroll preparation to service bureaus.

While many of the large hotels have extensive computer installations, most choose to use service bureaus rather than prepare their payrolls in-house. Keeping up with the continually changing formulas for deductions, not only state and federal taxes but also insurance, union dues, and so on, requires continuous program changes, too time-consuming for in-house computer staffs. As a result, the large majority of hotels (both large and small) and larger restaurants and clubs find it appropriate to place their payroll preparation function in the hands of service bureaus. In fact, most service bureaus prepare all necessary tax-reporting forms as well as filings required by insurance companies, banks, unions, and other regulatory bodies. They frequently mail the checks to the employees, handle the various tax remittances, and sometimes even reconcile the payroll bank account. Thus the role of the accounting department is one of control over input and entry of the final results into the hotel accounting system.

PAYROLL CONTROL

Since the majority of hotel employees are paid on an hourly basis, the most important area of input to control is the hours worked. However, it is also important to control the rate of pay and the calculation of deductions and even to verify the actual existence of the employee. It is not unknown in the industry for an unscrupulous department head to place fictitious or nonworking persons on the

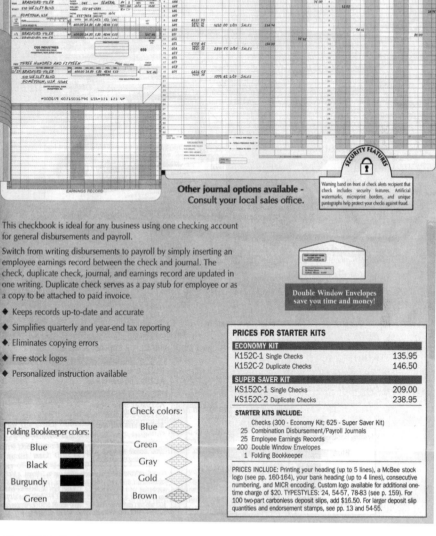

GENERAL DISBURSEMENTS/PAYROLL

Our popular checkbook combines bill paying with payroll capability

"I am very pleased with the one-write system & have bragged to my customers about the convenience compared to my previous system."

Bruce Summer
Home Brite, Sharpsville, IN

Other journal options available –
Consult your local sales office.

Warning band on front of check alerts recipient that check includes security features. Artificial watermarks, microprint borders, and unique pantographs help protect your checks against fraud.

This checkbook is ideal for any business using one checking account for general disbursements and payroll.

Switch from writing disbursements to payroll by simply inserting an employee earnings record between the check and journal. The check, duplicate check, journal, and earnings record are updated in one writing. Duplicate check serves as a pay stub for employee or as a copy to be attached to paid invoice.

- ◆ Keeps records up-to-date and accurate
- ◆ Simplifies quarterly and year-end tax reporting
- ◆ Eliminates copying errors
- ◆ Free stock logos
- ◆ Personalized instruction available

Double Window Envelopes save you time and money!

Folding Bookkeeper colors:

Color	
Blue	
Black	
Burgundy	
Green	

Check colors:

- Blue
- Green
- Gray
- Gold
- Brown

PRICES FOR STARTER KITS

ECONOMY KIT

K152C-1	Single Checks	135.95
K152C-2	Duplicate Checks	146.50

SUPER SAVER KIT

KS152C-1	Single Checks	209.00
KS152C-2	Duplicate Checks	238.95

STARTER KITS INCLUDE:

Checks (300 - Economy Kit; 625 - Super Saver Kit)
25 Combination Disbursement/Payroll Journals
25 Employee Earnings Records
200 Double Window Envelopes
1 Folding Bookkeeper

PRICES INCLUDE: Printing your heading (up to 5 lines), a McBee stock logo (see pp. 160-164), your bank heading (up to 4 lines), consecutive numbering, and MICR encoding. Custom logo available for additional one-time charge of $20. TYPESTYLES: 24, 54-57, 78-83 (see p. 159). For 100 two-part carbonless deposit slips, add $16.50. For larger deposit slip quantities and endorsement stamps, see pp. 13 and 54-55.

Figure 20-1 One-Write System

payroll. However, all payroll control fails if an unnecessary employee is hired. This can be avoided by establishing proper guidelines for the staffing of various positions.

Staff Planning

The initial effort at staff planning should take place during the preopening period of a hotel. The feasibility study in which the viability of a hotel project is analyzed should contain the rationale for the estimates of payroll costs. This rationale should provide estimated staffing required for varying levels of business as well as anticipated rates of pay. This is, in effect, the initial planning guide. After the startup period is over, those guidelines should be revised in line with actual experience.

Staffing guidelines should be determined for all departments. Staffing in the overhead departments will essentially be fixed (subject, possibly, to seasonal adjustments), while staffing in the revenue-producing departments will be fixed in some positions but for the most part variable relative to volume. Following are some of the more common measurements used in setting guidelines for variable positions:

Front desk receptionists—in relation to expected number of arrivals

Reservationists—in relation to reservation activity expected

Room attendants and floor housekeepers—in relation to anticipated number of rooms occupied

Servers, buspersons, and cooks—in relation to anticipated number of covers

Bartenders—in relation to anticipated volume

In many of the larger hotels at least one full-time employee, usually reporting directly to the general manager, is concerned exclusively with staff planning. The duties of this position are to assist the department heads in planning for the frequent temporary changes in staffing requirements and to make recommendations to top management for permanent changes. In the absence of a staff planner, these functions should be assumed by the controller.

The estimated gross sales and related statistics—percentage of occupancy, number of covers, and so on—are essential for any overall studies of long-term staffing requirements. But payroll savings can be realized only by reviewing current operations and expectations on a day-to-day basis. The reports used to make these studies are the forecasts projecting daily percentages of occupancy, arrivals, and departures. These are usually prepared each month for the following month and updated each week on a specified day for the following week.

Most front-office managers also regularly issue a daily forecast, to alert other department heads to any last-minute changes. However, these forecasts can be useless in controlling payroll costs unless the effectiveness of staff planning by department heads is checked. The methods that are used by the controller for this purpose depend to a great extent on the size of the hotel and the reports required by management. In some properties, department heads are required each week to estimate their staffing requirements for the following week. These reports usually show the estimated number of full-time employees, by category, needed for each day. These estimates are then compared daily or weekly with the actual payroll. Where there are substantial differences, the controller should review the results with the responsible department heads to ascertain the reasons for them.

The two categories of employees most affected by variations in the volume of business are room attendants and service employees in the restaurants. Control over these employees is best maintained through the use of productivity reports, comparing the actual productivity to an acceptable standard set by management. Productivity refers to the average number of rooms serviced or guests served by the respective employees. It is easily arrived at by dividing the number of occupied rooms, daily or weekly, by the number of room attendants employed for the same period, or the total number of guests served in each food outlet by the number of waiters and waitresses employed there. Again, variations from standards should be reviewed by the controller with the housekeeper or food and beverage manager.

Accounting Control for Payroll

Accounting controls start with the processing of new employees. This is primarily the function of the human resources department, and the many forms required were described in Chapter 6. But duties without related responsibilities are seldom properly performed. Therefore, in this phase of the operation, the human resources manager should share the responsibility of control with the controller.

The human resources department does not do the hiring or initiate status changes for existing employees; as previously mentioned, that function is the responsibility of the department heads. For this process, a multipurpose payroll and status-authorization form, shown in Figure 20-2, may be used, or else separate forms for new hires, terminations, changes, and so on. After the required approvals have been affixed, the forms are sent to human resources. There they are reviewed and checked, and copies inserted or proper notations made in the employees' permanent files. The originals, after being initialed by the human resources manager or their designated representatives, are then forwarded to the payroll department.

For proper control, this input into payroll must be checked and verified. Since most hotels' payrolls are on a computer, this is relatively simple. All it requires is a program designed to automatically produce a weekly list of all new hires, terminations, and changes. These three listings will be described separately, although they are usually incorporated into one list.

HOTEL GRAYLIG
PAYROLL AND STATUS AUTHORIZATION

CHECK PERSONNEL ACTION TO BE INITIATED BY THIS FORM		
☐ New Hire	☐ Personal Data Change	☐ Leave of Absence – Depart
☐ Job Change	☐ Contract Change	☐ Leave of Absence – Return
☐ Rate Change	☐ Termination	☐ Other (Explain in Comments)

EMPL. #	SOCIAL SECURITY #	LAST NAME	FIRST	MIDDLE

*ACTION EFFECTIVE ON >

*SALARY CHANGES EFFECTIVE ONLY ON FIRST DAY OF PAY PERIOD

FROM — COMPLETE BELOW ON ALL ACTIONS			TO — ENTER ONLY INFORMATION TO BE CHANGED		
DIVISION	LOCATION - CITY	Bldg. & Floor	DIVISION	LOCATION - CITY	Bldg. & Floor
DEPARTMENT		Dept./CC#	DEPARTMENT		Dept./CC#
POSITION TITLE		Sal Gr/Ex. Lev.	POSITION TITLE		Sal Gr/Ex. Lev.
IMMEDIATE SUPERVISOR			IMMEDIATE SUPERVISOR		

SALARY STATUS

	WEEKLY	ANNUAL	LAST INCREASE	REASON FOR CHANGE	IF MERIT, INDICATE PERFORMANCE LEVEL	POSITION IN RANGE
PRESENT SALARY	$	$	Date:	☐ Merit		
				☐ Promotion	☐ Meets Expectations	% Increase
CHANGE ±	$	$	Amount:	☐ Reclassification	☐ Above Expectations	
				☐ Contract	☐ Exceptional	New Position in Range
NEW SALARY	$	$	Reason:	☐ Other	☐ Other	

EMPLOYMENT, TRANSFER OR PROMOTION

Date of Birth	Date of Hire	Telephone (Area Code and Number)	Sex	EEO DESIGNATION	
				☐ White	☐ American Indian
Name of Person Replaced		Last Salary	Date Left Position	☐ African American	☐ Oriental
				☐ Spanish Surname	☐ Other

TERMINATION OR LEAVE OF ABSENCE

	WORKING DAYS	REASON FOR TERMINATION			ELIGIBLE FOR REHIRE?	LEAVE OF ABSENCE	
Severance Pay Due	#	☐ Resignation ☐ Layoff	☐ Death		☐ Yes ☐ No	☐ Disability ☐ Pregnancy	HOW LONG? _____
Vacation Pay Due	#	☐ Dismissal ☐ Retirement ☐ Other				☐ Military ☐ Other	

COMMENTS

APPROVAL
DATE

	DEPARTMENTAL		EXECUTIVE		PERSONNEL	
	IMMED. SUPVR.	DEPT. HEAD	DIVISION	CORPORATE	OPERATIONS	COMPENSATION
APPROVAL						
DATE						

PERSONNEL USE ONLY

Unit Rate	EEO	Sal. Chg.	MS	Term	Special Payment Amount & Reason
					$

NOTE: Minimum required is original and two copies: Original to Payroll Department, copies to Personnel and Originating Department head.

Figure 20-2 Multipurpose Form

For new hires, the list should show all the pertinent information—department, employee number, name, address, Social Security number, salary (both regular and overtime hourly rates), number of dependents, and so forth. If the employee is entitled to meals, that should also be shown, as well as the proper code for those classified as tip employees. If these reports are properly checked with the authorization forms by the designated employees in both the human resources and accounting departments, the possibility of error is almost eliminated. The termination report should show the department, employee number, name, and salary. The last figure should then be checked against the amount shown on the authorization for that employee's replacement. For the list of changes, the only information needed, in addition to the department, employee number, and name, is the new status, salary, address, number of dependents, and other such data.

Tip Employees

Earlier a reference was made to tipping as being the area where hotel and restaurant payroll preparation requires additional customization not encountered in other industries. The taxation of tips has always been a major problem for the Internal Revenue Service. The IRS maintains a firm policy that all tips received must be reported by the employee and requires that any employee earning over $20 a month in tips must maintain a daily record of tips received. However, the requirement that hotels and restaurants pay FICA on all declared tips has discouraged employers from enforcing the rules. The 1994 regulation permitting employers to take a credit against federal income taxes equal to FICA paid on excess tips has reduced the impact.

However, the main instrument used by the IRS to encourage tip declaration is the Tax Equity and Fiscal Responsibility Act of 1982 (TEFRA). This act requires that to the extent that actual declared tips do not equal at least 8% of sales, the employer is required to allocate the shortfall among the offending employees. This requires not only the filing of Form 8027 but creates a bookkeeping headache for employers. To avoid the bookkeeping many employers have encouraged employees to declare 8% of sales. However, this remains the prerogative of the individual employee and cannot be mandated by the employer.

In order to facilitate the handling of tips for payroll tax purposes, gratuities are divided into two categories: optional (tips) and prearranged (fixed gratuities). For this reason the special coding referred to in the preceding section is necessary. Gratuities to bellmen, when rooming or checking out individual guests, and to waiters and waitresses in the restaurants and coffee shops, are optional, although 10–15% is considered good etiquette in restaurants nowadays. Guests may give as little or as much as they please. However, for group or tour guests registering simultaneously, the bellmen's gratuities are often prearranged on a per-bag basis and charged to the sponsors. Banquet tips are always prearranged at a fixed percentage of the total food and beverage charges and are included as a separate item on banquet bills.

Both types are subject to all payroll and withholding provisions of the tax laws. In other words, for tax purposes they are treated the same as cash wages. At the end of each year, both totals are added to the employees' wages to arrive at the reported annual earnings. However, there is a difference in the payroll treatment.

Prearranged gratuities are processed through the payroll, included in the employees' cash wages, and offset in the general ledger against the amount collected from the guests. Declared tips are also processed through the payroll, taxed, but then deducted, since obviously they cannot be included in the employees' net pay.

Time Cards

The vast majority of restaurant and hotel employees punch a time clock. (In most hotels, exceptions are made only for department heads, their assistants, and possibly clerical help if they are nonunion.) However, time cards reflect only the time the employees entered and left the hotel, not the number of hours they worked. For proper control department heads should record on a time sheet, without reference to the time cards, the number of hours each of their employees worked each day. At the end of each pay period, the time cards should be sent by the timekeepers directly to the payroll clerks in accounting. There, as a test-check that should include at least 10% of the cards for each department, the hours punched are extended and compared with the hours worked as entered on the time sheets. In many hotels, however, there is not enough time while the payrolls are being processed for such extensive test-checks. In such cases, they can be made after a thorough investigation and review with each responsible department head and can be adjusted in the following pay period.

Overtime

Overtime pay is another area that requires careful analysis and strict controls. Most hotel and restaurant employees are entitled to overtime pay for all hours worked in excess of their normal work week. The federal minimum-wage laws mandate this for all employees except executives, their assistants, and other members of the administrative staff. For union members, the terms of their contracts would be in effect if more favorable to the employees.

The most important factor in the handling of overtime is not if it is authorized but *when* it is authorized. Authorization after the fact is pointless. If the employee has worked, he or she is certainly going to be paid. Except for emergencies or unusual circumstances, overtime should not be allowed unless it is authorized in advance. Properly planned occasional use of overtime saves money. However, analyses of overtime payments have often been unfavorable. They have shown that the establishments could have reduced their payroll costs by hiring one or more additional employees, thus minimizing the need for overtime. Later in this chapter we will address overtime reports.

Vacations

Vacations are necessary but costly, and only through careful planning and only with proper scheduling can this expense be controlled. Vacation lengths are fixed, determined by the period of employment. Management's only prerogative is to establish the time during which they can be taken. Obviously, the best time to schedule vacations is during slow periods, which depend on the location, type, and clientele of the hotel. Efficient department heads also try to spread their employees' vacations to minimize the cost of replacements. They should determine whether to cover for vacationing employees by paying other employees overtime or by hiring temporary, part-time help. Then, too, many employees request additional time off without pay. In such a case, if a replacement is not necessary, or if the cost of one is less than the employee's salary, the request should be not only granted, but encouraged.

Vacation scheduling is the responsibility of department heads. To perform this function properly, they must have a record of the employment date for each of their employees so they can determine the amount of vacation to which each is entitled. Then, wherever possible, they can give a choice of dates, based on seniority. Meanwhile, accounting checks payroll to ensure that employees receive only the amount of vacation pay to which they are entitled. This would be simple if all employees took their full vacations at one time. But many, with the consent of their department heads, break up their vacations. Some may elect to take an extra day or days off; others may divide the multiple weeks to which they are entitled into two or more single-week vacations.

Department heads should keep records and exercise reasonable control over their employees' vacation pay. Accounting must do so also.

A computer can be programmed to print out a monthly report and keep a record of each employee's vacation days due and taken. At the beginning of each year, the total number of vacation days due each employee for that year is entered into the computer as part of the payroll data. A separate program is then designed to deduct from that total any vacation days taken and paid for. It should also provide for an immediate printout, listing by department the names of any employees exceeding their allowed vacations, and showing the total vacation days due and paid to each employee so listed.

Test-Checks

There are at least two test-checks that should be made by the controllers or their assistants. The first, a periodic review of wage rates, should be made at least once a month for two or more departments at a time. It requires the cooperation and assistance of the staff in the human resources department, since it is best accomplished by comparing the rates as shown on the payroll with the wages as shown in the personnel files. If a complete check of all employees' rates is preferred, then the comparisons should be made every three or four months. As with every other control, differences must be thoroughly investigated; if any fraud is uncovered, the offending employee should be fired and, if the amount warrants, arrested.

The second test-check, of the distribution of payroll checks, should be made weekly. Its purpose is to verify that there is an actual employee for each check issued. The usual procedure on payday is for department heads to sign for, receive, and distribute the checks to all the employees in their departments. For the test-check, each week the checks for one department, chosen at random, are instead distributed by an accounting clerk. Either the affected employees are asked to come to the accounting office for their pay, or the clerk goes to their department to distribute the checks. Because personal recognition is almost impossible, the employees should be made to sign for their checks. One method of obtaining the signatures is to list all employees, usually in numerical order by employee number, and have each sign next to his or her name. Some hotels go one step further. They have some signatures verified each week by comparison with the ones in the personnel files.

Cash Payments

Cash wages have become almost extinct in the hospitality industry. In the event of immediate termination of an employee, a call to the payroll service will immediately provide the information on deductions required to prepare a manual check. This check can then be recorded in the preparation of the next payroll with specific coding so that a second payroll check is not issued. In circumstances where an employee is underpaid but will be receiving a payroll check the following period, a nonpayroll check can be issued for a payroll advance based on the estimated net underpayment. This advance can then be deducted in the following week.

Advances against future earnings are extremely poor policy. This only places the employee in the position of playing a continual game of "catch up." Furthermore, such requests usually come from an employee who has a prior history of the same problem. In situations of dire emergency, with the approval of management, a loan may be necessary. However, when such a loan is granted, the terms of repayment should spread the balance over a period of time within which the financial situation of the employees can be reasonably expected to allow repayment. Furthermore, a loan document, in writing, should be executed so that in the event employment is ended, legal action can, if appropriate, be instituted to recover the balance.

A singular exception to the demise of cash wages occurs in some major cities, in particular, New York City. In these locations it is common practice for banquet employees, in response to the need, to work in several hotels over a period of a week. This group of temporary employees includes dishwashers and housemen who are at the lower end of the pay scale. Need, combined with long-established practice, has resulted in these employees being paid in cash at the end of each shift. To facilitate these payments a payroll clerk must prepare a cash payroll voucher (Figure 20-3) from which the payment is subsequently entered into the payroll records. This is an area that is wide open to abuse and requires continuous audit and scrutiny. A periodic "check-off" should be held where the names of the employees are noted as they leave the hotel and the list is immediately

CASH PAYROLL VOUCHER

79-80-2-0

DATE _____   W/E _____

WAGES WILL NOT BE PAID EXCEPT ON PRESENTATION OF THIS CARD

AUTH. DEPT'S HEADS SIGNATURE

1-2 HOTEL	EXPLANATION/REASON	3-6 DEPT. #

7-15 SOCIAL SECURITY #

PRINT NAME OF EMPLOYEE AND ADDRESS

22-36 LAST	37-47 FIRST				48 INT.		
	49 M/S	50-51 Fed. Ex.	55 Sex	67 Res.		77 R	78 Un.

79-80-2-1

22-48 STREET ADDRESS

49-68 CITY	69-73 STATE (ABBN)	74-79 ZIP

79-80-6-0   EARNINGS   AMOUNT

28-31 REGULAR HRS. @	36-41	
32-35 OVERTIME HRS.	42-46	
47-48 OTHER CODE	49-53	
57-60 VACATION HRS.	61-66	
SERVICE CHARGES	67-72	

79-80-6-1

GROSS EARNINGS	73-78	$	
FICA	16-20		
FED. W/TAX	21-25		
STATE TAX	26-29		
CITY TAX	30-33		
UNION DUES	34-37		
UNION FEES	38-41		
OTHER (58)	59-62		
TOTAL DEDUCTIONS		$	
NET PAY 63-68		$	

RECEIVED PAYMENT IN FULL FOR SERVICES TO DATE AND CERTIFY THAT THE NUMBER OF WITHHOLDING EXEMPTIONS CLAIMED ABOVE DOES NOT EXCEED THE NUMBER TO WHICH I AM ENTITLED.

SIGNATURE

ADDRESS

PUNCHED		VERIFIED	

NOTE: Requires multiple copies, one for the employee and others as directed by the controller.

Figure 20-3   Cash Payroll Voucher

checked against the payroll vouchers prepared. Additionally, a specific schedule of hours to be worked should be prepared in advance and matched against the recorded hours.

Control of Deductions

As previously indicated, control over deductions is also a very necessary procedure. Employers act as trustees, temporary custodians of the money deducted from their employees' wages. Every deduction must be separately reconciled for each employee and in total. Each requires a separate form to balance and file reporting the deductions. Hotels, as a service industry, need many more employees in relation to size and volume of sales than any other type of business. They also employ a higher percentage of unskilled workers, which results in a larger turnover. Including part-time, temporary help such as banquet waiters and dishwashers, it is not unusual for a hotel to process through the payroll each year three or four times the number of employees on its permanent staff. Needless to say, the more employees involved, the more difficult it is to reconcile each deduction.

Computerizing the payrolls has eliminated most of these problems. However, an increasing number of hotels with in-house computers have turned this function over to an outside data-processing company. The results are better and the overall cost usually lower. Similarly, many restaurants and clubs utilize outside payroll services. These companies can better afford to hire specialists in the field and keep abreast of the many changes in laws and regulations affecting the payroll. Insofar as they can, they guarantee full and timely compliance with these regulations. Deductions are accurate and the reconciliations rarely, if ever, out of balance. It is not surprising that data-processing companies have steadily increased their volume of business in the hotel field.

Laws at state and local levels regarding taxes and employees' benefits differ in their provisions, so it would not be feasible to try and describe all the varied reports needed to satisfy these requirements. There are, however, many similar benefits enjoyed by employees in most hotels. Unionization of employees is quite common, and all hotels are subject to federal laws and Internal Revenue Service regulations. A brief review of the reporting forms and deposit requirements of these follows.

Reports and payments to the proper agency, at all levels of government, should be made on time. The interest and penalties if they are delayed can be very costly. Two separate reports must be submitted to the IRS; one combines the Social Security, Medicare, and Federal Income Tax withheld, and the other is for unemployment taxes.

The Social Security, Medicare, and Income Tax Report (Form 941) is due on the last day of the month following each calendar quarter. When the laws were originally enacted, payment in full was made quarterly and included with the returns. Regulations have since been changed to require deposits during each quarter. At the present time they range from no advance deposit, if the combined taxes are less than $500 in any quarter, to weekly for the larger hotels whose combined taxes exceed $50,000 per year. For the latter, deposits are due 3 banking days after the date wages were actually paid.

Withholding Tax Statements, W-2s, are prepared for the calendar year and due by January 31 of the following year. The IRS allows employers an additional month, until the end of February, to file copy A with them. They are individual multicopy, multipurpose forms, headed with the hotel's operating name, address, and employer number. Each employee is identified through his or her name, address, and Social Security number. The figures reported must show the total amount of each tax deduction made during the year and the gross wages used to calculate each one: Federal income tax, Social Security and, where required, state and local income taxes.

Two sets of W-2s are prepared simultaneously for each employee. One set is used to send reports to each taxing authority (the original to the IRS) and one to be retained as a file copy. The other set, with the same number of copies, is given to the employee. The total deductions must be reconciled to the amounts shown on the quarterly reports, which in turn are reconciled to the deposits or payments as required. For every deduction, a tape, either run on computer or adding machine, must be sent to the taxing authority with whatever summary sheet to be made on Form W-3, shown with the W-2 in Figure 20-4. Since the 1980s, the IRS has required employers filing more than 250 W-2s to use magnetic media. Most states are now either requiring or accepting similar filings.

Federal unemployment taxes are entirely paid by the employer and require no detailed reporting forms. Like all payroll taxes, they are based on a calendar year, with the maximum taxable wages for each employee set by Congress. The tax return (Form 940) is due by January 31 for the preceding year. Substantial credit is given for payment made to the state for unemployment insurance. Since the 1980s, the maximum rate has been 6.2% with a maximum credit of 5.4%, creating a net rate of 0.8%. The advance deposit requirements are relatively simple. If the accumulated tax liability exceeds $100 in any quarter, which is the case with most hotels, deposit of the total tax due is required before the end of the month following the quarter.

State laws have different deposit requirements and different regulations as to when or how their residents qualify for unemployment benefits. The amount of the payment, up to each state's maximum, depends on the individual applicant's earnings. Some states, commonly called reporting states, require detailed quarterly returns listing each employee's Social Security number, name, and taxable or total wages. Others, known as request states, require only quarterly summaries showing the computation of the total tax due. If a former employee files for unemployment benefits, a special form requesting detailed payroll information is sent to the hotel. This form must be completed and returned, usually within 7 to 10 days; otherwise a penalty for noncompliance may be assessed against the hotel.

a Control number 22222	Void ☐	For Official Use Only ▶ OMB No. 1545-0008		
b Employer identification number			1 Wages, tips, other compensation	2 Federal income tax withheld
c Employer's name, address, and ZIP code			3 Social security wages	4 Social security tax withheld
			5 Medicare wages and tips	6 Medicare tax withheld
			7 Social security tips	8 Allocated tips
d Employee's social security number			9 Advance EIC payment	10 Dependent care benefits
e Employee's name (first, middle initial, last)			11 Nonqualified plans	12 Benefits included in box 1
			13 See instrs. for box 13	14 Other

		15 Statutory employee ☐	Deceased ☐	Pension plan ☐	Legal rep. ☐	Deferred compensation ☐
f Employee's address and ZIP code						

16 State	Employer's state I.D. no.	17 State wages, tips, etc.	18 State income tax	19 Locality name	20 Local wages, tips, etc.	21 Local income tax

Form **W-2** Wage and Tax Statement **1999**

Department of the Treasury—Internal Revenue Service
For Privacy Act and Paperwork Reduction

a Control number 33333		For Official Use Only ▶ OMB No. 1545-0008		
b **Kind of Payer** ▶	941 ☐ Military ☐ 943 ☐ CT-1 ☐ Hshld. emp. ☐ Medicare govt. emp. ☐		1 Wages, tips, other compensation	2 Federal income tax withheld
			3 Social security wages	4 Social security tax withheld
c Total number of Forms W-2	d Establishment number		5 Medicare wages and tips	6 Medicare tax withheld
e Employer identification number			7 Social security tips	8 Allocated tips
f Employer's name			9 Advance EIC payments	10 Dependent care benefits
			11 Nonqualified plans	12 Deferred compensation
			13	
			14	
g Employer's address and ZIP code				
h Other EIN used this year			15 Income tax withheld by third-party payer	
i Employer's state I.D. no.				
Contact person	Telephone number ( )	Fax number ( )	E-mail address	

Under penalties of perjury, I declare that I have examined this return and accompanying documents, and, to the best of my knowledge and belief, they are true, correct, and complete.

Signature ▶   Title ▶   Date ▶

Form **W-3 Transmittal of Wage and Tax Statements** **1999**   Department of the Treasury Internal Revenue Service

Send this entire page with the entire Copy A page of Forms W-2 to the Social Security Administration. Photocopies are NOT acceptable.

Do not send any remittance (cash, checks, money orders, etc.) with FORMS W-2 and W-3.

Figure 20-4   Federal Forms W-2 and W-3

Other Deductions

Employee benefits and union contracts account for most of the other payroll deductions. All require special programming so that the necessary figures, statistics, and reports are automatically produced or available on demand.

Union contributions. Even though almost all benefits to union members require no employee contributions, the hotel's liability to the trustees administering each fund must be separately calculated, recorded, and paid. The benefits vary, but they usually include hospitalization, medical and life insurance, and pensions, and in some contracts dental benefits. Contributions are not necessarily based on cash wages; gratuities and meal allowances may be included, and the amount due a fund may be based on the total number of union employees in the hotel or on the total number of hours they worked. The percentages used to determine the cost of the benefits, regardless of base, are usually different. These factors must be analyzed and taken into account when setting up a computer program for processing the payroll.

Detailed reports listing the names of covered employees are usually not required. The unions control their membership through the dues and fees deduction reports. Dues are normally payable monthly and are deducted, by agreement with the union, in the same week of each month. Most unions either maintain their own employment bureaus or work very closely with their state's employment offices. A hotel is usually obligated under contract to try and hire all replacements of union employees through these offices. If they cannot provide a qualified union member to fill a position, then the hotel is free to hire any applicant that meets the requirements. However, since most union contracts call for a closed shop, new employees must join the union within a specified time and pay a fee for the privilege. These fees are rarely deducted in full in any one week; the usual procedure is to spread the total over a period of weeks.

Dues and fees thus require two separate functions to process and control them. The first is to deduct them and produce a detailed report listing the name, position, and amount deducted for each employee. The other controls the number of deductions for fees and stops them when the total amount due has been paid.

Shared benefits. Many hotels and restaurants offer their employees the option to upgrade some of their benefits by sharing the additional cost—by making voluntary contributions through payroll deductions. The internal administration of these programs may be a human resources or an accounting function, depending on company policy. Control of the income and expense is, as always, the controller's responsibility. However, this is an area where administration and control are so intermingled that it is often difficult to know where one ends and the other begins. Only through the complete cooperation of all concerned can the interest of the employees and the hotel be fully protected.

These plans usually involve a third party—a trustee, an insurance company, and a bank. The operation pays the total cost and is partially reimbursed by the employees' contributions. But this system can cause unnecessary expenses for the hotel and even loss of benefits for a few employees for the following reasons.

The insurance or administrators of the plan must have at all times a current list of all covered employees. Benefits such as hospitalization, major medical, dental, and life insurance cease when employment terminates (although the employee may have the option to convert to direct payments). Yet, unless they are so notified, the outside administrators will continue billing the hotel for its former employees. Conversely, in order to arrange for proper coverage, they must also be notified as new employees become eligible for the benefits, or when employees are given increases in wages that entitle them to an increase in benefits.

The other side of the coin involves payroll. Obviously, when employees are terminated, their deductions are no longer made, but deductions for new employees should start on the day they become eligible for benefits. Also, many employees are allowed to take time off without pay during slow periods. Since the benefits cannot be canceled, the deductions should not be stopped. If the time off is sufficient to create payless periods, then the deductions should be doubled up when the employee returns until the lost amounts are recouped. And additional benefits due to a promotion or a raise in pay may require an increase in the amount of the employee's contributions. All this points out the absolute necessity of communication and cooperation between the internal administrator and the paymaster.

But the dissemination of information, essential as it is, does not ensure proper coverage for the employees or control over expenses. Both can be achieved only by thoroughly analyzing the bills received from the administrators and in some way checking them with the payroll summary sheets. The totals shown in each pay period for each deduction should also be verified. This requires a worksheet listing by name and department the employees for whom changes in the amount of any deduction were processed during each pay period. The correct totals for any period are then the previous period's totals adjusted by the net differences of the listed additions and deletions. Prudence also dictates that each change be checked with the payroll to verify that it was not only correct in amount, but was processed for the named employee.

Some companies, such as Blue Cross and Blue Shield, submit as part of their bills itemized lists showing the name and charge for each covered employee. The charge denotes the type and amount of coverage. This is helpful if the plan includes an option for employees to upgrade their benefits. When checking the listings against the latest payroll summary sheet to verify that each person listed there is currently employed, clerks can also verify the deductions for those employees with excess coverage.

On bills for life insurance premiums, most companies will usually show, in addition to the rate per thousand, only the number and total dollar amount of all the policies then in effect. They should also attach a statement giving the figures at the close of the last billing period, itemization of all changes and adjustments in the interim, and the net totals for the current billing period. Most plans give the eligible employees basic coverage with an option to purchase additional amounts of insurance. This way, any worksheet set up to control these bills must start off with the number of eligible employees, which will always be the number of policies in effect, and the total basic coverage. As options are exercised, only the dollar amount need be adjusted. Once the original totals are set up, all that is required to keep the worksheets current is to enter all additions, deletions, and adjustments as they are processed. If they are properly updated and the insurance company is promptly advised of all changes, the totals on the worksheet as of any billing date should agree with the figures shown on the bills.

However, verifying the amount billed does not prove that each employee's share and the total deductions are correct. The amount of each deduction must be checked with payroll when the employees first exercise their options, and rechecked as soon as any changes are processed. Total deductions should be checked every month since a fixed monthly amount is usually charged for each thousand dollars of optional insurance. The total option insurance is the difference between the total amount of insurance in effect at the end of any month and the total amount given to all eligible employees without charge. This difference, multiplied by the rate per thousand charged for optional insurance, should equal the total deductions made each month for insurance.

Savings bonds. Deductions for savings bonds require detailed reports and individual accounts for every participating employee, in effect setting up a subsidiary ledger. As bonds are purchased for employees, their accounts are debited. Monthly, total net credits of all individual accounts should be compared with the net balance of the liability account in the general ledger.

The computer should be programmed to print out two monthly reports with all the required information. The first is a trial balance of the individual bond-deduction accounts with the activity for the month. The employees may be listed in alphabetical order or, preferably, alphabetically within each department. The headings for the amount columns should include the opening balance, total deductions, bonds purchased, and closing net balance. The second report is a list of those employees shown on the trial balance as having purchased bonds in that month. This report, prepared for the bank issuing the bonds, must have the employees' names and addresses, the face value of each bond, and, when required, the names of their co-owners or beneficiaries. The totals on the trial-balance reports should be checked every month: deductions against the payroll, bonds purchased versus the check drawn for that purpose, and final balance against the liability account in the general ledger.

PAYROLL ANALYSIS

As noted in the opening paragraph of this chapter, payroll is the largest single item of expense in a hotel. Obviously, to formulate its payroll policies, top management needs and must demand detailed reports and statistics with comments and analysis by the controller. Of course, such reports are useless unless corrective actions are generated by them.

To describe every report requested by or given to management is impossible. Many of them are described in our review of accounting controls and procedures: lists of new hires and payroll changes; department heads' estimates of their staffing requirements, with the accompanying comparison to the actual; overtime reports, with explanations of unauthorized payments; productivity reports, particularly for room attendants and restaurant and banquet-service employees; vacation reports; and special reports analyzing the paid-in-cash payroll for part-time, temporary employees. Budgets give management the opportunity to set payroll policies. Therefore, a prerequisite to budget approval is awareness of the staffing requirements and salary increments used in projecting payroll costs. Then, to review and, if necessary, revise its payroll policies, management should use the periodic updating of revenue forecasts and budget revisions.

For effective control, analysis of payroll costs must be made by job classifications within each department. This requires a worksheet showing the number of employees, the hours worked, and the wages paid for each classification. These figures are forwarded to management in a report showing comparable figures for the same week of the last year and the accumulated totals to date for the current and preceding year. In some hotels, this management report is prepared weekly—in most others, monthly.

It must be kept in mind that reports reflect only projections or actual expenses. Only management, with the assistance of the controller's analysis and explanations of differences, can formulate or revise policies to effectively control payroll costs.

CHAPTER SUMMARY

Payroll is usually the largest single item of expense, varying from 30% in properties with no food operations to over 50% in full-service properties.

Although income laws existed much earlier, payroll deductions started for most people in 1937 with social security.

Income taxes, union dues, and various types of voluntary deductions followed. Most deductions require a signed authorization by employees.

The most common early system was a one-write system where a check or payroll voucher, payroll journal, and earnings record were all created at one time. While some small establishments still use one-write, the vast majority of hotels now have their payrolls prepared by service bureaus.

Staff planning, based on productivity, is an essential element of payroll control. Accounting control requires the use of a form to record all changes in payroll status.

There are special procedures required to handle declared tips and banquet gratuities.

The recording of hourly payroll is based on time cards in most properties, although time sheets are also sometimes used.

The method of authorizing overtime is very important.

Vacation costs can be kept within control by proper scheduling.

Test checks are usually made on payroll distribution.

Cash payments are rare but are still used in some cities where part-time banquet employees circulate to various hotels.

Some deductions require control and reconciliation and may involve the filing of monthly and quarterly reports.

Certain reports may be used in payroll analysis.

REVIEW QUESTIONS

1. For most employees, when did payroll deductions start and what was the nature of the deductions?
2. What was the reason for the first income tax withholding?
3. List some benefits that may require voluntary deductions.
4. Other than social security and income tax, what payroll deductions do not require an authorization by the employee?
5. What is a pegboard or one-write system?
6. For what purpose do hotels usually use service bureaus?
7. What is the basis for staff planning in operated departments?
8. Explain the payroll treatment required for declared tips.
9. When should overtime be authorized?
10. When should hotel employees be required to take their vacations?

21

Accounts Payable

After studying this chapter, the student should:

1. Understand the purchasing and receiving of supplies.
2. Understand the requirements and use of a purchase order.
3. Know the procedures for properly recording accounts payable.

Accounts payable should be relatively easy to control. Yet there are few firms in any field of endeavor that have not paid for merchandise never received, or for more merchandise than was actually received, or twice for the same merchandise. The majority of these overpayments are made as a result of honest mistakes, and many are rectified by the creditors. Some, of course, are due to misrepresentation on the part of the vendors, collusion between the vendors and the buyers' employees, or dishonest accounts-payable clerks. Whatever the immediate reason, the underlying cause is usually the difficulty of handling the enormous volume of paper associated with this accounting function. This is particularly true in the hotel field, where the very nature of the operation generates a tremendous number of bills every day.

The heavy volume of bills has caused accounts payable, like payroll, to automate. However, this trend has not materially reduced the incidence of overpayment. Computers are used to accumulate the amount due to each vendor, compute cash discounts where allowed, print and sign the checks owed to the creditors, distribute the expenses to the designated subclassifications in each department, accumulate the month and month-to-date totals for profit-and-loss statements, and even check the extensions on each invoice. But they cannot verify the receipt of the merchandise or the accuracy of the number of units and unit prices shown on the invoices. They cannot check the quality of the merchandise, its delivery in accordance with desired specifications, or the return of all or part of an order to the vendor. In short, a computer can only substantially reduce the workload in the accounting department, often permitting a reduction of staff and, equally important, freeing the remaining employees to better check and control expenses.

To control expenses most successfully requires the installation of a complete payables system, involving the department heads, management, and accounting staff. The department heads must initiate requests for merchandise; management must approve purchases; and accounting must check, verify, record, and pay the invoices, distribute the expenses, and prepare financial statements.

The accounts payable process can be divided into four phases: purchasing, receiving, recording, and payment. Computerization has materially reduced the workload of the latter two phases. In a hotel, those two steps do not differ widely from the recording and payment procedures in use in most businesses. Therefore, adapting computer programs to meet the needs of hotel accounting was relatively simple. Due to the complex departmental structure of the hotels, the same statement cannot be made for purchasing and receiving. In the following sections, each of the four phases is discussed in detail. Purchasing and receiving of food and beverages is covered in Chapter 11. Discussion of food and beverages in those two areas only will, therefore, be omitted from this chapter.

PURCHASING

Department heads are expected to requisition needed supplies on a timely basis. This may or may not trigger a purchase order. When space is available, a hotel should keep all operating supplies in a central general storeroom. In a large hotel the general storeroom should be under the control of a storekeeper or possibly a receiving clerk who reports to accounting. However, in many hotels payroll economies have dictated that the purchasing agent perform that function. Some hotels are structured in such a manner that the storekeeper or receiving clerk reports to the purchasing agent. In those circumstances the principles of internal control are ignored, as receiving and inventory control are control/accounting functions while purchasing is an operational function.

Regardless, the individual with whom control of the general storeroom has been placed must assume the responsibility for maintaining adequate inventory levels. This can be done by use of a sheet or card, commonly called a *bin card* (see Figure 21-1) on which the quantity of an inventory item received or issued is recorded and the balance on hand is reflected. A minimum quantity on hand should be indicated clearly on the card so that when the balance drops below that level a purchase requisition must be initiated. It is particularly important that

BIN CARD

No. _____   Product _____   Size _____

Minimum Quantity _____

Date	Supplier	Quantity Received	Quantity Issued	Balance On Hand

Figure 21-1 Bin Card—General Stores

STOREROOM REQUISITION

Date _____

Department Ordering _____

Initiated By _____

Vendor*

Approved By
Dept. Head _____
Manager _____
Other _____

Quanity	Unit	Item Description**	

Figure 21-2   Storeroom Requisition

those supplies that are used by more than one department be controlled in a central storeroom, as this avoids excess quantities of the item being spread around the hotel and at the same time ensures that when the item has to be purchased, maximum use will be made of volume discounts. The existence of a central storeroom permits the individual department head to operate with a very limited quantity of supplies under his or her physical control, which in turn reduces the chance of employee pilferage. However, requisitioning on a daily basis places too large a burden on the storeroom and leaves very little margin for error or misjudgment by the department head. A policy should be set that each department should requisition on a weekly basis based on their normal seven-day consumption. A posted schedule for requisitioning should ensure that too many departments do not requisition on the same day, thus balancing the workload on the storekeeper. A sample of a storeroom requisition is shown in Figure 21-2.

Unfortunately, many hotels do not have or have a very limited central storeroom, frequently a few shelves in the purchasing agent's office for the most widely used items, for example, office supplies. The burden of controlling inventory levels and initiating purchases then falls on the department head. This should be accomplished by preparing, in duplicate, a *purchase requisition*, shown

<table>
<tr><td colspan="2" align="center">**PURCHASE REQUISITION**</td></tr>
</table>

PURCHASE REQUISITION

Date _____

Department Ordering _____   Initiated By _____

Vendor*

Approved By
Dept. Head _____
Manager _____
Other _____

Quanity	Unit	Item Description**	

PURCHASING

Vendor_____   Date Ordered _____

Terms_____   By _____

*From previous order
**As complete as possible

Figure 21-3   Purchase Requisition

in Figure 21-3. Purchase requisitions should differ from storeroom requisitions in order to avoid confusing the purchasing agent. Purchase requisitions must include information not needed for storeroom issues. The purchase requisition must briefly describe the items, quantity requested, date of the last order, quantity received, and vendor's name. The originals are sent to the general manager or other designated executive for written approval. Once approved, they are forwarded to the purchasing agent, who is responsible for actually ordering the merchandise.

Specifications as to size, type, or quality of any item should be originally approved by top management in consultation with the purchasing agent and affected department heads. Any deviation from these specifications when reordering should be approved.

Most requisitions are for items previously purchased, and many purchasing agents routinely reorder from the same vendor. However, they should periodically check the unit prices with those of other suppliers. Unit costs, particularly of printed forms, are materially reduced with increased quantities. *Bulk buying*, however, results in a net savings only if such purchases are carefully monitored and controlled. Adequate, safe storage and the rate of consumption should be prime considerations. Many hotels have ordered large quantities of stationery, office supplies, and cleaning supplies, only to have them stolen or misused by their employees, or to see them become obsolete long before the supply was exhausted. To help control this waste, the controller should review and approve all requisitions for printed forms.

When the price, quantity, and specifications have been checked, the purchasing agent should prepare a purchase order (see Figure 21-4). Purchase orders should be sequentially numbered and printed in at least five parts. The distribution, starting with the original, should be as follows:

1. Vendor
2. Accounts payable (accounting)
3. Department head initiating the purchase
4. Receiving or the department head in hotels with no receiving clerk
5. Purchasing

Department heads, by issuing requisitions, attest to the need for the merchandise; management approves the expense; and obtaining quotations and selecting vendors is the responsibility of the purchasing agent. However, the controllers have the overall responsibility for controlling expenses. They must exercise this responsibility by determining the reasonableness not only of the price charged but also of the quantity ordered. Prices can be periodically test-checked by calling rival suppliers for their prices, and care should be taken that the quality of the merchandise offered meets the requirements of management. Quantity can be checked only by estimating the usage based on the volume of business and comparing this figure to the actual consumption. To determine the consumption, the accounts-payable clerk need only maintain a worksheet listing all purchases of selected items, showing the date, quantity received, and unit cost for each order. Items usually listed are guest stationery, guest bills, registration cards, restaurant checks, and guest and cleaning supplies.

Although it was stated earlier that the impact of computerization in the purchase area has not had a substantial impact on the workload, some progress has been made. Most suppliers now provide the purchasing agent with a computerized list, preferably in quadruplicate, of available products and prices. The purchasing agent marks the quantities ordered and any agreed price changes on all

HOTEL		PURCHASE ORDER
GRAYLIG		**5900**

THE ABOVE NUMBER MUST APPEAR ON ALL INVOICES, SHIPPING BILLS, PACKING SLIPS AND ALL CORRESPONDENCE PERTAINING TO THIS ORDER

500 UNIVERSE AVENUE
GREAT CITY, U.S.A.

VENDOR

SHIP TO

DATE	TERMS	DELIVERY	F.A.B.
DEPT	REQUISITION	EXPENSE CODE	☐ PREPAY FREIGHT CHARGES AND ADD TO YOUR INVOICE ☐ NO FREIGHT CHARGES TO BE BILLED

QUANTITY	UNIT	DESCRIPTION	UNIT PRICE	AMOUNT

OTHER CONDITIONS REVERSE SIDE　　　TOTAL ▶

DIRECTOR PURCHASING　　　　　　　　　PURCHASING AGENT

SUPPLIER

Figure 21-4 Purchase Order

copies of the list. A summary purchase order can then be prepared reflecting "as per order form." One copy of the list is attached to the vendor's copy of the order while the other three copies are attached to the purchasing, receiving, and accounting copies. Systems have been developed that automate the payment to vendors, which eliminates the need to manually input and process their invoices. This concept has not yet received widespread use in the hotel industry where present efforts focus on the area of food and beverages. If successful in that area, it will be expanded to other types of purchases.

RECEIVING

While purchasing is an operational function subject to monitor and auditing by the controller's staff, receiving is an accounting and control function for which the controller is directly responsible.

Receiving procedures are determined to a great extent by the size of the operation. Larger hotels need, and usually have, a separate receiving department. The others will either assign this function to their timekeepers or route deliveries directly to the department heads. The receipt of merchandise may be recorded on a special receiving form, usually favored in hotels with separate receiving departments, or on the receiving copy of the purchase order. In effect, these are the only two receiving procedures. In both, the department heads should be solely responsible for the contents of all packages. Receiving clerks and timekeepers should only indicate the number of packages received and immediately forward them to the right department heads. Furthermore, for proper control, the complete cycle of the receiving-form routing should take no longer than 48 hours. With this in mind, here is an examination of the two methods.

Where a special form is used, it should be printed as a four-part form (see Figure 21-5). When the merchandise is received, the receiving clerk should complete the form and indicate the number of packages received. The packages and three parts of the form are sent to the department head who ordered the merchandise. The department head then signs one copy of the receiving form (keeping the other two) and returns it to the receiving clerk, indicating that the number of packages shown has been received. The clerk should attach it to the copy of the purchase order and file it in a processed folder. The fourth copy is sent, that night, to accounts payable, where it is checked for numerical sequence and filed. The fourth copy can also serve as a check on the department heads in the event the cycle is not completed within the specified time.

If a receiving form is not used, the receiving clerk should indicate the number of packages received on the copy of the purchase order. The delivery should then be listed on a sheet showing the purchase order number, the name of the department or department head, and the number of packages received. The purchase order is then forwarded with the packages to the department head. Each night, the list should be sent to the accounts-payable clerk. In hotels with no re-

```
                                              No. _____

                RECEIVING SLIP               Date_____


Supplier _____
        Name


        _____
        Address
                              Department
        _____ Routed To_____

Purchase Order No. _____

Merchandise Received
Description; No. of
Packages _____

                    Statement of Condition

        ☐ All in good condition   ☐ Damaged

Remarks and Disposition


                              _____
                              Receiving Clerk's Signature
```

Figure 21-5   Receiving Slip

ceiving department, the timekeeper or other authorized personnel would perform the same functions.

In the last stage of the receiving cycle, the department head should have in his or her possession the unopened packages and two copies of the receiving form or the receiving copy of the purchase order. As the final step, the department head opens the packages and checks the quantity and quality of the merchandise against the specifications on the purchase order. If the number of items is correct and the quality satisfactory, the department head should attest to both facts by a signature. The purchase order, since it shows the number of items ordered as well as the number of packages received, requires only a signature as a sign of approval. However, the receiving form shows only the number of packages received and, where this form is used, the department head must enter the quantity received on both copies before signing. Then, one copy is sent to accounts payable and the other should be attached to the departmental copy of the purchase order and filed. If there is anything wrong with the quantity or quality, this fact must be noted on the receiving slip so that accounting may adjust the vendor's invoice and take whatever other action is deemed necessary.

Proper handling of the receiving slips by all concerned is the key to minimizing losses due to overpayments. These forms are essential in checking the vendors' invoices and serve, together with the purchase orders, as authority for the accounts-payable staff to process and pay the invoices.

RECORDING ACCOUNTS PAYABLE

Computerization has made the recording of accounts payable a very simple process. Computers have no problems in handling the large number of accounts found in the Uniform System. The computer software provides several options relative to the accumulation of totals and entry into the general ledger. Given the ease in the recording process many hotels have opted to revert to having each invoice individually posted in the general ledger. However, given a proliferation of invoices for a specific account, each of which has the same characteristics (for example, same account number, same vendor, same date), hotels will usually group those particular invoices into a single entry. The actual recording of an invoice can only follow the completion of various audit procedures conducted by the accounts-payable personnel.

When the approved receiving slip reaches the accounts-payable department, it should be immediately matched against the purchase order copy sent to the department by the purchasing agent. Where the receiving copy of the purchase order is used, the clerk need only attach the two forms together and file them in a pending file until the vendor's bill is received. Where a special receiving form is used, the quantities shown must be carefully matched with the purchase order and a notation of the receiving slip's number made on the purchase order before it is placed in the pending file. Any bills received before the receiving slip should be attached to the purchase order and filed in the pending file until the approved slip is received. A few vendors may enclose their bills with the delivery slips, but the vast majority mail them shortly after the merchandise is delivered. The employee opening the hotel mail should be instructed to forward all bills directly to the accounts-payable department.

At least once a month, every purchase order in the pending file should be carefully examined. The purpose of this review is to clear the files of all purchase orders except those calling for deliveries at a future date. Purchase orders in the files that call for delivery on a prior date, and those with either a bill or a receiving slip attached, should be immediately investigated. To ensure future compliance, the controller should personally review any infractions of the receiving regulations with the offending department heads.

The audit procedures for checking, recording, and processing invoices for payment start when all three forms—purchase order, approved receiving slip, and invoice—are on hand. The accounts-payable clerk, as we stated in a previous chapter, only records and processes food and beverage invoices for payment. Verifying the receipt of food and beverage purchases, and the quantity, price, and total due as shown on each invoice, is the responsibility of the food and beverage controller.

All invoices for food and beverages received should, accompanied by a receiving sheet that shows each vendor's name, invoice number, itemization, and cost of merchandise received, be forwarded to accounts payable on a daily basis. The work of the food and beverage controller in verifying the accuracy of those invoices is described in detail in Chapter 11. To ensure that no invoices were lost in transit, the accounts-payable clerk should check each bill against the receiving sheet immediately upon receipt.

Checking all other invoices starts with matching the quantity received, as shown in the approved receiving slip, to the purchase order. When the invoice is received, the quantity and unit cost billed are checked against the purchase order. If they are in order, the extensions are checked and the invoice total verified. The accounts-payable clerk performing this function should initial the totals shown on the invoices to signify the quantities, unit costs, extensions, and totals were checked.

Normally, it is not necessary for the department heads to review or approve the invoices. They initiated the orders, they have a copy of the purchase order on file with the current unit price and vendor's name, and they have signified their approval for payment by signing the receiving slip. Any action taken by management regarding the invoices depends entirely on the desires of the individual managers.

There are many options available to management. Some authorize payment of all invoices without their approval. Others insist on personally approving each invoice before it is processed for payment. For the controller's protection and, in a sense, better control, the latter is much more desirable; yet it would certainly not be feasible to ask the managers of large hotels to personally approve the thousands of invoices processed each month. Alternatively, requiring no approvals by management is even less desirable. A procedure followed in many hotels is a compromise between the two extremes: invoices for nonrecurring expenditures exceeding a specified amount must be approved by the manager; all others can be processed for payment without their approval.

CODING AND INPUTTING INVOICES

When all the necessary approvals are affixed, the invoices are ready for coding and input. Many hotels require the department head to record the department and number of the account to be charged on the purchase requisition. This procedure not only helps the department head to understand what each item on the operating statement represents but should also permit them to track expenses against their budget on a monthly basis. This does not, however, relieve the accounts-payable personnel of the responsibility to ensure that coding is correct. Each invoice must have a designated department and expense classification in accordance with the guidelines established by the Uniform System of Accounts.

Computerization permits the processing of each bill individually. However, it is common practice to attach a simple purchase voucher, shown in Figure 21-6, to the invoice. The completed purchase voucher permits easy entry of the invoice into the computer or, if not computerized, a mechanical or manual accounting system.

The key information to be recorded on the purchase voucher is the following:

1. Vendor number: This should be a combination of the vendor's name and a number, for example, Wilcox Dairy could be WILC 01. This permits the accounts-payable clerk to recall the vendor numbers without the need to look each one up.
2. The vendor's invoice number: This specifically identifies each invoice.
3. The date of the invoice: This permits aging.
4. The total of invoice and discount (if any).
5. The breakdown by account number to be charged.

The account numbers are based on the chart of accounts in use, which, in conformity with the Uniform System of Accounts, consists of both the department number and the individual expense account within the department.

Consideration should always be given to any discounts reflected on the invoice or generally received from the vendor—such discounts are known as *trade discounts* and should be reflected on the purchase order. These should be automatically taken and accounted for as reductions in the invoice price. *Cash discounts,* however, are inducements to settle the invoices promptly. Whether they are taken or not taken is a question of management policy directly related to the overall financial resources of the hotel. These should be taken when possible, as they usually exceed the rate of interest, which could be earned by investing the funds. However, when taken, the discount should be recorded separately as a credit to "Other Income—Cash Discounts."

Care should be taken when entering invoices that are more than 5 or 6 weeks old. While the computer should be programmed to red flag any invoices previously entered, an additional review should be made to ensure that payment was not made under another invoice number. This is extremely important in a noncomputerized system.

Certain invoices, such as insurance, dues, subscriptions, service contracts, and so forth, cover an expense for a period of several months. Such items should be charged to a prepaid expense balance sheet account and recorded on a worksheet. They become the basis for standard monthly journal entries, as described in Chapter 23.

Similarly, invoices may be recorded for items that have been accrued, by standard journal entry, for several months, such as taxes or utilities. To the extent that they relate to prior periods and are covered by an *accrued expense liability*

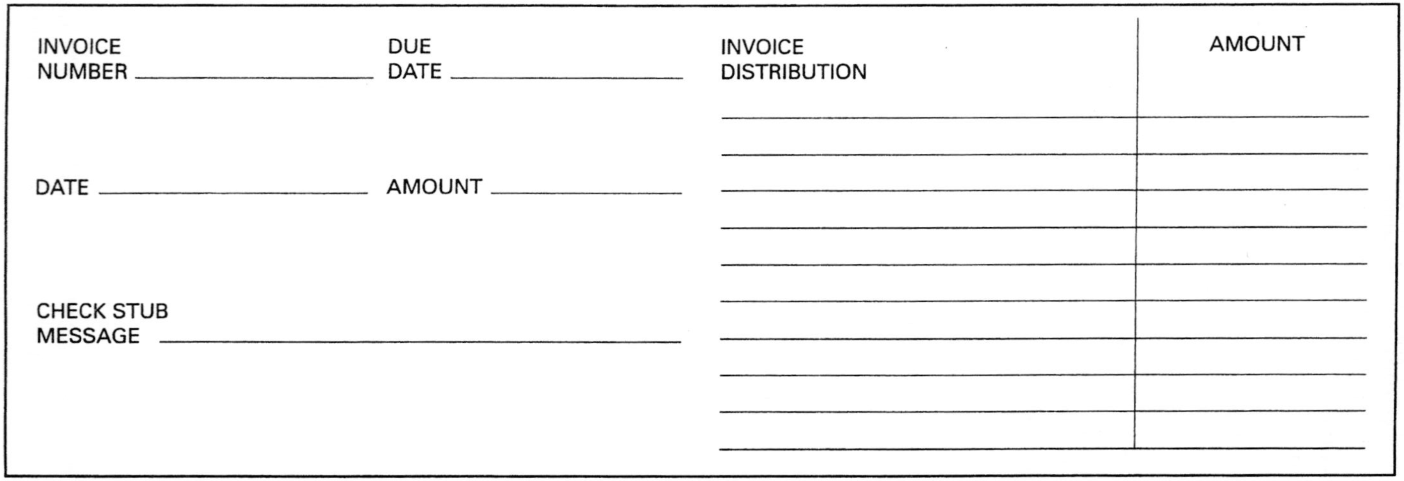

Figure 21-6 Purchase Voucher

account, they should be charged thereto. An accrued expense liability account is used to record an estimated liability for an unreceived invoice.

A category of invoices that merits special attention is for items exclusively ordered for and charged to a particular guest. These purchases, usually made for banquet guests, are of such items as flowers, wedding cakes, printed matchbooks, or other wedding favors; they might also be rentals of special audio or other electronic equipment by sponsors for their meetings. The invoices should not be vouchered and processed for payment unless approved by the income controller or other employee responsible for checking them with the guest charges. A detailed worksheet should be set up to properly control these disbursements. Checking the invoices against the guest bills without adequate notations may increase, rather than reduce, the possibility of error. When receipts and disbursements for such items cannot be matched, there is no alternative but to write off the difference, the open balance. With inadequate records, it is difficult to analyze the account and so discover and try to correct the error causing the open balance. Hence the importance of up-to-date worksheets checked monthly against the balance in the general-ledger accounts.

Regardless of who is designated to approve the invoice, the worksheet or the list of all such guest charges that is then transcribed into the worksheet should be prepared by the income controller as part of the daily routine. The total charges listed each day should equal the total entered, either in one amount or by category, in the earnings journal. At the end of each month, they are posted as credits to the *contra accounts* in the general ledger. Contra accounts are accounts used to offset debits and credits for the same item. Worksheets need only be spreadsheets with sufficient columns to record the following data:

Date of function
Name of guest
Banquet check number
Description of item
Total guest charge
Vendor name
Invoice number
Total amount due
Markup, if any
Date invoice is approved

All headings, with the possible exception of "Markup, if any," are self-explanatory. Markup is a service charge, added at management's instructions to the cost of many of these items. Thus, the total amount due on the invoice plus the required markup should equal the total guest charge. On all invoices, the employee approving them should indicate the account number to be charged.

In addition, where there is a markup, the employee should enter, with appropriate account numbers, the total guest charge as a debit to the contra account, the markup as a credit to income, and the net as the amount due to the vendor. In any month when invoices are not processed in time to offset the revenue, the net balance in all contra accounts is shown on the balance sheet as a current liability. The net balance should also equal the total on the worksheets of all open items.

While Figure 21-6 is a suggested format for a purchase voucher, the most important factor in designing the voucher is to have the information available for quick and easy entry into the computer. Therefore, the computer software design for accounts payable input is the most determining factor in the voucher layout.

The vouchers should be batched, that is, assembled in a stack, alphabetically by vendor, and totaled to arrive at a control total. A schedule should be established for entering batches, once or twice a week depending on volume. Since certain vendors may have a seven-day due date, at least one batch per week should be entered. The computer will automatically provide a total amount entered to be agreed back to the batch total.

Payment of Invoices

Most accounts-payable programs provide the ability to print an "authorization for payment" list by due date. This list should be reviewed relative to the intended due date through which it is the intention to make payment. Where necessary, due dates should be changed to add or delete invoices from the intended payments. After these corrections are made, checks can be printed through the designated date.

In certain instances it may be necessary to create a *pro forma* invoice for payments (such as sales tax), which must be made periodically but for which invoices are not received. Pro forma invoices are documents created in the invoice format and used to substitute for actual invoices.

Accounts-payable checks should be signed by at least two people, usually the general manager and the controller. All supporting documents, invoices, purchase orders, and so on, should be attached to the checks when presented for signature. When paid, the invoices should be voided with a "paid" stamp to avoid reuse and filed with a copy of the check. As a further element of internal control, the checks, when signed, should be given to, and mailed by, someone other than the accounts-payable clerk, purchasing agent, or anyone else involved in the purchasing process. The computer systems usually have a feature where the issuing of checks and the printing of a check register (a listing of checks issued for a specific date) initiates an automatic entry in the general ledger, debiting the accounts payable account and crediting the bank account with the total amount of checks issued. If this does not happen, the same can be accomplished by a manual journal entry.

Suppliers' Statements

Most vendors send out monthly statements showing balances owed and outstanding invoices. These statements should never be used as a basis for recording or paying invoices. However, they should be reconciled to the accounts-payable balance in the books, and copies of missing invoices should be requested from the vendor.

CHAPTER SUMMARY

The accounts payable process includes purchasing, receiving, recording, and payment.

Purchasing is initiated by department head requisitions and involves the preparation of multicopy purchase orders.

Storeroom controls normally use bin cards and where applicable pars or minimum quantities initiate purchases.

Larger hotels have a receiving department, but in many hotels receiving is done by the department heads, who under either scenario are ultimately responsible for checking the merchandise.

Copies of purchase orders, receiving reports, and invoices are used by accounts payable to process invoices.

Most hotels use a computer program to, after coding, record the invoices. Trade discounts are taken automatically, but a policy must be established for cash discounts.

Payments of invoices are based on payment cycles and are controlled through authorization for payment lists. Suppliers' statements should be reconciled at month end.

REVIEW QUESTIONS

1. What is the most common way of recording supplies inventories?
2. How frequently should a department requisition supplies?
3. What is the difference between a storeroom requisition and a purchase requisition?
4. How many copies of a purchase order should there be and how are they distributed?
5. What documentation should accounts payable receive in addition to the invoice?
6. What is the difference between cash discounts and trade discounts?
7. What is an authorization for payment list?
8. Should suppliers' statements be used to support payments?

22
Credit

After studying this chapter, the student should:

1. Know the elements of a credit policy.
2. Understand the functions of a credit department.
3. Know the steps in credit management before and after the event.

The proper control of credit is the most serious problem confronting business today. More than half of all Americans carry at least one credit card, a fact that makes the credit industry the biggest in the nation. But such widespread use of credit can foster, and even encourage, impulse buying and overspending, all too often beyond the individual's means.

Credit management is not a new business. Businessmen in ancient Babylon and Rome faced many of the same problems their modern counterparts do. However, the greatest growth in this field came in the twentieth century. There are many reasons for the increase in the use of credit—and the resulting need for more and better credit management—but most of them are related directly or indirectly to two factors: inflation and business and industrial expansion.

Inflation directly affects the use of credit. As the purchasing power of the dollar shrinks and the cost of an article increases, the desire and the ability of the consumer to make immediate payment decreases.

Business growth in this century quickly outdistanced the ability of owners to provide the necessary capital from their personal funds. They were faced with two alternatives: to share their businesses by selling stock or to borrow the funds needed to expand; most used both. As the demand for borrowing increased, so did the cost. Businesses and individuals not only increased the use of credit for their purchases but delayed payments as much as possible. "Slow pay," letting bills sit a little longer, an easy and cheap way of stretching cash reserves, caused serious problems for creditors, whose need for cash in many cases exceeded that of their customers.

The hotel industry has, throughout its history, been particularly plagued with credit problems. The innkeeper, as the genial host, was never particularly inclined to enforce credit procedures. Guests were accepted at face value, with little if any attempt made for proper identification. Losses due to skippers—guests who registered under fictitious names and addresses and left without paying their bills—were considered a normal operating expense, a necessary risk of doing business.

As the concept of hotel operations changed and innkeepers became profit-oriented businessmen and women, excessive credit losses could no longer be tolerated. The increased use of credit, the longer time taken by guests to pay their bills, and the cash requirements of the operation also contributed to the greater stringency of the credit procedures now in effect in most hotels.

A credit policy based solely on sound financial principles is difficult, and a uniform policy, even for a group of hotels under one management, is impossible to establish. A hotel room is the most perishable article sold in any type of business. The income from today's vacant room is lost forever, as is the income from a banquet or other function lost to a competitor. Often a hotel must accept business, whether for a guestroom or a banquet, even though it may involve a credit risk. What is an acceptable degree of risk must be a management decision, it cannot be incorporated into written credit policies or procedures. Credit limits obviously depend on the operation, the level of charges, and the type of guest.

ELEMENTS OF A CREDIT POLICY

A hotel chain's general credit policy rules may be interpreted, changed, or modified by the management to fit their one particular hotel. This authority is necessary if the managers are to be held responsible for the success or failure of their operation.

A credit policy, since it can affect every facet of the operation, must take into account the marketing objectives of the organization. A liberal policy tends to expand the market, but it entails a certain amount of risk; conversely, the tighter the policy, the more restricted the market. A new hotel has a greater need to solicit and attract business than does a well-established hotel, which can depend on its reputation to attract new guests and repeat business from former guests. Within the hotel itself, a more liberal credit policy may be adopted in a dining room with empty tables than in a busy coffee shop.

Distinction must also be made between in-house guests and nonhotel guests. In-house guests are those who occupy sleeping rooms: nonhotel guests are those who do not, but who use one or more of the hotel's other facilities—banquet rooms, restaurants, bars, nightclubs, stores and concessions, and so on. Credit privileges extended to in-house guests are for room charges, food, beverages, laundry, valet, items purchased in the stores and concessions, telephone services, entertainment, and cash. Every item except cash represents profit. Hotels are not banks, but they usually permit their guests to cash personal checks. Like every other service performed for the convenience of their guests, this is intended to build goodwill, ensure repeat business, and evoke a recommendation from the guest to his or her friends and business associates. Obviously, the only result of an increase in the number of checks cashed is the possibility of greater losses. For this reason, the "sale" of cash must be tightly controlled.

FUNCTIONS OF THE CREDIT DEPARTMENT

The credit department in a hotel is small. In the largest hotels, it consists of only a credit manager, a secretary, and a few assistants. They are members of the accounting-department staff, and the credit manager reports directly to the controller. In smaller hotels without a credit department, the policy must be administered by the accounting department.

In most industries, the credit department has two primary functions: to investigate the financial standing of and approve limits of credit for each prospective client and to try to collect the amount. In the hotel industry, there is never enough time to check the financial status of each guest, as individual credit limits are impossible to establish. Rather, an attempt must be made to control credit while charges are accumulating, with no idea as to what the final total will be. Bad debts can be prevented, or at least kept within reasonable limits, only while the guest is still in the hotel; after checkout, it is too late.

Automation has reduced the workload of credit department personnel. A computer program can be used to provide a daily list of guest balances that exceed a specific amount, and other analyses of the individual guest bills that the credit manager requires. Obviously that eliminates the tedious and time-consuming daily review of each guest bill. But full automation of the front office does not change the basic principles of a good credit policy or the credit manager's responsibility to carry them out. For these reasons, and to better explain the duties and responsibilities of the department, all the functions of a credit department will be reviewed as if they had to be manually performed.

Ideally, each guest's bill should be under constant surveillance by one member of the credit personnel. However, there may be a thousand or more bills and only a few people to monitor them. Furthermore, the staff has many other duties to perform and thus cannot devote full time to this function. Other than hiring more credit people than are economically feasible, the only solution to this imbalance is to make credit everyone's business. In a hotel, it must be. In fact, this co-operation is so necessary that it requires the expertise of the controller to organize and supervise the training needed to obtain it and the authority of top management to enforce it. Some of the ways in which others can help the credit department succeed in its job follow.

INTERDEPARTMENTAL COOPERATION

The bellman who rooms the guests should note on every *rooming slip* (a slip issued by the front desk showing the room number) the number and condition of the bags. Some record only negative comments, such as poor or light baggage. If no such comment appears, a member of the credit staff who is reviewing the slips cannot be certain that the guest had good or excellent baggage; the bellman could have overlooked or forgotten to record its true condition.

The room-service cashiers should immediately alert the credit department of any unusually large orders of food and, more particularly, beverages. The room-service waiter or waitress should report unusual activity in a room: a large number of people, a party, many bottles of liquor not ordered from the hotel, and the like, as well as unusually large tips (over 25% of the check). Skippers usually prefer room service to restaurants, order the finest food and beverages available, and are generally very liberal tippers.

The room attendant indicates the status of the room in her morning report, but she should be trained to recognize and report any conditions that might indicate that the guest had departed without notice. A favorite trick of skippers is to remove all personal toilet articles except perhaps a half-empty can of shaving cream or hair spray and to leave an old dress or pair of trousers hanging in the closet and an old, broken-down bag in the room. The room attendant's report will not help to stop the skipper, but it will prevent the accumulation of additional room charges and possibly a loss of revenue if the room could be rerented that day. Restaurant, bar, and nightclub cashiers should also alert credit personnel of any unusually large gratuities authorized by guests on their checks.

The most important aid to the credit manager is, however, the actual activity on a guest account. The front-desk staff and the night auditors are, for a variety of reasons, continually looking at guest folios. They are in the best positions to spot unusual activity, both in the numbers of charges and in the amounts involved. If guests, immediately after arrival, start ordering from room service, incur charges in the restaurants or bars, send out clothes to the valet or laundry, or charge purchases from the stores and concessions, they are suspect, and someone in credit should be advised to review their bill. This is particularly important if the guest has made no long-distance telephone calls. Of all possible guest charges, long-distance calls are the only ones that may be used to trace a former guest when the hotel does not have a valid address.

Night auditors should be instructed to monitor the **high balance report** (a listing of guest balances exceeding predetermined limits) and ensure that copies go to the credit manager, front-office manager, and controller.

THE CREDIT POLICY IN DETAIL

The assistance given the credit department does not in any way alter or reduce the credit manager's responsibility to carry out the credit policy of the hotel or to maintain adequate controls over all guest charges. Others can only alert the credit department. They cannot make any determination as to a guest's honesty or ability to pay. Once alerted, the credit staff must review the charges and determine what action, if any, to take.

Excluding city-ledger billing and collection procedures, the credit policy should cover three periods:

1. Prior—before a function or registration.
2. During—while the function is in progress or while the guest is in residence.
3. After—at the end of a function or at the checkout of the registered guest.

Prior to the Event

The credit manager's efforts during this period are primarily confined to checking the financial standing of small or relatively unknown companies, associations, groups, or individuals who have booked banquets or conventions.

To assist the credit manager in checking ratings, most hotels with banquet and convention facilities sign up with one or more credit bureaus or national or local credit associations and the larger ones with Dun & Bradstreet (D&B).

Subscribers to D&B receive a reference book listing the estimated financial strength and credit rating of thousands of companies and individuals. Financial ratings are shown by a series of symbols, each indicating a dollar amount, ranging from under $5,000 to over $50 million. A separate symbol, and a number from 1 to 4, is used to designate the credit rating. The four classifications are high, good, fair, and limited. Cards issued to subscribers explain the dollar range for each symbol, and the credit-rating classifications. In the case of listings that are not rated, the absence of the rating is also explained. When a name is not listed in the reference book, D&B will provide on request a special report on that company or individual. Many hotels extend or refuse credit solely on the basis of a D&B rating.

Credit managers who have no access to the D&B reports can obtain similar information from credit bureaus or associations. Other valuable sources of credit information are the bank used by the sponsor of the affair and, if a company is responsible for the bill, its suppliers or creditors. References can also be requested from other hotels who have previously hosted the group or convention.

Most credit policies do not establish definite procedures or define the class of guests whose financial standing should be checked. They leave the decision to be made by the credit and sales department heads in consultation with the controller and, if necessary, with the general manager. Since the credit manager cannot know of any future business until notified by sales, the credit policy must require sales to notify credit immediately when a banquet or convention is booked. It should also mandate frequent meetings between these department heads to review the coming events and the steps needed to ensure prompt and full payment.

Verifying credit in advance on individual guests has become a very minor element of the credit process, as almost all hotels require a credit card guarantee on individual reservations. The credit card information is entered into a computer at the time the reservation is made and its validity verified. For those guests who make cash deposits or have no reservations, little can be done prior to arrival.

During the Event

For this period, specific rules and procedures for individual guests can be incorporated into a credit policy, applicable either to one hotel or to a group of hotels under one management. The following paragraphs will discuss the areas generally covered, the procedures, and, wherever possible, the rationale behind the rules.

Guest registration. As management has become more aware of credit problems, new credit policies have been formulated and, more to the point, enforced. All arrivals, except well-known former guests, are asked for some form of identification. Hotels go one step further and ask for a national credit card that the guest will use to settle his or her account at departure. The average traveler carries more than one credit card, and the controller can reduce the credit card commission expense by taking advantage of this fact. The receptionist should mention first the card with the lowest discount rate, pause for a few seconds, and then mention the other cards accepted by the hotel. Many guests will automatically use the first card mentioned.

When a guest presents a credit card, the receptionist should immediately imprint it on the back of the registration card. If it will be used to settle the bill, the clerk should also imprint it on the proper charge slip and staple the slip to the registration card. Some credit policies require the receptionist to indicate in code, on the hotel's copy of the guest bill, walk-ins, same-day telephone reservations, and claimed reservations. Finally, the policy should clearly indicate the responsibility of the bellmen to note on the back of the room slip the condition of the guest's baggage. All rooming slips for guests with light or no baggage should be immediately returned to the receptionist, who should then note that fact on the back of the registration card and have it initialed by a member of the credit-department staff.

Credit-department billing procedures. Most credit policies require the credit manager or a member of the credit staff to review each day every guest bill. Policy should indicate what to look for and, in a general way, what action to take. The bills customarily listed for special attention are for those accounts that exceed a specified amount, those that seem to have an unusual number of charges—especially when coded or marked for light or no baggage—and finally, any bill that, for a few days, has no charges other than room and tax. The specified amount can vary from guest to guest, depending on the credit card limit and the house limit.

The reason for checking the last-mentioned accounts is that the guest may have checked out, but for some reason the bill was not pulled, and the room continues to be carried as occupied when in fact it is vacant. The policy should also specify the number of days a guest can remain as a resident before receiving a bill for all charges to date. Formerly, most credit managers were instructed to bill every guest except those with established credit at the end of three days and to follow up the three-day bills on the next day with a request to establish credit or a demand for immediate payment. Today, because of the better credit procedures at registration, three-day bills have been phased out. Our opinion is that all guests, regardless of affiliations, should be billed at the end of each seven days. The night auditor should bring the total balance forward to a new bill and forward all copies except the guest's to accounting. The guest's copy is left for the credit manager, who should review the account, and if it is a personal charge, see that it is placed in the guest's box, and be responsible for following through for payment. If the account is to be charged to a firm, the credit manager should determine the requirements for billing, and if they are in order, give the bill to the city-ledger clerk with proper mailing instructions. Every account, regardless of the credit rating of the firm involved, should be followed through for payment, and any deviation in the payment from the amount billed should be questioned immediately—principally, because after a long stay, it is difficult to analyze and break down the unpaid balance of any account with partial or on-account payments.

Group and convention billing. A uniform policy cannot be established for billing an organization, company, or corporation hosting these functions. Not only do the charges for which they will accept responsibility vary, but most will specify exactly how their bill is to be prepared and to whose attention it is to be mailed. This is very important, particularly when dealing with a large company; many hotel bills have been lost or payments seriously delayed because the mailing address did not include the department and name of the person authorized to process them. These varied requirements emphasize once more the need for cooperation between the sales and accounting departments.

Salespeople make the contacts, sell and supervise the functions, and are usually the only people privy to the billing instructions. Therefore, management should require that all billing instructions, whether written or verbal, be immediately turned over to the controller, who then issues the proper instructions to his or her staff. In fact, because the salesperson may misunderstand or misinterpret the billing instructions, it is suggested that the controller meet with the group's representative to review the billing procedures personally, particularly in the case of large companies or groups.

Since *group billing*—the master bill as well as the individual members' charges—must be closely monitored and frequently reviewed, the billing instructions should be updated daily if necessary, while the guests are in residence in the hotel rather than after the function is over or the group has checked out.

Check cashing. Every state has a "bad-check law" that makes it a crime to issue a check with intent to defraud—that is, in the knowledge that insufficient funds are on deposit to cover the amount of the check. In most states, the act of issuing a bad check is in itself proof of intent to defraud and, depending on the amount, is a misdemeanor or a felony, punishable by a fine, a jail sentence, or both. Therefore, it is essential that the credit manager be thoroughly familiar with the bad-check law of the state in which the hotel is located and at least have access to the general provisions of these laws in other states.

Management in each property must set its own limits on the total dollar amount of checks it will cash for guests during any one stay or period of time; but here are some guidelines and restrictions that should be incorporated into an overall credit policy:

1. *Credit cards*: Cards are used primarily to settle the guest's accounts, but some cards carry certain check-cashing privileges. National companies—American Express, Diners' Club, and Carte Blanche, among others—will guarantee their cardholders' checks up to a specified amount, provided that the cardholder is a registered guest of the hotel, that the credit card is valid, that the card is imprinted on the back of the check, and that at departure the full amount of the bill is charged to the credit card. If all conditions are met, the company will reimburse the hotel, deducting only the normal discount, for any bad checks cashed by its cardholders. Every member hotel is given a form specifically designed for filing these claims. The credit policy, therefore, should list the companies extending this privilege, the dollar limits, and restrictions involved.

2. *Approvals*: A credit policy should clearly define, with a definite dollar limit, the responsibility and authority of all employees or executives empowered to cash a guest's check. These are the front-office cashiers, the credit manager and staff, assistant managers, night auditors, night managers, and all other department heads, as well as the general manager

and controller. The last two are usually given unlimited authority in this matter, and if so, this should be stated in the policy.

3. *Restrictions:* There are certain types of checks that should not be approved for cashing but may be accepted in payment of a guest's account. These are:

   a. *Postdated checks:* A postdated check is in effect a note receivable, a promise to pay at some future time. The hotel cannot deposit it, and should not record the payment, until the date shown on the check. Also, the hotel loses its rights to prosecute and recover under the bad-check law if the check is returned for nonpayment. However, it is at least a written acknowledgment of the debt, and if that is all a guest can or will give, the controller may have no choice but to accept it in payment of an account.

   b. *Second-party checks:* A check may be drawn to the order of the guest by a second party—an individual, association, company, or corporation. A second-party check should be cashed or accepted in payment of an account only if the payee is personally known to the hotel executive who is specifically authorized to approve such a transaction. Otherwise, no credentials should be accepted for purposes of identification, because they, as well as the check itself, could be found, stolen, or forged.

   c. *Checks payable to a corporation, company, or organization:* Such checks should never be cashed or accepted in payment of a guest's account even if the guest is known to be the president of the company or organization involved. By accepting such a check, the hotel would be subject to a lawsuit by any stockholder or member of the organization should the guest be convicted of misappropriating funds and might even be in trouble with the tax authorities if the guest was siphoning company funds to hide income and reduce taxes.

   d. *Money orders:* Few people carry money orders or purchase them for any reason except to mail in payment of a debt or for a purchase. Therefore, they should never be approved for cashing unless the payee is personally known to the hotel executive. As with second-party checks, credentials are worthless. It is no exaggeration to say that more than 50% of all money orders cashed at hotels without personal identification are found to be stolen; the hotels never recover their money.

4. *Recording:* There is only one way to control the number and the dollar amount of all checks cashed by each guest during any one stay and that is by keeping an accurate and complete record of every check cashed. For a registered guest, the entry can be made on the back of the registration card. The only information needed is the date, the bank on which the check is drawn, the amount, and the initials of the person who approved it for cashing. This means in effect that the entry should be made by that person, not by the front-office cashier who actually pays out the money, unless he or she is authorized to cash the check without other approval.

The reason is obvious. No one can intelligently approve a check without knowing the number and amount of any checks previously cashed for that guest. Where this rule is not strictly enforced, bad-debt writeoffs may include three or more checks cashed in one day by a guest, each one approved by a different executive so authorized. Recording the payer bank is helpful only in that rare instance when a guest presents a check drawn on a different bank from the one on which a prior check was cashed, and then only to indicate the possibility of fraud. People rarely carry blank checks drawn on more than one bank, so such a deviation from normal custom should be thoroughly investigated, even to the point of calling both banks to verify the validity of the checks.

For nonregistered guests, if they are permitted this privilege, a similar entry should be made, again by the person approving the check, on a card with the guest's name and address. The cards, filed in alphabetical order, should be kept in a secure place but must be readily available during the hours that such transactions are permitted.

5. *Traveler's checks*: It is common knowledge that traveler's checks can be freely accepted without risk of loss if a few simple rules are followed. Each check must be countersigned on its face in the presence of the cashier, who can accept it without further identification. Yet this simple safeguard has all too often been disregarded by both the guest and the hotel cashier, and traveler's checks are sometimes improperly accepted. Some have only one signature on the face, with the second, usually affixed in the presence of the cashier, on the back as an endorsement. Others are correctly signed in both places, but before the guest comes to the cashier's desk. And in neither case does the cashier verify the signatures.

Accepting these improperly signed checks may not result in any loss to the hotel, provided that the guest was the purchaser. But the most important reason for carrying traveler's checks is that if they are lost or stolen, the purchaser can notify the issuing company of the loss and receive prompt replacements. The company then stops payment, and anyone improperly accepting them suffers a financial loss. It is for this reason that we recommend that the procedures for accepting or cashing traveler's checks be included in the overall credit policy, and that the credit manager be specifically given full responsibility for enforcing them.

6. *Restaurant and other cashiers*: The credit policy should limit or prohibit the handling of any type of check, except traveler's checks, by any cashier in the hotel other than the front-office cashiers. Restaurant, bar, garage, and other cashiers may be authorized to accept traveler's checks up to a specified amount in payment of an account and to give cash for the excess over the amount of the charge. If a restaurant or bar guest is not required to pay at the cashier's station, then the second signature should be witnessed at the guest's table by the person in charge of the room, who should then initial the check as proof.

7. *Stamp*: Whenever a cashier gives cash on any check (with the possible exception of traveler's checks), whether for the full amount of the check or for the excess over an amount applied to the guest's bill, the guest should be required to sign for it. The cashier needs only a stamp to imprint on the back of the check, with spaces for the amount of cash paid out, the amount applied to the bill, the guest's room number, and a blank line for the guest's signature, all to be entered in ink. This procedure not only helps the hotel control its cashiers and avoid serious disputes with the guests; it should be implemented primarily for the benefit of the guests, to help them verify the amount paid on their bill and to have any error easily corrected.

8. *Group and convention guests*: The procedures outlined regarding checks cashed for individual guests apply equally to personal checks presented by in-house guests who are members of a group or convention. However, second-party checks issued to their members by the company or organization holding the function are normally accepted or cashed without further approval by the front-office cashiers. Advance arrangements should always be made to handle these checks, not only so that the controller can set up proper controls, but also to make sure the cashiers have enough money on hand to cash them. The payer should provide a list of those authorized to sign the checks, the dollar range with a maximum amount that can be accepted, an estimate of the total dollar amount to be issued and, if possible, the amount the hotel cashiers may be expected to handle in any one day. The payor should also assume full responsibility for lost or stolen checks, unless either the controller, the credit manager, or, in their absence, the hotel salesperson servicing the account is immediately notified of such a loss. The person so notified must then alert the front-office cashiers and post in a conspicuous place the check number, name of the payee, and the amount. He or she should also alert the staff of all nearby hotels, in case some members of the group or convention are registered there.

Guest charges. Guests may purchase almost anything and charge it on their room bills. Normally, these charges are incurred within the hotel itself; in the restaurants, bars, nightclubs, stores, and concessions; but sometimes they involve C.O.D. purchases from outside stores and even outright cash advances.

Obviously, not every guest charge that originates within the hotel can be checked; rather, the credit staff must try to monitor and control them through the daily review of each guest's bill. The credit policy can only require that procedures ensure that all charges, whether posted automatically from a point-of-sale terminal or physically given to the front desk, are posted promptly to the guest account.

C.O.Ds and cash advances, where they are permitted, are not sales for profit but an outlay of the hotel's cash, so they must be strictly and individually controlled. The front-office cashiers should not have the authority to pay out any cash without the written approval of the credit manager or other authorized executive. Packages sent C.O.D. should not be accepted unless the guest has left written instructions stating that an article was being delivered, by whom, and the amount of the total charges—in effect approving in advance the charge to his or her account. This authorization should be stapled to the C.O.D. voucher, which should be signed by the person delivering the package.

Charges from nonregistered guests. Few hotels, except those owned by companies issuing their own credit cards, will accept charges from their stores and concessionaires for persons who are not registered guests of the hotel. However, they all permit charges in the hotel-operated restaurants, bars, or other facilities. Most of these charges are made through national credit cards and, if properly accepted, pose no credit problems. Many hotels also establish individual or company accounts for executives of firms whose offices are located nearby. Again, the hotel sales representative making the original agreement should have forwarded it to the controller for review and, if needed, a check on the company's credit standing. The cashiers and personnel in charge of the restaurants and bars should be given a list of the companies with such accounts, together with the names of executives authorized to sign, either as individuals or as company representatives.

All these charges, whether on credit cards or on company or individual accounts, should also be processed through the front-office system. However, instead of being posted to individual room folios, they will be posted to a house account folio. For customers with frequent charges, separate accounts should be opened for each customer. Such accounts can be closed out through a transfer to city ledger and billed on a monthly basis. Random or infrequent charges should be posted to a specified "city-ledger restaurant charge" folio and the individual charges cleared by the night auditor to the city ledger on a nightly basis.

After the Event

At checkout. The general tightening of credit procedures prior to guest arrival and at the time of registration has greatly eased the burden of the credit staff and front-office cashiers at checkout time. And by reducing the time needed for this process, it has also contributed to better guest relations. Long lines and delays at the check-out counter frequently lead to complaints, which former guests remember and may mention when discussing the service they received and the efficiency of the hotel staff.

The procedures themselves have not changed, and the front-office cashiers still have the principal responsibility for checking out guests. The manner in which they carry out these duties directly affects the present and future earnings of a hotel. The correct procedure follows.

The guest usually asks for the bill by room number. After printing the bill and pulling the registration card from the pit, the cashier should check for unposted charges and then ask the guest, by name, if he or she made any telephone calls or incurred any restaurant or other charges within the last few hours. Since many guests make a telephone call or order a meal, particularly breakfast, immediately before checking out, these two items should be specifically mentioned, and most cashiers are required to do so. The guest should be addressed by name if for no other reason than that it is good guest relations; most people relate better to the hotel staff when so addressed. However, there is a more pressing reason: to prevent the guest from settling the wrong account. The cashier may pull another bill or the guest may give a wrong room number and in the rush to check out the guest may not immediately catch the error. When this happens, the result is not easy to straighten out, and it is certain to irritate two guests, the one who settled the wrong account and the one whose account was wrongly settled.

Since the method of settlement was established for most guests at the time they registered, and since the credit staff has had sufficient time to check it where necessary, the cashier can then proceed to close out the account. If a guest's payment method was not established or if it has been changed, the cashier must determine if he or she has the authority to complete the transaction, and if not, must refer the guest to the credit manager. A disputed charge, if incurred on the day the guest is checking out, should be checked and adjusted by the cashier. Previous days' charges must, if time permits, be referred to the credit manager, since the vouchers are not available. If the guest is unable to wait, the cashier should circle the item, mark it "disputed charge," deduct it from the total, and settle the balance with the guest, leaving the amount of the disputed charge open. The night auditor should transfer this open balance to the city ledger, and the city-ledger clerk then has the responsibility to check it the next day and take whatever action is necessary to properly charge and collect the item. Charges for local calls, in hotels with telephone registers, are not subject to these restrictions, and most cashiers have the authority to allow them if disputed by a guest.

Although cashiers rarely are given authority to cash personal checks for guests without approval, many are permitted to accept them in payment of an account up to a specified amount, provided the check is made payable to the hotel and is in the exact amount of the bill. A guest whose account exceeds that limit, or who writes a check for an amount greater than the total bill and requests cash for the excess, should be referred to the credit manager for approval.

Charge accounts fall into two categories, those charged to a personal or business account in the city ledger and those charged on a credit card. The information regarding the method of settlement, requested from most guests at registration, can greatly facilitate and speed the handling of either transactions. During daily review of the guests' bills, the credit staff should use this information to check the guests' credit or, if the account is to be charged to a credit card, take some of the steps necessary for the proper acceptance of these cards. Credit approval should be indicated by initialing the bill; then the cashier need only make sure all charges are posted and obtain the guest's signature to show acceptance of the total amount due.

All checkout procedures outlined here apply both to individual guests and to those who are with a group or attending a convention, insofar as their personal charges are concerned. The master bill, as previously mentioned, should be under constant review by the credit manager or a member of the accounting staff. In addition, it is often advisable for the controller and credit manager to periodically review the account with the group's representative or person in charge of the function. Review and approval of the charges while the group is still in the hotel usually results in more prompt payment.

Collection. When guests check out, their bills are printed and any open balance is transferred by the night auditor to the city ledger. This includes all charge accounts and paid bills that, because of a disputed or after-departure charge, were not settled in full. Restaurant, bar, banquet, and other charges for nonregistered guests are charged directly to the city ledger. It then becomes the responsibility of the city-ledger clerk or clerks to bill these accounts.

There is one primary credit principle: the only way to collect an account is to bill it. Any delay in billing automatically delays payment. This means that the first bill should be sent out by the city-ledger clerk as soon as possible after the guest has checked out or the function has been held. This is followed by monthly statements on whatever billing dates are established by the hotel. Nonregistered guests with either personal or business accounts in the city ledger are rarely billed after each restaurant or bar charge. Rather, they are billed once a month for the total charges incurred through the billing date.

Credit policies are exclusively a management decision and so can vary from hotel to hotel or among groups of hotels. Most policies do not mandate any special collection effort, assuming the address is correct, until at least the second monthly statement has been mailed out. A possible exception might be a message printed on this second statement asking the guest if payment has been held up because of an error or question regarding the charges. With the third statement, most hotels will include a formal demand for payment, which, depending on the amount due, may be followed by a telegram, a personal call, or even an attorney's letter, especially if the hotel is owned by a company with an in-house legal department. Hotels with outstanding banquet or convention accounts will often include the banquet or sales managers and their staffs in this collection effort, on the theory that, since they booked and supervised the functions, they are known to the people involved and should be more successful than the credit clerk in collecting. However, many salespersons are reluctant to press for payment, because they feel that any such pressure will alienate their clients and cause them to lose business. Therefore, a wise policy will limit the time given the banquet or sales staff to effect a collection, and will require that at the expiration of that time the account be returned to the controller for whatever action is deemed necessary.

Almost all small balances, under $10, can be traced to disputed charges at checkout that are subsequently found to be correct in whole or in part, or to after-departure charges. Each requires different handling.

Every guest who disputes or questions a charge at departure should be given the courtesy of a letter of explanation, with an apology if the charge was totally or partially incorrect. A photocopy of the actual charge and a duplicate or corrected bill should always be included to substantiate any remaining balance.

After-departure charges on a paid account should be billed as soon as possible after the guest's departure. Many hotels use for this purpose a preprinted form that merely states that a copy of the charge is enclosed that had not reached the cashier in time to be included on the guest's bill at departure, expressing regret for any inconvenience caused, and requesting payment. Accounts under two or three dollars are rarely rebilled and are often transferred directly to a house account in the city ledger. Any money received from the one-time billing is credited to this account with no attempt made to identify the original charge. The net balance of the account is usually written off each month. Late charges from stores or concessions, which some hotels even refuse to accept, and for long-distance calls in states where the telephone company will accept responsibility for uncollected calls, must be segregated and controlled so that they can be charged back in the event payment is not received within a specified time.

After-departure charges on charge accounts require a slightly different billing procedure. For a personal or business account, a form letter of explanation, with a copy of the late charge and a corrected bill, will usually suffice. Guests who charged their accounts on credit cards must also be informed but, in addition, the charge slip must be corrected or a supplementary one (in the amount of the late charge) prepared. The amount signed for by the guest should never be altered. Some charge slips have a blank space where the city-ledger clerk can enter the corrected total, which will be accepted by the credit card company subject to the cardholder's approval. If the incidence of after-departure charges is high, the causes should be investigated and corrective action be instigated.

However, at some point, all unsuccessful efforts by the hotel personnel must cease and other collection methods be employed. At what point outside assistance is to be implemented, and the form it should take, should be clearly spelled out in the overall credit policy, particularly since most controllers and credit managers are understandably reluctant to write off uncollected accounts or to turn them over to an attorney or collection agency. Unfortunately, waiting too long will sometimes cause an uncollected account to become uncollectible.

Collection efforts, like controls, must be carefully evaluated and studied before being put into operation. Costs, salaries, and other expenses involved sometimes exceed the amount collected. Collection staffs are relatively small, and the time and effort needed to collect a $1,000 account is approximately the same as that to collect a $100 account. For these reasons, many collectors are instructed to concentrate their efforts on accounts with a minimum past-due balance of at least $200.

The following procedures are recommended for consideration and inclusion in a credit policy:

1. Imprint an "Address Correction Requested" stamp on the first billing to any guest who did not have a confirmed reservation. If the debtor has moved, the post office will send the new address, providing your correspondence was sent by first-class mail.

2. Immediately investigate all returned mail. Sending further statements without first verifying the address on the bill, registration card, or reservation correspondence, if any, is a waste of time and money. If no other address is available, then that guest must be considered a "skipper" and a decision made as to the disposition of the account. Unless there are long-distance calls or a record of checks cashed by the guest, which might enable the hotel staff or an outside collection agency to trace the guest, the only available alternative is to write off the balance due.

3. Small balances—say, from $10 to $25—if not paid in 90 days, should be deemed uncollectible and written off.

4. Accounts from under $50 up to $200, depending on the type of hotel and the rates, should not be assigned to the hotel collection staff for personal attention. Collection efforts would then be limited to the normal billing routine—monthly statements, demands for payment, and attorney's letters. After 90 days to a maximum of 120 days, all unpaid balances should be turned over to an outside agency for collection. Many agencies offer a so-called letter series, whereby for a nominal amount they send three to eight letters to the guest. The hotel retains full control over the accounts, and the letters normally specify that all payments be made directly to the hotel. By introducing a third party, hotels have been fairly successful in collecting a substantial percentage of their accounts, and many hotels use this service before turning accounts over, on a percentage basis, to a collection agency of their choice. The percentage charge is usually in the range of 25 to 50%.

5. With the small balances written off and other accounts assigned for routine billing, the hotel's collection staff can concentrate its efforts on accounts with substantial open balances. Letters on hotel stationery, like repeated monthly statements, are often completely disregarded by the former guests. They are fully aware of the outstanding balance, and until they are ready to settle the account, mail from the hotel is discarded without being read. The best way to contact such people and be sure of getting their personal attention is to call them. If the telephone number is not available, because of a private listing or for any other reason, a telegram or registered letter should be sent requesting immediate payment or, if that is not possible, a call to the person assigned to collect the account. Complete and accurate records must be kept of all telephone

conversations, and any promises to pay that are not kept should immediately be followed up by another call. Some collection managers instruct their staffs to make these follow-up calls collect if they are outside the local call area.

Even though the overall credit policy cannot prescribe detailed credit procedures, it can and should be very specific as to the point at which accounts should be assigned to the collection staff and when these efforts, if unsuccessful, should cease. The suggested timetable is assignment of these accounts to specific collectors at 90 days and termination of their efforts on all balances still unpaid when they are 180 days past due. At that time, all accounts, except those specifically withheld by the general manager or controller, should be turned over to an outside agency for collection.

At 90 days, no special collection efforts need be made. The collector should be given statements demanding payment, the attorney's letter, and any form letters normally sent. These should be mailed and a file opened for the account. Ten to 15 days later, if no payment is received, the collector should obtain the original bills, individual charge vouchers, and any other pertinent information that is available in order to discuss the open balance with the guest intelligently and answer any questions that arise.

Of course, this process can be carried out only if the aged trial balance is received and analyzed each month by the controller, along with the credit manager, an investigation clerk who keeps the data on skippers and disputed charges, and a collection clerk to report on the status of the over-90-day accounts. The general manager may participate in some of these meetings; if not, he or she should be briefed on any actions taken and should review the monthly trial balances with the controller.

Checks returned unpaid by the bank require special and immediate attention. Many hotels redeposit them on the next business day without notifying the guests, on the theory that their own bank will let them know when the checks are returned for "insufficient funds" or "drawn against uncollected funds." The results are excellent; most checks clear on the second try. Those that don't, as well as checks returned for other reasons ("account closed," "payment stopped," and the like), should be turned over to the credit manager for immediate action and, if not paid within 30 days, given to an attorney for collection.

Bad debts. Few city-ledger accounts, except those of skippers, are deemed to be uncollectible in the same accounting period, fiscal or calendar year, in which the charges were incurred. Therefore, a reserve for bad debts is set up each year, the expense being charged to current operations, to offset any such losses that might occur in the future. When the account is actually written off, it is charged against the reserve and does not affect the operating results for a future year. The amount set up as a reserve is usually a percentage of room sales, from .25% to 1%. The reserve should be reviewed at least twice a year to determine if the balance is sufficient to cover any possible losses from doubtful accounts. A percentage of the totals shown on the city-ledger aged trial balance as being 60 days or older should be considered uncollectible; in addition, 2% of 60 days; 5% of 90 days; 10% of 120 days or more; and 50% of all accounts not yet written off but turned over to outside agencies or attorneys for collection. If the reserve is more or less than the total of these percentages, the monthly provision can be decreased or increased.

Comparisons between hotels is difficult, even between hotels under one management. Too many factors must be considered—deterioration of the neighborhood, a change in the class of guests, and, of course, the charge-sales percentage (excluding credit cards) of total sales—before the annual amount written off as bad debts can be properly evaluated and determination made of its reasonableness. A hotel with 75% of its total sales paid for in cash or charged on credit cards should certainly have a smaller annual bad-debt loss than one with the same volume but 75% of sales charged and only 25% paid in cash or through credit cards. In any event, barring very unusual circumstances, the annual write-off should not exceed 1% of room sales. If it does, the credit policy should be reviewed and its enforcement strengthened.

Legal aspects of collection. Until well into the 20th century, collection practices were rarely challenged; debtors could be harassed and coerced into paying their accounts. Slowly at first, but accelerating very rapidly in the 1960s and 1970s, consumer-protection laws were enacted at all levels of government—local, state, and federal. In addition, the courts have been very liberal in interpreting these laws in favor of the debtor. Today, credit managers must be aware of what actions are illegal. However, they should also be made aware of what steps they can take to properly protect the hotel, and must make a strong and determined effort to collect the amounts due. Management can help by incorporating in the credit policy some general information as to what actions are proper and which are illegal.

If possible, this section of the credit policy, as well as the formats of all collection letters and telegrams, should be reviewed and approved by an attorney. Too many creditors have found themselves not only accused but convicted of extortion or of committing a libelous action while trying to collect a just debt. The courts have been judging any action calculated to harass or coerce a debtor a form of extortion. Some of the more common credit procedures found to be offensive are repeated telephone calls at all hours of the day or night, collection letters that appear to be legal documents, summonses or complaints intended to frighten the debtor into paying, threats of criminal prosecution, and dissemination of an unfavorable credit report to force the debtor into bankruptcy. Naturally, the creditor can legally threaten to turn the account over to a collection agency or to an attorney for legal action if the debt is not paid within a specified time.

Libel laws prohibit the publication of any material that might injure a person's reputation or invade his or her right to privacy. Defamatory telegrams and postcards, or envelopes on which are written words or symbols indicating the debtor to be delinquent, have been judged to be libelous actions, on the grounds that they could be seen by others. Mailing such cards or envelopes is also in violation of postal laws and subject to a fine, imprisonment, or both.

Collection agencies should be thoroughly investigated before they are used. Any illegal acts they commit as agents will reflect on the hotel's reputation and possibly subject the hotel to legal action. Most reputable agencies have, or will purchase, an insurance policy to protect the hotel against such a possibility.

Credit policy should also include some reference to the provisions of the Equal Credit Opportunity Act and the "Truth-In-Lending" Act. The first is not of much concern to most hotels. It prohibits discrimination in the extension of credit on the grounds of sex, marital status, race, color, religion, national origin, or age. It does not prohibit any credit practices that are uniformly administered. Thus, a policy is legal that requires everyone without a confirmed reservation to produce proper and sufficient identification before being accepted as a guest and allowed to register.

The other, the Truth-In-Lending Act, does mandate certain procedures. It requires that with any statement of a current charge that is mailed to a guest, a notice outlining specific procedures for handling disputes be enclosed. The notice is not required if the statement shows only a previous balance due. However, since it is too costly to sort the statements, most hotels enclose it with each.

The Act not only outlines the procedures but sets a time limit for each step. It specifies the time within which a guest must file a written complaint and the time within which the hotel personnel must acknowledge receipt of the complaint and handle it. The guest is then given the option to accept or reject the settlement within a specified time. Finally, the Act outlines the rights of each party during and after each interval.

There are also many local and state laws or statutes with respect to the extension of credit, particularly in the sale of alcoholic beverages, that should be reviewed by management and included in the overall credit policy.

CHAPTER SUMMARY

The hotel industry has always had credit problems, but the use of credit cards has reduced the problems with individuals.

Hotels must have an established credit policy administered by the credit department or if the hotel has no credit department, by the accounting office. However, it is the responsibility of all departments.

Policies must consist of actions both before, during, and after the event. Before the event, action relates mostly to groups and involves checking credit ratings and history.

During the event, individuals and groups are monitored on a daily basis.

A policy must be established for check-cashing.

After the event, credit activities are instigated by the accounting department. Action by the accounting department for a specific period of time is followed by the use of a collection agency, or if the account is large, a lawyer.

Specific policies should be established to handle returned checks. The final decision to write off an account should be made by a credit committee.

Various government laws may restrict certain actions to collect an account.

REVIEW QUESTIONS

1. Which is more likely to have a liberal credit policy—a new hotel or an established hotel?
2. How can a bellman or a room-service cashier help in the area of credit?
3. How can information on the credit status of a corporation be obtained?
4. Should postdated checks, second-party checks, and money orders be accepted?
5. When should small balances be written off?
6. When should accounts be turned over to a collection agency?
7. How should returned checks be handled?
8. What is a reasonable percent of sales to establish a reserve for bad debts?
9. What does the Truth-in-Lending Act specify?

23

Other Responsibilities
of the Accounting
Department

After studying this chapter, the student should:

1. Understand the importance of internal controls.
2. Understand the elements of internal controls.
3. Understand the Daily Revenue Report.
4. Know journal entries and the entry into the general ledger.
5. Know the elements of financial statement analysis.

INTERNAL CONTROLS

The authors have two favorite sayings in relation to accounting-department functions. The first is rather obvious: "The only serious mistakes are those not caught and corrected before the work leaves the department." The second is a variation on, and interpretation of, "Physician, heal thyself": "Controller, control thyself." This points up the primary responsibility of a controller: to set up internal controls in the accounting department.

But, since it is the controller's responsibility to set up controls in all departments, the question could very well be asked: Why start in accounting? The answer may be expressed in one word: cash. Accounting personnel are primarily involved in the collection of cash receipts and the deposit of all money received, and the department has the sole responsibility for checking and verifying the income of the hotel. In addition, accounting personnel initiate and approve all payments to creditors, commissions to travel agents, refunds to guests, and so on, certifying the accuracy of the amounts due. Following are the procedures needed to properly implement these controls.

There are two principal reasons for developing any type of controls. The first is to ensure accuracy—to prevent or discover and correct mistakes. The second is to reduce employee theft, and the controls used for this purpose are based on the theory that most people are honest but not many could resist temptation were it not for the fear of being caught. Since fear is all too often the only deterrent, it follows that rules must be strictly enforced and dishonest employees punished. Punishment should always include immediate dismissal and, if the amount involved is substantial, arrest and prosecution. It is also advisable to publicize this among the other employees, not to further discredit the guilty person, but in the hope that emphasizing the consequences will discourage others from stealing. The procedures employed in internal controls are designed to achieve both objectives: accuracy and theft prevention.

The final step is the reconciliation of the bank statements. Common sense, as well as good accounting practice, dictates that people directly or indirectly involved in handling receipts or disbursements should not be allowed to perform this function. Included in this category would be the general cashier and all billing, investigation, accounts-payable, and payroll clerks, or anyone supervising or checking their work.

An important element of internal control relative to daily procedures is the verification by the controller or assistant of the deposit processed by the general cashier. Not only should the total be checked, but receipt by the bank should also be confirmed. To truly verify a deposit, the bank should be asked to mail a duplicate receipt to the hotel, to the attention of the controller or an assistant. Again, merely checking the amount shown against the daily report is not enough. Good accounting procedures mandate that deposits be made daily, in consecutive order, with all weekend and holiday deposits made on the next banking day. Manipulating the sequence of deposits and misusing the cash included in each is a method frequently used by dishonest cashiers to cover up their thefts. Checking the consecutive order of the deposits and immediately investigating a missing receipt eliminates this possibility.

In addition to approving petty-cash disbursements, the controller should personally review and approve all rebates to the guest accounts. Rebates, except to write off bad debts or unidentifiable charges, are meant only to adjust errors in the amount charged. A hotel operates and reports its income daily, hence today's revenue should not be reduced by yesterday's overcharges. Such adjustment must be made through a rebate. (The reverse, when the guest was not charged or was charged less than the amount due, must be included as additional income on the day when the error is uncovered.)

Rebates, as was pointed out in discussing duties of the investigation clerks, are often made for charges that were incurred by another guest and should have been transferred to that guest's account. Therefore, a proper and complete explanation must be made on each rebate voucher. It should not only include the reason for the adjustment, but clearly indicate how the total was arrived at. Where the hotel is required to charge room or sales taxes, adjustment of any items subject to either must include a proportionate amount of the tax charged, and the rebate should clearly show both figures in arriving at the total credit. The reason for this breakdown should be obvious. Taxes are not an expense of the hotel. Any amount rebated is deducted from total collections and only the net remitted to the taxing authority. Not separating the amounts only increases the chance that the total will be charged against income, thus needlessly creating an additional expense.

Two basic requirements of good internal controls are the following:

A set of rules with specific instructions and procedures for implementing them; and a system for checking—the assigning of a supervisor or staff member to review and verify the accuracy of the work of another employee. However, a rule not enforced is far worse than no rule at all. Employees may decide that if they can get away with one thing, they can try to get away with everything. In a sense, then, controls are like recurring orders, and it is the obligation of the supervisor—in this case, the controller—to make sure that they are clearly understood, to train the personnel needed to carry them out, and finally to see to it that they are never disregarded.

Cash is the most important asset in any business. In the final analysis, no income is truly income until it has been converted into cash and the cash deposited in the bank. Therefore, there is a need for strict adherence to the controls outlined above. Controls in other departments besides accounting have been dealt with in Section III, and in the chapters to come that cover specific items of income and expense, the applicable controls will be discussed.

DAILY REVENUE REPORT

In Chapter 18, the night audit function is described in detail. Reference is made to the production of the daily revenue report (Figure 23-1) as a part of the night audit function. The format should be tailored to meet specific requirements of the hotel. A comparison on a month-to-date basis is made against budget and prior years' numbers.

Following are comments and explanations regarding some of the items shown in the daily revenue report.

Room revenue. The revenue is broken down into the basic segments of transient (individual) and group business. It is then segmented into specific categories that are significant to that specific hotel. Other hotels may require different segmentation.

ROOM REVENUE	Today	(— Month to Date —) Actual	Budget	Last Yr.
TRANSIENT ROOM REVENUE				
TRANSIENT INDIVIDUAL	5,188	80,431	23,957	42,957
GOLF/SKI INDIVIDUAL	535	8,525	13,036	0
CORPORATE INDIVIDUAL	0	2,775	1,330	3,108
TOTAL TRANSIENT REVENUE	5,723	91,731	38,323	46,065
GROUP ROOM REVENUE				
GROUP CORPORATE	1,900	12,359	40,837	19,114
GROUP TOUR AND TRAVEL	485	5,690	15,738	18,078
GROUP ASSOCIATION	0	0	15,834	0
TOTAL GROUP ROOM REVENUE	2,385	18,049	72,409	37,192
TOTAL ROOM REVENUE	8,108	109,779	110,732	83,257
FOOD AND BEVERAGE REVENUE				
FOOD REVENUE				
MAIN DINING ROOM FOOD	1,434	16,480	13,667	10,003
TAVERN FOOD	1,979	21,508	13,363	8,246
	0	0	0	429
ROOM SERVICE FOOD	0	0	0	0
BANQUET FOOD	0	9,082	31,688	16,311
TOTAL FOOD SALES	3,413	47,070	58,991	34,989
BEVERAGE REVENUE				
MAIN DINING ROOM LIQUOR	0	1,173	1,219	435
MAIN DINING ROOM WINE	0	1,709	1,499	439
TAVERN LIQUOR	466	6,363	6,608	3,483
TAVERN WINE		237	3,463	689
POOL TERRACE LIQUOR	0	0	0	109
POOL TERRACE WINE	0	0	0	21
BANQUET LIQUOR	13	2,424	4,038	1,427
BANQUET WINE	0	321	3,218	2,159
TOTAL BEVERAGE REVENUE	716	15,453	17,271	9,592
MISC FOOD AND BEVERAGE INCOME				
PUBLIC ROOM RENTALS	0	0	715	100
BANQUET MISCELLANEOUS COMM.	0	0	0	0
AUDIO VISUAL RENTALS	0	0	0	980
TOTAL FOOD & BEV MISC INCOME	0	0	715	1,080
TOTAL FOOD AND BEVERAGE INCOME	4,129	62,523	76,704	45,661

	Today	(— Month to Date —) Actual	Budget	Last Yr.
TELEPHONE REVENUE				
LOCAL & LONG DISTANCE REVENUE				
LOCAL TELEPHONE	12	117	70	157
LONG DISTANCE TELEPHONE	57	1,008	2,447	695
TOTAL LOCAL & LONG DISTANCE	69	1,125	2,516	853
TELEPHONE COMMISSIONS	0	0	187	0
TOTAL TELEPHONE REVENUE	69	1,125	2,703	853
GIFT SHOP REVENUE				
SALES CLOTHING AND GIFTS				
SHEPPARD'S STORE CLOTHING	36	331	1,972	309
SHEPPARD'S STORE GIFTS	270	2,087	1,972	746
TOTAL SALES-GIFTS AND CLOTHING	306	2,418	3,944	1,055
SALES OTHER				
MAGAZINES AND PAPERBACKS	57	214	81	74
NEWSPAPERS		32	391	162
VERMONT FOOD PRODUCTS	76	340	162	44
SUNDRIES	19	142	0	238
GIFT SHOP COMMISSIONS	6	221	0	145
TOTAL SALES-OTHER	190	1,308	404	704
TOTAL GIFT SHOP REVENUE	496	3,726	4,348	1,759
GUEST LAUNDRY & VALET REVENUE				
SALES-LAUNDRY	0	207	0	130
TOTAL GUEST LAUNDRY & VALET	0	207	0	130
TOTAL STORE RENTS & OTHER INC	5	11,779	2,236	13,965
COUNTRY CLUB REVENUE				
SALES-FOOD & SODAS				
COUNTRY CLUB FOOD	940	4,772	5,409	0
TOTAL SALES-FOOD & SODAS	940	4,772	5,409	0
SALES-LIQUOR & WINE				
COUNTRY CLUB LIQUOR	134	832	3,302	0
COUNTRY CLUB WINE	25	351	296	0
TOTAL SALES-LIQUOR & WINE	159	1,183	3,598	0
TOTAL COUNTRY CLUB REVENUE	1,099	5,955	9,006	0
SPA REVENUE				
A LA CARTE SERVICES	268	3,412	2,263	1,202
FACILITY CHARGE	11	749	0	676
LOCAL PROGRAMS & MISC SPA	62	961	1,742	134
SPA PRO SHOP	93	757	404	0
TOTAL SPA REVENUE	434	5,880	4,409	2,011
GOLF REVENUE				
GREEN FEES	4,980	35,248	44,825	0
CARTS	1,197	8,113	10,409	0
PRO SHOP SALES	337	4,267	6,577	0
OTHER GOLF INCOME	0	0	0	0
Total Hotel Income	20,853	248,602	271,949	147,635

Figure 23-1   Daily Revenue Report

Food revenue and beverage revenue. These categories are broken down by specific outlets. The actual name of the outlet can be used as a caption.

Miscellaneous food and beverage income. This reflects miscellaneous income sources related to food and beverage, usually banquet operations.

Telephone revenue. This revenue is broken down into local and long distance.

Gift shop revenue. In the example used, the hotel operates its own gift shop. Revenue is broken down by type of product sold.

Guest laundry and valet revenue. This is revenue received from laundry and valet services provided to the guests.

Store Rents and Other Income. This category contains income from shops leased out (as opposed to being hotel operated) and income from concessions and miscellaneous sources. If so desired, this section can be further segmented.

The remaining sections reflect revenue from the other profit centers operated as departments within the overall hotel structure. It should be noted that the daily revenue report should have a statistics page that gives daily information on occupancy, average rate, number of covers, and so forth.

ENTRY OF REVENUE INTO GENERAL LEDGER

While old systems require that the daily revenue numbers be entered into the general ledger from the daily revenue reports, most property management systems have an interface between the front-office functions and back-office accounting that transmits the revenue numbers from the night audit directly into the general ledger. The interface can be activated during the night audit or the following morning after review by the accounting department.

OTHER BOOKS OF ORIGINAL ENTRY

Up to this point, we have dealt only with the entry of revenue into the general ledger. In the chapter on accounts payable, we addressed the recording of expenditures and cash disbursements. In the chapter on payroll, the payroll recording process was reviewed, although many hotels utilize an outside payroll service to prepare their payrolls. In those circumstances, general journal entries are prepared from the data provided by the payroll service. The preparation and entry of journal entries is discussed next.

JOURNAL ENTRIES

Journal entries can be divided into two categories: *standard* journal entries and *regular* journal entries.

Standard journal entries are those entries that occur every accounting period in the same amount (subject to periodic review and change). In a computerized general ledger system, these entries can be programmed to be automatically recorded each month. The most common types of standard journal entries are write-offs of prepaid expenses; monthly accruals for an expense paid quarterly, semiannually, or annually; depreciation and bad debt provisions; and predetermined allocations or distributions of expense.

Regular journal entries are required not only for the abnormal or nonrecurring entries, such as corrections of errors, but also for those entries that occur

ACCOUNT NUMBER	ACCOUNT DESCRIPTION	DEBIT	CREDIT	SOURCE	REFERENCE
3901 - 320	Food - Cost of Sales	3121^{50}			To adjust closing inventory
1105 - 000	Food Inventory		3121^{50}		
5027 - 320	Food - Guest Supplies	862^{17}			To correct coding of charge
5027 - 310	Rooms - Guest Supplies		862^{17}		
4121 - 330	Beverage-Salaries & Wages	1121^{00}			To allocate portion of
4021 - 320	Food - Salaries & Wages		1121^{00}		F&B Mgr to Beverage Dept
1445 - 000	Prepaid Expense	600^{00}			To defer portion of large
5060 - 500	Sales - Office Supplies		600^{00}		purchase of supplies

Page #_____
MONTH ENDING:_____

Figure 23-2   Regular Journal Entries

each period but in varying amounts, such as inventory adjustments. Such entries are usually recorded on manual journal entry forms and entered into the computer on a batch processing basis. Figure 23-2 is an example of regular journal entries.

THE GENERAL LEDGER

General ledger balancing is automatic in a computer system. When all entries have been completed, trial balances both for the period and on a year-to-date basis can be printed for review purposes. The financial statement format is programmed into the computer and can be readily printed after the trial balances are reviewed. Normally a preliminary financial statement will be printed for further review before a final statement is printed.

The various exhibits in this chapter reflect, where required, those changes in financial statement presentation mandated by the ninth edition of the *Uniform System.*

FINANCIAL STATEMENT ANALYSIS

Occupancy

The most commonly used statistic in the hotel industry is the percentage of occupancy. It is the measurement of the level of rooms business enjoyed by the property. To arrive at the occupancy, the number of rooms occupied is compared with the number available. (In Europe, occupancy is sometimes measured by comparing beds occupied against beds available.)

The mathematical formula to arrive at the percentage of occupancy is as follows: Rooms occupied × 100 ÷ rooms available = percentage of occupancy. For example, assume that a hotel has 200 rooms and that on the night in question 120 rooms were occupied. Then the occupancy was:

$$\frac{120 \times 100}{200} = 60\%$$

However, occupancy is not measured only on a per-night basis. Assume that in the example 130 rooms were occupied on the following night; then the combined occupancy for two nights is:

$$\frac{250 \times 100}{400} = 62.5\%$$

Thus, occupancy can be calculated for one or more nights, a month, or a year.

Average Rate

The average rate is almost as significant as occupancy, since it indicates the amount of revenue obtained per occupied room. The formula is: Rooms sales ÷ occupied rooms = average rate. For example, assume that the rate charges for 120 occupied rooms were these:

Number of Rooms		Rate	Revenue
56	at	$ 90	$5,040
27	at	100	2,700
21	at	110	2,310
16	at	115	1,840
Total 120			$11,890

The average rate is $11,890 ÷ 120 = $99.08. As with occupancy, average rate can be calculated for any period of time.

Group And Transient Statistics

It is frequently desirable to a hotel to further break down its occupancy and average rate into group and transient business. This is particularly important where groups form a major element in the overall occupancy. If meaningful, group statistics can be further broken down into market segments, such as corporate, association, or tour and travel.

Analysis Of Statement Of Income And Expenses

To illustrate the key ratios in the statement of income and expenses, Table 23-1 shows such a statement for a hypothetical 400-room hotel for a 12-month period. The figures used are about what might be expected for a hotel of this size.

The income after deduction of undistributed operating expenses is commonly known as "gross operating profit" and is the level at which the effectiveness of the management of a hotel can best be measured. Expenses shown below the line—property taxes, insurance, interest, and depreciation—are beyond operational control; they depend on several factors that have no relation to day-to-day operations, such as construction costs and terms of the mortgage. The ratio of gross operating profit to total revenue thus becomes the measurement of management's ability. In the case of the Graylig Hotel, this ratio is:

$$\frac{4,860 \times 100}{16,000} = 30.37\%$$

The ratio depends to some extent on the relative volumes of room sales and food and beverage sales, and its merits must be judged in this light. However, in general, a ratio of 30% or better is viewed as desirable.

Since the rooms and food and beverage departments are usually the principal contributors to a hotel's income, the degree of profitability of these departments is obviously the key to a hotel's success. The financial statements will usually include, in addition to the statement of income and expenses, a detailed schedule of the results of each department. These analyses are particularly important for both the rooms department, the food department, and the beverage department, and Table 23-2 shows the figures reported for these departments for the same time period. The ratios provided by these analyses are examined next.

In these departments, the percentage of departmental profit is the most important. In the rooms department, the profit ratio is $7,800 \div 10,000 \times 100 = 78.22\%$; in the food department, it is $300 \div 3,200 \times 100 = 9.38\%$. In the beverage department the profit ratio is $780 \div 1,400 \times 100 = 55.71\%$. It should be mentioned that in the latter, the actual mix of business—food versus beverage, and banquet food sales versus regular outlets—can materially affect the department profits. A high proportion of beverage operations, which have a lower overall cost than food operations, will result in a higher combined percentage profit; and banquet sales, which have preestablished numbers of covers and a fixed menu, are usually more profitable than sales through the regular outlets. Therefore, a hotel with a popular bar and a high volume of banquet business should have a good departmental profit.

Table 23-1 Hotel Graylig, 400 Rooms, Statement of Income and Expenses (000s and Omitted)

Operated Departments	Net Revenue	Cost of Sales	Payroll and Related Expenses	Other Expenses	Income (Loss)
Rooms	$10,100	—	$1,450	$750	$7,900
Food	5,200	$1,000	1,720	180	300
Beverage	1,400	280	280	60	780
Telecommunications	600	300	100	20	180
Guest Laundry	200	120	10	30	40
Rentals and Other Income	500	—	—	—	500
Total Operated Departments	16,000	1,700	3,560	1,040	9,700
Undistributed Operating Expenses					
Administrative and General			1,140	900	1,340
Human Resources			80	40	120
Security			65	15	80
Marketing			300	1,500	1,800
Property Operation and Maintenance			400	400	800
Utility Costs			—	700	700
Total Undistributed Operating Expenses			1,285	3,555	4,840
Totals	$16,000	$1,700	$4,845	$4,595	$4,860

Income after Distributed Operating Expenses

Management Fees	(700)
Property Taxes and Insurance	(160)

Income before Interest, Depreciation, and Amortization and Income Taxes $4,000

	Assets		
Current Assets			
Cash on Hand and in Bank			
House Banks	$ 22		
Demand Deposits	118		
Total Cash		$140	
Receivables			
Guest Ledger	$132		
City Ledger	328	460	
Inventories			
Food	47		
Beverage	38		
Other	21	106	
Prepaid Expenses		42	
Total Current Assets			$748
Property and Equipment			
Land	3,000		
Furniture and Equipment	520		
Building	5,130		
China, Glassware, Silver, and Linen	430		
		9,130	
Accumulated Depreciation		1,270	
Net Property and Equipment			7,860
Total Assets			$8,608

Table 23-1 *(Continued)*

	Liabilities and Equity	
Current Liabilities		
Accounts Payable	$280	
Accrued Expenses	172	
Advance Deposits	88	$ 540
Long-term Debt		
Mortgage Payable		3,110
Shareholders Equity		
Capital Stock	2,000	
Retained Earnings	2,958	4,958
Total Equity		
Total Liabilities and Equity		$8,608

Not only is "payroll and related expense" the largest single departmental expense category, but it is very controllable, so its ratio to departmental sales is extremely significant. In the Graylig Hotel, we find that in the rooms department it is $1,450 \div 10,100 \times 100 = 14.35\%$, and in the food department $1,720 \div 3,200 \times 100 = 53.78\%$. However, a reduction in payroll expense of 10% in the latter department would result in a profit increase to 20%. This illustrates the importance of carefully monitoring the payroll percentage and acting on unfavorable variances.

Other departmental expenses can be measured against revenue both in total and individually. Significant variances either from a predetermined budget or from normal ratios call for detailed analysis and explanations. However, inasmuch as some of these expenses are relatively insignificant in total, examination of individual months may show distortions while the year-to-date ratio is normal.

In the food and beverage departments, there are two other very important ratios: the food-cost ratio and the beverage-cost ratio. (The cost of food sales is the total cost of sales less the cost of meals consumed free of charge by employees.) In each case, the cost of sales is measured against the revenue. Thus, we find that in the Graylig hotel the food-cost ratio is $1,000 \div 3,200 \times 100 = 31.25\%$, and the beverage-cost ratio is $280 \div 1,400 \times 100 = 20\%$. A poor food- or beverage-cost ratio is indicative of one or more of the following problems:

1. Too-low selling prices.
2. Too-high prices being paid for the ingredients as a result of poor purchasing.
3. Too much waste in the preparation process.
4. In the case of food, an improper balance of structuring in the menus; that is, too many items that have a high cost and produce a lower-than-normal profit margin.
5. Inadequate controls, permitting employees to steal the proceeds of sales or give away free drinks or meals.
6. Physical theft in the storerooms, kitchens, or bars.

Table 23-2 Hotel Graylig, 400 Rooms, Department Schedules (000s omitted)

ROOMS DEPARTMENT SCHEDULE

Revenue:		
Room Sales		$10,100
Departmental Expenses:		
Payroll and Related Expenses	$1,450	
Contract Cleaning	50	
Laundry and Dry Cleaning	200	
Linen	140	
Uniforms	30	
Travel Agent Commissions	85	
Guest Supplies	75	
Cleaning Supplies	75	
Printing and Stationery	75	
Other Expenses	20	($2,200)
Departmental Profit:		$7,900

FOOD DEPARTMENT SCHEDULE

Revenue:		
Food Sales		$3,200
Cost of Sales:		
Food		($1,000)
Gross Profit:		$2,200
Departmental Expenses:		
Payroll and Related Expenses	$1,720	
China and Glass	25	
Silver	15	
Linen	25	
Laundry and Dry Cleaning	21	
Kitchen Fuel	14	
Contract Cleaning	18	
Uniforms	17	
Paper Supplies	15	
Guest Supplies	20	
Cleaning Supplies	20	
Other Expenses		($1,900)
Departmental Profit:		$ 300

BEVERAGE DEPARTMENT SCHEDULE

Revenue:		
Beverage Sales		$1,400
Cost of Sales:		
Beverage		280
Gross Profit:		$1,120

Table 23-2 *(Continued)*

Departmental Expenses:		
Payroll and Related Expenses	$280	
Glass	5	
Laundry and Dry Cleaning	5	
Music and Entertainment	30	
Uniforms	5	
Paper Supplies	5	
Guest Supplies	5	
Cleaning Supplies	3	
Other Expenses	2	$ 340
Departmental Profit		$ 780

Balance Sheet Analysis

In addition to the hypothetical statement and schedules described, a hypothetical balance sheet for the Graylig Hotel has been prepared. The balance sheet in Table 23-3 is representative of what one might expect for a 400-room hotel.

Before examining the ratios that can be developed from the balance sheet, the makeup of certain sections of it need to be explained.

"Cash on hand and in bank" includes, in addition to the operating funds needed to carry on day-to-day operations, the floats required by the front-office and restaurant cashiers and the general cashier.

"Inventories—other" consists of guest supplies, cleaning supplies, printing and stationery, engineering supplies, and any other inventories required in the operation of the hotel.

"Prepaid expenses" covers any expense that has been prepaid for a period beyond the balance-sheet date. The most common such items in hotel operations are insurance and maintenance contracts.

"Accumulated depreciation" represents the cumulative amount of charges against income for depreciation of the building and furniture and equipment.

"Accrued expenses" is the opposite of prepaid expenses. It is the liability for expenses incurred but not included in accounts payable because the costs on the billing period will extend into the following year. Most commonly found in hotel accounts are utilities, payroll, and telephone; legal and audit fees and similar items are also included.

The balance sheet represents the financial picture of the hotel at a given time, whereas the statement of income and expenses reflects the results of operations for the period covered by the statement. Consequently, although the statement of income and expenses and the related schedules are the sources of most of the necessary analysis, certain conclusions can be reached by relating the balance-sheet data to the operating results.

BUDGET PREPARATION

The preparation of the financial statements marks the end of the recording functions of the department and is in a sense the beginning of the controller's management responsibilities—the analyses not only of the statements but of the many reports prepared to assist top management in setting the operating policies of the hotel. Where these policies relate to income and expense, as many do, the controller has the additional responsibility of monitoring them and making certain they are carried out. This is done through spot checks, by establishing and maintaining adequate controls, and through frequent consultations with top management and fellow department heads.

Most of the special studies and reports are discussed, as are controls, in the chapters covering specific departments or functions—credit, food and beverage, housekeeping, payroll, and so on. Some cannot be anticipated, because they depend solely on the desires or priorities of management. Finally, there are the studies that concern the budget, primarily those required by management to explain variations between actual and projected results. They may involve an in-depth study of departmental operations, a review of the methods and factors used in compiling the budget, consideration of any changes since the budget was prepared, and certainly rechecking of the accuracy of the actual figures submitted. To try and standardize or even to describe these procedures is not feasible, since they depend entirely on the desires and priorities of management. There may be many variations from the budget, but only those deemed important by management need to be analyzed and explained.

A budget, as we have said, is an estimate of future income and expense. It is a projection used by management to plan, control, and shape future operating policies. When so used, it is possibly management's most valuable operating guide, so it requires the combined efforts of all the department heads. The controller is the coordinator who guides and helps each one to assemble the necessary figures, then reviews, records, and if necessary revises, the estimates before presenting them to top management for approval. The budget usually follows the format of the profit-and-loss statement and is prepared for the calendar or fiscal year used by the hotel for its financial reports. Because it must be submitted for approval at least two to three months before the start of the year covered, many hotels require that it be updated monthly throughout the year, usually for the following three months. Generally, these reports are only intended to give management a continual opportunity to review the forecasts in light of current information, and to make any policy changes deemed necessary to meet or exceed the goals set in the fiscal budget. The revisions usually do not affect the financial statements or analyses of variations in actual results; these are still compared to the approved fiscal budget. The formats for this report may vary in context but usually show only departmental totals and related percentage for each item of income and expense. Figure 23-3 shows the format we favor showing the complete operating budget for the first month, with only sales projections for the next two months.

There are, however, some companies that require their controllers to completely revise the fiscal budget each month by incorporating the updated three-month forecast into the original budget. The actual operating figures are then

Figure 23-3   Three-Month Forecast

Months of		19 ___			19 ___			19 ___		
Revenue: Rooms		$	$	$	$	$	$	$	$	$
Food–Banquets										
Restaurants										
Misc										
TOTAL FOOD	$									
Beverage–Banquets										
Restaurants										
Misc										
TOTAL BEVERAGE	$									
Minor Operated Depts	$									
Other Income										
TOTAL REVENUE	$	$	$	$	$	$	$	$	$	
Departmental Profit Rooms		%	%	%	COMMENTS					
Food & Beverage										
Minor Operated Depts										
Other Income										
TOTAL DEPARTMENT PROFIT ·		% $	% $	% $						
Operating Deductions (Incl. Payroll)	% Revenue	$	$	$						
Adm. & General										
Sales & Public Relations										
Property operation, maintenance & energy										
TOTAL OPER. DED.		$	$	$						
Gross Operating Profit		$	$	$						
		%	%	%						
Statistics Rooms: Available										
Occupied										
% of Occupancy		%	%	%						
Avg. Rate Per Occ. Rm.		$	$	$						
PERCENTAGES										
Rooms Payroll & Related										
Food–Cost of Sales Net										
Payroll & Rel.										
Beverage–Cost of Sales										
Payroll & Rel.										
Payroll & Related										
Minor Oper. Depts.										
Adm. & General										
Sales & Public Relations										
Property operation, maintenance & energy costs										

compared with the revised forecasts. This is a very time-consuming and costly process, since it in effect requires setting up a detailed three-month operating budget each month. In addition, it seems that these constant revisions circumvent the basic concept of a budget, which is to serve as an operating guide—indeed, a goal—for management to attain. The incentive for operating efficiently is lost, since poor results can be incorporated into the budget by adjusting the figures for the following three months.

Budget preparations is a team effort by the general manager and the primary department heads, each of whom is required to submit an estimate of projected income and expenses for the department. The controller's active participation and assistance are essential in assembling the information necessary to make these forecasts.

To project income, past performance must be reviewed, trends analyzed and interpreted, repeat business evaluated, and any function, group, or convention already booked taken into account. Possible increases in room rates or in banquet and restaurant food and beverage prices must also be considered, and the additional revenue, as well as its effect on statistics (percentage of occupancy, average rate, and such) calculated and incorporated into the budget. Since price changes must be initiated or approved by top management, this phase requires consultations with the general manager to ascertain if such increases are considered and, if so, their effective dates. And once all the income projections have been made by the department heads, it is advisable that the controller review them with the general manager before starting to assemble the proposed budget.

For expenses to be intelligently analyzed and projected, they must be broken down into at least the following eight categories:

1. Payroll and related expenses
2. Operating supplies
3. Cost of goods sold—food and beverages
4. Advertising
5. Heat, light, and power (cost of utilities)
6. Repairs and maintenance
7. Replacement of china, glass, linen, and silverware
8. Capital improvements

Payroll and Related Expenses

Projecting payroll costs entails adjusting present costs by contractual obligations for union employees and estimated increases for all other employees. "Related expenses" are such items as payroll taxes, disability and compensation insurance, and employee benefits such as hospitalization, life insurance, major medical, and pensions. The rate for each is available, obtainable, or relatively easy to estimate.

Once the estimated costs have been ascertained, they should be thoroughly reviewed by the controller and general manager with each department head. At these departmental meetings, a decision should be made as to the future employment policy of the hotel. Unfortunately, it is not always possible to pass on to the guests all increases in payroll costs; sometimes they necessitate a reduction in staff.

Operating Supplies

Many department heads keep a permanent record of quantity and price for major operating supplies purchased for their departments. This enables them to better estimate their needs for the period covered by a fiscal budget and, more important, by monitoring the frequency of purchases to exercise some control over the use of these supplies. Excluding price adjustments and assuming proper supervision and control, the total cost of operating supplies generally increases or decreases in direct ratio to changes in the volume of business. Thus, for a reasonably accurate forecast of operating supplies, the current cost should be adjusted by a percentage that takes into account the effect of any projected changes in both the volume of business and the unit price. Where the actual consumption for the major items is available, it is relatively simple to compute the estimated cost of these items for any period by multiplying the quantity by the projected unit cost (present cost increased by a percentage judged sufficiently to compensate for inflation).

Cost of Goods Sold—Food and Beverages

This is primarily a management decision. It should be made by the food and beverage manager in consultation with the general manager. The controller should be present to help evaluate the effect of any increase in the cost due to inflation.

Advertising

The total advertising budget, whether it is a fixed dollar amount or a percentage of income, is also a management decision. In multihotel chains, it is usually made by a home-office executive. However, each general manager and director of sales should at least have the authority to select the media best suited to cover the local market.

Energy Costs

Energy costs started rising rapidly in the 1970s. While the percentage of increase has slowed down somewhat since, there is little doubt that it will continue to rise, possibly more rapidly in some sections of the country than in others. Thus, a general rule for estimating this expense is difficult, if not impossible, to establish.

What we recommend is that each controller compare the figures for at least three prior years and try to establish an average percentage of increase, which he or she can then apply to future years' expenses.

Repairs and Maintenance

There can be no specific formula applicable to all hotels, even those operated by the same management, for forecasting this expense. Although management must define the overall policy for the upkeep of the building and its contents, the application varies with each hotel, depending to a great extent on the age and condition of the property. In a newer building, maintenance costs should be low but it might be prudent to set up a reserve for future repairs and to practice preventive maintenance of equipment to minimize future breakdowns. Older buildings require more upkeep, and the forecast must provide for it.

Within the framework of the overall schedule set by management, each budget must include, in the months mandated for this work, the estimated cost of painting and decorating the guestrooms. Public rooms, halls, lobbies, and the like should be inspected by department heads and a recommendation made to management in regard to any improvements deemed necessary. Additionally, many hotels use outside contractors for the maintenance of some equipment, furniture, upholstery, and possibly carpet repair. This maintenance, together with that of elevators, electric outdoor signs, television sets, accounting and front-office computers, and calculators must also be included in the budget.

Replacement of China, Glass, Linen, and Silverware

The requirements in this area should be estimated by the affected department heads: the housekeeper for room linens and glassware; the food and beverage manager, with his or her subdepartment heads, for the restaurant, bar, and banquet linens, china, glass, and silverware. The quantities needed can be estimated on past performance and adjusted to compensate for any change in volume of business as forecast in the budget. The controller can assist by reviewing the methods used by the two department heads to make this adjustment, and by helping them project the increase in unit prices that must be anticipated. The final figures must be approved by management.

Capital Improvements

Capital improvements are not operating expenses and are therefore not included in the budget. However, although the plans may be drawn up far in advance, management must be in a position to make the necessary financial arrangements to implement them, and this requires some knowledge of the hotel's cash position in any given period. The budget is the only report designed to provide management with this information. In addition, some improvements require the use of hotel personnel and supplies, and since it is not always feasible to capitalize these expenses, they affect the operating costs and should be considered in preparing the budget. What better time for management to review, with the department heads, plans for any major improvements scheduled during the period covered by the budget than during the many meetings and discussions required for its preparation?

CHAPTER SUMMARY

Controls are necessary to ensure accuracy and reduce employee theft.

Of particular importance are bank reconciliations, petty cash approvals, and rebates.

The daily revenue report should be used by department heads to verify their revenue.

Many entries to the general ledger are done by interfaces but journal entries, some standard, are required.

Important statistics are occupancy and average rate, also by group and transient business.

The income statement and the balance sheet should be analyzed monthly.

The annual budget requires input from all departments. Forecasts and updates of expectations are also important.

REVIEW QUESTIONS

1. What is the purpose of internal controls?
2. Why should deposits be verified?
3. Explain the reasons for the daily revenue report.
4. What are the sources of entry into the general ledger?
5. What are the most important statistics and how are they calculated?
6. What is usually the largest departmental expense?
7. What problems can create a high food cost?
8. Explain the process of budget preparation.

24
Franchising

After studying this chapter, the student should:

1. Understand the legal aspects of franchises.
2. Know the services provided by a franchiser.
3. Know the obligations of a franchisee.

In the last 20–40 years, franchising has been one of the fastest-growing phenomena in not only American but international business. Franchises cover many fields and are limited only by the scope of the business to which they relate. Types of franchises range from fast food (McDonald's) to income tax preparation services (H&R Block), dance studios (Fred Astaire), and our particular area of interest, the hotel and motel field.

Franchising can be described as the selling by the franchiser of the right to market a proven product. Thus, in the hotel and motel industry, major franchisers first established the quality of their product and their expertise in the field by operating company-owned properties, and only after demonstrating the success of these properties were they able to make their franchises marketable packages. Through establishing a format for a successful product, franchisers have provided a means for small investors to get into the hotel and motel business with a reasonable assurance of success. Many investors have found franchising a suitable area in which to employ their capital. Banks and lending institutions look with favor on the better-known franchises and, indeed, are often reluctant to make loans to potential investors in the lodging industry unless an affiliation with a referral organization has been established. The most common way to develop such an affiliation is by the acquisition of a franchise.

Originally, the major player in hotel/motel franchising was Holiday Inns. However, the current leader is Best Western with 3,983 properties (311,276 rooms). However, the combined numbers for Holiday Inns Full Service and Holiday Inns Express are 2,104 properties (292,193 rooms), making them still a major factor in the field. Other franchisers of note are:

Comfort Inns	1,736 properties (133,251 rooms)
Super 8	1,870 properties (112,000 rooms)
Ramada	1,030 properties (129,689 rooms)

Franchising must be looked at as a two-way street: the franchiser provides certain services and conveys certain rights to the franchisee, and the franchisee in turn has certain obligations to the franchiser. Therefore, this chapter will explore franchising from both points of view.

FRANCHISE SERVICES

The services offered by a franchiser can be broken down into three general categories: methods, technical assistance, and marketing.

Methods

Each reputable franchiser should have established operating procedures that the franchisee can use to run the business in the fashion that has proven successful. These procedures are usually provided to the new franchisee in the form of operating manuals covering each phase of the operation. The manuals should be continually updated as the franchiser amends and improves its procedures.

In opening a new operation, the greatest problem is always the availability of qualified personnel. Training of staff prior to opening is therefore of prime importance, and many franchisers provide training programs for this purpose. These programs require a certain number of the franchisee's staff to spend a training period in a company-owned operation, during which they familiarize themselves with the operating procedures used by the chain.

Franchisers usually employ regional managers or inspectors to visit each franchise operation periodically. Although their primary responsibility is to ensure compliance with the franchiser's standards, as shall be discussed later in the chapter, they also provide advice and assistance to the operator covering all facets of the operation. At the time of such a visit, staffing should be reviewed and suggestions made regarding areas in which payroll savings can be obtained. Recommendations should also be made regarding possible reductions of operating costs in other areas, such as food and beverage, purchasing, operating supplies, and equipment. The quality of food and beverage preparation and service should be discussed, and advice should be given about marketing techniques, in particular menu presentation and layout.

Technical Assistance

Those services described in the preceding section are standard and usually covered by the basic fee. However, many franchisers make available to the franchisee various forms of technical assistance that are optional and obtainable by the payment of an additional fee, a sum that is proportional to the amount of technical services provided.

The logic of such a policy is most clearly apparent as it relates to assistance during the development and construction phase. Certain chains will aid in the study of potential sites and the eventual selection of one. Advice and assistance will also be given to a potential franchisee in obtaining financing—sometimes only in the preparation of cost budgets and feasibility studies to give to the proposed lender, but in some cases by introducing the franchisee to sources of capital, or even working with the franchisee in negotiating a mortgage from the lender.

Architectural services may also be provided by the franchiser. Holiday Inns, for example, has its own firm of architects, whose services can be obtained through Holiday for the complete architectural design of the hotel or motel. Interior design services, project management, and construction supervision can similarly be obtained from certain franchisers.

Purchasing services are another form of technical assistance very commonly provided by franchisers. Such services are, of course, extremely valuable for a new franchisee who must acquire furniture and equipment, but their continuing availability is also very important. These services are more commonly used in the areas of operating equipment (linen, china, glass, and silver) and consumables such as paper supplies and guest supplies than for purchasing food and beverages.

The charges for the purchasing services can take various forms. Some chains actually stock or even manufacture certain items, particularly identity items that embody the name of the chain. In such circumstances, the chain will invoice the franchisee at a price that includes a profit factor. In other cases, the chain does the purchasing, taking advantage of its available volume discounts, but the manufacturer ships directly to the franchisee. The manufacturer may invoice the chain, which in turn reinvoices the franchisee at a marked-up price, or the franchisee may pay the vendor directly but pay a fee to the chain, usually a percentage of the total price. In either instance, the franchisee benefits, since, although there is a markup or fee, the substantial volume discounts (sometimes over 50%) reduce the overall cost to far below what an independent operator would pay.

Marketing

The most important ingredient in any franchise agreement is marketing. The franchiser's marketing techniques, which have been tested and proven, must be utilized to sell the franchisee's property.

The company name itself is, of course, a key element in the marketing. It appears on signs, menus, glassware, napkins, and many other places. But the continued marketing of the name is much more important.

The nucleus of any hotel/motel-chain marketing program is the reservation system. A properly functioning system should provide a steady flow of reservations to the individual property. Many of these reservations come through what is known as the "referral" process. Individual members of the chain accept reservations for other member properties and pass them along through the reservation network. The more franchises in operation, the more potential sources of business for the individual franchise, particularly since many of these reservations are derived from guests currently staying at another property. Various reservation systems in use and their methods of operation are discussed in detail in Chapter 7.

An extensive integrated advertising program is almost as important as the reservation system. It is the advertising campaign that continually keeps the name of the chain in the public eye. This is commonly called "joint advertising," since it is intended to promote the chain as a whole rather than any single property. Thus, most advertisements, regardless of the media used, are designed to emphasize the consistency of quality to be found in all properties bearing the company name.

However, a number of specifically identified properties are sometimes grouped in a chain-sponsored advertisement. Quite often, this is done on a regional basis, with all chain properties in the specific geographical region identified in the same advertisement. Similarly, grouping can be done by the type of hotel, as where all resort properties are identified in an advertisement specifically aimed at the resort market.

Joint advertising is not limited to newspapers and magazines; radio, and particularly television, are very commonly used by chains.

The last element of a franchise marketing package should be a sales network. The chain places at strategic locations throughout the country regional sales offices, whose staffs sell not only the properties in their regions, but all member properties of the chain. Such selling is principally aimed at the group and convention market, but limited selling can also be done in the corporate and travel-agent areas.

Thus, the franchiser offers the three key ingredients of hotel marketing: advertising, sales, and reservations.

OBLIGATIONS OF THE FRANCHISEE

Earlier in the chapter, we referred to franchising as a "two-way street." In return for the services rendered by the franchiser, the franchisee is obliged to meet the standards of the chain, so that the reputation and the name of the franchiser are not blemished by an inferior operation. Such standards can broadly be divided into two categories: definitive standards and operational-quality standards, and observance of both is policed by the visits and reports of the regional managers or inspectors.

Whether or not the property meets the definitive standards is usually a question of fact rather than opinion, requires no arbitration, and is therefore seldom an area for disagreement between franchiser and franchisee. Such standards define the physical characteristics required of a franchised property. Some of the more common definitive standards relate to the following:

1. Size of the rooms
2. Amount of furniture
3. Size of the beds
4. Existence of food and beverage outlets
5. Hours of operation of outlets
6. Parking
7. Television
8. Swimming pool

Of these, only the hours of operation can be readily changed, and this matter to some degree falls into both categories of standards.

Operational-quality standards are less easily definable, so whether they are being met is sometimes a source of dispute between franchiser and franchisee. These standards commonly relate to the following:

1. Cleanliness
2. Politeness of staff
3. Quality of service
4. Rates charged
5. Checkout times
6. Changing of linens
7. Use of identity items, that is, items bearing the name of the chain

Obviously, failure to meet such standards can be excused as occasionally unavoidable, but continued violation cannot be permitted. This is where differences of opinion and controversy arise.

FRANCHISE COSTS AND FEES

Most franchisers require the payment by the franchisee of an initial fee that is not refundable should the agreement be terminated as a result of actions or violations by the franchisee. It is the possible loss of this fee that principally motivates franchisees to comply with maintenance of standards.

In addition to the initial fee, which can run as high as $400–$500 per room, a monthly franchise or royalty fee or combination of fees is payable to the franchiser. Various methods are used for computing this fee, the following being some of the more common:

1. A fixed monthly fee
2. A fixed monthly fee plus an amount per reservation originating from the reservation system
3. A percentage of room sales treated either as an overall fee or separate fees for royalties and reservation services
4. A percentage of total sales treated either as an overall fee or separate fees for royalties and reservation services
5. A fixed dollar amount per available room
6. A fixed dollar amount per occupied room

A combination of two or more of these is also feasible. Provided the fixed fee is low, alternative 2 is the more desirable from the point of view of the franchisee, since it obliges the chain to provide reservations in order to generate fees.

FINANCING THE FRANCHISE

Although the franchiser will, as noted, frequently work with the franchisee in the search for financing, it is the responsibility of the franchisee to obtain the necessary mortgage.

First mortgages are obtained from several sources—banks, insurance companies, investment trusts, and private sources of financing. The potential sources will require information as to costs and probable return, so a feasibility study must be made. Many chains assist in the preparation of the study, and some will pay part or all of the cost.

Certain companies in the franchise business enter into joint ventures with franchisees. The land is acquired and the facility constructed by the chain, after which a joint venture is created, giving the franchisee 50% of the operation. The degree to which franchising companies actually invest varies from chain to chain. Some make no investment and derive their income solely from franchise fees and from profits on purchasing services and other forms of technical assistance. Others take active equity positions in the franchise operation.

PROTECTION FOR FRANCHISEES

It would be unfair to close this chapter without commenting on some potential pitfalls that may be encountered by franchisees.

The most important protection the franchisee must seek is that against competition. Such protection must define the distance between the new franchise and any future franchise. Obviously, the same rules cannot apply in New York City and New Mexico; 15 city blocks may be reasonable protection in New York City, and 200 miles may be reasonable in New Mexico. At the same time, the franchise owner must realize that the protection obtained today may be a saleable product sometime in the future. Frequently, franchisees have received substantial remuneration for giving up part of their territory. When it appears obvious that a previously quiet area suddenly has a tremendous potential for business, a partnership can be created between a resident franchisee and a possible new franchisee with an infringing site.

Every new franchisee should ensure that certain services are properly defined in the agreement. If a training program is provided, it should be defined in terms of both the number of employees to be trained and the period for which they will be trained.

Clauses applicable to purchasing services should define the maximum markup or commission the franchiser can receive. In particular, franchisees should protect themselves against the cost of so-called "identity items" that must be used under the terms of the franchise agreement.

Certain franchise agreements call for the purchase of computerized equipment or the provision of reservation services. In the event that the chain devises new procedures, the equipment purchased by the franchisee should be compatible with the changes. If not, the franchisee should not be required to incur additional costs to replace it.

The preceding comments should not be interpreted as suggesting that we are antifranchise. Indeed, particularly in the motel field, it is strongly recommended to have an association with a recognized name in the franchise field. However, new franchises should make sure that the scope of services described in this chapter are obtained.

CHAPTER SUMMARY

Franchises are not unique to the hotel business. However, they have been valuable in enabling small investors to get into the hotel and motel business.

Major companies in the field are Best Western and Holiday Inns, but there are many other companies in the field.

Services offered by the franchiser include operating procedures, technical assistance, and marketing reservations and advertising.

Obligations of the franchisee include payment of fees and maintenance of standards, both definitive and operational quality.

Franchisees receive help in financing.

The franchisees should obtain protection against competition, increased costs of purchasing services, and the costs involved with changes in the reservation system.

REVIEW QUESTIONS

1. What is the basic description of franchises?
2. Name the top chains in the franchise field.
3. Explain methods provided by the franchiser.
4. Explain technical assistance provided by the franchiser.
5. Explain the elements of marketing provided by the franchiser.
6. What are the obligations of the franchisee?
7. Explain the difference between definitive and operational standards. Give examples.
8. Explain various methods of calculating franchise fees.
9. What types of financing help can be provided?

CASE STUDY

Robert Williams is in the process of negotiating a franchise for his 200-room motel. He is concerned about adverse effects that could jeopardize his operation. What in particular could create problems and what protection should he seek in the franchise agreement?

25

Casinos

After studying this chapter, the student should:

1. Understand a casino's organization and staffing.
2. Know the nature of the games offered.
3. Know the functions of the cage.
4. Understand casino controls.

In recent years, casinos have been the fastest growing area of the resort industry. Casinos first appeared, in Nevada, as an integral part of hotel operations in 1945, but it was not until 1979 that they made an appearance in another state, New Jersey. In the 10 years from 1983 to 1993, 36 states passed some form of new gaming ("gaming" is the more proper word for legalized gambling) legislation. Indeed, today, only two states, Hawaii and Utah, offer no legalized form of gambling, and even Utah has legalized horse racing—but with no betting.

While casino operations do not necessarily require a hotel location, both hotel and casino operators, dating back to the early days in Las Vegas, have recognized that casinos and hotel operations are closely interrelated, one element serving and at the same time feeding off the other. Many of the new casinos have diverged from the traditional Las Vegas format of excessive noise, glitter, and intensity, that often scares away the gambling novice. At Foxwoods Casino, in Connecticut, we find a perfect example of the new trend. The lighting and decor is subdued, the noise level acceptable, and courtesy and attention to the customer's needs is the order of the day. Even daylight can be seen through the windows, disputing the old Las Vegas belief that a player should not be able to distinguish between night and day. Foxwoods has quickly become one of the most successful casinos in North America.

CASINO ORGANIZATION

From a structural point of view, casino management usually has a higher degree of independence than the management of a normal hotel—operated department.

The magnitude of operations of a casino hotel dictates that there be a level of authority above the hotel general manager, usually a managing director or a vice president of operations. The casino manager also reports to this individual, and is essentially at the same authority level as the hotel general manager. The relationship between the two managers can be somewhat delicate, requiring both to display a strong sense of cooperation and understanding. The hotel provides many areas of service to the casino, including rooms and food and beverage to the casino clientele and the services of the overhead departments, that is, engineering and marketing. Other recreational departments, such as the golf course and the spa, also provide recreational activities to casino customers.

Most of the services provided by the hotel take place outside the physical confines of the casino. The reservations, front desk, and housekeeping staffs and most of the food and beverage operate within their respective areas. However, beverage service is usually provided inside the casino. The employees providing that service primarily report to food and beverage management but also have a dotted line of authority to casino management.

All staff directly involved in the operation of the games are completely under the authority of the casino manager. This includes assistant managers, supervisors, or "pit bosses" as they are commonly referred to, and the dealers who operate the games. It also includes hosts, public relations personnel, and casino security. Two further categories of staff deal with the financial and control functions of the casino: the cage staff and the casino credit personnel.

Having reviewed the staffing, we should now examine the games of chance commonly found in casinos.

GAMES

In the United States, the best known game is dice, or, as it is commonly called, craps. This game in a casino is much refined from the game that used to be played down at the corner. Dice games have a tremendous fascination for the average person, so they generally draw the most people and the most play. Casinos are usually located in or adjacent to the lobby of the hotel, thus taking advantage of the traffic going through to draw people to the noise and excitement of the dice table.

Craps is a game in which one player, called the "shooter," rolls a pair of dice and all the players, including the shooter, bet on the result of the roll or combination of rolls. The various odds are calculated on the premise that each die may land with any one of its six faces uppermost and that the probability for each of the six faces is equal. Thus, skill at craps is a combination of knowledge of the odds and management of money.

Dice is played on a table that holds from 15 to 25 players. The table is covered with green felt, on which is printed the betting alternatives. Dealers handle the bets of the players, while the dice are handled by a dealer known as a "stickman," because he or she uses a long bamboo stick or pole that is bent on the end to rake in the dice. In front of the stickman is an area called the "box," which contains the layout for special fixed-odds bets known as "proposition bets." Each bet reflects a different percentage, and thus the actual percentage advantage to the house depends on the combination of bets placed.

Blackjack, or 21, is also a very popular game. A dealer deals cards to the players and to him- or herself. The object is to draw cards that when added up amount to 21, or as close as possible to 21 without exceeding it. If your hand is closer to 21 than the dealer's, you win; if it is a tie, you break even. Each player and dealer receives a minimum of two cards. The player may then draw additional cards or "stand"—retain just the two. After the player draws all the cards desired, it is the turn of the dealer. However, the dealer must draw up to a certain total and cannot draw above it. In certain circumstances, the player may convert the hand to two hands or increase the initial bet.

Although dice and blackjack are increasing in popularity in Europe, roulette is still the favorite game there. Roulette is strictly a matter of luck. The layout consists of black and red squares numbered 1 to 36, and possibly a zero and double zero. A wheel containing slots numbered to correspond with the layout spins in one direction while a lead ball spins in the opposite direction until it falls into a slot, which is the winning number. Players bet on a color, a number, or a combination of numbers at varying odds. Regardless of the bet, the odds are always the same, 5-5/19 percent in favor of the house (using a zero and a double zero).

Baccarat and *chemin de fer* are games with a European background that have gained some popularity on this side of the Atlantic. They are nearly identical card games in which players draw cards to get as close as possible to a specific number. Wagering is for very high stakes. The only difference between them is that in baccarat the players play against the house, whereas in *chemin de fer*, they play against each other, with the house only receiving a commission.

As in many other areas of hotel operations, computerization and new technology has invaded the casino scene. While the major impact has been in the area of slot machines (discussed in the next paragraph), certain table games have become "online." Blackjack tables have been equipped with electronic tracking devices that track each gaming chip, which have imbedded microchips enabling the tracking system to record all action at the table. This provides casino management not only with increased security but better information on the individual players.

However, the major technological advances in the area of games are found in slot machines. For many casinos slot machines have been the real backbone of their income. For the house they are the only sure thing, since the only ways to beat them are illegal. Traditional slot machines required players to obtain two or three symbols (usually fruit) in a row in order to win, with the combination of symbols on a wheel dictating the odds against winning. The odds can vary not only from casino to casino but within an individual casino based on location, volume of business, and clientele. For the typical slot-machine player, the desire to play is highly emotional and most winnings are speedily reinvested.

Technology has impacted slot machines in various ways. Games now played on the slots include poker, blackjack, roulette, and others. Of particular significance has been the popularity of progressive slots. The basic type of progressive slots is the single property progressive slots where a group of machines in a casino are linked together. A percentage of all play, for example, 4%, is accumulated electronically and paid out on a deferred basis to a patron lucky enough to hit the required progressive jackpot combination. More advanced and complicated but much more exciting from a player's point of view is where machines in several casinos are linked up, all contributing the same percentage to the deferred jackpot, which can be won at any of the participating casinos. Each casino, naturally, contributes the amount it collected to the overall payout.

As a result of new technology, the use of coins in slot machines is disappearing, being replaced completely by paper money. The machines are capable of accepting and reading the paper currency and issuing credits to the player for the equivalent amount. The player receives a card telling them of the number of credits they have. These credits can be redeemed at the cage for real money at any time. Also, for casinos the counting and handling of currency is much less time-consuming than handling coins.

The Cage

In every casino, there must be a location where chips and cash are stored and transactions settled. This area usually consists of a room constructed adjacent to the casino, with a window or windows that open into the casino, and it is usually called the *casino cage*.

The cage is the control center for the flow of chips to and from the tables. Such transfers are made whenever a table has a shortage or an excess of chips, and they are controlled in a systematic fashion that is described later in this chapter. The cage is also the focal point for the handling of credit granted to individual players for the purpose of gambling.

The cage is under the authority of a cage manager, who usually has the overall responsibility not only for the cage personnel but, more important, for the total casino bank. The casino bank consists principally of three forms of money: chips, cash, and markers (outstanding debts owned by gamblers). An initial chip bank in a predetermined amount is issued to the cage and, together with an adequate supply of cash, forms the initial casino bank.

From the chip bank, chips are issued to the tables, to be exchanged with the players for cash or markers. At the end of each shift, the number of chips at each table is restored to the original amount either by issuing additional chips from the cage or by returning excess chips to the cage. Thus, the amount of the chip float at each table remains fixed and forms a part of the total cage bank.

Cash floats are issued to cashiers who staff change booths and change cards in the slot-machine areas. Change booths provide change to slot-machine customers to speed up play and avoid congestion at the cage windows. The change-booth floats also form a part of the total cage bank.

Casino Controls

Casino gambling involves a high volume of cash and credit transactions, so strict control is required. In order to obtain as much control as possible, the play and results are controlled on an individual table basis rather than in total for all games.

Chips are, of course, exchanged for cash or approved credit at the cage window, but they are usually obtained at the tables. Each table is equipped with a steel lockbox, which locks in place beneath the table. While the box is in place, it has an open slot through which all cash received from players is dropped. When the box is removed from the table, the slot is automatically locked and can be reopened only by keys that are under the control of the count team. The boxes are locked up in the count-room area and, at a specific time, all boxes are opened and the contents counted carefully under strict supervision.

When chips are issued to a player for credit, the player is required to sign a *marker* acknowledging the debt (see Figure 25-1). Extra care must be exercised in granting credit to foreign residents, as the markers may not be collectible in their country of residence. A duplicate copy of this marker is dropped through the table slot, so the combined total of the cash and the markers in the box equals the income of the table for chips issued.

However, this figure does not reflect the final result for the table. If the table returns excess chips to the cage during or at the end of a shift, the table must receive a credit for these chips. A credit slip denoting the chips returned is completed and sent in duplicate to the cage together with the chips. When the count is verified by the cage, the duplicate is signed and sent back to the table, where it is dropped through the slot. An example of a credit slip is shown in Figure 25-2.

Finally, winnings by players may deplete the supply of chips at a table, necessitating the issuance of more chips by the cage. When an additional supply of chips is required, a "fill slip" (Figure 25-3) is completed in duplicate and sent to the cage. The cage keeps the original and returns the initialed duplicate with the chips to the table. The duplicate is then dropped through the slot. Thus, the net

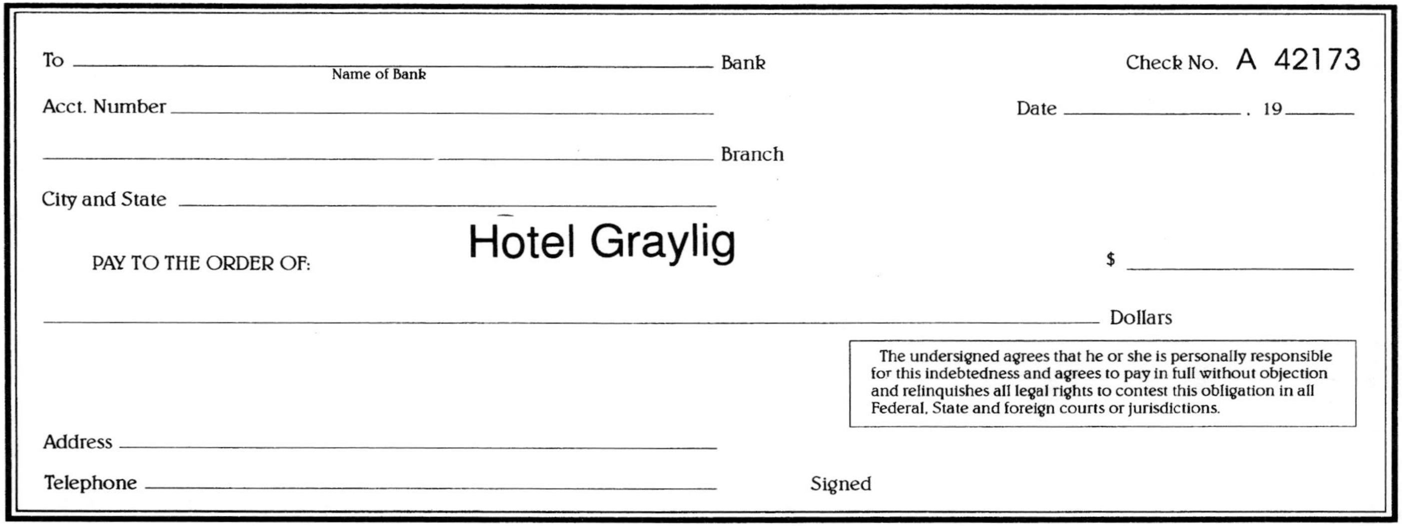

Figure 25-1 Casino Marker

The form shown contains the following fields:

Check No. A 42173

To _____ Bank
Name of Bank

Acct. Number _____ Branch

City and State _____

Date _____, 19 ___

Hotel Graylig

PAY TO THE ORDER OF:

$ _____

_____ Dollars

Address _____

Telephone _____

The undersigned agrees that he or she is personally responsible for this indebtedness and agrees to pay in full without objection and relinquishes all legal rights to contest this obligation in all Federal, State and foreign courts or jurisdictions.

Signed _____

Hotel Graylig

CREDIT SLIP

DATE			TIME

SHIFT	GYD	DAY	SWING

Game	Number	Denomination	Amount
CRAPS			
21			
ROULETTE			
BIG WHEEL			
TOTAL			

MEMO   RETURN CHIPS ☐

RUNNER	FLOOR MAN
CASHIER	DEALER - BOXMAN

Figure 25-2   Credit Slip for Chips Returned

```
┌─────────────────────────────────────────┐
│                                           │
│                                           │
│          HOTEL GRAYLIG                    │
│                                           │
│           FILL SLIP                       │
│  ┌──────────────────┬──────────────────┐ │
│  │ DATE             │ TIME             │ │
│  ├──────────────────┴──────────────────┤ │
│  │ SHIFT    GYD      DAY      SWING     │ │
│  ├──────┬──────┬──────────┬────────────┤ │
│  │ GAME │NUMBER│Denomination│ AMOUNT    │ │
│  ├──────┼──────┼──────────┼────────────┤ │
│  │Craps │      │          │            │ │
│  ├──────┼──────┼──────────┼────────────┤ │
│  │21    │      │          │            │ │
│  ├──────┼──────┼──────────┼────────────┤ │
│  │Roulette│    │          │            │ │
│  ├──────┼──────┼──────────┼────────────┤ │
│  │Big Wheel│   │          │            │ │
│  ├──────┼──────┼──────────┼────────────┤ │
│  │      │      │          │            │ │
│  ├──────┼──────┼──────────┼────────────┤ │
│  │      │      │          │            │ │
│  ├──────┼──────┼──────────┼────────────┤ │
│  │      │      │          │            │ │
│  ├──────┴──────┴──────────┼────────────┤ │
│  │ TOTAL                  │            │ │
│  ├────────────────────────┴────────────┤ │
│  │ MEMO        RETURN CHIPS  ☐          │ │
│  │                                      │ │
│  │                                      │ │
│  ├──────────────┬───────────────────────┤ │
│  │ RUNNER       │ FLOOR MAN             │ │
│  ├──────────────┼───────────────────────┤ │
│  │ CASHIER      │ DEALER-BOXMAN         │ │
│  └──────────────┴───────────────────────┘ │
│   MCC-5-0-8-75       F  0601              │
└───────────────────────────────────────────┘
```

Figure 25-3   Fill Slip for Chips Issued

result of any table is the cash plus markers and credit slips, known as the "drop," less the total of the fill slips. The net is known as the "win."

The individual results, by shift, for each table game are recorded on a form known as the "stiff sheet." This form is used to tabulate the opening and closing inventories of chips, the drop, credit, and fill slip totals and markers for each table. The resulting win is calculated for each table game and the totals for the shift, by game, are determined. The individual stiff sheets for each shift are then combined in the preparation of the casino balance sheet.

The calculation of the drop and the win for the slot operation is tabulated in a different manner. The drop is determined, not by the amount of coins inserted into the machine, but by the amount contained in the "drop buckets," which are removed at the end of each shift. When coins are inserted into a machine, they fall into a holding area known as a "hopper." Only when the hopper is full do the coins get diverted to the drop bucket. When the hopper is emptied due to a jack-pot, it is replenished with a "fill" of coins or tokens, similar to the chip fills re-plenishing table inventories. Very large jackpots are usually paid by hand. The "win" for the slot operation is the drop minus the machine fills and hand-paid jackpots.

The completion of the daily cage balance sheet (Figure 25-4) is the responsi-bility of the cage manager or appointee. This sheet is a mathematical summary of the results by table and by game in the manner explained in the preceding para-graph. The time-consuming but most important part of the daily process is the physical count. The number of shifts operated for each table (normally a maxi-mum of three) will determine the number of actual boxes required to be counted. The boxes should, for proper control, be replaced with an empty box at the end of each shift. The locking mechanisms on the tables require that a new box must be inserted in order to remove the old box.

A separate subcount sheet (Figure 25-5) should be prepared for each box. The physical count of all currency dropped should be rechecked by a second indi-vidual. The counting should also be observed by supervisors who do not partici-pate in the actual count. The individual table counts are then combined for each table and carried forward to the master sheet.

The results of each shift by table number should be tabulated on a day-by-day basis for review of variance and unusual results. This tabulation is facilitated by use of a computer. It is important that the names of the actual personnel work-ing that shift also be included in the tabulation. Thus by regrouping, a record of results by individual dealer and/or supervisor can also be obtained.

The last tabulation that must be completed on a daily basis is the nightly balancing of the cage bank. This balancing can also be facilitated by the use of a specially designed form (Figure 25-6). Certain items on the bank count sheet re-quire explanation.

Foreign Chips

In locations where more than one casino is in operation it is common practice to accept chips from the other casino(s). Those chips are not accepted at the tables and must be exchanged at the cage window for the casino's own chips. Those chips are then returned to the originating casino in exchange for cash. Until that exchange is completed, they are carried in the casino bank as "foreign chips."

Checks Held

Frequently, a player, normally known to the casino personnel, will cash a check but ask that it be held and not deposited until a specific date. This must be a rela-tively short period of time, possibly 1–2 weeks or until the end of the month. Be-yond that length of time, the normal practice is to have the player sign a marker since legally a postdated check is simply a promise to pay.

Hotel Graylig

CASINO BALANCE SHEET FOR _September 1919_

Game	Cash Drop	I.O.U.s	Gross Play	Credit Slips	Less Fills	Net Wins	%
CRAPS							
Table 1	2,486,000	758,000	1,728,000	53,000	1,559,000	222,000	12.3
Table 2	637,000	62,000	575,000	11,000	503,000	83,000	10.9
Table 3	103,571	—	103,571	2,000	90,000	15,571	15.0
Total Craps	3,226,571	820,000	2,406,571	66,000	2152,000	320,571	13.3
BLACKJACK							
Table 1	493,400	72,300	421,100	7,000	366,000	62,100	14.7
Table 2	83,500	11,500	72,000	3,000	66,000	9,000	12.5
Table 3	114,100	13,000	101,100	6,000	91,000	16,100	15.9
Table 4	7,223	—	7,223	800	4,800	3,223	44.6
Table 5			—			—	
Total Blackjack	698,223	96,800	601,423	16,800	527,800	90,423	14.8
ROULETTE							
Table 1	683,300	51,000	632,300	11,500	552,500	91,300	14.7
Table 2						—	
Table 3	184,123	—	184,123	2,000	169,000	17,123	9.3
Total Roulette	867,423	51,000	816,423	13,500	721,500	108,423	13.3
SLOTS	322,911	X	322,911	X	Jackpots 42,300	280,611	86.9
Total Casino	4,247,705	967,800	5,215,505	96,300	3,441,600	800,028	15.3

Figure 25-4 Daily Casino Balance Sheet

375

HOTEL GRAYLIG

COUNT SHEET

DATE: TABLE: SHIFT:

CURRENCY	NO. OF BILLS	TOTAL
$1		
$5		
$10		
$20		
$50		
$100		
$500		
$1,000		_____
		_____

FILL SLIPS   AMOUNT

NO.

_____

_____

CREDIT SLIPS   AMOUNT

NO.

_____

_____

SIGNATURES OF COUNTERS   SIGNATURE OF SUPERVISOR

_____   _____

_____

_____

Figure 25-5 Casino Shift Count Sheet

HOTEL GRAYLIG
CASINO BANK COUNT FOR SEPTEMBER 19__

OPENING BANK$12,930,300
ADD: IOUs RECEIVED   967,800
LESS: IOUs COLLECTED   930,300
NET CHANGE IN IOUs $12,967,800
CLOSING BANK
BANK COUNT

CURRENCY	NO. OF BILLS	TOTAL	
$1	25,000	25,000	
$5	5,000	25,000	
$10	10,000	100,000	
$20	5,000	100,000	
$50	5,000	250,000	
$100	5,000	500,000	
$500	4,000	2,000,000	
$1,000	5,000	5,000,000	8,000,000

TOTAL CURRENCY	NO.	TOTAL
CHIPS IN CAGE		
$1	3,500	3,500
$5	19,200	96,000
$10	30,000	300,000
$20	20,000	400,000
$50	20,000	1,000,000
$100		
$500		
TABLE BANKS	80,000	
SLOT BANKS	40,000	
SLOT CHANGE BANKS	60,000	
FOREIGN CHIPS	21,500	
TOTAL CHIPS	2,000,000	

CHECKS HELD

IOUs	2,967,800	4,967,800

TOTAL CHECKS AND IOUs

CLOSING BANK $12,967,800

DAILY DEPOSIT RECONCILIATION

NET WIN   800,028
NET CHANGE IN IOUs   37,500
ACTUAL DEPOSIT $762,528

Figure 25-6   Casino Daily Bank Count

Good casino practice mandates that all travelers checks and foreign currency be deposited as part of the deposit on a daily basis.

It is important to understand that the exact net win cannot be deposited, as the markers (IOUs) included therein must be added to the casino bank. However, on the other hand, the markers collected will be deposited. Thus, the casino bank will fluctuate to the degree that the markers increase or decrease. The total chips counted will differ from the total chips in circulation by the amount of uncashed chips still in the hands of customers. The casino bank is simply holding additional cash in substitution for uncashed chips. Over a period of time, the amount of uncashed chips will increase as they are lost, misplaced, or kept for souvenirs. At the time that a casino completely changes its chips (by changing design, color, etc.), the amount of the uncashed chips can, in accordance with sound accounting practice, be written into income. The income should not, however, be realized for at least three months, permitting the chips that are "floating," but with the intention of ultimate cashing, to be actually redeemed.

Issuance And Collection Of Markers

In the preceding section related to the casino bank, the term "IOUs" is sometimes used instead of markers. While markers is the more correct term, IOUs is a part of the normal casino language used internally between gaming employees and usage thereof is common practice. Readers should understand that they are synonymous.

The mechanics of the issuance of markers has been addressed, but it is now necessary to review their control within the overall casino credit and collection procedure.

All players desiring credit are required to provide the information necessary to complete a credit application, specifying the credit limit desired and providing bank references and a history of credit limits previously obtained in other casinos. After checking these references, the casino credit office can make a judgment as to whether to grant the full amount of credit requested, a lower amount, or no credit.

A player should never be permitted to exceed his or her credit limit. Should a casino negligently or knowingly permit a player to exceed the requested limit, the player may, with some justification, refuse to pay the excess. Most players are not local residents but visit the hotel periodically, either on their own or on *junkets*—casino-sponsored trips. On a return visit, it is desirable to ask a player to settle any markers outstanding from a prior visit before granting additional credit.

Since markers form a portion of the casino bank, they are physically kept and controlled in the casino cage. Each player has a marker envelope on the front of which a record of all markers issued, payments, and the current balance is displayed. Careful recording of issuance and payment must be made. If the markers are removed from the envelope for delivery, upon payment, to the player, this must be carefully noted. Some casinos prefer to have only the records in the cage while the actual markers are under the control of the casino credit manager, who has the responsibility for collection. This can create problems, however, since players will go to the cage to redeem their markers at any time, day or night.

Because casino debts are usually of a rather confidential nature, most of the collection effort must be made by telephone, with a careful record kept of all calls. Letters requesting settlement can also be used, particularly if the debtor has resisted efforts to collect by telephone.

Before a debt is written off as uncollectible, consideration should be given to using an outside collection agency. However, the degree of success is limited since, in many locations, payment of casino debts is not enforceable under the law.

CASINO INCOME AND EXPENDITURES

The following is a brief explanation of the method by which casinos tabulate and record their financial results.

Gross Play (or Drop). In table games, the gross play is the total amount wagered by the players, whether cash or credit. The gross play for slot machines is the total amount of cash removed from the machines.

Less **Paid Outs.** In table games, this is the actual winnings paid to players. In slot play, it is the total of jackpots paid out. Incidental winnings at slot machines of smaller amounts, which the machines automatically eject, are not considered paid outs but merely reduce the gross play.

Equals **Net Win.** While the volume of slot play can distort the net win, a net win at table games of 12–15% is very acceptable.

Less **Expenditures.** This includes payroll and benefits, maintenance, supplies, travel, customer entertainment, advertising, and commissions to junket operators. When a hotel operates a nightclub primarily for the purpose of attracting casino gamblers to the premises, it is common industry practice to also charge the cost of music and entertainment to the casino.

The net result of the above items is the Operation Profit.

JUNKETS

Junkets are casino-sponsored groups of gamblers brought in from elsewhere. The casino bears the cost of the rooms, food, and beverages of the group, and the transportation cost, usually of a chartered airplane.

Because the casino pays the hotel operation either in full or at discounted rates for all hotel services, a large volume of junkets can have a material effect on the hotel results in both the rooms and food and beverage departments. Shops and concessions in the hotel are usually also beneficiaries of high casino volume.

The junket policy must be continually evaluated to determine whether the benefits of a higher casino win exceed the costs involved. Precautions must be taken to ensure that junket guests do, in fact, play and are not taking advantage of the casino. Casinos normally grade players using the rating to determine the extent of the benefits to be provided. A grade "A" player, for example, might receive first-class airfare and all hotel expenses underwritten by the casino while a grade "B" player might receive free transportation, coach class, on a charter. A "C" player would possibly not receive any airfare.

It is common practice to ask junket guests to put up "front money"—an advance payment in cash as evidence of their intention to play. The players can then draw chips against their front money. If they do not play, the cost of rooms, food, beverages, and transportation can be deducted from their front money and the balance refunded. The organizers of junkets are paid a commission, usually related to the credit limit of their players.

Casinos also have programs (for nonjunket players) similar to frequent traveler programs where players receive points based on game choices, frequency of visits and play, and amounts wagered. Based on their records, players receive complimentary bonuses and are placed on a mailing list.

CHAPTER SUMMARY

While for 34 years casino operations were limited to Nevada, they are now legal in many states.

Casino management is usually independent of hotel operations, with a manager reporting only to the highest level of management.

Hotel services are provided in the areas of rooms and food and beverage.

Casino staffing, in addition to the casino manager, includes assistant managers, supervisors, dealers, hosts, public relations, security, cage personnel, and credit personnel.

Games offered include dice (craps), blackjack, roulette, and possibly others. Slot machines are a major and highly profitable part of operations.

The cage controls the bank, the flow of chips, and provides change for the slots.

Casino control is very important to the success of the operation.

Markers (IOUs) are used to provide credit to qualified players.

Junkets sponsor gamblers by offering transportation, rooms, food, and beverage. Gamblers are rated and this determines what they receive.

REVIEW QUESTIONS

1. Explain the usual casino staffing.
2. Explain the game of dice (craps).
3. Explain the game of blackjack.
4. Explain the game of roulette.
5. Explain slot machine operations.
6. What are the functions of the cage?
7. Explain fill slips and credit slips.
8. What are foreign chips?
9. Explain the use of markers.
10. What are junkets?

CASE STUDY

Sam Quick has been appointed junket manager for the new Golden Chance Casino. His first duty is to define a junket policy. What would you expect to see in his policy?

26
Health Spas

After studying this chapter, the student should:

1. Know the history of spas.
2. Understand the difference between spa hotels and hotels that provide a spa as an amenity.
3. Be knowledgeable of spa activities.
4. Be knowledgeable of spa services.

Another area of hotel amenities that must be addressed in this last section is health spas. An ever-increasing emphasis on physical fitness and overall health has provided a new and major amenity that many resort hotels can offer: the health spa.

Health spas were for many years essentially a European phenomena—in fact, the word "spa" is derived from the name of a town in the Liege province of Belgium in the Ardennes mountains near the German border. Its mineral springs and baths were frequented from the 16th century on, and it was an extremely popular resort destination in the 18th centuries. The German army used it as their headquarters in 1918, and it was the site of the famous Spa Conference on repatriation payments held between Germany and the Allies in 1920.

The original concept of spas was associated with springs producing mineral waters containing various mineral salts, such as the carbonates, phosphates, and sulphates of metals such as magnesium, calcium, lithium, potassium, and sodium.

The presence of gases such as carbon dioxide, particularly in springs that contained iron, produced a bubbling or sparking effect. While many of the mineral springs were thermal in nature (hot springs), some were cold. The waters were considered to be effective in the treatment of such ailments as rheumatism, gout, liver disorders, and other diseases of the organs and body.

In addition to the above-mentioned town of Spa, other European locations (frequently mentioned in novels and motion pictures) were Carlsbad, Baden-Baden in Germany, Aix-les-Bains in France, and in England the appropriately named town of Bath.

The United States was not without its mineral springs locations, notably Saratoga Springs, New York; White Sulphur Springs, West Virginia; Hot Springs, Arkansas; Poland, Maine; and French Lick, Indiana. However, in recent years the popularity of the traditional mineral water destinations has decreased, and they have been replaced as destinations in demand by new modern-style spas offering a wide range of facilities and services. California has been a leader in such development, with the Golden Door in Escondido and The LaCosta Resort in Carlsbad being two of the best known. Many of the original mineral water spas have, however, continued to remain heavily in the public eye by bottling their health-inducing waters for resale on a commercial basis throughout the country and, in some instances, on an international scale.

SPA ADMINISTRATION

Spas must be divided into two categories: the spa hotel and the resort spa. The *spa hotel* caters exclusively to spa clientele. All guests must participate in the spa program, which includes room, dietary meals, treatments, and physical exercise. The rates charged daily or weekly are all inclusive. In those hotels the overall administration must be in the hands of an administrator or manager who has knowledge of health/medical operations as well as experience in the hospitality field. A *resort spa* is a spa located within a resort, its programs available as an option to the hotel guests. The spa should be run as an operating department of the hotel, but the management of the department and the spa facility should be in the hands of a professional spa manager.

Where spa programs or facility usage is offered as an alternative hotel amenity or recreational outlet, spa services may be sold as part of an overall package, or ala carte charges may be made for general facility usage and for each individual program.

Consideration may be given to making programs or facility usage available to nonhotel guests at an equitable charge.

FACILITIES AND SERVICES

Spa facilities can best be described as both recreational- and exercise-oriented. Many of the more recreational facilities are commonly found as part of a hotel's guest facilities.

Swimming Pools

Swimming pools, both indoor and outdoor, are a fundamental element of spa operations and find a substantial degree of usage, dependent, of course, on the weather conditions. This particular facility will commonly be used not only by spa activity participants but also by regular hotel guests.

Tennis Courts

Most of the criteria relative to swimming pool usage also applies to tennis court usage. Again both indoor and outdoor courts can be found. Indoor courts require a substantial investment both in dollars and in space. Quite frequently a collapsible bubble is used during winter months, converting outdoor courts to all-weather use.

Handball and Racquetball Courts

These facilities also require considerable monetary investments and space utilization. Badminton courts are a further alternative, both indoor and outdoor, with the possibility of convertible all-weather facilities.

Jogging/Running Tracks

Many hotels have chose, as part of their guest facility programs, to lay out jogging or running tracks, quite frequently with the only investment being the printing of maps to lay out the track over existing roadways or terrain. Indoor tracks do require an indoor exercise area of a reasonable circumference to make indoor jogging practical.

Weight Training

The use of various forms of exercise machines in a controlled and supervised environment are also an integral part of health spa operations. Emphasis is on professional direction to acquire proper form and body alignment. These exercises are conducted with careful monitoring of key body functions, including heartbeat and pulse rate. Frequently, spas employ full-time medical professionals to direct the exercise and dietary programs.

Figure 26-1   Completion of a successful hike to the summit of Mt. Equinox by Susan Wheeler (on right), manager of the Equinox Resort Spa and a member.

Aerobic Training

Televised and videotaped classes have made aerobic exercises popular to many people. Normally organized and directed by staff members, aerobic classes (outdoor and indoor) have become a fundamental element of any spa program.

A new form of aerobics, known as "spinning"—a complete body workout—makes an innovative contribution to cardiovascular fitness. The class is conducted on stationary bicycles.

The successful spa combines cardiovascular exercise with a low-fat food menu. The desired effect is to have a balanced physical and nutritional program.

Of particular interest is the increase in spa programs designed to heighten interest in the environment. Hiking in natural settings, such as in the woods, up mountains, and along beaches, has become a major element of most spa programs. Figure 26-1 is a photograph of the manager of the Equinox Resort Spa (in Manchester, Vermont) and a member who have just completed a successful hike to the summit of Mt. Equinox.

SPA PROGRAMS

In addition to facilities designed to promote various forms of exercise, spas also provide varying types of programs designed to provide health benefits to the spa participants, as well as behavior modification programs to enhance lifestyles.

Dietary Programs

As the basic objective of most participants in spa programs is improved physical well-being, dietary programs are an essential element. Some programs begin with a computerized analysis to determine the percentages of fat, water, and muscle in the participant's body.

A menu is developed consisting of meals designed to be appealing to the spa participants, while at the same time contributing to the overall intent of the programs. In some instances, these meals will be served in the regular facilities of a resort, which at the same time provides a regular menu selection for guests who are not participants in spa programs. Those resorts that cater exclusively to persons enrolled in spa programs provide an array of fare designed to completely meet the requirements of the dietary programs, with an emphasis on low-fat eating.

Massage

The full body massage is the most common form of treatment offered in spas. These services are provided by professional masseurs or masseuses.

Herbal Wrap

This is another form of treatment commonly available in spas. The participant is wrapped in muslin sheets that have been boiled in aromatic herb recipes to relax and soothe muscles and detoxify the skin. Face, neck, and shoulder massage is applied during this treatment.

Exfoliation

This is a treatment designed to exfoliate the dead outer layer of skin from the face or body. The proper degree of abrasiveness is achieved by use of salts or other materials selected by the therapist. After the dead skin has been exfoliated, a soothing lotion or gel is applied with a gentle massage.

Thalasso Therapy

Thalasso Therapy is a seaweed treatment evolved in Europe. The body is covered with seaweed and wrapped. The treatment stimulates circulation and nourishes the skin.

Facial Treatments

This is a program designed both for health and beauty. The face is rubbed with oil or lotion and massaged or covered in a mud-type shell that is allowed to harden and is then removed. In the process, the facial pores are opened and cleansed of undesirable fluids and solids. Skin analysis determines the best type of facial for a particular individual.

Hydrotherapy

This treatment takes place in special tubs. The feet and face are treated to hydrate skin and increase circulation.

STAFFING

Staff within the spa facility should be highly qualified professionals, not only at the management level but also at the program operational level, which requires persons experienced in massage, health care, and organized athletic activity leadership. Numbers will be dependent on the size and diversity of the facility and the types of programs offered.

Adequate general administrative personnel will be required for reception, record maintenance, bookkeeping, and facility engineering and maintenance.

A friendly, warm, and caring staff is essential to ensure that guests will return to the resort. The importance of a satisfied guest experience cannot be overstated, as spas have a high level of both repeat business and referrals from guests.

CHAPTER SUMMARY

Health spas had their origin in Europe and many resorts had names that were associated with spas. The popularity of mineral springs carried over to North America and the springs were the location of some of the earlier resorts.

It is important to differentiate between spa hotels and resort spas.

Spa hotels cater only to spa clientele, and all guests must participate in the meals, treatments, and exercises. One the other hand, resort spas are amenities that are available to the guests, and charges are made for the various usages of the spa.

Administration of spa hotels heavily involves people with a medical background, whereas resort spas are merely operating departments of the resorts.

Exercise-oriented facilities are swimming pools, tennis courts, handball and racquetball courts, jogging trails, hiking, and weight and aerobic training.

Spa programs include dietary programs, massage, herbal wraps, exfoliation, thalasso therapy, facials, and hydrotherapy.

Under both scenarios, staffing involves people experienced in the programs and administrative personnel.

REVIEW QUESTIONS

1. Name several spa locations in Europe.
2. Name several spa locations in the United States.
3. Explain the difference between spa hotels and resort spas.
4. What are the most common exercise programs found in a spa?
5. What is a herbal wrap?
6. Explain exfoliation.
7. Explain thalasso therapy.
8. What is the purpose of facial treatments?
9. What staffing is required in a spa?

CASE STUDY

The Shining Mountain Resort, a 300-room property, is adding a spa and hired Juanita Fitz as manager.

Her first task involves deciding on activities and programs. What would you expect her to suggest?

27
Trends in the Industry

After studying this chapter, the student should understand various trends that are taking place or may take place in the industry.

PROBLEMS IN THE INDUSTRY

In Chapter 27 of the third edition written in 1992, we noted certain problems that we felt the industry must face and address.

ENERGY CONTROL SYSTEMS

We felt that continuing increases in energy costs necessitated that new systems be built to properly monitor the use of energy, whatever the form, to both public areas and guests, particularly when unoccupied. Uncertainty as to the future direction of energy costs has created a need to build into new facilities the ability to properly monitor and control energy consumption. Such systems are designed to reduce the use of energy, whatever the form, in both public areas and guestrooms, particularly when unoccupied.

Timing devices control the supply of heat, air-conditioning, and light in public areas, reducing the supply when unneeded. Programmed computers direct the flow of energy to both guestrooms and function areas, keeping temperatures within predetermined limits and cutting off the supply of air-conditioning or heat to unoccupied areas. Such controls also monitor lighting, not only in public areas and corridors within the building but also in parking lots, gardens, and other outside areas.

In the late 1980s and early 1990s, there was considerable interest and activity in this area. However, in the mid-1990s the price of crude oil dropped, and with it, energy costs. As a result, hotels lost interest in energy costs as a major problem. In particular, very little was done in finding new sources, and, in fact, because of political pressure, atomic energy plants either were dismantled or simply closed. Interest in solar energy diminished, and in some areas, such as northern Vermont, small hydroelectric plants ceased to be used. However, in 1999 increases in the barrel price of crude oil has once more rekindled the concerns. Notable increases in gasoline prices can severely impact resorts due to less travel by guests. Airlines are also heavily affected and, of course, there is a direct impact on hotels using oil as their primary energy source.

LABOR: AVAILABILITY AND COST

Labor continues to be the largest single problem facing the hotel industry, in both cost and availability, and regarding both supervisory and nonsupervisory personnel.

Perhaps the most serious effect has been felt in the food and beverage operations, which have traditionally employed the highest number of nonsupervisory personnel—dishwashers, cooks, waiters, and buspersons. Many workers in this area are service personnel, paid the minimum wage permitted by law, and dependent on gratuities from patrons as their main source of income. However, authorities have become increasingly effective in taxing gratuities received by service personnel, rendering this form of income less attractive than in the past.

Furthermore, the sources of supply of such personnel are gradually depleting. The hotel industry must compete for such labor with manufacturing companies and with the construction and building trades. Wage rates in these fields have risen to levels with which the hotel industry is unable to compete. Also, growth in the service industries, notably fast food, competes seriously for the same labor. There have also been the addition of casino hotels to the industry and an increase in the number of cruise ships. To reduce the problem, efforts are being made to make it easier for immigrant workers to obtain visas.

Additionally, increased union activity in the hotel field, together with increases in the minimum wage, has resulted in higher payrolls and shorter working hours with no noticeable increase in productivity. Prices can be increased only at a certain pace, so it is not possible to pass along the total increase in labor costs to the customer. This makes the long-range outlook bleak for profitability in hotel food and beverage operations.

The industry can take certain steps to try to combat these problems, particularly in personnel management. More work challenge and room for creativity must be developed as well as more opportunities for job advancement and promotion from within. Training programs should teach personnel the most effective use of their time, and the image of the industry in the eyes of the workforce must be improved. The hotel industry has long had a poor image for careers, advancement, and remuneration. The industry must make progress in this area.

The increasing interest in technological development—mechanization and labor-saving devises—will reduce the size of the required workforce, as will the use of semiprepared foods and disposable products. At the same time, more sophisticated equipment, while reducing the total workforce, will require additional skilled labor to operate it. The replacement of people with computers does, however, impact a hotel's reputation for hospitality.

There will be a gradual reduction in luxury-type restaurant operations that require large numbers of service personnel and an increase in self-service operations; that is, more buffets and less French service. As mentioned earlier, the demise of most room service is also anticipated.

Unions must cooperate by permitting the more effective use of personnel, such as the combining of certain jobs, particularly in the kitchen. Vegetable cooks should not be restricted to cooking vegetables but should be permitted to cook soups or prepare salads when necessary. Failure of the unions to permit such flexibility will compel more and more hotels to lease out their facilities to restaurant operators who either employ nonunion staffs or operate with fewer restrictions than are placed on hotel operators.

Most of the comments directed to food and beverage operations also apply to housekeeping. This department, with its large contingent of attendants and housemen, usually employs the largest number of nonsupervisory personnel. However, because the profit margin in the rooms department is much higher, the problem of rising labor costs has not yet received as much emphasis as it has in the food and beverage areas.

Lack of adequate supervisory and management personnel has long been a problem of the hotel industry, and that situation cannot be expected to improve. Salaries have traditionally been lower than in other industries, and the current growth in the number of motel units requiring capable management has even further drained the pool of available people. It must be recognized that higher management skills will be needed in the future. Developments cited earlier will require more technical knowledge on the part of managers rather than the knowledge of food service or the ability to interact with people that was formerly sought.

A knowledge of accounting and financial planning will also become much more important than in the past. Many of the chains and hotel operations owned by conglomerates place great stress on budgets and long-range forecasts. The ability to prepare these and to analyze the financial results thus becomes a vital part of a hotel manager's duties.

Again, the image of the hotel industry must be improved. More emphasis must be placed on on-the-job training for middle-management and supervisory positions, in preparation for higher levels of responsibility.

A faster rate of promotion would also help. The industry has a reputation for failing to promote capable people, frequently only because they do their present jobs too well. Hotels must make efforts of turn entry-level employees into managers by extensive training in additional areas to food and beverage and finance. These areas include front desk, housekeeping, engineering, security, and in certain areas, gaming.

Salary benefit programs must be expanded to compete more effectively with business and other industries. Fringe benefits in the hotel industry, such as travel, meals, and sometimes accommodations, should be stressed.

Future government legislation in areas affecting employees could create new challenges for the industry.

TECHNOLOGICAL DEVELOPMENT

Much of the technological development taking place in the industry is in communications, where high-speed computers and the lower costs of hardware and software are providing opportunities not previously available. In an earlier chapter, the processing of reservations through a computerized reservation system was detailed. Such systems are being integrated with other computerized hotel systems.

Property management systems, of which reservation systems form an integral part, are being expanded on an ever-increasing scale. In addition to automating the front-desk check-in/checkout and billing procedures, they interface with other hotel systems.

Telephone service and utilities, such as heat, air-conditioning, and lighting, can be turned on or off at check-in and checkout. Similarly, computerized room-locking devices can be controlled by the front desk.

New maintenance and engineering systems will permit the removal and immediate replacement of defective or broken parts, eliminating the need for in-house repairs.

Greater emphasis is being placed on environmental controls. In addition to the energy-saving systems previously discussed, new controls will be directed to air and noise pollution.

Continued research will result in the use of new synthetic materials that will withstand more wear and tear and require less maintenance.

There will be a greater emphasis on modular construction, complete with preinstalled systems, whereby major segments of a hotel can be constructed in an off-site location and transported to the hotel site for assembly and finishing. Some motel chains are already widely using this type of construction.

REDUCTIONS IN FRONT-DESK OPERATIONS

Technological improvements are gradually diminishing the role of the front desk—perhaps to a point in the future where it may be completely eliminated as we know it.

The capture of credit card and billing information at the time of the reservation makes 90% of check-ins in most hotels simply a matter of signing to acknowledge preprinted information. This does not require a full-scale front desk, as automatic "check-in" terminals directly deliver a programmed plastic key for the guest. Only walk-in guests actually requires the capture of information.

When billing or credit card information is precaptured, checkout can be handled in the guestroom by giving the guest the ability to review his or her account on the television screen and the opportunity to call down for an explanation or correction. Checkout can then be a matter of signing a slip and dropping it in a slot on the way out. (A provision would have to be made for the handling of exceptions.) Many hotels are already using a "speedy checkout."

RATE STRATEGIES

In Chapter 2, we reviewed the ever-increasing types of hotels and mentioned the impact of competition on rates. We should also mention the increasing competition from cruise ships for resort business.

Some of the hotel chains have adopted schemes similar to the airlines. High discounts have been offered for reservations made several weeks in advance. Attempts, however, to impose guarantees in the event of cancellation produced a negative response from business travelers for whom changes in travel plans are frequently necessary. Increases in discounts on slow nights have increased substantially. The use of yield management systems has greatly improved the rate strategies.

Chains also all have developed frequent travel plans where guests receive points for nights stayed. These points can be used to obtain free rooms in other hotels, but many of the plans provide alternative uses for these points.

ENVIRONMENTAL CONSIDERATIONS

The chapter cannot be closed without mentioning the high level of environment-related issues being addressed by the hotel industry. These vary from selecting sites to the use of recycled productions and control over waste disposal and fuel emissions.

CHAPTER SUMMARY

Although this chapter is titled "Future Trends of Hotel Operations," some of the topics have already seen some action. We are suggesting, however, that more intensive action is required in the future. All the topics have one thing in common: They address major industry problems.

Topics are:

1. Energy—Energy conservation must be practiced and new sources of energy developed. Related to this are concerns about conservation and protecting the environment.
2. Labor—The industry suffers from a decreasing labor supply. Technology will replace people in some areas. Nevertheless, the existed labor supply must have its skills improved, wages increased, and the image of the industry improved to attract more people.
3. Technology will be further developed in the following areas:
   a. Reservations and front desk.
   b. Energy control.
   c. Environmental protection.
   d. Modular constructions.
4. Rates—New rate strategies will be developed.

REVIEW QUESTIONS

These questions attempt to get the student to develop their own ideas.
1. What actions do you feel hotels should initiate to counter the energy problem?
2. What actions do you feel hotels should initiate to counter the shortage of labor problems?
3. What actions do you feel hotels should initiate to address the environment and conservation?
4. What other areas do you feel must be addressed and what actions do you suggest?

Glossary

Abstracting the menu   A term used by restaurants for counting the menu items sold.

Accrual expense liability   An amount shown on a balance sheet that is a estimate for unbilled expenses.

Address correction requested   A request to the post office to forward mail when an address has changed.

After-departure charges   Charges that were not on the guest's bill when they departed.

Afternoon report   A report prepared by housekeeping reporting the status of each room.

A la carte   A menu that prices each item individually.

Ale houses   A historic term for inns and taverns.

All-suite hotels   Hotels in which every room is a suite of varying sizes.

American plan   A plan in which the rate includes three meals.

Apartment-hotel   A hotel that has apartments leased to permanent guests.

Bad debts   Uncollectible accounts receivable.

Banquet audit   A daily audit of banquet revenue.

Bin cards   An inventory tracking system using quantities only.

Botulism   A type of food poisoning.

Budget motor hotels   Hotels with limited services offering a low rate.

Budgetary control   Controls exercised to keep the operations within budget.

Builder's risk policies   Insurance carried by builders during construction.

Bulk buying   Buying in large volumes to obtain lower prices.
Business interruption   Insurance that covers expenses and profits when business is interrupted due to a fire.

Call accounting system   A system to measure the length of phone calls, calculate the charge, and post to the guest account.
Cash discounts   Discounts received for early payment of bills.
Cash reserves   Funds held to protect against possible losses.
Casino bank   The total amount of cash, chips, and markers in a casino. It varies daily because of the markers.
Casino cage   The place in a casino where chips, cash, and markers are handled and controlled.
Central reservation offices   Offices that record reservations for a chain or group of hotels.
Checkouts   Rooms that have checked out of the hotel.
Chip float   The amount of chips maintained at a table in a casino.
Circulation   A term used for linens, china, glass, and silver in use.
City ledger   A term used for nonguest accounts receivable.
Closed-circuit television   Television used by hotel security departments to monitor activity in various areas.
C.O.D.   A term for payment on delivery.
Comfort foods   A new style of menu items that actually goes back to old-style meals.
Computerized reservation systems   Computer systems used to take reservations.
Contra accounts   An accounting term used when the revenue and the expense are offset in the same account.
Convention hotels   Hotels that primarily cater to conventions.
Corporate account   An account receivable from a corporation.
Credit card authorization   Authorization received from a credit card company for a guest charge.
Cycle billing   Billing of accounts on a period that does not end at month end.

Daily quotation sheet   A sheet used to record daily quotations on food.
Daily receiving sheet   A sheet prepared each day that records all items received by a hotel.
Declared tips   Tips declared by service staff for tax purposes.
Departmentalization   A term that refers to the various departments in a hotel operation.
Deposit requirement   The amount of deposit required by a hotel for a room reservation or function.
Dietary programs   Programs in spa operations that maintain certain diet requirements for guests during their stay.
Direct purchases   Food purchases that go into the kitchen on delivery.

Double locks   A term used when rooms are locked and require a special key to open them.

Drop bucket   The bucket where coins lost in a slot machine eventually fall.

Electronic locking systems   Computerized systems used in hotel room locks.

Elevator starters   Employees who control the operation of elevators.

End-of-shift reports   A balancing report prepared by servers at the end of their shift.

Exfoliate   A term used in spas for a treatment that removes dead skin.

Expediter   Person in a hotel or restaurant kitchen who speeds up the supply of food to servers.

Expense and Payroll Dictionary   A dictionary used in conjunction with the Uniform System to define and classify expenses.

Experience rated policies   Insurance policies whose premium is based on actual experience.

Fair rental value   The amount considered to be a reasonable rental for a shop or other area.

Fixed charges   Charges on a financial statement that have no relation to volume. Usual charges are rent, taxes, insurance, interest, and depreciation.

Floor supervisor   An employee in housekeeping who supervises the cleaning of a group of rooms.

Food cost percentage   The percentage of food cost to food sales.

Function sheet   A sheet prepared for a function that specifies all details, for example, number of people, requirements, guarantees, and prices.

Game rooms   Rooms in a hotel where various games are available to the guest.

Garage ticket   Ticket used to control the in and out of vehicles.

General cleaning   Cleaning in a hotel not normally done on a daily basis.

Guest history   A record maintained on a guest after departure for marketing purposes.

Guest ledger   Accounts receivable of guests in a hotel.

Handheld terminal   Computerized terminals used by servers where orders and settlement are recorded on a terminal held in the server's hand.

High balance report   A report prepared nightly reflecting guests who have exceeded their credit limits.

Hospitalization, dental and major medical policies, pensions, and savings plans   Various benefit programs offered by some hotels.

House account   Accounts used in a hotel for nonguest activity.

Hydroelectric plants   Plants generating electricity using water flow.

In and out fees   Fees charged to hotel guests who take their vehicle in and out of the garage.

In-house parking   Hotels that have on-premises parking facilities.

Input and output terminals   Computer terminals to input and output information.

Interface   A term used where two computer operations communicate with each other.

Internal control   Controls exercised on revenue, expenses, and protection of assets.

Investigation clerks   Clerks in the accounts receivable department who handle guest problems.

Joint advertising   Advertising that promotes a group of two or more hotels. Also used to promote hotels in conjunction with airlines, etc. It is commonly used by the chains.

Junkets   Free transportation and other services given to good customers by casinos.

Khans   Structures used for overnight stays of travelers in Persia a long time ago.

Labor contracts   Contracts made between workers and employers relative to conditions of employment.

Lease   A rental agreement on property.

Linen cart   A cart on which a room attendant carries his or her supplies.

Lobby attendant   A member of the housekeeping staff responsible for keeping the lobby clean during the day.

Lobby porters   Members of the bell staff whose function is to carry luggage to the rooms and handle baggage; more common in Europe.

Magnetic stripe reader   A device to read the magnetic stripe on the back of a credit card.

Markers   Forms used in casinos to formalize credit granted to players.

Market   The area or group from whom a hotel or restaurant draws its business.

Metering devices   Devices attached to liquor bottles that measure and count the drinks poured.

Minimum, standard, superior, deluxe, and suite   Room rate categories used by hotels.

Morning report   A report prepared by housekeeping staff in the morning recording room status.

Multiple-line protection   A type of insurance where various types of risk are included on the same policy.

Natural recreation area   Resort location where the main attraction is natural, for example, a waterfall or a mountain used for skiing.

Night audit report   Report prepared nightly providing the day's revenue and key statistics.

One-number system   A reservation system where all hotels receive their reservations through calls to the same telephone number.

One-write systems   Manual systems where transactions are recorded on more than one document through use of carbonized paper.

Operated departments   Hotel departments such as rooms, food, or beverage that have revenues.

Order in which information is requested   The order in which reservation information is obtained.

Outside valet   A valet service used by a hotel but not using employees.

Overhead departments   Departments such as sales that provide support to the operated departments.

Par stocks   Inventory quantities considered necessary for operation.

Payroll deductions   Various deductions made from an employee's gross income.

Pegboard systems   A refined form of one-write systems.

Permanent financing   Finances obtained for the life of the hotel.

Perpetual inventory   An inventory control system that uses dollar values as well as quantities.

Personal exemptions   Deductions from taxable income based on family statistics.

Point-of-sale systems   Computed control systems used in food and beverage operations.

Price fluctuations   Fluctuation in the price of food, mainly meat, seafood, and produce.

Productivity reports   Reports that measure the volume of business handled by individual employees.

Property management systems   A computer system that handles reservations, check-in and checkouts, guest accounting, and guest history.

Purchase requisitions   Requisitions to make purchases sent by department heads to the purchasing agent.

Purchase specifications   Specifications (based on government standards) used in ordering food.

Purchasing agent   The person in charge of purchasing for the hotel.

Recruitment   A program of hiring new employees.

Referral organization   An organization whose hotels' members refer reservations to other member hotels.

Regional American cuisine   Food that is associated with a geographical area in the United States.

Regional offices   A term used for chain reservation offices in various locations.

Registration desk   The desk where guests check in to a hotel.

Rental agreements   Agreements signed between a hotel and tenants for shop rentals.

Reserve for bad debts   A reserve on a balance sheet provided to cover possible bad debts.

Requisitioning, storage, and control   Terms used in hotel inventory control.
Room status information   Computer information advising the status of each guestroom.
Rooming slip   A slip issued to a guest at check-in specifying room particulars.

Salmonellosis   A type of food infection.
Sanitation   A term for cleanliness.
Self-standing   A term used for independent restaurants within a hotel.
Service bureaus   Companies who provide computer services.
Service charge   A fixed charge, usually a percentage, added to the check for functions.
Settlement   A restaurant term used for payment of a charge.
Skippers   Hotel guests who leave without checking out.
Sole proprietor   A business owned by a single individual.
Staff planning   The procedure in a hotel for using certain standards to determine needed staff.
Staphylococcal   A type of food poisoning.
Subsidiary   A corporation that is owned by another corporation.
Systems management   A term used for management of hotel systems.

Tabernae   A Latin word meaning an inn. It is believed to be the origin of the word "tavern."
Table d' hote   A menu where one price covers the whole meal.
Technical assistance   Assistance provided by a franchiser in various areas before and during operations.
Technological developments   Changes that have resulted from new technology.
Touch screens   Screens in a point-of-sale system where an order is placed by touching an item on the screen.
Trade discounts   Discounts offered to special customers, usually related to volume.
Trichinosis   A type of food infection.
Turnover   The amount of employee replacement in a period.

Use-and-occupancy   A type of insurance that covers fixed charges during a nonoperating period.
Uniform System   A system developed by the New York Hotel Association that defines departments and expense classifications.

Valet Parking Attendants   Attendants who park guests' cars.

Working capital   Funds required to finance daily operations.

Xenodocheions   A Greek word used in the Middle Ages for accommodations for travelers (usually run by a monastery).

Index